THE LOGIC OF
ECONOMIC REFORM IN
RUSSIA

THE LOGIC OF
ECONOMIC REFORM IN
RUSSIA

JERRY F. HOUGH

BROOKINGS INSTITUTION PRESS
Washington, D.C.

Library of Congress Cataloging-in-Publication data

Hough, Jerry F., 1935–
    The logic of economic reform in Russia / Jerry F. Hough.
        p.   cm.
Includes bibliographical references and index.
    ISBN 0-8157-3754-8 (cloth : alk. paper) — ISBN 0-8157-3753-X
    (pbk. : alk. paper)
    1. Russia (Federation)—Economic policy—1991– 2. Russia (Federation)—
Economic conditions—1991– 3. Privatization—Russia (Federation) 4. Russia
(Federation)—Politics and government—1991– I. Title.
    HC340.12.H68   2001   00-012817
    338.947—dc21   CIP

9 8 7 6 5 4 3 2 1

The paper used in this publication meets minimum requirements of the
American National Standard for Information Sciences—Permanence of Paper
for Printed Library Materials: ANSI Z39.48-1984.

Typeset in Sabon

Composition by
Betsy Kulamer
Washington, D.C.

Printed by
R. R. Donnelley and Sons
Harrisonburg, Virginia

To close friends and collaborators,
Iosif Diskin, Mikhail Guboglo,
Tatiana Guboglo, Susan Goodrich Lehmann,
and Sergei Tumanov

Foreword

THE HIGH HOPES for Russian economic reform in the early 1990s have been deeply disappointed. After the collapse of the ruble in 1998, many causes were given for the failure of the reform and many different people blamed. Those in the West naturally have had a strong tendency to blame preexisting conditions in Russia or the corruption of Russian officials, or both.

Jerry F. Hough reminds us that the preexisting conditions were well known in 1991 and that economic theory sees corruption as the rational response of economic actors to a particular incentive structure. He accepts the argument of Nobel Prize laureate Douglass North that markets are not self-forming mechanisms, but a set of institutions and incentives that are created. The challenge in 1991 was to establish a set of institutions and incentives that took account of the preexisting conditions and promoted economic progress.

On the basis of eight years of work between 1992 and 2000, Hough probes beneath the surface to describe in detail how Russia's economic system works. As a political scientist, he analyzes how that system emerged from the politics of Russia of that period.

His basic task is not to assess blame, but to demonstrate the basic rationality of Russian economic actors. As was expected, they did respond to the real incentives they were given, but these incentives were not those of the abstract neoclassical economic model. The implication, paradoxically, is optimistic. The incentive system can and should be changed to induce them to act in more productive ways.

Hough is particularly interested in the phenomenon of corruption. It was widespread in Europe, the United States, and the Pacific Rim countries in their early stages of capitalism when these areas had their respective periods of highest economic growth. As a result, it is utopian to think that corruption can be wiped out completely. Nor can eradication of corruption be a necessary precondition for economic growth. The problem is to try to ensure that the inevitable corruption contributes to growth rather than destroys it.

The secret, Hough argues, is to understand the problems flowing from the great lack of trust in the early investment process and the role of government in overcoming these problems. The collaboration of large numbers of government, economic, and military officials in domestic investment projects not only provides the basis for secure investment, he contends, but also the incentives for the development of property rights and constitutional restraints on government. This point has implications not only for Russia, but also for the development process in the rest of the world.

The research for the book was begun in 1992. Four major independent surveys conducted in Russia from 1993 through 1997 are the basis for key analysis in two chapters. As a consequence, Hough finds it impossible to acknowledge all the help he has been given and the intellectual debts he has incurred in the process. He will only mention a few of the most prominent, but is deeply grateful to countless others as well.

The Russians, especially in Yaroslavl, who were willing to discuss the system anonymously were of invaluable assistance. David Johnson has provided an enormous service to Russia and specialists on Russia with the publication of his "David Johnson's List" two or three times a day through the Internet. The list not only is full of information from Russia, but has become a forum for discussion that led Hough to many participants who communicated with him privately.

A few specific individuals played a particularly key role in various aspects of the project. Ralph Clem of Florida International University, Timothy Colton of Harvard University, Evelyn Davidheiser of the University of Minnesota, and David Laitin of Stanford University were collaborators on various of the survey projects. Laitin, George Breslauer of the University of California–Berkeley, and Michael Munger of Duke University provided major intellectual criticisms of the manuscript at later stages. Jean Marshall Crawford read the manuscript through many stages and made many suggestions.

There were, however, five friends who worked so closely with the author over the years that he dedicates the book to them. Without these friends and colleagues this book could not have been written. Iosef Diskin, deputy director of the Institute of Socio-Economic Problems of Population of the Russian Academy of Sciences, had a key role in helping to illuminate the details of the economic reform and the debates within the Yeltsin and Civic Union camps. Sergei Tumanov, director of the Sociological Center of Moscow University, and Mikhail Guboglo, deputy director of the Institute of Ethnology and Anthropology of the Russian Academy of Sciences, were the leading collaborators on the surveys in Russia, along with regional scholars who conducted them. Tatiana Guboglo was unbelievably efficient and patient in organizing the projects and the entry of the data.

Last, but far from least, Susan Goodrich Lehmann, now institutional research manager of the American Councils for International Education: ACTR/ACCELS, was the closest collaborator on all the surveys. She shared all the struggles to obtain funding (indeed, she played the central role in several cases), to ensure the questions were right on the questionnaires, to have the surveys conducted, to get the data organized, and then to try to figure out what they meant.

Last, the Brookings Institution Press has provided invaluable support in getting the book into print, notably, Debbie Styles, who did an outstanding job in editing the manuscript, and Inge Lockwood and Mary Mortensen, who provided proofreading and indexing services. In the Foreign Policy Studies program at Brookings, Susan Jackson and her successor, Todd DeLelle, ably handled the verification.

The views expressed here are solely those of the author and should not be ascribed to any persons or institutions acknowledged above or to the trustees, officers, or staff members of the Brookings Institution or the funders.

MICHAEL H. ARMACOST
President

February 2001
Washington, D.C.

Preface

PART OF THE ARGUMENT advanced in this book is based on data that originated in four different surveys: (1) a 1993 Russian parliamentary election survey conducted in November and December 1993; (2) a 1995 Russian parliamentary election survey conducted in November and December 1995; (3) a 1996 Russian presidential election survey conducted in May and June 1996; and (4) two simultaneous and overlapping surveys of Russian youth and young adults conducted in the spring of 1997, one a national sample of those aged 17–18, 23–24, and 31–32, the other a sample of high school seniors in the capitals of the former autonomous republics.

The principal investigators of the 1993 survey were Jerry F. Hough, Timothy Colton of Harvard University, and Susan Goodrich Lehmann of American Councils for International Education: ACTR/ACCELS. Funding was provided by the Carnegie Corporation of New York, the John D. and Catherine T. MacArthur Foundation, the Brookings Institution, and National Science Foundation grants SBR-94-02548 and SBR-94-12051.

The study was conducted by two groups of scholars in fifty-two oblasts and krais (all but three of them), the cities of Moscow and St. Petersburg, and all sixteen former autonomous republics. The scholars in the oblasts were supervised by Sergei Tumanov, director of the Center for Sociological Study of Moscow State University, and Mikhail Guboglo, deputy director of the Institute of Ethnology and Anthropology of the Russian Academy of Sciences. Data entry and cleaning were supervised and double-checked by Tatiana Guboglo, a candidate of science (Ph.D.) in mathematics, who has worked for decades in a similar role on her husband's sociological studies.

The regional scholars were sociologists and ethnographers engaged in survey research. Most had years of experience conducting surveys in their regions, and all worked concurrently as scholars in local universities and institutes. Many had their own survey research centers with as many as fifteen people on staff or as few as five. The members of the network received a complete data set for their own use so that they could publish from it. The expectation was that the surveys would help foster the development of Russian social science.[1] The surveys were designed jointly by the Russians and the Americans. The Americans know Russian; they went to Russia and negotiated the wording of the questions in Russian. With the exception of the 1997 survey of high school students, which was a written questionnaire filled out by the students in the classroom under the supervision of one of our regional sociologists, all interviews were conducted in person by members of a local research team who interviewed people one-on-one in their homes.

The core 1993 national study was based on a stratified random sample of 3,848 respondents interviewed at approximately 170 sites within Russia. The questionnaire contained approximately 150 questions. The respondents were revisited for a postelection survey containing new questions a few days after the election. The postelection study was written and supervised by Timothy Colton.

A computer-generated list randomly selected raions (the equivalent of an American county) within the oblasts and republics (both equivalent to American states) in which the interviews were to take place. Depending on the overall population of the administrative unit, 40, 80, or 120 interviews were conducted in each oblast and ethnic republic. The only exceptions were the cities of Moscow and St. Petersburg, where more interviews were conducted to reflect their proportionately larger populations. The interviews were conducted in the capital city and in several surrounding cities and villages within each oblast. The respondents were chosen randomly from voting lists for the raion.

In the United States, a set sample of respondents is chosen at the outset of a national survey, and those who are not found or who refuse to participate are not replaced. Hence the scholars report such data as response rates, and their results are based on a sample smaller than that with which they began. In traditional Soviet practice, interviewers were instructed, by set rules, to replace respondents who refused or who could not be interviewed after several attempts. Indeed, Soviet scholars often used a quota system in which regional interviewers were instructed to choose specified numbers of respondents from different categories. Often interviewers simply chose friends and acquaintances who met the demographic profile; this practice led to the well-known liberal bias in so many Russian polls.[2]

When most Americans conduct scholarly surveys in Russia, they adopt the American methodology and report the standard American data. The insistence on the American methodology increases, we think, the likelihood of fraud, for the firms in Moscow and interviewers in the field do not believe that westerners will be satisfied with a high nonresponse rate. The response rates and methodology of selection that they report to westerners may not, we fear, correspond to their actual practice. They may even use unacknowledged quotas based on the candidate supported.

In theoretical terms, samples distorted by nonresponse and those distorted by replacement should not be that different as long as the replacement is done by strict rules. We thought that results would be more reliable if the Russian leaders of the survey were instructed categorically to avoid the quota method, but then allowed to use the replacement method that they thought would allow them better to control interviewers in doing a random sample. It was also thought that if the Russians were permitted and even encouraged to publish out of their own data, their own reputations inside Russia would be affected by the quality of the survey work, and this would increase their incentive to do honest and top-quality work.

Whatever sampling method is used, scholars usually choose to weight the data to bring them in line with census data. All the surveys in this study were weighted by age, education level, gender, and urban/rural residence by Susan Goodrich Lehmann. The data used in the weighting were from the 1994 Micro-Census of 5 percent of the population of Russia collected by the State Committee of Statistics in February 1994. The survey data were adjusted simultaneously along four parameters: age group (18–19, 20–24, 25–29, 30–34, 35–39, 40–44, 45–49, 50–54, 55–59, 60–64, 65–69, 70+), educational level (no education, primary education, incomplete secondary=1; secondary, specialized secondary, incomplete higher=2; higher and advanced degrees=3), gender (male, female), and urban/rural (village=rural, all others=urban).

In addition to the 1993 national sample, separate regional surveys of 1,000 respondents were conducted at the same time with the same pre-election questionnaire in each of thirty-one oblasts, the cities of Moscow and St. Petersburg, and sixteen former autonomous republics (including Chechnia, where no election was held).[3] The sample in each oblast and republic was stratified by city size to include a representative collection of cities of various types. Within city and rural districts, respondents were selected randomly from voting lists. The regional scholars were instructed to interview a third of the respondents in each of the three weeks of the election campaign and to keep the mixture between different types of population points more or less equal in each week. This was meant to ensure some 3,000 more or less representative respondents for every day of the campaign so that the shifting attitudes and allegiances could be examined on a day-to-day basis.

The questionnaire included sixty very detailed sociological questions in the hope that the respondents, although not a strict random sample, could be aggregated into a huge data set that could be used to do detailed sociological cohort analysis of a type never done in usual sociological work.[4] Given the standardization in occupations, educational experience, and salaries produced by the Soviet planning system, it was thought that the overrepresentation of residents of smaller regions and underrepresentation of residents of larger regions would not have a major impact on the results. In this book, this data set of 50,827 respondents is the basis for table 2-3 on base salary of different occupations of those in the data set who were employed.

Conclusions about political attitudes from such a sample are obviously more unreliable, but when the 1993 unweighted data from the aggregated data set of respondents from the oblasts, Moscow, and St. Petersburg alone were used in a preliminary article, the results proved to be remarkably similar to those from the later weighted data from the national sample.[5] The day-to-day poll also caught the rise of Vladimir Zhirinovsky that was missed by other polling agencies.

The 1995, 1996, and 1997 surveys were all led by Professors Tumanov and Guboglo in Moscow, and the regional scholars of 1993, with a few exceptions, were also in charge in the regional teams. The basic methodology was also used, and the same raions surveyed in 1993 were revisited. No efforts were made to contact the respondents from the 1993 survey, but the similarity in methodology and team should make the data quite comparable from study to study.

The 1995 survey was conducted between November 30 and December 10, 1995, just before the 1995 Duma election. The principal investigators were Hough and Lehmann from the 1993 study and Evelyn Davidheiser, assistant professor of political science of the University of Minnesota. The sample comprised 3,860 respondents and again was a national random sample stratified by oblast and republic. The questionnaire comprised approximately 150 questions, a large number taken from the 1993 questionnaire to ensure comparability. Funding was provided by National Science Foundation Grant SBR-96-00413 and the United States Information Agency.

The 1996 election study was a panel study. The pre-election study was conducted two weeks before the first round of the June 1996 presidential election. The national random sample consisted of 3,781 persons, selected as before. The election had a runoff round since no candidate received a majority on the first ballot. The respondents were revisited between the first and second round in the expectation that memories about the vote in the first round would be fresher and that fewer would be on vacation than after the second round; 3,260 respondents were found and agreed to answer a second questionnaire. The principal investigators were the same as in December 1995. The funding for the pre-election study was provided by the John D. and Catherine T. MacArthur Foundation and that for the postelection study by National Science Foundation grant SBR-96-01315 and the United States Information Agency.

The 1997 youth survey was conducted in the spring of 1997 and had two parts. One was a national sample of 3,839 respondents within the oblasts (but not the republics). The principal investigators were Hough and Lehmann. The survey was conducted by the same group as the election studies and included many of the same questions as the election studies. It also had large blocs of questions on marriage, childbearing, life choices, and leisure time values. It was funded by the John D. and Catherine T. MacArthur Foundation.

The youth survey included 1,068 respondents who were aged 17 and 18, 1,390 respondents who were aged 24 and 25, and 1,381 respondents who were aged 31 and 32. The purpose of the survey was to have a substantial subgroup of those who were becoming adults just before perestroika, at the time of the disintegration of the Soviet Union, and at the time of the survey. The sample was chosen by the same methodology as the election studies, with one exception. In order to ensure an excellent sample of persons of the desired ages, we chose respondents from the housing lists, for they not only list all residents, but also show their year of birth. Thus the sample is extraordinarily good in comparison with others that limit themselves to specific age groups.[6] The 1997 data in this book are drawn from the national survey.

In addition, a simultaneous survey was conducted of 13,600 high school students in the capitals of fifteen former autonomous republics, the sample stratified to provide a sample comprising half ethnic Russians and half those of the titular population. The survey was conducted in the high schools, with the classrooms chosen to include both ethnically heterogeneous and homogeneous ones. That study focused more on nationality issues. It was funded by the National Council for Soviet and East European Research.[7]

Contents

ONE   *Introduction*

On October 28, 1991, Boris Yeltsin addressed the Fifth Congress of People's Deputies and proclaimed his intention to conduct radical economic reform "decisively, abruptly, and without wavering."[1] The reform, he said, would feature economic stabilization, privatization, and price liberalization, and he warned that conditions would be very difficult for six months. A week later President Yeltsin took over the premiership himself and appointed a team of radical young economists to carry out the reform. Thirty-six-year-old Yegor Gaidar was the leader of this team.

Yeltsin declared in his October 28 speech: "We officially invite the International Monetary Fund, the World Bank, and the European Bank of Reconstruction and Development to participate in the working out of the detailed plan for cooperation and participation in the economic reforms." He called for technical assistance "in the analysis and working out of recommendations on key economic, ecological, and regional questions."[2] Yeltsin's young economists in turn announced their complete dedication to the economic reform package of the International Monetary Fund—"the proven answers of economic theory and practice."[3] In February 1992 they promised to accept the IMF conditions completely.

From early 1992 onward, however, real economic reform in Russia clearly deviated from that which the IMF had been promised. Despite these deviations, western supporters of the Russian reform package remained highly optimistic. As early as October 1994, Anders Aslund was asserting that Russia had become a market economy:

1

The main goal of the Russian economic transformation has been accomplished. Russia has become a market economy. The essential feature of such an economy is that the market is the main instrument of allocation. . . . The economy had been emancipated from politics. . . . Ownership had been depoliticized. . . . Bureaucratic directives were gone (with rare exceptions), and allocation had been depoliticized. . . . The problem is no longer one of lack of monetarization but the stabilization of the ruble. . . . Credit and pricing have . . . been essentially (although not completely) depoliticized.[4]

In 1995 Stanley Fischer, the first deputy director of the IMF, examined the experience of the countries of the former Soviet Union and predicted, "Growth in these countries will on average increase in 1995 and will turn positive in most of these countries by 1996 or 1997."[5] Russia was surely among the former Soviet republics he viewed as having a rosy future. This optimism infused the thinking of the American investment community.[6]

The optimism vanished with the Russian financial crash of August 1998. The ruble lost over 70 percent of its value, and banks defaulted on their debts and forward currency contracts. An unseemly debate ensued on "who lost Russia," with all participants generously giving credit to others, especially to the Russians. Nevertheless, the explanations almost all pointed to factors that had been well known during the period of optimism. Everyone was aware in 1991 that Russia did not have a capitalist culture, a rule of law, secure property rights, a regulated and trusted banking system, or enough trained personnel. Everyone knew Yeltsin was elected in June 1991 as an extreme populist promising reform without pain. In the postmortems, no one explained why these obvious problems proved more dangerous than anticipated and why the reform program did not take them more into account.

Some in the West said that the Russian state was "weaker" than expected. It was the West, however, that had pushed Russia to have democratic elections, and Yeltsin's government actually was far more authoritarian than anticipated in 1991. Others said that weak meant insufficient government regulation of the economy. Nobel laureate Douglass North expressed this view in 1997: "There is no such thing as laissez faire—that means anarchy somewhat akin to what we have been observing in Russia."[7] Nevertheless, as this book will document, the

Russian government under Yeltsin maintained a strong directing role in the economy from the beginning of 1992 through 1999. The system remained in place at the end of 2000.

The real problem was that the state was using its power and involvement in the economy to do the wrong things. The deviations from the announced economic reform actually went far beyond those usually acknowledged in the West. The Russian economy functioned in a manner almost the reverse of what Aslund had described. Russia was far closer to the old centrally directed Soviet economy, with its nonmonetary delivery and receipt of goods, than to a market economy. The large "privatized" enterprises and banks remained essentially state or quasi-state entities acting on the direction of the central government. Inter-enterprise loans, barter, and tax arrears were depicted as the independent actions of enterprise managers, but they usually were approved or ordered by the government. Government often required the enterprises to deliver goods free; in return it excused them from tax payments. The reform politicians idolized by the West deliberately deceived the West on these and many other questions.

As a consequence, the same need exists to probe behind the façade of the official version of the relationship between government and the economy in the 1990s as in the Soviet period.[8] The first purpose of this book is to show the real nature of policy while Yeltsin was president and the real way in which the economy functioned. The usual analysis of the "independence" of the Central Bank, the enterprise directors, the financial oligarchs, and the regions is precisely as accurate as that rare analysis in the Soviet period that treated the soviets as independent from the Communist party organs.

The second purpose of this book is to try to explain why the economic reform went wrong. Everyone assumed that Russian economic reform would face difficulties—although, of course, the Chinese economic reform did produce nearly 10 percent growth a year for twenty years—but no one in 1991 expected that the situation would be disastrous a full decade later. In 1997 one major participant stated, "Given the scope for restructuring, the need for new capital, the relatively low labour costs by international standards, and the high level of human capital, one might have expected transition to be associated with high rates of capital accumulation."[9] A year later, another recalled that the transition period was expected to be relatively short and that no major and prolonged drop in production was anticipated.[10]

This book argues that the answer is not found in the Soviet past, in Russian national character, or in the lack of a capitalist culture. Adam Smith and David Ricardo developed their analysis well before Europe had a well-developed capitalist culture or a set of modern financial and regulatory agencies. Indeed, "naked self-interest," to use Karl Marx's phrase from this period, logically should be the decisive motivating force for people whose old cultural restraints have been shattered and who are not yet enmeshed in new ones.

The core assumption of the economic reform was right. Russians possessed the rationality assumed in the neoliberal economic models, and in that sense they were "normal economic men."[11] They did, in fact, respond rationally to the incentives they were given. The corruption, mafia, capital flight, lack of investment, and lack of economic growth were not the product of Russian culture or history, but the natural consequences of the response of rational people to the incentive system created by economic reform. That is the meaning of the title of this book.

The third purpose of the book is to draw theoretical lessons from what happened. That process has already begun, and scholars agree on the first implication: institutions are more important than the neoliberal economic community supposed in 1990. In the jargon of the 1980s, many had believed that Russia could and should cross the chasm from socialism to capitalism in a single leap, as if a functioning capitalist system, culture, and legal system existed full-blown on the other side. That belief was wrong. The agreement about the importance of institutions is universal, however, because the word institution is vague, and people define it in quite different ways. The problem is illustrated by a speech by Alan Greenspan, chairman of the U.S. Federal Reserve Board, in 1997:

> Much of what we took for granted in our free market system and assumed to be human nature was not nature at all, but culture. The dismantling of the central planning function in an economy does not, as some had supposed, automatically establish a free market entrepreneurial system. There is a vast amount of capitalist culture and infrastructure underpinning market economics that has evolved over generations: laws, conventions, behaviors, and a wide variety of business professions and practices that has no important functions in a central planned economy.[12]

It is difficult to disagree with Greenspan's statement, but what is the concrete meaning of "capitalist culture and infrastructure" in an analysis of Russian economic reform? Is it the informal norms, expectations, and conventions that must take generations to evolve? Will they make economic growth impossible for a prolonged period? Or are there concrete laws and organizational infrastructure that can and should be put in place and that may fairly quickly produce the growth of the Chinese transition from communism? What is the normal or optimal sequence of the development of formal and informal constraints?

Douglass North, who received the Nobel Prize for his work on institutions (work from which Greenspan's ideas were drawn), has been utterly forthright in recognizing that neither he nor the scholarly community as a whole understands how durable, socially desirable institutions are developed where they do not exist. "We simply do not know how to create efficient political markets. . . . We simply have no good models of politics in Third World, transition, or other economies. The interface between economics and politics is still in a primitive state in our theories, but its development is essential if we are to implement policies consistent with intentions."[13]

This book hopes to make a contribution to the development of such a theory. By insisting that corruption, the mafia, capital flight, lack of investment, and lack of economic growth were produced by concrete incentives created by government action, I intend to show that the role of informal institutions should not be exaggerated, at least in an analysis of change. People usually do act in a habitual, unthinking manner rather than by constant calculation, but the habits develop in response to real rewards and punishments. The effort to introduce change must focus on the establishment of real rewards and punishments.

This book does not focus on institutions in general, but on the problems of generating capital investment in early and middle stages of capitalism and on the reasons why the role of government must be different at these stages than at later ones. The book begins by suggesting another look at the work of Alexander Gerschenkron, but it insists that we move beyond a general acceptance of the importance of the role of the state to recognize that the state is not simply the king, but a range of individual government and military officials with their own interests. It argues that the individual officials have the correct concrete incentive to engage in activities that protect investment and promote economic growth. This often involves what is called "corruption." It is not a coincidence that the periods of highest economic growth in the United States, Europe, and the Pacific Rim were periods of high corruption. The problem in

Russia was that the corruption was not associated with protected investment inside Russia, but with capital flight.

The Impact of the Western Economic Community

By demanding formal Russian compliance with an economic program
that they knew the Russians were not carrying out, the officials of the
International Monetary Fund (IMF) put themselves in a bureaucratically
comfortable position.[14] The officials did themselves no honor by accepting the same formal assurances from the Russian government year after
year, long after it was patently obvious the promises would not be kept,
but this meant they could always claim they were not to blame. All the
failures of the Russian economic reform could be attributed to the deviations from the program, and the deviations could be attributed to some
factor inherent in Russia.

In fact, no one would blame the IMF entirely or primarily for the economic failure in Russia. A great variety of factors produced that failure,
and historians will spend decades and even centuries trying to assess
their weight. The most important factor was Boris Yeltsin. IMF advice
may be right or wrong, but government leaders decide whether or not to
adopt it. Wisely or not, the United States did not raise interest rates in
the 1990s as much as the IMF staff wanted. Wisely or not, the Chinese
and Pacific Rim leaders did not follow the IMF program in many partic-
ulars. The leaders of those countries ultimately deserve the credit or the
blame. Yeltsin was an authoritarian leader with the power to change
policy when it was not as successful as promised. He did not do so
although often advised to do so by critics of the IMF.

The problem was that Boris Yeltsin was not a modern ruler trying to
build either a smoothly functioning democracy or authoritarian regime;
both require strong laws and rules, and Yeltsin did not want to introduce such laws.[15] He refused to create a presidential political party, he
never relied on a well-organized military or police force, and he would
not establish the kind of rational-technical bureaucracy that Max Weber
thought inherent in modern industrial society. He sensed a point emphasized by Weber, namely that laws, bureaucracies, and organizations
restrain leaders as well as citizens.[16]

Yeltsin was the patriarchal head of the Russian family, and he
adopted an extremely personalistic style of rule.[17] He often referred to
the young neoliberal economists as his children—as the sons he never

had. He was the familiar Russian father who drank too much, was indulgent toward his children, but knew what was best and brooked no challenge. He tolerated an enormous amount of corruption. Perhaps he calculated that if everyone high in the system engaged in corrupt or illegal activities, everyone would fear removing him from office. Or perhaps the personalism inherent in what Weber called "patrimonial bureaucracy" naturally led to activity that those in rational-technical society would call corruption.[18]

Yeltsin's preferences about the relationship of king, court, bureaucracy, and economy were quite typical for the early and middle stages of capitalist development. The off-budget subsidy of consumption in Russia fit well with Yeltsin's personalistic system of rule. Nevertheless, the more usual result in early capitalism is an industrial policy in which the line between government official and entrepreneur is blurred, but in which both become rich on the basis of profitable investments and economic growth, not through the redistribution of poverty.

Everything in Boris Yeltsin's background and the structure of Russian politics suggests that an industrial policy would have been a natural outcome in Russia without outside influences. Yeltsin was the quintessential party apparatchik, a construction engineer with twenty years of work in construction management before he became the governor (*obkom* first secretary) of a major heavy industrial center (Sverdlovsk) noted for its conservatism. The leading industrial and regional forces of Russia wanted an industrial policy, and the Russian population favored gradual economic reform. Yeltsin could have ruled in a personalistic way with investment subsidies, as easily as with direct consumption subsidies. This would have satisfied all his instincts as a construction engineer and administrator.

China had an industrial policy that focused on investment, and it erected barriers against imports while promoting export-led growth. This program, which should have seemed so congenial to a construction engineer, produced excellent growth. The Chinese model seemed the natural one for Yeltsin to emulate, all the more so since it was associated with an authoritarian political system. Nevertheless, Russia did not choose concrete indicators of success such as economic growth or level of construction, but monetary factors: inflation, money supply, and budgetary stringency. This choice can only be explained by the advice of the international community and the conditions it set.

Although the IMF program was not enacted completely, the IMF and western neoliberal economists seldom criticized the worst aspects of

Yeltsin's policy vociferously. They called for property rights, but supported the violation of the property rights of those who actually owned industrial property—the insider-owners. They talked about a rule of law, but never confronted the system of nontransparent, personalistic off-budget subsidies that destroyed both property rights and legal predictability. They never declared that creation of a well-functioning, well-financed bureaucracy was crucial, but instead defended privatization as a step needed to weaken state control. Indeed, this remained the main defense of privatization when it could no longer be defended on economic grounds.

Worst of all, the international community never treated neglect of investment as the key flaw in the reform. Indeed, it almost never mentioned the problem or discussed how to cure it. The West, impossible as it is to believe, never pushed for marketization of the wholesale agricultural trade system that was the key to exploiting agriculture to subsidize urban food prices and that made any form of agricultural reform impossible. Incredibly, the West said that the epitome of a good reformer was Anatoly Chubais, the architect and chief administrator of Yeltsin's personalistic subsidy program, Yeltsin's patronage man, and the chief destroyer of property rights.

To some extent, the position of the western neoliberal reformers reflected a lack of knowledge. However, the character of the off-budget subsidies, the directing role of the quasi-ministerial state organs, and the role of the government in interenterprise loans were quite clear by the winter of 1992–93.[19] As it became clear that Yeltsin was deviating from his promises and trying to hide the deviations, the IMF made no serious attempt to publicize the real situation, but often contributed to the effort to reduce the transparency.

Douglass North suggested that the problem might be that the neoliberal economists reacted as they did because they did not know what to do. He insisted that they could not create an institutional framework for a market because, as he argued in his 1993 Nobel Prize speech, they did not have the tools, acting by themselves, to do so:

> Neoclassical theory is simply an inappropriate tool to analyze and prescribe policies that will induce development. It is concerned with the operation of markets, not with how markets develop. . . . How can one prescribe when one doesn't understand how economies develop? The very methods employed by neoclassical economists have dictated against such a development. That theory

. . . modeled a frictionless and static world. When applied to economic history and development, it focused on technological development and more recently human capital investment but ignored the incentive structure embodied in institutions that determined the extent of societal investment in these factors. In the analysis of economic performance through time it contained two erroneous assumptions: first, that institutions do not matter and, second, that time does not matter.[20]

The most important problem, however, was that the experience of neoliberal economists and the assumptions of their model led them to assume that Yeltsin's deviations were not all that important. They had seen personalistic rule and deviations from an optimal economic model in Latin America and Africa, and they had seen their policies work despite them. That is why they could say that Russia had achieved a normal market economy by 1994, that monetary stabilization would produce growth in 1995 and 1996, and that westerners could confidently invest in 1996 and 1997. The question is the nature of the assumptions of the model.

The Assumptions of the IMF Program

Only two months passed between the failed coup d'état in Russia in August 1991 and Yeltsin's appeal for a program from the IMF and the West. No one had time to develop a reform program specifically for Russia. If the international community had studied Russian reality closely from 1992 onward and tried to make adjustments as seemed necessary, no one would criticize them for early mistakes. Instead, they accepted all the worst changes made to Yeltsin's sound early privatization program because the rent-seekers who benefited from them (the mislabeled reformers) clothed them in ideologically acceptable garb. When Yeltsin compromised with the Congress and decided to introduce an industrial policy in early 1993, the West offered to support his dissolution of the Congress and his establishment of authoritarian rule if he would reject the industrial policy. This was the key mistake.

Before October 1991, top western economists had concentrated their thinking about the transition from communism only on eastern Europe, and really only the countries of northern eastern Europe at that—Hungary, Poland, and Czechoslovakia. It was inevitable that they would think about reform in Russia in the same terms. In April 1992 Lawrence Summers, then the chief economist of the World Bank and soon to be the top Clinton administration official dealing with Russia, reported that "a striking degree of unanimity exists in the advice that has been provided to the nations of Eastern Europe and the FSU."[21]

At another conference the previous year, Summers asserted:

> The elements of reform can be grouped into four categories:
> 1. Macroeconomic stabilization: tightening fiscal and credit policies, and addressing internal and external imbalances;
> 2. Price and market reform: removing price controls, liberalizing trade, and creating competitive factor markets;
> 3. Enterprise reform and restructuring: private sector development: establishing and clarifying property rights, facilitating entry and exit of firms, restructuring of enterprises;
> 4. Institutional reform: redefining the role of the state: legal and regulatory reform, social safety net, reform of government institutions (tax administration, budget and expenditure control, monetary control).
>
> While there is general consensus over the nature of the reforms to be implemented, the sequencing of those reforms has been intensely debated. [However], there is broad agreement that macroeconomic stabilization, followed by price and trade reform, should occur at the very beginning of the reform process. Tax reform, the development of a social safety net, and measures to encourage the private sector should follow quickly thereafter.
>
> Restructuring, privatization, institutional, regulatory and legal reform can be addressed early in the reform process, but completion of reform in these areas will take more time. Financial liberalization, full convertibility of the capital account and full wage liberalization should come in later in the reform sequence.[22]

The universality of Summers' language accurately reflected his belief that these principles of reform could improve the performance of almost any economy in which they were not being fully applied. The language corresponded to what John Williamson called "the Washington consensus" that had flowed from the reform experience of Latin America in the 1980s.[23] Indeed, the order of Summers' points was similar to that of Williamson's ten points of the "Washington consensus" on Latin America and also to that in Stanley Fischer and Alan Gelb's major World Bank paper on Eastern Europe of 1990.[24]

As Summers recognized in the long statement cited above, the sequencing of steps was crucial. The ranking of his points—and those of Williamson and Fischer—was not meant as a precise sequence of steps, but it was not random. It represented a reasonable ordering of priorities in Latin America, where the immediate problem was financial stabilization. A social safety net was not thought crucial in Latin America, because it already existed to some extent and because all agreed that "the recessionary . . . effects of fiscal contraction . . . are short-lived, especially under conditions of financial crisis."[25] Economists could be strident in insisting on free trade, deregulation, privatization, and property rights in Latin America because they knew that Latin American politicians would take political considerations into account and introduce change slowly at best.

Obviously, everyone understood Russia was different. It did not have a seriously distorted market economy as did Latin America, but rather almost no market at all. As Stanley Fischer and Alan Gelb noted in 1990, Russia was not only much larger than any of the East European countries, but also had a more centralized system, more centralized even than China. As Jeffrey Sachs emphasized at a 1993 conference, the Soviet Union, like India and China, did not have the Roman law tradition of western and eastern Europe.

Despite subsequent charges to the contrary, neoliberal economists all understood that institutional change would be more important in Russia than in Latin America. Stanley Fischer explicitly stated: "One of the most difficult intellectual challenges the Washington consensus faces" is to develop an understanding of "how to create an enabling environment. The issue goes well beyond property rights to the creation of legal, accounting, and regulatory systems, and the need for efficient government administration."[26]

Nevertheless, Fischer's statement reflected the general realization of the neoliberal economists that creating institutions was a "most difficult challenge." A similar comment in Williamson's discussion of institutional change in Latin America was even more revealing. "I suppose that I was provoked into adding property rights to [the bottom of] the list by an article . . . that derided me as a "hydraulic economist" [this was presumably intended to be an abusive term for a macroeconomist] who was indifferent to such legal institutions as private property, which the author was convinced were at the core of Latin America's problems."[27]

The real problem in Summers' analysis of the sequence of the steps of economic reform was his casual statement that "institutional, regulatory and legal reform can be addressed early in the reform process, but completion of reform in these areas will take more time."[28] "Can," not "must." "Addressed," not "resolved." It obviously would take decades for Russia to develop a smoothly functioning institutional, regional, and legal system, but Summers and his associates did not share North's insight that institutions establish incentive structures and that rational individuals respond to the real, existing incentive structure, not to the incentive structure in some abstract model in the minds of scholars.

The crucial starting point for economic reform in Russia was to realize that incentives were going to exist from the beginning and that the top priority was to do something, even if imperfectly, to ensure that the incentives were not counterproductive. The notion that optimal institutions would arise spontaneously contradicted everything that had been learned in the decades of work on the logic of collective action. Every step in the reform should have been analyzed in terms of the incentives—the real incentives—they would create in the conditions prevailing in Russia at the time. Leading economists such as Larry Summers, Stanley Fischer, and Kenneth Arrow were very cautious about assembly plant privatization at first, for they understood the potential problem. But when, for reasons that are not clear, they supported Chubais's enthusiasm for voucher privatization, they never rethought the implications for the incentives that were created.

There was no reason to abandon the basic assumptions of the neoliberal model; they were the correct starting point of policy. But it had to be understood that those assumptions did not rest on the rosy optimism about the state of nature (that is, human nature) of Jean Jacques Rousseau, but on the harsh pessimism of Thomas Hobbes. The central point of the neoliberal model, often not emphasized in polite company, was expressed by Dennis Mueller in a succinct summary of the current state of American public choice literature in 1989:

> Probably the most important accomplishment of economics is the demonstration that individuals with purely selfish motives can mutually benefit from exchange. If A raises cattle and B corn, both

may improve their welfare by exchanging cattle for corn. . . . [However], the choices facing A and B are not merely to trade or not, as implicitly suggested. A can choose to steal B's corn, rather than give up his cattle for it; B may do likewise. . . . In an anarchic environment, the independent choices of both individuals can be expected to lead both to adopt the dominant stealing strategy.[29]

Just as crime is a rational response to the incentives imbedded in a certain set of costs and benefits, so too is political corruption. Gordon Tullock implied this point when he equated anarchy and government corruption:

In a situation in which there is no government it would be possible to motivate people to do anything you wish by offering them suitable compensation. In a completely corrupt government, officials could be motivated to do anything you wish by suitable payments and, hence, there would be no difference between this society and that of anarchy. If, as I believe is correct, people under anarchy are every bit as selfish as they are now, we would have the Hobbesian jungle. In any event, we would be unable to distinguish a fully corrupt government from no government.[30]

The market is not something that exists in the state of nature, to be released by the collapse of state institutions. Over the thousands of years of human history, the institutions of many great civilizations collapsed, but a well-functioning market did not emerge as a result, only the collapse of civilization. Markets are created and maintained by government, and there is no single "market" that can be introduced in Russia or anywhere else. The pure neoliberal model would not be tolerated anywhere, certainly not in the United States, and real market incentive structures vary with time and place. The incentives of the United States market system today are not the same as those in 1928 or in 1828—or even before the bank crisis of the 1980s or the rise of the unregulated Internet of the 1990s. The incentives in the United States are not the same as in the markets of Sweden, Japan, or India. People respond to the incentives that exist at their particular time and place.

Yet the creation of a proper set of rules, laws, and incentives (North's definition of institutions) is the epitome of a public good. The well-studied problems of aggregating individual rationality in achieving a collective good are nowhere so severe as in this realm. Neither the entrepreneur nor the uncontrolled public official has any individual self-interest to expend individual effort for the public good.

To the extent that individuals can help shape the rules and regulations, public choice literature insists that individuals have an interest in shaping them in a way that gives themselves an advantage and helps them maximize personal profit. Business lobbying over the incentives in tax laws provides only a hint of what should be expected when more fundamental laws and rules are at stake.

Nothing in economic theory suggests that neoliberal economists are any less self-interested than other human beings. Indeed, their ideology should lead them to be more self-conscious in pursuing their self-interest than those they see as misled by moralistic propaganda. Stanley Fischer made this point directly in 1993 when he criticized a paper by Andrei Shleifer and his Russian colleagues for using the word "politician" to refer only to opponents. Yeltsin and those in his government were politicians as well, Fischer insisted. "So this is really a paper about the good guys versus the bad guys, and we do not know what drives the good guys, and what differentiates them, except that we are on their side and they on ours."[31] Fischer was implying that "the good guys" were driven to rent-seeking like other politicians, and he was absolutely right. The drive of the Russian neoliberal economists to acquire property through state action was a key element in the Russian economic reform. The mystery is why the West did not base its policy on Fischer's insight.

The State and an Investment-Centered Analysis

The root of the word capitalism is no accident. All economists agree on the crucial importance of capital for economic growth, and the strength of capitalism is its ability to allocate investment to projects where the societal demand is the greatest. The basic reason that the Russian economy did not grow in the 1990s is quite clear: investment fell even more rapidly than production. The problem was not just new investment, but the most basic capital upkeep of buildings and equipment. The Norilsk Nickel combine on the Arctic Circle earned hard currency, but made no capital repairs from 1985 to 1997, the latter a year in which the plant had five major accidents.[32] The amount of chemical fertilizer used in agriculture was cut 90 percent. Grain production fell from 116 million tons in 1990 to less than 50 million tons in 1998, the level of the immediate post-Stalin period in the mid 1950s.

But if the failure of long-term and short-term investment was the basic proximate cause for the failure of Russian economic reform, the reason that investment failed to emerge is the most basic question of the Russian reform. Nevertheless, it is almost never analyzed. The reason is that both the western and Russian neoliberal economists and the architects of the Yeltsin off-budget program had virtually identical assumptions on the question. All strongly favored a reduction in investment in 1992 to maintain consumption, and all thought that no special efforts would be needed to stimulate investment. The investment would develop spontaneously if macroeconomic conditions—the "hydraulics"—were correct.

The basic assumptions of self-interested economic behavior illuminate why large investment is so problematic, especially in the early and middle stages of industrialization. There is no activity in modern industrial society that rests to such an extent on trust in such a range of actors. Depositors must feel confident in putting their money in impersonal banks; banks must think that borrowers whom they do not know will not disappear; companies must be able to issue stock in whose general honesty investors can believe; entrepreneurs must trust contractors to do reliable construction work, and they must assume that their project and its fruits will not be stolen when the project is finished. Investors know they may make a bad investment decision with respect to future market demand, but at least they want the assurance that a stable market will exist at that time. Neoliberal economists even insist that investors must have assurances about rates of inflation.

In modern society, much is done on implicit trust, but abstract trust is not enough even in modern society. Even in the United States today, people demand a government guarantee on their bank deposits, and business personnel demand legal guarantees against fraud at all stages. When a savings and loan crisis occurs or a hedge fund makes very bad decisions, the government is expected to intervene in extraordinary ways. Even when no crisis occurs, a *New York Times* reporter could note in 1999 that "judging from the cases streaming out of prosecutors' offices recently, it seems as if securities fraud rivals the internet as the nation's hottest growth industry."[33] A year later the *Wall Street Journal* published an article nearly one page long making the point: "In what may be one of the oddest aspects of the New Economy, [American] businesses . . . are reporting an upturn in old-fashioned petty cheating."[34]

However, in earlier stages of industrial development, trust in unknown persons and impersonal organizations is far more fragile at every link of the chain. Paradoxically, this point was never made more eloquently than in the case of Russia, but the Russia of the 1890s and 1900s, by Alexander Gerschenkron. Gerschenkron was a Great Russian émigré economist who taught at Columbia and Harvard universities in the 1940s and 1950s, who wrote much about the economic development of southern and eastern Europe, but who thought most about his native Russia.

Most of the conditions and problems Gerschenkron described in Russia of the 1890s seem similar to those in the 1990s, but not the role of government. Gerschenkron noted the importance of "the great judicial and administrative reforms" of the 1860s in "creating a suitable framework for industrial development." Nevertheless, he strongly emphasized that "the main point of interest [in Russia of the nineteenth century] is that, unlike the case of western Europe, [the creation of a well-functioning legal system] did not per se lead to an upsurge of individual activities in the country."[35] By contrast, although the legal reforms of the 1990s were less thorough than those of the 1860s, the reformers of the 1990s assumed they would work automatically.

According to Gerschenkron, the reason that legal reform was insufficient in Russia in the nineteenth century was that conditions did not lead to the creation of the banking system requisite to support investment:

> The scarcity of capital in Russia was such that no banking system could conceivably succeed in attracting sufficient funds to finance a large industrialization: the standards of honesty in business were so disastrously low, the general distrust of the public so great, that no bank could have hoped to attract even such small funds as were available, and no bank could have successfully engaged in long-term credit policies in an economy where fraudulent bankruptcy had been almost elevated to the rank of a general business practice.[36]

The difference between the nineteenth century and the 1990s was that western economists demanded real bankruptcy in up to 60 percent of the enterprises, thus making loans even more dangerous.

Gerschenkron's conclusion was clear-cut, and the Russian model that he described became the basis for the so-called Asian model of the twentieth century:

> Supply of capital for the needs of industrialization required the compulsory machinery of the government, which, through its taxation policies, succeeded in directing incomes from consumption

to investment. There is no doubt that the government as an *agens movens* of industrialization discharged its role in a far less than perfectly efficient manner. Incompetence and corruption of bureaucracy were great. The amount of waste that accompanied the process was formidable. But when all is said and done, the great success of the policies pursued under Vyshnegradski and Witte is undeniable.[37]

Modern neoliberal economists fear that a government assuming such a strong directing role, often tainted by corruption, will not relinquish it, but Gerschenkron pointed out that the role of government naturally changed in Russia after 1890. By the 1907–14 period, the direct role of the state was "very greatly reduced," as the conditions for private investment were being created.

The retrenchment of government activities led not to stagnation but to a continuation of industrial growth. Russian industry had reached a stage where it could throw away the crutches of government support and begin to walk independently—and yet, very much less independently than industry in contemporaneous Germany, for at least to some extent the role of the retreating government was taken over by the banks. . . . As industrial development proceeded apace and as capital accumulation increased, the standards of business behavior were growingly Westernized. The paralyzing atmosphere of distrust began to vanish, and the foundation was laid for the emergence of a different type of bank. . . . In short, after the economic backwardness of Russia had been reduced by state-sponsored industrialization processes, use of a different instrument of industrialization, suitable in the new "stage of backwardness," became applicable.[38]

Gerschenkron used the word industrialization, but of course he meant "market industrialization," and hence his words were as applicable to the marketization of the 1990s as to the industrial development of the 1890s. One of the great mysteries of Russian economic reform is that virtually none of the reformers or politicians looked back to the economic model of the Russian industrialization drive of Tsar Nikolai II that Gerschenkron described.

The history of economic reform in Russia in the 1990s, laid out in this book, will show, therefore, that the problem was not simply a weak state or a lack of institutions. Russia had a strong state and ample institutional rules. The Russian state and the international organizations created a powerful set of incentives (that is, real institutions). Unfortunately, the logic of those incentives led normal economic men to the behavior that is rightly deplored.

What economic reform in Russia lacked was a government (and international economic organizations) that was aware that the incentives for investment had to be carefully structured, that trust was based on legal restraints and concrete economic incentives, and that government is required to compensate as that trust is being built. Investors needed assurance on far more questions than inflation alone. As this book describes the state actions and the incentive system they created, it will point to other actions and incentive systems that may be helpful in correcting the situation.

Ultimately, however, the crucial fact to understand is that government is not a single actor. The establishment of a strong state is not enough. Individual government officials and individual military officers must have close relationships with individual entrepreneurs in order to create the trust necessary for investment. The periods of greatest growth in Europe, the United States, and the Pacific Rim countries were the periods of the closest such personal, "corrupt" relationship. Corruption builds the trust necessary for investment. The problem in Russia was not corruption, but the incentive of the corrupt and noncorrupt alike to invest in Swiss bank accounts rather than in their own emerging markets.

TWO   *Economic Reform*
and the Role of
Government

A CLEAR RESULT OF ECONOMIC REFORM, even
under Gorbachev, was that Russians learned to use western language to
describe the Russian economic system. A reader without knowledge of
Russian has little problem translating "barter," "makroekonomich-
eskie," "kommercheskie banki," "Tsentralny Bank," "privatizatsiia,"
"piramida," and "diler" (pronounced "deeler"). Unfortunately, these
words usually do not mean the same thing in Russian as in the West,
except "piramida." Most economic activities in independent Russia
were described in the language of classic economics and were explained
as the response of actors to economic incentives, not to government
directives. In fact, this had almost no relation to reality.

From early 1992, the Russian government proclaimed it was powerless vis-à-vis other actors both to avoid responsibility for economic difficulties and to justify strengthening its power. An article written in
March 1992 by a top American economist, when the only information
came from pro-government sources, emphasized "regional semi-
autarky" in which "local authorities and top enterprise management,
i.e., the local *nomenklatura* have taken effective control of economic
operations."[1] Five years later Douglass North spoke of "anarchy somewhat akin to what we have been observing in Russia," a reflection of
similar disinformation.[2]

Much of the detailed scholarly work on the Russian economy of the
1990s is similar. Anders Aslund's *How Russia Became a Market Economy* is typical in attributing almost all the nonmarket phenomena docu-

19

mented in great detail in his book to the actions or the power of those outside the government. "Direct deals between producers became the dominant form of trade in producer goods." "Rosnefteprodukt, the former State Committee for the allocation of petroleum products, still insisted on allocating gasoline." "Many exporters were so powerful that they could blackmail the government into exempting them from export taxes by threatening to stop exporting." "The natural gas price was kept very low at the insistence of Gazprom. . . . [It] needed to keep the price low if it was to sell all its output." "The agrarian lobby holds its own as the most potent lobby in Russia [but] the agrarians were remarkably slow to realize that Roskhleboprodukt [the former Ministry of Grain Procurement] cheated them, exacting state subsidies meant for farms while not paying those farms for deliveries made."[3] Since the agrarians who controlled the agriculture committees of the legislature were collective farm chairmen, and since they were not receiving the payments they were voting for themselves in the legislature, they must, indeed, have been remarkably slow!

The foremost scapegoat of the neoliberal reformers was the Russian Central Bank. Despite the frequent assertions that Yegor Gaidar and his team followed a tight money policy in their first months in office, Jeffrey Sachs and Anders Aslund were damning the Central Bank and its allegedly uncontrolled emission of money as early as January 1992. "Either the government wins control of credit in a matter of weeks, or it falls." They described its chairman as "the demon."[4] In fact, although the Central Bank was formally accountable to the Congress, the Congress had little power on economic questions, and the Central Bank was never independent of Yeltsin on fundamental questions.

The Gaidar team may have wanted to follow a tight money policy in the first months of 1992, as it told westerners, but the Yeltsin government did not—and Yeltsin was both president and premier. Boris Yeltsin always was extremely sensitive to any slight or perceived slight, and he reacted dramatically to them. No doubt Gazprom, Rosnefteprom, and the Central Bank could and did present their cases to Yeltsin, but the notion that they could insist that Yeltsin carry out their preferences or blackmail him is quite bizarre.

In fact, Yeltsin and the Russian government were deeply involved in all the decisions Aslund mentioned from the first days after independence. By mid-January 1992, Yeltsin spoke of "correctives" to the reform program, including a 50 percent limit on prices, control of prices by monopoly suppliers—and the press said virtually all suppliers had a monopoly position—and social protection for the masses.[5] A month later Yeltsin was deliberately distancing himself from Gaidar in public: Gaidar, the president reported on television, had told the government that the ruble was stabilized, but he, Yeltsin, disagreed and saw very difficult times ahead.[6]

Gaidar was to tell many scholars and reporters that his big mistake had been not to release controls on energy prices in the first months of 1992. In fact, Gaidar never had this option. Yeltsin not only refused to endorse such a measure, but also emphasized his disapproval of the idea by removing Gaidar's minister of oil, a fellow young economist, in a humiliating manner, as Yeltsin reported with pleasure in his memoirs.

In May 1992, at a meeting of the Cabinet of Ministers, I announced the dismissal of [Vladimir] Lopukhin [the minister of the oil industry]. I remember two faces: one was scarlet, almost crimson—that was Gaidar; the other was as white as a sheet—that was Lopukhin. . . . There was a very concrete reason for Lopukhin's dismissal. Using him as a battering ram, Gaidar was putting pressure on me to release prices on energy resources simultaneously with other prices without any restrictions. Future historians will determine which one of us was right, but I will always remember Lopukhin's deathly pale face.[7]

The Yeltsin government not only deliberately instituted a number of subsidies, but also often did so in a covert manner while still leaving fingerprints that would appear under closer scrutiny. Less clear was the variety of mechanisms that were used to direct the economy, the way in which they interacted, and the way in which they evolved. This chapter begins to analyze the relation of government and economy in the Yeltsin period, to clarify how the Russian economy was ruled.

Yeltsin's Reform Program and the Paradox of Unemployment

The policy that Boris Yeltsin enunciated in October 1991 and that his government endorsed in a memorandum to the IMF in February 1992 was everything that the IMF could have desired. In October 1991 Yeltsin promised not only a liberalization of prices, but "free prices:" "a one-time transition to market prices—a difficult, forced, but necessary measure." He pledged rapid privatization (at least of small-scale enterprises in services, trade, and industry, where 50 percent of the enterprises were to be privatized in three months), together with a tight money policy and a sharp reduction in government expenditures. After six months of inflation and a decline in living standards, the rate of inflation would slow, he expected. Living standards would start to rise by the fall of 1992.[8]

Gaidar announced that industrial prices, except for energy and freight transportation, would be unregulated. The same was true of the prices for most consumer products and services except bread, milk, medicines, rents, and utilities. Gaidar promised to reduce the budget deficit to 1 percent of gross domestic product (GDP) in the first quarter of 1992. Wage increases would be kept lower than inflation, and heavy taxes would be imposed—a value added tax of 25 percent, a wage tax of 37 percent, and a profit tax of 32 percent.

In an interview at the beginning of 1992, Gaidar described the most favorable scenario of economic reform. It would entail an inflation rate of 100 percent in January and February, of 10 to 12 percent a month by March and April, and of a few percentage points by the end of the year. He saw it as "fully realistic."[9] In early January 1992, the minister of foreign economic relations spoke of freeing all petroleum and gas prices by March and April. The ruble would be made convertible, and the exchange rate (then around 100 rubles to the dollar) would drop to 15–35 rubles to the dollar.[10]

An urgent goal was a major reduction in industrial employment. Everyone recognized that the Soviet system had given managers the incentive to hoard labor and that, as a result, the labor force of Soviet factories had been much too large for a long time. Indeed, as table 2-1 indicates, the Soviet Union had far too many people employed in agriculture, industry, construction, and transportation; a normal number in areas such as education and health; but far too few in the consumer and financial services. Within industry, far too many were employed in the smokestack and defense industries and too few in the computer and electronics industry. Within transportation, too many were working in railroads and too few in trucking. All branches of the material economy had far too many production workers and too few white-collar staff members.[11]

Both proponents and opponents of economic reform acknowledged that its effect—and its intention—was deindustrialization. The huge

Table 2-1. *Employment by Sector, Selected Countries, 1990*
Percent[a]

Sector	USSR	USA	Sweden	Korea	Brazil
Agriculture	18.2[b]	2.8	3.3	18.3	24.2
Manufacturing, mining, gas, electricity, water	28.3	19.9	22.2	27.7	17.0
Construction	10.0	6.5	6.9	7.4	6.3
Transport	8.2	5.6	7.1	5.1	3.8
Trade, restaurants, hotels	7.8	20.6[c]	14.4	21.7	11.6[d]
Community, social, and personal services	25.1	33.2	37.4	14.6	31.1
Finance, real estate, insurance, business service	.6	11.3	8.6	5.2	6.0
Other	1.7	0.0	0.1	0.0	0.0

Source: From Susan Goodrich Lehmann, "Costs and Opportunities of Marketization: An Analysis of Russian Employment and Unemployment," in Richard L. Simpson and Ida Harper Simpson, eds., *Research in the Sociology of Work*, vol. 5, *The Meaning of Work* (Greenwich, Conn.: JAI Press, 1995), p. 205–34. Based on International Labour Organization data.

a. Percentages may not total 100 as a result of rounding.

b. USSR agriculture includes state farmers (*sovkhozniki*) and collective farmers (*kolkhozniki*).

c. United States: hotels are included in community services.

d. Brazil 1988: hotels and restaurants are included in community and social services.

state heavy industry sector—especially the defense industry subsector—was to be drastically reduced in size. With nowhere else to go, redundant workers would stream into the understaffed services sector. The smaller number of industrial workers would be more productive, their wages would be higher, and the larger service sector would allow them to enjoy their money.

One of the strongest arguments for rapid marketization was that it would change the managers' incentives and encourage them to lay off excess workers. This is what restructuring meant. The industries with the greatest excess of workers were precisely those that suffered the greatest decline in production. The need to reduce a labor force that had always been too large and further to cut workers not needed because of the decline in production should have resulted in a massive decline in industrial employment.

Such a decline was widely expected. The deputy minister of the economy predicted 5 million unemployed in early 1992,[12] while a Soviet scholar estimated that a 20 percent decrease in production would result in unemployment of between 10 and 15 percent of the labor force, increasing to more than 30 percent in later years.[13]

In January 1992 Gaidar estimated that production would fall 19 percent in the first quarter.[14] Industrial production in 1992 was later reported to be 75 percent of the 1990 level and then 65 percent in 1993 and 51 percent in 1994.[15] Western supporters of Russian economic reform often claimed that official Russian figures on the decline of GDP were exaggerated, but it is unquestionable that a very major decline occurred in industrial production across the board. Table 2-2 presents data on a range of products on which there is little dispute about the comparability of data over time. Indeed, in many cases the decline in the sales of products was greater than in their production, and it was greater still in industries such as machinery and defense, where production must be measured in rubles and is harder to compare.

Analysts had to face a jarring fact from the beginning. Soviet factories had been greatly overstaffed, but unemployment rose very slowly despite a precipitous decline in industrial production in the first three years of Yeltsin's economic reform. While industrial production fell to 75 percent of 1990 levels by 1992, 65 percent by 1993, and 51 percent by 1994, employment in industry itself was 95.6 percent of 1990 levels in 1992, 91.6 percent in 1993, and 82.2 percent in 1994. The wages of skilled workers in heavy industry had always been higher than those of most professional and managerial personnel, and, as table 2-3 shows, this remained true in October 1993. The wages of industrial workers were also generally kept at high levels.[16]

Although many westerners, even at the end of the 1990s, believed that Yeltsin never had a policy of social support, this is not accurate. From the beginning, the Yeltsin government had a very deliberate, sophisticated policy of social support, although almost never articulated, especially to westerners. It was deliberately trying to maintain consumption in the cities in the face of declining production. It was using the factory and other places of employment as its major social welfare institution and was paying wages rather than unemployment insurance to employees even when they were not working. The use of earnings from exports and foreign loans for consumption rather than investment goods had the same purpose, as did the policy of exploiting agriculture to ensure that cities would receive food more cheaply than if prices were market-based.[17]

The former Soviet Union did not have a comprehensive social service system, but used the factory and other places of employment to provide a range of services. Factories built housing with ministerial funds and distributed it to employees through the place of work. They often maintained their workers' housing in the settlement (*poselok*) or district and

Table 2-2. *Production of Selected Items, 1990–96*

Category	1990	1991	1992	1993	1994	1995	1996
Petroleum (million tons)	516	462	399	354	318	307	301
Coal (million tons)	395	353	337	306	272	263	257
Steel (million tons)	90	77	67	58	49	52	49
Tractors (thousands)	214	178	137	89	29	21	14
Excavators (thousands)	23	21	15	13	7	5	4
Trucks (thousands)	665	616	583	467	183	142	134
Bicycles (thousands)	3,671	3,390	2,402	1,812	869	563	348
Metal-cutting machinery (thousands)	74	68	53	42	20	18	12
Mineral fertilizer (million tons)	16	15	12	10	8	10	9
Agricultural pesticides (thousand tons)	111	87	65	39	19	16	13
Timber (million cubic tons)	304	269	238	175	119	116	97
Cement (million tons)	83	78	62	50	37	37	28
Cattle (million head)[a]	n.a.	57	55	52	49	43	40
(without cows)	n.a.	36	35	31	29	25	23
Pigs (million head)	n.a.	38	35	31	28	29	23
Grain (million tons)	117	89	107	99	81	63	69
Canned goods (million)	8,206	6,944	5,353	4,517	2,817	2,428	2,158
Refrigerators (million)	3.8	3.7	3.2	3.5	2.7	1.8	1.1
Shoes (million pairs)	385	336	220	146	77	52	37
Cloth (billion square meters)	8.4	7.6	5.1	3.7	2.2	1.8	1.4
Synthetic fiber (thousand tons)	673	529	474	349	198	216	134
Socks, stockings (million pairs)	872	743	677	547	353	285	209
Antibiotics (tons)	4,672	4,524	3,577	1,898	1,556	1,582	1,468

Sources: 1990 grain: *Narodnoe khoziaistvo RSFSR v 1990 g.: Statisticheskii ezhegodnik* (National economy of the RSFSR in 1990: Statistical yearbook) (Moscow: Goskomstat, 1990), p. 420; *Rossiiskii statisticheskii ezhegodnik: Statisticheskii sbornik* (Russian statistical yearbook: Statistical collection) (Moscow: Goskomstat, 1998), pp. 399, 402, 404, 410–14, 417, 419–21, 423, 436, 459, 480.

n.a. Not available

a. Figures are end-of-year. The handbook actually lists them for January 1st of the next year.

subsidized the police and fire protection for it. The factory built and partially financed clinics, owned and managed farms to provide food for its employees, furnished preschool day care and summer camps for employees' children, repaired schools and roads, and so forth. Free or cheap vacation passes were provided for resorts owned by the plant or ministry. The main meal of the day was lunch (*obed*), and most meat

Table 2-3. Average Monthly Wages, Skilled and Unskilled Workers and Professionals, October 1993

Rubles

Professional	Salary	Skilled worker	Salary	Other workers	Salary
Economic manager	94,100	Locomotive engineer	129,000	Truck driver	67,600
Engineer	93,600	Miner	125,700	Fireman	59,500
Physician	71,600	Metallurgist	107,400	Weaver	56,000
Scholar	64,400	Paper industry worker	95,400	Tractor driver	47,800
High school teacher	63,700	Excavator operator	89,100	Barber	45,100
Accountant	60,200	Welder	89,000	Shoe factory worker	44,700
Pharmacist	54,000	Machinist	86,000	Clerk	44,600
Agronomist	51,300	Construction hard hat	80,900	Cook	36,000
Dentist	49,700	Mechanic	69,800	Unskilled agricultural worker	26,800
Librarian	40,000	Chemical worker	69,400	Janitor	26,600
Preschool teacher	40,900	Lathe operator	64,100	Porter	24,000

Source: These data are from a survey of 50,827 Russian adults conducted in December 1993. The survey was funded by the MacArthur Foundation, the Carnegie Corporation, the National Science Foundation, and the Brookings Institution. In addition to the usual question about family income, the questionnaire asked for the monthly salary at the basic place of employment. The purpose was to collect data on average income of occupations, not just of individuals.

consumption took place in the factory cafeteria at prices well below cost. Kiosks at factories often sold at subsidized prices meat and other goods that were in short supply to workers to take home. Managers had an incentive to employ the semi-employable. Single-factory towns or districts took on the character of American factory towns or districts.[18]

The restructuring planned under the official economic reform program would have destroyed most of this social infrastructure. All the services provided by the factory were highly subsidized, and any manager interested in maximizing profit would try to reduce them as much as possible. In the long run, it was desirable to privatize these services or transfer the subsidized ones to local government, but in the short run, unemployment would have deprived employees of their social support when no replacement was available. The maintenance of employment at the factory, even of people not actually working forty hours a week, was a brilliant administrative solution to the immediate problem.

The government did, however, have to resolve a series of concrete questions about how to use the factory as a social support instrument. First and foremost, how was the factory to get the money to support a quantity of workers that was excessive in the Soviet period and that became even more excessive as production fell?

Those who talked about a normal market economy remained silent about these facts. They talked about the enterprises' making interenterprise loans to cover their purchases of supplies from one another. But where were the managers obtaining money to pay for wages, social services, and also taxes? The role of government in the economy somehow clearly was far from the role the Russian economic reformers and the government itself acknowledged.

The Development of Off-Budget Subsidies

Gaidar announced from the beginning that the prices on certain consumer goods would be controlled, at least in the near term, and these included medicine and food. The government then kept its reported budget deficit relatively low by failing to pay for the subsidies that it officially announced. For example, the cost of medicine produced in Russia rose tenfold during the first quarter of 1992, and the price of imported medicine even more. To cushion the blow on consumers and hospitals, the regime increased the price of medicines sold to them only fourfold. This was a reasonable policy, officially announced, but the regime should have provided a subsidy to the wholesale pharmaceutical distributors to cover the difference. To maintain the appearance of budgetary stringency, it did not do so.

When pharmaceutical plants threatened not to ship medicines for which they were not being paid, the government told the distributors— which were completely state owned—to go to the banks for loans to pay for the medicine. The debt of the regional distributor in Yaroslavl rose from 3 million rubles on January 1, 1992, to 20 million on April 15. The total budget for medicines for Yaroslavl hospitals alone for the first quarter of 1992 was 7 million rubles.[19] All this took place before the Sixth Congress in April and continued afterward.

Since the loans to the pharmaceutical distributors were to pay for medicines already sold below cost, the banks knew that the government would pay off the debts through budgetary appropriations, that the loans would never be repaid, or that they would be effectively wiped out by inflation. Either the government was postponing the deficit until later in the year, when it was promising the IMF it would have a lower deficit, or it was engaging in deliberate off-budget deficit financing. Bank officers, who read the press reports of government promises to the IMF, had to know that their loans to the distributors were very high risk, but they still made them. The reason is that they were really state officials, so they did what they were told.

Similarly, Gaidar retained price controls on twelve basic food items, but the controls were administered regionally. However, the regions were not given the necessary money for the subsidies at first. Thus in January 1992 Riazan oblast needed 3 billion rubles for food subsidies, but received only 35 million from the government. It was reported in mid-January that the region asserted it had no choice but to lift all price controls.[20] This problem was quickly solved. Local governments included many of these subsidies in their budgets (although labeled as agricultural subsidies rather than urban ones), along with expenditures for education, health, highly subsidized housing and utilities, and the like, and so they were not part of the budget deficit.

But what was the source of the taxes for these local government budget items? Local government had neither a property tax nor any other significant independent tax. There were three major tax sources: a value added tax, a profit tax, and a wage tax. In March 1992, 19.3 percent of total Russian taxes came from excise or individual taxes (the vast majority withholding taxes from the paychecks of workers in state enterprises), 41 percent from the value added tax, and 31 percent from the profit tax. By May 1992 the proportion provided by the profit tax rose to 53 percent.[21]

Table 2-4 shows just how unimportant most taxes—and particularly taxes from the private sector—were in the budget of Yaroslavl, a city with a population of 650,000. The budget of the city government rose precipitously from month to month as wages and supply costs increased with inflation, and tax revenue rose in tandem. In May 1992, 68 percent of Yaroslavl taxes were coming from a tax on profits of enterprises.

The local governments were not assigned some fixed percentage of the taxes collected by the federal government in their regions and then allowed to raise additional taxes, nor were they forced to cut expenditures in case of tax shortfalls. In official jargon, there were no "fixed norms" on taxes. The regional expenses were decided first, and then the national Ministry of Finance calculated the percentage of taxes that it would assign each region to finance them. The Russian national budget was in deficit, but local budgets remained in balance as the local governments were assigned the percentage of local tax receipts necessary for local expenditures. The frequent allegation that local governments were

Table 2-4. *Changing Revenue Budget, City of Yaroslavl, First Six Months of 1992*
Rubles

Source of income	1st quarter 2/28/91	1st quarter 1/23/92	2d quarter 5/13/92
Total income	317,063	225,966	811,459
Enterprise profit	205,285	155,546	551,024
Cooperative profit	1,502	1,502	0
Public organization profit	323	323	0
Public cooperative profit	90	90	0
Value added tax	7,672	4,603	70,000
Excise tax	4,500	11,656	15,500
Enterprise property	0	6,643	0
Payment for water	647	647	1,000
Individual taxes	72,198	40,110	162,000
Tariffs	1,821	1,821	2,135
Fees and other tax income	3,025	3,025	3,500
Property	n.a.	n.a.	1,800
Privatization	n.a.	n.a.	4,500

Source: Budget data provided to author by Yaroslavl city soviet, June 1992.
n.a. Not available

not "submitting" their taxes to Moscow was simply disinformation: they had no taxes to submit or not to submit.

All of this would have been fine if the large state-owned enterprises had been making a profit. However, they already had excess labor force, and their level of production was falling without a commensurate reduction in the work force. The plants were usually not being paid for the goods they produced and delivered, but they still were paying wages. They were being assessed a large tax on profits based on the difference between prices of supplies acquired at one time and goods shipped at a later date at inflated prices, but usually without being paid for the goods shipped. Indeed, the head of administration of Yaroslavl hypothesized privately that inflation was tax-push, that it was deliberately created by the government to ensure that a paper profit could be made. The enterprises presumably were getting the money to pay these taxes through loans from the same types of banks that lent to the wholesale pharmaceutical distributors.

A major reason for this practice was that the IMF demanded that the government reduce the budget deficit sharply. Both publicly and privately many in Russia referred to double bookkeeping in which a hidden part of the budget was financed by credit. As shall be seen, the chairman of the Budget, Planning, Taxation, and Price Committee of the Supreme Soviet often complained that this practice unjustly destroyed legislative power.[22] The answer was that the international financial institutions made assistance dependent on a relatively small deficit in the official budget.

Such statements did not come only from Communist forces. The committee chairman just cited was Aleksandr Pochinok, an economist trusted enough by Boris Yeltsin to be named deputy minister of finances. They spoke on television and wrote in papers like *Izvestiia* that surely were read by IMF staff and diplomats. Neoliberal economists were concerned about control over money as well as a democratic budgetary process. Surely they also tried to persuade the IMF in private and provided detailed information on the hidden budget. Those fighting with ministers of finance such as Boris Fedorov were surely trying to persuade the IMF that such people were playing a fraudulent game and were not worthy of support.

The West, however, seemed little concerned as long as the verbal formalities were observed. In the Soviet period, the Russians had become accustomed to treating legal institutions and procedures as formalities, and they were happy to continue the practice. The foreigners never reflected on whether their own policy was undercutting any effort to build respect for law or whether it was contributing to an utter contempt for international organizations as fools whose loans were properly targets of private corruption.

Detailed evidence has not yet emerged on the process through which decisions on off-budget subsidies were being made. The Ministry of Finance, the Ministry of Economics (the old Gosplan), the Ministry of Industry, the presidential administration, and the chief regional officials surely were involved, but the old officials must pass from the stage before new ones will speak and write freely.

Nevertheless, it can be confidently asserted that the Russian economy was centrally regulated and directed from January 1992 through the end of 2000. The central government had overwhelming power vis-à-vis the enterprises, the oligarchs, the banks, and the regions. Neither the neoliberal western economists nor the author of this book approve of the decisions made by the central government, although often for different reasons. However, no one should continue to assert that the Russian government was not strong or that institutions did not exist. In the 1990s the Russian economic system was closer to that of the Soviet Union in 1990 than to a market system.

The Mechanisms of Control

This chapter can only suggest the workings of the mechanisms of control. There were, however, a multiplicity of them, and they all were deliberately hidden from view. Hence the following material should be seen as a research agenda rather than a definitive explanation.

The Ministerial "Holding Companies"

The abolition of the industrial ministries in 1992 gave the impression that authority in economic management, except in the natural gas and petroleum industries, had totally collapsed. The new Russian government had only two industrial ministries—the Ministry of Industry and the Ministry of the Fuel and Energy Industry. While the Ministry of Industry had a series of departments that duplicated most of the old industrial ministries, these departments (a non-Soviet term was used, *departement*) usually had a staff of only some one hundred persons.

Government spokesmen strengthened the impression that central control had disappeared by claiming that plant managers had become a law unto themselves in setting prices and wages and in making loans to one another. Appearances, however, were deceiving. The Gorbachev government in the last two years of its existence had initiated a little-noticed and still little-understood policy of abolishing the industrial ministries and replacing them with branch "concerns," "holding companies," and "corporations" that dealt with the same enterprises as the old ministries. In July 1989 Leonid Abalkin, deputy premier, had told Hedrick Smith that one of the important elements of reform was the "step-by-step elimination of 'production ministries.'"[23] The first, Gazprom, was created in 1989 from the former Ministry of the Gas Industry and remained a state institution throughout the Gorbachev years. The successors of the ministries created in 1991, however, were formally more privatized.

After the Soviet Union collapsed, all these institutions became instruments of the Russian government. The successors to the ministries were called Roschermet (Russian Ferrous Metallurgy), Rosobshchemash (Russian "General Machinebuilding" or Rockets), and so forth, even though they oversaw Ukrainian plants as well.[24] The result was paradoxical in light of the denunciation of the ministerial nomenklatura: the network of coordinating institutions that had managed and regulated the ministries was destroyed, but the new quasi-ministerial institutions continued to exist and to deal with the non-Russian republics.

Russian reformers seldom mentioned these new institutions, except occasionally as something that old ministerial forces wanted to create.[25] Other westerners thought that they coexisted with the old ministries, or else they were given a very misleading impression about their functions by their Russian sources. The best but extremely brief western discussion of the new entities used the terminology of Soviet informants and called them "trade associations":

> Although interviews suggested considerable variation across associations, the main functions they performed were lobbying for state subsidies with the government and central bank, coordinating input supplies and production, providing investment and financial assistance, marketing, and research and development. Some associations offered a menu of services, and members could purchase only the services they wanted.

The associations appear to have played a very important support role for their enterprises in the 1990–1991 period. By the summer of 1992, however, it was clear to many of the associations that the need for some of the functions they provided would decline as their member enterprises learned how to operate independently and other supporting institutional arrangements emerged. [26]

Some of the words of this paragraph are accurate, but the overall impression created is quite misleading. The associations did not play an important support role for their enterprises until the last months of 1991, because they were not established before then. In the late 1980s the ministries had often transformed their chief administrative units (*glavki*) into associations and concerns,[27] probably in order to claim that the size of the ministerial staff was being reduced, but they were quite different institutions. The first ministerial associations, such as Gazprom, were state entities indistinguishable from the old institutions called ministries.

The function of the bodies formed in late 1991 was not to lobby, except to the extent that all government bodies in all countries always lobby in the budgetary process. It was not to provide services, nor to serve a support role except to the extent that all bureaucratic officials do so. In "coordinating input supplies and production," they were maintaining the old supply ties in the same basic way that the ministries and the central planning organs had always done. In "providing investment and financial assistance," they, alas, provided no investment assistance at all, but instead were the main conduit for state subsidies for wages and taxes and the main organizers of "interenterprise loans."

Another euphemism that insiders used in interviews with me was "wholesale trading firm." The chairman of Pharmindustriia, the successor of the former Ministry of the Medical Industry, said in March 1992 that his staff was about half the size of that of the former ministry, but this was a substantial group of officials. In October 1992 the Automobile and Agricultural Holding Company (Avtoselkhozmashkholding) was said to be staffed by 500 people. They acquired supplies and then sold them to their plants for a 5 to 6 percent commission.[28]

In fact, the holding companies and corporations, together with the branch commercial banks, were brought under the effective, if unacknowledged, control of the Ministry of Industry and its departments and then of more specialized ministries when they were formed. The nature of their relationship is clear from their location. The Tractor and Agricultural Machinery Department and the Automobile Department of the Ministry of Industry were both located in the old building of the Ministry of the Automobile Industry and the Ministry of Tractor and Agricultural Machinery Industry. The heads of the two departments occupied adjacent offices—the offices of the respective former ministers.[29] On the same floor, less than 100 yards away, was the office of the head of the industry's holding company, Avtoselkhozmashkholding. In October 1992 the sign on the wall gave the name of the head of the holding company: Nikolai A. Pugin, the USSR minister of the automobile industry from 1986 to 1991. The head of the Tractor and Agricultural Machinery Department of the Ministry of Industry said in an interview that the holding company was independent of the ministry, but a cynic might wonder about the independence of a holding company headed by a former USSR minister located on the same floor as the department.

A major reason that the key role of the holding companies was not being acknowledged was that their existence called into the gravest doubt the various explanations for economic developments that Russian reformers gave to foreigners. The enterprises supposedly were engaged in autonomous activities, but the holding companies closely associated with the industrial ministries were organizing the procurement and delivery of all their supplies. Thus the holding companies had to be deeply involved not only in the organization of interenterprise loans, but also in setting the prices of supplies, which presumably had to include their own commissions. The branch banks making the loans that the plants needed for wages were also closely associated with the industrial ministries. It thus makes no sense whatsoever to say that enterprise managers autonomously set prices and wages, causing virtually uncontrolled inflation.

It also would be wrong to suggest that the holding companies and concerns had finished serving their function by the summer of 1992 and were disappearing. My interview on Avtoselkhozmashkholding took place in October 1992. However, as will be discussed in the next chapter, the Yeltsin government did begin seriously to attack the power of the holding companies in the summer of 1992. Most of the large enterprises were turned into stock companies and became, in reality, the property of their management. The top managers in the holding companies saw that they had to be at the enterprise level to acquire riches. For example, Pugin of Avtoselkhozmashkholding once more became director of the Gorky (now Nizhnii Novgorod) Auto Works.

This "nomenklatura privatization" at the enterprise level was severely criticized by the radical reformers, but, in fact, the alternative at the time was the strengthening of the ministry-like holding companies. In March 1992 the head of Pharmindustriia told me that he was giving a great deal of thought to acquiring shares in his plants and maintaining control of them as they were privatized. The income from the "wholesale trade" was meant to be the source of capital if the concerns were to turn into large corporations and acquire their production plants, but the holding companies were accumulating debt from the enterprises and hoped to transform it into equity as well.

Such a pattern might have been desirable from an economic point of view. Soviet enterprises were comparable to western assembly plants rather than to large western corporations. The continued domination of the holding companies and their transformation into giant corporations that owned their production or assembly plants would have been one of the better ways for Soviet economic reform to evolve. Once these companies became the equivalent of the original Standard Oil of New Jersey, government control could have been loosened and an antimonopoly policy could have divided them into competing mini-ministries (companies), such as were created from Standard Oil and are the dominant units in the modern western economy. Then they could have become more genuinely privatized. If conditions had simultaneously been established for the creation of new enterprises that, like Compaq and America Online, could become giant corporations, Russia might have been in a position for a transition to a modern market economy over the medium term.

However, the radical Russian reformers were not thinking in terms of the nature of the modern western economy and the role of giant corporations and their production plants within it. They were planning to privatize assembly plants. Moreover, whatever was economically desirable, the heads of the holding companies were the last ministers appointed by Gorbachev. Indeed, the head of Pharmindustriia, with whom I talked, had even been a close lieutenant of Gorbachev in the party apparatus of Stavropol. Yeltsin absolutely did not want him and those like him to be the great beneficiaries of privatization. The radical economists totally agreed with Yeltsin.

The evolution of the holding companies after 1992 remains obscure. Many, if not most, continued to exist, and the press reports suggested that they did become more like trade associations over time. However, Roslespom (Russia Timber Industry) remained a state company that controlled the timber industry, and Rosugol (Russian Coal) had a similar role in the coal industry.[30] A new Rostekstil was formed in 1993 "on the basis of the Ministry of Textiles," and almost all the private plants became part of it to receive orders, financing, and subsidies. Since textile production fell ten times between 1991 and 1997, Rostekstil was mainly providing subsidies. A 1998 article, for example, discussed how the governor of Vladimir persuaded Rostekstil to give more orders and raw materials to Vladimir textile plants.[31]

The key point for the transformation of the role of the holding companies was the first half of 1993. The Central Bank reduced direct credits to the branch banks that were closely associated with the holding companies, or perhaps ended most of them. "Independent" funds (the Pension Fund, for example) were put under the control of the regional governors. Yeltsin at this time had decided to dissolve the Congress and to introduce a new constitution in which a federation council composed of regional officials had a dominant role, and he wanted to give these regional officials a greater role in distributing subsidies.

The Banks

The crucial instruments in off-budget financing were the "privatized" commercial banks or, at least, the type of "privatized" commercial bank that became dominant in Russia. For the great majority of citizens in the old Soviet Union and in independent Russia, Sberbank, the Savings Bank, was the only bank of importance. Personal checking accounts did not exist, and Russians had long used their saving accounts in Sberbank as the depository for both their long-range savings and any funds for consumption they would not use in the immediate future. Throughout the 1990s Sberbank remained the only bank whose deposits were guaranteed by the government, and Russians continued to place the great bulk of their savings there. Sberbank never lent money to the population or enterprises, and one way or another its money was at the disposal of the central government.

Besides the Savings Bank, the old Soviet system had a banking system that served little purpose other than as a clearinghouse for state enterprises. Since money had very little importance for economic producers, the banks that handled money had little economic or political significance. Membership in "elected" organs of party committees was a reliable status indicator in the Soviet period, and it dramatically documented the status and power of different institutions. The chairman of Gosplan (the distributor of concrete goods) was always a member of the republican Central Committee and sometimes a member of the party bureau, the minister of finances was almost always a member of the republican Central Committee, but the chairman of Gosbank was usually only a member of the Auditing Commission, lower in rank than even a candidate member of the Central Committee.

Obviously, if money were to become more important, the Ministry of Finance and the banks had to assume a more important role, and the economic reformers of the Gorbachev period increasingly turned their attention to bank reform. The leading economic reformer from 1988 to 1990, Leonid Abalkin, was much attracted to the Japanese economic model, and he and the central government tried to create a banking system that brought the banks into close association with the top industrial organizations. In 1987, as a first step in this direction, the USSR Gosbank was split. Five specialized banks were created, corresponding with the major sectors of the economy and the deputy premiers who supervised them.

In 1988 and 1989 these specialized banks were supplemented by an increasing number of "commercial banks," and then the specialized banks and their subdivisions themselves became "commercial" banks.[32] Some of the commercial banks were small and served the new cooperative enterprises that were beginning to be created. It was rumored—surely with frequent accuracy—that they often were "mafia banks" that laundered money from various types of illegal activities in the West.[33] Some of them also accepted deposits from customers, but paid interest at rates so high they obviously were—and proved to be—pyramid schemes.

The major commercial banks created in 1989 were branch banks that were closely tied with the ministries and large enterprises. The largest and best publicized was Avtobank. In early 1990 the new Bank for the Development of the Automobile Industry of the USSR (Avtobank) was described both as a stock society whose stockholders were almost all automobile and agricultural machinery enterprises and as "a component part of the state apparatus." The branch banks were to perform the short-term banking functions for the enterprises and pay them interest on their money, but they were also to provide long-term investment to both their own plants and their suppliers.[34] The manager of the bank was the head of the finance department of the Ministry of the Automobile Industry, and the bank was located in the building of the Ministry of the Automobile Industry—presumably the same building where Avtoselkhozmashkholding was located.[35]

The role of these branch commercial banks could be seen through several prisms. Since reform was somewhat chaotic, many in the banking system showed considerable independence during the period, but this independence took place within limits. The primary function of the commercial banks was to serve as the conduit of funds between the government and the plants, and they remained basically under the control of the ministry or plant that founded them. The branch banks were meant to give the ministries and their plants more financial flexibility in an era when supply procurement was becoming more decentralized and interenterprise payments more unreliable.

As long as the industrial institutions were fundamentally solvent, the branch commercial banks played a useful role as inside banks of the industrialists. They gave the enterprises the opportunity to earn interest on their funds and to obtain quick loans at a time of economic instability. They were an intelligent transition step on the road to more independent banks or at least to German- and Japanese-type banks. That surely is how Abalkin saw them.

Of course, the increasingly chaotic administrative system and the "war of laws" between the USSR government and the republics allowed the semi-independent banks to finance various types of semilegal trading, currency speculation, and the like. This meant that the branch banks could also serve the personal interests of those working in the banks and the ministry. At a minimum, the banks paid dividends to their shareholders,[36] and at some point these shareholders came to include individuals as well as institutions.

After Russia became independent, the branch banks not only continued to exist, but became more important. Eleksbank, for example, was the bank for all enterprises in the electronic industry that were in the quasi-ministerial corporation Eleks. In the Soviet period, the bank had fifty people on its staff and clearly played a relatively minor role. With Russian independence, its staff was almost immediately increased to 1,800 people.[37] It essentially became a ministry-like institution. The process of financing the subsidies to the enterprises was a complicated administrative task.

The financial crisis of early 1992 also fundamentally changed the role of the commercial banks. By mid-1992 four-fifths of the industrial enterprises had overdue accounts with their suppliers, customers, or both, and half were behind in their wages. In January 1992 the arrears totaled 37 billion rubles, less than four percent of Russian GDP. By July 1992 they totaled 3.2 trillion rubles in current prices, 80 percent of the GDP of the first six months of the year.[38] This translated into the most severe financial problems for the enterprises. To solve those problems for the enterprises, the commercial banks began providing them with short-term loans, often three months in duration, at interest rates well below the rate of inflation.[39]

Once the commercial banks were required to provide loans for such purposes, they inevitably assumed the enormous liquidity problems of the enterprises as well. Because they provided loans at interest rates well below inflation, they needed constant new infusions of funds. The only major sources were the government, foreign currency speculation with government deposits, or delayed transfers of payments. The banks were essentially as bankrupt as the enterprises.

In early 1994 a scholar speaking at the annual convention of the Russian Association of Bankers documented the situation that the bankers already knew all too well. By then, 40 to 50 percent of all loans had been prolonged so that they would not have to be declared nonperforming. Most banks prolonged the same loan repeatedly, and the scholar admitted, "There is little basis to hope for its repayment." Most loans rested on little collateral: 26 percent were totally unsecured; 22 percent were secured by a guarantee of the bank, 27 percent by material goods, 14 percent by others (legal persons), 7 percent by hard currency, and 1 percent by property and insurance.[40]

The banks were closely tied with the new holding companies and the departments of an industrial ministry. For example Stankinbank, the machine tool and instrument "commercial" bank that served the industry once administered by the USSR Ministry of Machine Tools and Instruments, was physically located in the same building off Pushkin Square as the Department of the Machine Tool and Instrument Industry of the Russian Ministry of Industry. Top IMF officials working with the Russians could not distinguish between bank and government because there was no distinction.

At first the commercial banks received credits directly from the Russian Central Bank in huge amounts—13 to 15 percent of GDP in 1992 and 6 percent in 1993.[41] Western supporters of reform were told that the practice of direct Central Bank credits was ended in 1993, but this was not accurate. In May 1993 the domestic credit issued by the Central Bank to the government and to the commercial banks became the basic control indicator of monetary policy and was restricted. Yet a year later the chairman of the Central Bank reported that it still was only "gradually" withdrawing from direct crediting of specific branches of the economy.[42]

The Central Bank and its chairman, Viktor Gerashchenko, were often used as a scapegoat in the West because of the credits and excess money, but, in fact, the direct credits the bank provided for the branches and their commercial banks reflected government policy. The branch commercial banks themselves did not make loans to enterprises independently, but responded to instructions from the Ministry of Finance and the Ministry of the Economy (the new name for Gosplan or the State Planning Committee, which retained a staff of some 2,000 persons) and from the holding companies.

The result was, in the words of a Moscow professor, "a quasi-budget system of specialized banks that have little in common with market principles of distribution of credit resources."[43] Michael Bernstam and Alvin Rabushka summarized the situation well:

> Commercial banks in Russia were not, and still are not, normal banks as found in market economies. They do not accept deposits paying a market rate of interest or make loans on the basis of commercial criteria. They do not fulfill the normal role of intermediating household deposits to enterprises, thereby converting savings into investment. Instead, Russian banks have served primarily as government agencies that redistribute public funds to enterprises, mostly to favored ones, or as profit centers trading in foreign exchange, government bonds, or insider lending. The banks may look and feel as though they are private enterprises, especially to outsiders, but in fact they have largely served the government's discretionary allocation of subsidies to other enterprises and also financed political causes.[44]

The enterprises themselves never gained real independence in choosing suppliers or deciding whom to pay. In jargonized Russian scholarly language, "Numerous deviations are permitted from the policy of granting enterprises the principles of freedom of choice in forms of payment [and] order of payments."[45] Indeed, it was said that the overwhelming majority of the loans was made to trade structures handling enterprise supplies, not to the enterprises.[46] It is not clear to what extent this meant loans went to the quasi-ministerial holding companies, local mafia-controlled organizations, or "trade structures" established by the enterprise directors in order to enrich themselves.[47] Probably most went to the holding companies, but it is not even clear how much difference there was between mafia organizations and "trade structures" established by directors.

The direct subsidies provided by the Central Bank in the first year ultimately, of course, came from the government's export earnings. As the government had to change this system of direct subsidies and replace it with "loans" from "private" banks, it had to find methods of getting funds to these banks for them to lend. The deeper one probes, the more imaginative are the devices one discovers as the regime sought methods that would at least temporarily survive the scrutiny of the IMF. Many of the actions that were explained to the West as personal corruption actually were covert means of financing the off-budget loans.

Increasingly the foreign trade banks were allowed to retain more of the earnings so that they could make the subsidies themselves. The important foreign trade banks all were "authorized" (*upolnomochennye*) banks that served one or another purpose for the government and were paid for their services. The heads of these banks were called oligarchs by the press, but the banks were government creatures and, to all intents and purposes, government banks. In practice, the banks usually were each the patrimony of the key figures in the Yeltsin government and their institutions, and the top bankers were their bagmen rather than oligarchs. When top officials fell, their bagmen and their banks tended also to disappear.

Oneximbank was, for example, not created until 1993, and it was headed by a seemingly obscure foreign trade official, Vladimir Potanin. It quickly became one of the most important banks because it was given responsibility for all money from all customs payments. Potanin proposed, and the Ministry of Finance agreed, that importers pay their customs before the goods arrived so there would be no delays. It was suggested that importers keep a sum deposited in Oneximbank for this purpose. In the interim, Oneximbank was able to use this money to serve government functions or to benefit itself.[48]

Only fragmentary knowledge is available about the complex network of banks that issued subsidies. The "privatized firm" with the most wealth, Gazprom, used its Gorbachev-era commercial bank, Gazprombank (Gas Industry Bank), to handle its domestic accounts. It remained "one of the most closed financial institutions of the Russian Federation." Together with Lukoil, Gazprom founded Imperial Bank, one of the giant banks of 1995 and 1996, and presumably used it for handling foreign currency accounts. It used the National Reserve Bank for the acquisition of Ukrainian bonds to "pay" for natural gas sent to Ukraine. Then in early 1998 it bought a quarter of the shares of two other giant banks, Promstroibank and Inkombank. Since these two banks were in the most difficult financial shape (and were both declared bankrupt after the financial crisis of the summer), the purchase seemed less an investment than another form of government-forced subsidy.[49]

The same pattern was found in local banks. The St. Petersburg Industrial-Construction Bank, for example, seemed to make its "loans" primarily to the unprofitable defense industry of the city, but 65 percent of its earnings were from interest payments from those to whom it was making loans.[50] In 1995 it provided dividends of 1000 percent on the ruble shares and 35 percent on the hard-currency shares. This was only 6 percent of 1994 profits.[51]

The character of the bank shareholders is shrouded in mystery. Normally the banks were "founded" by groups of enterprises or institutions, but in 1995, 58.3 percent of the shares of Uralpromstroibank (Ural Industrial-Construction Bank) were held by nonstate enterprises, 27.7 percent by state enterprises, and 13.2 percent by individuals.[52] To the extent that shareholders, as originally was the case, were the enterprises being subsidized, the "dividends" were just another form of subsidy. As many bank shares came to be held by individuals, the situation changed.

No information has been discovered about the nature of such individuals, but surely they include the officials of the banks and founding enterprises, and probably political officials as well. The mystery is increased because the banks had the ability to issue new stock. In early 1995 one of the big seven banks, Menatep, announced its fifth issuing of new stock—60 billion rubles, including $50 million in hard currency.[53] It is most unclear whether these shares went to individuals and were a way of distributing corruption or whether they went to government and were a way for the government to finance Menatep.

Some of the activity that was reported to the West as corruption was almost surely a cover for the transfer of money for off-budget purposes. By contrast, much of the real corruption of the system was not recognized as such because it was quite legal. The banks had annual meetings, they all reported profits, and they all paid dividends. The precise dividend varied, but that of Tveruniversalbank was said to be average: 387 percent for the value of the ruble shares and 20.4 percent for the dollar shares. The total dividends equaled 20 percent of the profits.[54] Tokobank had sold a packet of shares to the European Bank for Reconstruction and Development for $35 million, and the EBRD had pushed for the capitalization of all income to build bank reserves. But Tokobank still decided to distribute dividends.[55] The giving of such dividends to individuals by what were really state institutions was the worst form of graft in the Yeltsin period, but it was never denounced by international organizations.

Regional Government

One of the perennial themes of the Yeltsin-controlled or Yeltsin-oriented media in the 1990s was the danger of Russian disintegration. The regional governors were said to be acting independently: they supposedly withheld their taxes, they refused to carry out central orders, they either prevented privatization or they privatized corruptly, they were going to seek independence like Chechnya. The list was endless.

All this was little more than an attempt to provide official justification for Yeltsin's authoritarian rule and Moscow's central control over the regions. Yeltsin was, in fact, quite willing for the Communist governor of Ulianovsk to follow policies that differed from those pursued by the liberal governor of neighboring Nizhnii Novgorod. He tolerated corruption everywhere and was not a disciplined administrator in any part of the political system. Without question, this gave regional governors, as well as ministerial officials, a certain leeway even beyond that recognized in official policy. Nevertheless, their basic independence was extremely limited.

In 1993, as chronicled in chapter 5, a major political and bureaucratic battle broke out over who would assume the detailed administrative responsibilities of the "iron triangle" of holding company, branch banks, and ministerial department that was disappearing with the weakening of the holding company. The Ministry of Economy had been dealing with this complex of bodies, but a new minister of economy, Oleg Lobov, wanted to extend the power of the ministry and take over the holding companies' detailed control of the enterprises. The neoliberal economists favored ending central direction of the enterprises, and Yeltsin shifted a large part of the power of the semiministerial holding companies to the regional governors.

Perhaps Yeltsin, by conviction and instinct, believed in regionally based government. He first became a manager when Nikita Khrushchev was running the economy through Gosplan and regional economic councils (the *sovnarkhozy*). He then served in the regional party organs as governor (regional first secretary) when those organs had lost their powers to the reconstituted and hated ministries.[56]

Surely more important, Yeltsin in the spring of 1993 was moving toward a new constitution in which the Federation Council, a legislative body composed of regional officials, would, if loyal, give him virtually complete control over the other house of the legislature, the Duma. Yeltsin's shifting of the subsidy-making power to the governors while giving them no independent source of income was part of his strategy of ensuring their loyalty.

The regions had no independent tax base, and they received subsidies through an arbitrary allocation of taxes, bank "loans" that were not to be repaid, petroleum and energy for which payment might not be made, and so forth. The regional officials were totally dependent on the central government for their finances. Yeltsin's decision to put his political fate in the hands of a body composed of regional officials showed his supreme confidence in his ability to ensure their loyalty, especially the governors'. The fact that no governors became involved either in political parties in 1993 and 1995 or in the presidential politics of 1996 showed that his confidence was justified.

Just as the old *obkom* (regional party committee) first secretaries had begun as officials with their greatest power in agricultural production and procurement, so the first major economic role of the governors (or heads of administration) was to coordinate the relations between city and countryside and to ensure that the cities received food at minimal cost. This role of the governors was already embodied in the earliest "barter" or "interenterprise loan" agreements. In 1992 I interviewed the chief engineers of Avtodizel, the largest plant in Yaroslavl, and of one of the main plants to which it sent engines, the Kharkov Tractor Plant in

Ukraine. In return for the engines it sent to Kharkov, the Yaroslavl region received grain and sugar from Ukraine, as it always did, and these major "barter" agreements were signed by high Russian officials. The head of the administration (mayor) of the city of Yaroslavl said in April 1993 that the system was more centralized than that under Brezhnev. This may well have been an exaggeration, but the arrangements were unquestionably quite centralized.

As the holding companies became weaker and subsidies became more selective, the regional banks were the main instruments for distributing direct subsidies, and the governors came to assume a more important role in determining who would get the subsidies and when. Most of the regional banks remained under the general supervision of the Moscow banks of which they were formally a part, but they also came under the supervision of the governors, who assumed the broader coordinating role of the old regional party first secretaries.

S. Iu. Yevseev, a top Soviet specialist on the Russian banking system, quite accurately described the situation that had developed in "the illusion of market self-regulation":

> The regional banking sector was formed under the influence of the previously existing administrative system and transformed itself under the force of inertia into the following features: dual subordination (federal, regional); the tradition of central control, the limitation of the rights of the region in the sphere of taxation; the absence of an effective scheme of inter-regional redistribution of financial resources (especially budgetary means), the existence of extra-budgetary funds that are weakly controlled, arbitrary granting of preferred conditions (transfers and subsidies).[57]

The tip of the iceberg emerged when Sergei Kiriyenko, a protégé of Boris Nemtsov, was appointed Russian premier in March 1998. Kiriyenko was an engineer who had been a Komsomol secretary at a Gorky (Nizhnii Novgorod) defense plant and then second secretary of the Gorky Komsomol *obkom*. The Nizhnii Novgorod head of administration, Boris Nemtsov, had appointed Kiriyenko head of the Graniti Bank in March 1993 at the age of thirty. A *Washington Post* correspondent reported on the basis of an interview with Kiriyenko that he had "made his mark . . . with a bank that helped dispose of state assets, such as oil, abroad, and then plowed some of the profits back into local pension funds, which were suffering."[58] A later critical article accused him of enriching himself by stealing from poor retired people.

Both stories missed the essence of what was happening. The creation of regional pension funds and regional banks to handle them was part of Yeltsin's plan to take power from the quasi-ministerial holding companies and to strengthen the position of the governors. The petroleum in Nizhnii Novgorod surely was being refined by the Norsi Refinery in the city, the third largest in the country, and Kiriyenko, a man without experience in the oil industry, moved on in a few months to become its director, by one report while still holding his bank job. Basically, however, the governor was making the key decisions on the priority of social expenditures: when could pensions be postponed a few months to pay workers, or vice versa; when petroleum revenues were to be used for other purposes.

Any notion that Kiriyenko was showing initiative in transferring bank and oil refinery profits to the pension fund is far-fetched indeed. Kiriyenko's biography shows clearly that he was the personal financial agent of the governor, Boris Nemtsov. When Nemtsov became the first deputy premier, he brought Kiriyenko with him, first as deputy minister of fuel and energy and then as minister.

But this bank was not the only one in Nizhnii Novgorod. In 1992 the Nizhnii Novgorod Banking House had been formed to finance industrial conversion. It was the "authorized" bank of Nemtsov's regional government, and its twenty-four-year-old head, Boris Brevnov, also served as Nemtsov's economic adviser. When Nemtsov became vice premier, Brevnov moved with him to Moscow to take a leading position in the "privatized" United Energy Systems.[59]

The major bank of the oil refinery industry, "Oil-Chemistry Bank" (Neftekhimbank), must also have dealt with the Norsi Oil Refinery—and probably concentrated on export financing. Nizhnii Novgorod also had a regional affiliate of the Industrial-Construction Bank, and it too was surely in dual subordination to the central bank officials and the local governor. It must have directed its loan subsidies to other industries. We do not have a comprehensive understanding of the channels through which funds came into the region and the criteria by which decisions were made, but it is clear that the complex network of threads converged on the governor. The powers held by the old party *obkom* first secretary still existed, but were now held by the regional governor.

Tax Offsets

Soviet authorities never collected significant taxes from individuals through income, sales, or property taxes. They had simply added "taxes" (to the extent the term had meaning) to prices. Since government "owned" the entire economy, it could simply set wages and prices in ways that left it with resources to pursue its various goals. It could also take arbitrary deductions (*otchislenii*) from plants with large financial balances to use for other purposes. This process could be seen either as arbitrary additional taxes or as extraction of profits by the owners.[60] Independent Russia would not be able to develop an American-like tax collection system for years, and special attention needed to be devoted to public finances in the interim.

After 1991 the government could easily collect a value added tax from the state enterprises or large corporate "privatized" enterprises dependent on the government, and the enterprises could withhold an income tax from their employees. However, a thriving private sector, especially in the services, would be almost impossible to tax effectively for a prolonged period. The obvious answer was to base public finances on tariffs, export earnings from natural resources, and several lucrative potential sources of revenue that might remain nationalized—for example, alcohol and tobacco. Nevertheless, both western advisers and economists in the government insisted on a free trade policy as well as the privatization of the export industries, the alcohol industry, and foreign-trade firms. In fact, Yeltsin gave the right to import alcohol and tobacco to tax-exempt organizations that apparently became highly criminalized. As a result, $10 billion in commercial credits from western governments in 1992 were lost in what was universally called "massive state corruption."[61]

In early 1992 Russian newspapers were already reporting problems with tax arrears and with tax shortfall, and by 1995 the IMF had come to perceive that tax collection was a major, if not the major, Russian financial problem. The IMF tried to insist on stricter tax collection as a main condition for loan dispersal in 1995. Reformers in the Russian government responded by making tax dodgers, especially among the financial oligarchs and the oil and gas companies, the main scapegoats for the failure of economic reform. The Russian media followed their lead in denouncing the omnipotent oligarchs, and so did the western media. By 1997 and 1998 western editorial writers almost universally suggested that a crackdown on tax fraud was a panacea that at last would permit the Russian economy to begin growing rapidly.

It was all high melodrama, but the issue was just one more element in the web of deceit that surrounded Russian economic reform. The definition of the tax collection problem was shifted continually to confuse the issue, especially for foreigners, and clear distinctions had to be made.

First, every year the official budget had an unrealistically small deficit based on predictions of tax collection that everyone knew from the beginning could never be attained. Each year, this fact was proclaimed loudly in the budget debates. Indeed, when Gaidar first submitted a budget to the Supreme Soviet on January 24, 1992, the radical chairman of the Committee on Property and Economic Reform, Sergei Krasavchenko, rightly charged that it contained very unrealistic assumptions about both revenues and expenditures.[62]

Nothing changed over the years. The draft 1997 federal budget projected 434 trillion rubles in revenues and 524 trillion in expenditures. The head of the budget committee of the Duma, Mikhail Zadornov, was among those stating that the revenue figure was unrealistic.[63] In fact, the 1997 receipts, including tax credits, were 313 trillion—252 trillion as measured by the IMF (real cash). A substantial amount of the shortfall resulted from the unrealistic assumptions of the original projection. The 1998 budget then called for an increase in tax revenues from 252 trillion, as defined by the IMF (that is, real cash), to 351 trillion.[64]

At the end of each year, the West was, of course, shocked—positively shocked—when it discovered that the original budget estimates had not been reached and that the government had a shortfall in its tax collections. The rules of this game were so blatantly obvious that the IMF must have been a willing player. The targets of the deceit were outsiders—western governments and investors, but also other potential recipients of IMF aid who thought they should receive the same easy conditions accorded Russia.

There were, of course, real problems with tax collection, but the different reasons for them must be carefully distinguished. The fundamental reason for low tax collection was that the economy was in a severe depression. This inevitably lowered all tax receipts, regardless of the form of taxation or the level of tax evasion. The only way to maintain the volume of tax revenues without economic growth was to raise the tax rates, and this is scarcely the policy advocated when the United States enters a recession, let alone a depression.

The other problems with tax collection were left deliberately murky. In particular, the phenomena of tax avoidance and tax arrears were often confused in order to distract attention from a third phenomenon—tax credits and tax write-offs. Tax avoidance involves the attempt by citizens to hide income, wages paid, and/or production from the tax collector in order to avoid taxes being assessed on them. Without question large numbers of people in the private sector and the semilegal economy in Russia found ways to hide their economic activity and their income from the tax collector. Without question the Russian government needed to create a mechanism that collected taxes more effectively on this type of activity.[65]

Nevertheless, tax avoidance needs to be seen in perspective. No country—certainly not the United States—effectively taxes the illegal economy (for example, the cultivation and trade of marijuana) and the small-scale handyman and people in the service sector (baby sitters, for instance). The American rich manage to shelter much of their income, and big American enterprises avoid much taxation through write-offs for depreciation and the like. Because the Russian tax code has relatively few legal shelters and exemptions for individuals, and the illegal and corrupt sector has been abnormally large in Russia, so too has been the size of the untaxed sector.

Although the problem of tax avoidance definitely needed to be addressed, anyone who suggested that the reduction of tax avoidance could make a major impact on the Russian deficit in the near future was being either naive or duplicitous. Police and legal protection for economic activity are preconditions for effective extraction of taxation of such activity. When economic activities such as the sale of alcohol, gambling, and prostitution have been illegal in the United States and hence not protected by the police and courts, gangs and mafias have arisen to protect them. When the sale of many drugs was illegal in the second part of the twentieth century and thus also not protected by the law, new urban gangs rose to fill this need. The mafias and gangs collected "taxes" for the protection they were providing in lieu of government. In Russia, providing police and legal protection to economic actors, reducing the size of the illegal sector, and creating a more effective system for taxing the private sector were going to be slow and difficult at best.

Tax arrears are a very different problem, involving the nonpayment of taxes that have been assessed on income, wages, and production reported to the tax collector. Most of the arrears in Russia were not the result of willful tax avoidance by enterprises and individuals, but of deliberate government policy. Many of the "tax arrears" were really "tax credits," although the latter phrase is misleading in implying the application of impersonal rules and regulations. As the direct subsidies via Central Bank credits were decreased in 1993, they were replaced in significant part by tax write-offs. Thus combined taxes to the federal and regional government constituted 27.3 percent of GDP in 1992 and 18.7 percent in the first quarter of 1994.[66]

The tax arrears became enormous. One suspects that they would have been even larger if they had not been periodically written off. They involved the huge enterprises—often the exporting enterprises—that posed few administrative problems for the tax collector. Any immediate improvement in tax collection would have had to center on these arrears, not on the collection of taxes that had been evaded. The problem was not one of tax collection, however, but of changing the state subsidy program.

The criticism of Gazprom was particularly demagogic. Gazprom brought in more than half the hard currency earned by Russia and employed more than 7 percent of the Russian work force.[67] It paid one-quarter of Russian taxes, and by the spring of 1998 it was reported to collect only 10 to 15 percent of its revenues from gas sales in cash. In 1996 it owed $2.8 billion in back taxes, while its customers owed it $8.9 billion.[68] The director of PetroStudies in Sweden correctly noted the "hybrid function" of Gazprom: "a blue-chip company . . . a *de facto* arm of the federal government, an auxiliary central bank, an auxiliary tax collector, or a foreign aid bank."[69] Gazprom was typical of a large number of institutions. In early November 1996, for example, Minister of Finance Aleksandr Livshits said 46 trillion rubles were owed to the coal ministry, including 38 trillion from nonbudgetary sources and 8 trillion from the federal budget. Among the debtors were the electric power generating stations, which owed 4.1 trillion, up 2.1 times from the beginning of the year.[70] In 1998 United Energy Systems, the national electrical utility, collected only 21 percent of its bills in cash, and its debts to the coal company were probably high.[71]

Whatever the term used, government officials were permitting enterprises such as Gazprom not to pay the taxes that came to be classified as arrears. In the case of the exporting firms, the real taxes—and they could approach 100 percent—were "assessed" through directed free deliveries. In the case of nonexporting firms, the arrears were simply another form of subsidy to permit the enterprises to pay wages, at least from time to time.

The free deliveries for which tax write-offs were given were made not only to enterprises, but also to federal government agencies. For example, the army might get trucks from a plant in exchange for tax payments.[72] Free electricity often was provided to military installations. When the IMF protested, the government would cut the power to nuclear submarine bases or missile command posts and frighten the West into silence.

City governments too were major recipients of such subsidies. They received virtually no rent or utility payments from the population for the huge stock of housing that they administered. One partial response was to end repair work on housing, but heat and hot water in the cities came from centralized urban steam plants, and fuel was required for the boilers. The city government should have paid for this fuel and electricity from its budget, but often it did not.

This practice of nonpayment was not limited to the impoverished provinces. Thus Mosenergo (the Moscow electric utility) owed Gazprom $512 million in 1997 for natural gas. The Moscow city government in turn owed Mosenergo $342 million and $218 million a year later. The total debt owed to Mosenergo was 16.1 billion rubles, including 1.4 billion by enterprises, 1.1 billion by the defense industry, and 0.6 billion by the Ministry of Defense.[73] Moscow's economy was growing, and it was being hailed as the great example of successful market reform. In fact, the prosperity of Moscow and St. Petersburg, often much proclaimed in the West, was based on a series of such hidden subsidies and foreign aid.[74]

A normal government would have paid for electricity for the military or natural gas for the cities and included these expenses on its budget. Because of IMF pressure, however, Russia was compelled to keep its official expenses as low as possible and preferred to reduce tax revenues so that it would have a scapegoat for its budgetary deficits. "Taxes" was just one of the largely irrelevant accounting categories that the bookkeepers tried to apply after the transactions were completed as they always had.

The amount of tax arrears was not, of course, a constant number, and it could vary with the extent to which other subsidies were used.

From the beginning the Yeltsin government subsidized enterprises, the federal and local governments, and the former republics of the Soviet Union with very low energy prices. If energy prices were low, recipients did not face such an enormous problem in paying them.

The IMF waged a long struggle to raise Russian energy prices to world levels, and the Russian government now and then would bow to pressure and raise energy prices a little. Since the new price usually was set at a fixed ruble rate, inflation and depreciation of the ruble quickly widened the differential between world and domestic price once more, especially as long as inflation remained high. Even as inflation slowed, the problem was particularly severe in the first nine months of 1994, when the world price of petroleum rose 24 percent at the same time as the value of the ruble was declining.

As a condition for receiving a large IMF loan in 1995, Russia agreed to increase domestic petroleum prices substantially. Because inflation had slowed sufficiently, the prices did not decline immediately. The IMF hoped that this would help marketize the economy, but it merely shifted the type of subsidies. Simply put, the higher prices only meant that the government permitted a larger number of enterprises and institutions not to pay their bills. As enterprise and governmental indebtedness to oil and gas companies increased, the government forgave more of the oil and gas companies' taxes, and the shortfall in tax revenues deepened.

When the western media called for more aggressive tax collection from the oligarchs, they never understood that there were few taxes to be collected. The problem existed throughout the economy. By June 1998 *Financial Times* was reporting that the officials of Gazprom were threatening not to export gas because the real taxes on it were higher than the amount they were receiving.[75]

Tatneft had qualified to be listed on the New York Stock Exchange. It succeeded in borrowing more than $1 billion abroad—more than its annual export earnings—and, *Business Week* reported later, "was funneling loan money from foreign banks into the treasury of the Tatarstan regional government," which was using it as its "cash cow." It often could not pay its own workers on time because it was not being paid.[76] Where was it to get money to pay its taxes? It, no doubt, was a typical example of a company with tax arrears.

The real reason that the West focused on a demand to improve tax collection was unclear. At some level it reflected the argument that the firms should stop providing oil and natural gas to cities and enterprises without payment, stop sending manufactured goods without payment, and cut the number of workers to the level needed for production for which payment would be made. Then, presumably, the producers would have money to pay more taxes. This the western neoliberal economists almost surely understood.

But the implications were not thought through. First, the weather was always cold or soon to turn cold, and the government always faced political consequences if it cut off fuel when people would need heat and hot water. More fundamentally, the major customers who were not paying their bills could not afford to do so, and hence energy producers would find a sharp drop in the demand for their product if they insisted on payment.

In particular, the call for an immediate improvement of tax collection was a call to bankrupt the oil and gas companies and bring in new owners. The head of the tax agency in 1998 was, in fact, quite clear about this. Not surprisingly, the so-called economic reformers wanted to do this so that they might acquire the property. But, of course, this was also a call for the bankruptcy of the very firms in which westerners had invested. It scarcely was going to help the ruble and the value of the short-term government loans (GKOs) in which westerners had also invested if the heart of the stock market were destroyed. It was this unsolvable dilemma that lay at the heart of words such as "pyramid" and "Ponzi game." That so many westerners did not understand this point to the end is evidence of the skill of the Russian con men among the reform economists.

Miscellaneous Types of Subsidies

Many of the subsidies of the early 1990s and even the irregular means of delivering them seemed quite rational. Social protection was needed during the period of sharpest inflation and drop in production, and the factory was the only realistic safety network. If the Russian economy had begun to revive in the mid-1990s, as the leading neoliberal economists predicted, then foreign investment would begin to pour in. The indirect consumption subsidies could have been phased out and replaced by a more legitimate social welfare system. The branch and regional industrial banks could have turned into German- and Japanese-like investment banks as official policy proclaimed they would. The architects of the subsidy program would have emerged from hiding to compete for the credit.

But when the economy did not begin to revive, the situation became increasingly desperate. A deliberate starving of investment to support consumption may sometimes be a desirable and even necessary short-term policy, but it is a deadly long-term strategy. The economic base begins to deteriorate and to be less productive. Grain production dropped from 116 million tons in 1990 to 48 million in 1998 because of a decline in yield produced by the deprivation of inputs. It symbolized what was happening elsewhere in the economy. The problem was particularly severe in Russia because of the great amount of capital needed for reconstruction, conversion, and the development of new products.

Russia always had the option of abandoning its early course and adopting a vigorous industrial policy. Such an industrial policy produced spectacular short-term results in Germany in 1933 and 1934 and in the United States in 1942, but, for reasons that will be explored in chapters 5 and 6, this step was not taken in Russia. Except for a strong but general criticism in 1996 from the new chief economist of the World Bank, Joseph Stiglitz, western officials and institutions never called for such a change. Indeed, the IMF and the Treasury Department continued explicitly to condemn a change in policy.

But if support of consumption was necessary in 1992 and 1993, it became no less so as the economy continued to deteriorate. However, the decline in inflation made the old policy technically more difficult to implement, and the Russian reformers found a wide range of the most ingenious methods to try to keep money flowing to the banks and enterprises.

Thus banks that handled export earnings made "interbank" loans to subsidizing banks, a fact highlighted in the first great interbank loan crisis of August 1994, when the Central Bank had to provide one of its major loans precisely to one of the most important (and, therefore, most affluent) export banks, Menatep. When the IMF pushed the government to issue government bonds and sell them to the banks to increase their stability, the government responded. It sold short-term loans (GKOs), first of three-month and then of six-month duration, to banks at interest rates well above the rate of inflation as a way of subsidizing them. But again the money went to subsidies, not to loans or to building bank reserves.

The primary technique of financing subsidies, to be discussed at length in chapter 7, was to attract money from foreigners. Shares were sold in the export industries; the government did not officially sell high-interest GKOs to foreigners, but it did so informally; and the banks began obtaining short-term hard-currency loans abroad in one form or another, and so did municipalities, regions, and enterprises. The $1 billion debt of Tatneft was not unique.

Precisely because foreign money became increasingly important, it became increasingly important to try to keep the subsidies hidden. One of the most spectacular and successful such efforts was the so-called loans-for-shares program of 1995. According to the official version, accepted by the West, the shares of oil companies, but also unprofitable enterprises and newspapers, were bought by the oligarchs who "owned" the large foreign trade banks. The operation was depicted as the scandalous and corrupt acquisition of wealth by the financial elite. In fact, the banks were primarily required to acquire unprofitable properties in order to provide them with subsidies, and the few profitable properties they obtained were meant to help provide the means for this purpose.[77]

The problem with relying on foreign loans was that an increasing amount of foreign earnings had to be used for interest payments and a decreasing amount to subsidize consumption. Unless production or export commodity prices rose, it was a classic pyramid scheme. When the economy did not revive and commodity prices (especially those of petroleum) fell, foreigners began to flee and the pyramid collapsed.

The techniques became more desperate. The timber industry had been run by a state company, Roslesprom (Russian Timber Industry), and it included Roseksportles (Russian Timber Export Company), presumably so that export earnings could be distributed at least in part back to the industry. In early 1998, Roseksportles was taken away from Roslesprom so its earnings could be used for more general purposes.[78] The car plant AvtoVAZ owed 5 billion rubles to the budget and was pressured to pay. It had 10,000 unsold cars, but said it would try to raise money for its debts by raising prices.[79] Cheliabinsk Tractor was declared bankrupt, and Gazprom loaned it 630 million rubles to pay off its debts even though there was no promise of increased production. The bankruptcy and change in ownership were said to be a victory for local government, and one imagines that local firms held most of the debts to be paid.[80] Regional governments required profitable local enterprises to acquire unprofitable ones.[81]

Conclusion

It is not a new discovery that the Yeltsin government provided heavy subsidies to large sectors of the economy, much of it off budget. Jeffrey Sachs and Katarina Pistor have estimated that the Russian Central Bank transferred as much as 40 percent of GDP as direct subsidies in 1992 and 20 percent in 1993.[82] Scholars have not perceived as much consistency over time as they might—for example, the similarity or even identity between the early "interenterprise loans" and the later "barter." They have not always seen clearly how direct subsidies through lower energy prices were being replaced by greater tax arrears for the energy companies. But if knowledgeable observers may disagree with details, they will not dispute the emphasis on deliberate off-budget subsidies.

Western scholars have, however, been slow to integrate what is known about the subsidies into their analyses of other aspects of economic reform. The reduction in the inflation rate was, for example, often hailed as one of the great successes of the Russian reform process. Yet, if goods were being exchanged or simply shipped at government direction without payment or at least without full payment, prices could be set high to achieve high profits or set low to end inflation. In both cases they would not have much macroeconomic significance. In the words of Jean Foglizzo, an IMF representative in Moscow, "How can you run a tight monetary policy when money has no meaning?"[83]

Similarly, the implications of the subsidy program for the privatization program need to be given greater consideration. All knowledgeable westerners understood the hybrid nature of Gazprom and were correctly cautious about investing heavily in it. But when the success of privatization was being emphasized, Gazprom, with 40 percent of its shares in the hands of the state and its product often given away free, was, no doubt, proudly included in the privatized sector by westerners hailing the success of reform. The banks being formed and subsidized were proclaimed not only part of the private sector, but part of the private services sector, whose growth was an even more important symbol of the success of reform. When Viktor Chernomyrdin was removed as premier, many of Gazprom's "powerful," "oligarchical" banks disappeared with him, looking even more like patrimonial state institutions than they had previously.

These are points that need to be seriously considered by political scientists who have spent a great deal of time drawing implications from official versions of the economic reform that are far from the complex reality. They have often seen the state as "weak"—too little involved in establishing a well-enforced set of laws and forcing through a tough monetary program. In fact, the state has been quite "strong" in the sense of being deeply involved in the economy and forcing through the "king's" preferences and maintaining tight control over major economic actors who would want more freedom and security.

If the policy had produced major economic growth or a successful transition to the market, the duplicity embodied in the subsidies would have little more than theoretical interest for scholars. It did not, however, have such positive results. All can agree that the lack of transparency contributed to the level of corruption and was, therefore, a negative in itself. The major question, however, is whether, at one extreme, the government intervention destroyed an excellent economic program that would otherwise have been successful, or whether, at the other extreme, the government intervention was a desperate attempt to ward off the utter disaster that the economic program itself would have produced. The answer to these questions lies in an examination of the ways in which the incentives established by the economic program actually functioned.

THREE *Privatization*

ALTHOUGH PRICE LIBERALIZATION and monetary stabilization were key parts of the reform process, market prices and a controlled money supply would, of course, solve nothing by themselves. Economic actors would have to respond to the incentives created. These actors could be managers of state enterprises,[1] but both the IMF and Russian reformers had a strong bias in favor of privatization. In Russia, as Anders Aslund pointed out, there was a "reverse Marxism, which implies that no market can exist before private property has achieved hegemony."[2] In addition, no one in the Soviet Union had the security and wealth associated with ownership of property, and a broad range of the administrative and educated elite, including the so-called conservative nomenklatura, wanted it desperately.

The privatization program has been described in several different ways, and by far the most common ways have been normative. Few condemn the privatization of housing or small enterprises, but the privatization of large enterprises has received enormous attention, especially the voucher program and the sale of state shares that occurred in the wake of the insider privatization that took place in early 1992. Critics of the program focus on the large amount of corruption and favoritism in the program and correctly conclude that it did not achieve its goal of equitable distribution of property.

The proponents of privatization, however, always expressed more concern with efficiency than equity, and they wanted ownership to be concentrated in what they called efficient hands. Their expressed concern was that relatively little restructuring was occurring and that insider managers maintained control. They then used this unquestioned fact as an excuse to explain why economic reform failed. They said that the "old-line managers" in industry and agriculture—the "nomenklatura"— were too corrupt and too old-fashioned to adjust to new conditions and to invest, restructure, and develop new products as they should have.

Both proponents and critics of privatization seldom go beyond the purported virtues and defects of the program. Few analyze the real incentives created by the program or try to analyze its consequences as the response of rational economic actors to these incentives. After all, while the insider owners may not have been ideal, they were not nearly as incompetent as their opponents charged. None of the many critics of Gazprom doubts that its production engineer managers are highly competent executives. All specialists on the Soviet economy in the 1970s believed that other heavy industry managers were of similar quality. Economic theory suggests that they—or even state managers—should have responded reasonably well to the right kind of economic signals.

The fundamental problem in the privatization program was the incentive system embedded in the program itself. It created three powerful incentives—all of them detrimental to economic growth—to which rational economic actors should and did respond:

—The widespread privatization of property at extremely low prices meant that rational entrepreneurs should concentrate their attention on acquiring privatized property rather than on creating new enterprises.

—The privatization of the resource-exporting industries and of the export firms that handled them meant that the rational entrepreneur should ignore the less profitable manufacturing sectors and concentrate on the realm where large amounts of hard currency were instantly accessible without managerial effort.

—The two-stage privatization—first insider privatization and then voucher privatization designed to bankrupt large numbers of the insider owners—meant that the insiders usually had a strong incentive to take a short-term view, even to strip assets. This incentive was strengthened by the policy of subsidizing the plants through loans the plants could not repay.

Privatization under Gorbachev

Marx and Lenin insisted that private ownership of the means of production was the source of all evil in society. Then, in the propaganda wars with the West in the 1970s, Leonid Brezhnev defined freedom from unemployment and economic exploitation as the essence of human rights. Thus the Soviet population entered the era of perestroika strongly suspicious of private ownership, especially of large enterprises and of land. The modest privatization of trade that Lenin had permitted in the New Economic Policy of the 1920s was not as frightening.

Gorbachev tried to reassure conservatives by using a series of euphemisms. Land would not be sold, he said, but only leased for a long period of time, as in China. For years Gorbachev and his economists avoided endorsing private ownership, except for very small-scale property, but instead spoke of cooperatives, collective property, destatification of property (*razgosudarstvo*, a favorite of deputy premier Leonid Abalkin that was as awkward in Russian as in English). Radicals insisted that the failure to use the words "private" or "privatization" showed the moderate reformers were hopelessly conservative, but this was wrong. Abalkin always emphasized that shareholder-owned companies such as General Motors and IBM were not private property, but collective or even socialized. He clearly wanted analogous forms of property in the Soviet Union.

Privatization was not limited to words in the Gorbachev years. In 1986 individuals were granted the right to engage in individual private work and to create cooperatives. This initiative was not properly supported by government action, but some 6 percent of the work force was employed in such ways by the end of 1991. In 1989 managers were permitted to lease enterprise assets, including ultimately to the collective, and the lessee could sell products at uncontrolled prices. Another 9 percent of those employed in the Soviet Union worked in leased or stock enterprises that were at least semiprivate from a formal point of view.[3]

Westerners correctly cautioned that this "private sector" should not be seen in American terms, and limitations frequently were placed on leased enterprises or subunits, often ex post facto.[4] The changes did, however, give managers ways to enrich themselves personally. A manager would, no doubt, tell superiors what the director of Uralmash (Urals Machinery Works) told Hedrick Smith about the leasing of a "deadweight" subsidiary (a crane factory) 100 miles to the north: "That factory is working badly. It would simply die without some reorganization."[5] One suspects that the managers who took over the factory did not find it such a burdensome deadweight, but quite profitable for themselves. And the factory may actually have functioned more efficiently under the new regime.

The rights of managers in the financial realm were also being increased. The Soviet economic system had made a clear distinction between cash (*nalichnoe*) money that could be used for a variety of purposes and "funny" or "accounting" (*beznalichnoe*) money that could be used only for goods allocated by the State Planning Committee at set prices. The Gorbachev reforms permitted some transfer of money from the *beznalichnoe* to the *nalichnoe* category. This was one of the causes of the wage inflation that occurred during that period, but it also allowed managers to engage in activities that benefited themselves.[6]

In 1989 Premier Nikolai Ryzhkov proposed a privatization plan that was as radical as that proposed by Boris Yeltsin in October 1991, but it was quickly denounced as too conservative. The radicals developed a 500-day plan of privatization that was embraced by the Moscow intellectual community in the fall of 1990. It was utterly utopian, promising full privatization of all branches of the economy in a 500-day period as well as the virtual or total disappearance of the USSR government and any economic regulatory role for it. Gorbachev should have rejected the plan outright for its foolishness, but instead he partially endorsed it, then backed away and, as was his wont, called for a "centrist" position between Ryzhkov's plan and the 500-day plan. As Ryzhkov's position became the conservative alternative, it became politically impossible for anyone to embrace anything approaching the Chinese model of privatization.

The USSR Law on Property, which was passed on March 6, 1990, legitimated a variety of forms of property, including "collective property," which "shall be the common property of its collective."[7] By early 1991 the managers of the Saratov Aviation Works, among others, had taken advantage of this law to buy out the enterprise and transform it from a state enterprise into a collective one. These plants, however, never were converted to workers' management, and collective property often was synonymous with managers' property.

The most interesting privatization of the Gorbachev period is the least discussed. As has been seen, the Ryzhkov government began a concerted policy of transforming the ministries into "concerns" and "holding companies" and of creating branch and regional "commercial banks" that were both private and state institutions. As Leonid Abalkin told Hedrick Smith in July 1989, he already wanted at that time to turn the ministries into nonstate institutions.[8] His goal was to create financial-industrial complexes such as existed in Japan, and he had a key role in creating branch and enterprise "commercial" banks in 1989 and 1990. The transformation of ministries was accelerated by the government of Valentin Pavlov in 1991. These were logical steps toward the Japanese system, but the intended speed and character of the transformation was not made public—if, indeed, the question was ever firmly decided.

The Law on Enterprises and Entrepreneurship passed by the legislature of the Russian republic in December 1990 did not mention the "collective property" of the USSR Law on Property but rather the joint-stock company (*aktsionernoe obshchestvo*). The managers of the Saratov Aviation Works responded by changing their plant from a collective to an employee-owned stock company. They claimed they chose the joint-stock form as a way of increasing the motivation and enthusiasm of the workers. Peter Maggs is probably right that they were thinking of how to gain control over the plant at a very cheap cost and establish a legal structure—a poison pill—to keep outsiders from acquiring it.[9] In addition, however, they surely were betting that the Russian government was going to control privatization and that they should align their structure with Russian law.

The word "privatization" (*privatizatsia*) was quite alien to the Russian language, because the Russian word for "private" ("*chastny*") had a different etymology. A word that was very familiar to Russians—*prikhvatit'*, to grab—did, however, sound very similar. Critics of the privatization program coined a new word for it: *prikhvatizatsia,* or "grabification."[10]

The word "grabification" reflected a real phenomenon. Without question, managers sometimes used the laws expanding the rights of state enterprise directors and legalizing cooperatives to spin off valuable properties or functions to "cooperatives" controlled by themselves or relatives. They used the new "commercial banks" to make insider loans to themselves. That was the purpose of the reform.

Since most enterprises would require subsidies, licenses, police protection, or other support from the government, they often had only ephemeral value except to those already managing them. Even the managers had extremely insecure property rights in their plants, for they remained subject to ministerial control and dependent on ministerial support subsidies. They could easily be bankrupted if higher authorities wished. For an individual, the most desirable "grabification" was of financial resources, petroleum or minerals that could be sold abroad for cash, equipment that could be sold on the private market or turned into metal scrap, and small buildings and equipment that could be sold to the mafia or to foreigners, who then would have the problem of protecting their rights in them.

As the Soviet Union began to disintegrate, the process became chaotic, or as the Russians put it, "wild." After the August 1991 failed coup, almost all the economic ministers resigned or were removed and were not replaced. The result was summarized by Yegor Gaidar: "The all-Union economic ministries administer nothing. Their staff is preoccupied with seeking work in the private sector, creating commercial firms, and transferring state money and property into them."[11] Much of this activity involved the creation of the quasi-ministerial organizations described in the previous chapter, but much was individual.

The state properties most subject to "grabification" were the dachas or country homes of the ministries and enterprises. High officials often did not have their own private dachas, but simply occupied those of the institution that employed them while they were in office. The people who occupied the dachas in 1991 strove to turn them into their own private property. Sometimes, as in the case of the State Supply Committee, the dachas were sold to officials at low cost; sometimes, as in the case of the Ministry of Defense, they were given to top military officials after August 1991 in an obvious and successful effort to give them a compelling incentive not to conduct a coup to restore the old system;[12] sometimes, as in the case of the writers and officials who occupied the famous dachas of the Union of Writers in Peredelkino, they were simply seized by their current occupants.

Nevertheless, private seizure of the fixed property of the USSR ministries without some formal purchase document, and sometimes even with such a document, was never really secure. Throughout 1990 and 1991 the Russian ministries—and those who occupied the top posts in them—claimed that they owned any USSR ministerial property on their territory. The property of USSR ministries seized by their officials might be reseized by RSFSR officials.

This meant that the disintegration of the Communist party and its subsidiary institutions—the Komsomol or Young Communist League—was the catalyst for an even wilder grab for property than the disintegration of the state. No one would have a strong claim to much of this property in the future. Gorbachev had essentially destroyed the power of the party and allied organs in early 1990, but the party controlled large amounts of property (rest homes, dachas, buildings, stores, clubs, camps, printing presses), as well as bank accounts containing large sums of money from activities such as publishing and dues paid in the past and those still being paid.

In 1990 the Communist party and subordinate groups had begun placing their funds in commercial banks.[13] For example, the Soviet magazine *Ogonek* published a party document about a bank (Rossiia) created by the Leningrad regional party committee on June 27, 1990, and its request for deposits of some central party funds.[14] By December 1991 two Russian prosecutors had discovered more than 1.5 billion rubles belonging to the Communist party deposited in twelve Russian banks.[15] In December 1991 the two prosecutors had also found 100 commercial party enterprises in Moscow and 600 in Russia, many of them headed by significant people in the Russian White House. In the main, they were probably publishing houses, rest homes, sanatoriums, and other preexisting party properties rather than new enterprises created with party money.

Articles in the Soviet press late in 1991 treated these developments as scandalous, but this was not true. The party was running into financial difficulties as the amount of dues collected fell and as inflation increased its expenditures. It made perfect sense for it to try to earn interest or dividends from its legal funds and also to sell property that was no longer needed.[16] Political parties in the United States engage in such activities and would be remiss if they did not.

The same process took place in the "nonstate" institutions controlled by the party—the Komsomol (Young Communist League), trade unions, the Peace Fund, and so forth. They too put their funds into commercial banks, often as founding capital, but in addition lower-level officials were encouraged to use clubs and the like to generate funds for the organization. They took advantage of this to sell and appropriate such property for their personal use.[17] Thus when the journalist Stephen Handelman interviewed a leading mafia figure in Ekaterinburg at the Urals Machinery Works (Uralmash), they met at the former Komsomol club of the enterprise, which apparently had been sold to the local mafia.[18]

The abolition of the Communist party by Yeltsin in August 1991 had little to do with the destruction of a political force, because the party was already politically dead. The real purpose was to legalize the seizure of its property by others rather than the old insiders. Similarly, the real struggles between Russia and Ukraine in the early months of 1992 over the Crimea seemed to have less to do with the public issue—ownership of the Black Sea fleet—than with the ownership of party sanatoriums and rest homes that were located in Ukraine on the Black Sea (for example Foros, where Gorbachev was held in August 1991).

There is a real question about what the banks did with the party and Komsomol money and what happened to it and other party property after 1991. Did the banks make "loans" to insiders, to be repaid in the inflated rubles of 1992 and 1993, or did the money disappear? How much of the property illegally grabbed under Gorbachev was then just as illegally regrabbed after the August 1991 coup? The amount was probably substantial. For example, two-thirds of the party money was said to be in Avtobank, the branch bank of the automobile and agricultural machinery industry. Did this money simply become part of the bank resources that were eaten up by the subsidy policy of 1992? Did it become part of the bank "capital" controlled and owned by new officials? The "oligarch" (bagman) most associated with Boris Yeltsin was Boris Berezovsky, a man who made his fortune by financing the sale of Lada cars. It would not be surprising if Avtobank thrived after 1991 because of this connection and became part of Berezovsky's patrimony. But we simply do not know.

The Debate over the Character of Privatization

As the economist Peter Murrell emphasized, there is a major difference between the concepts of "privatization" and "creation of a private sector."[19] Privatization is not the only way of creating private property, and privatization will not succeed without the creation of new private property. Both practically and theoretically, there is much to recommend the Chinese model of privatization: the government does not privatize large-scale enterprises, especially in the raw materials industries that naturally would provide instant unearned wealth. Individuals or companies are allowed to create new private firms, but land is not sold to individuals, only leased. The state privatizes its own property in a gradual, orderly manner, beginning with trade and small enterprises that are the easiest to privatize. The government thereby creates incentives for those still working in the state sector to continue to produce, and those seeking the wealth associated with private production or trade are driven to create their own enterprises and therefore contribute to economic prosperity.

The striking thing about the Soviet Union in the last years of Gorbachev's rule is that economic reformers thought little about the creation of new private property, as occurred in China, but they took privatization for granted. Reformers of all stripes were concerned with the "private good" of enriching themselves quickly, not the optimal reform plan. The issue of how and what to privatize was, however, highly controversial, for different people would benefit from different plans, and many of the issues remained hidden beneath the surface. Thus the debate on the free sale of land had little to do with agricultural reform, but primarily involved the right of urban individuals to buy urban land or, perhaps, rural land for nonagricultural use. Similarly, reformers saw privatizing large enterprises that could not survive without subsidies as a way of forcing them to close or to reduce their labor force drastically. These hidden issues were politically sensitive and therefore seldom fully discussed in public.

The open debates focused on the method of privatization. The gradual reformers associated with Premier Ryzhkov focused on investment and savings as the way to absorb excess purchasing power and to fight inflation. They naturally wanted to sell property rather than give it away. Most wrote about small-scale privatization of property that small investors would find safe and familiar—privatization of apartments on the basis of long-term mortgage loans, the creation of shops, and so forth.

In 1991 Premier Valentin Pavlov insisted that the economic enterprises administered by the USSR ministries were USSR property and their privatization solely the prerogative of the USSR government acting through its Fund of State Property. Pavlov intended to privatize property by selling it on a ten-year time-payment program, usually to the enterprise's own workers, but sometimes to foreigners or other Soviet individuals who might buy it. He expected to receive 200 billion rubles within a year or a year and a half and 350–400 billion rubles in three years.[20] Those were huge sums at the time.

If the USSR owned all "its" property until it was sold, and at least retained final title for ten years while payments were being made, it held the economic base of the republics in its hands for a long time. This was the key issue. If the republics owned the property, they logically deserved its fruits immediately. On this basis, Yeltsin as president of the

Russian Republic claimed all the foreign and domestic earnings from the oil and natural gas fields on Russia's soil as well as the taxes and proceeds from the large plants.

Yeltsin's claim to all economic enterprises on Russian soil meant that the USSR would have no financial base, not even what it needed to repay foreign loans, and no meaningful economic role. Gorbachev inexplicably failed to resist Yeltsin, and virtually every high official in the USSR government supported the August 1991 coup in a desperate effort to save the Soviet Union.[21] But when the coup failed and Gorbachev continued not to resist republican claims to industrial property, the questions of USSR ownership and the existence of the USSR were decided by default.

When the republics gained control of property, they might well have adopted Pavlov's proposed method of privatization and sold property on time payments at a reasonable market value. Indeed, foreigners generally favored the sale of state assets as a method of privatization.[22] This method would help absorb any excess monetary supply, at least as long as inflation did not wipe out the real value of future payments. Unfortunately, only insider managers, foreigners, and those in the illegal second economy had the resources to acquire property outright, and thus this policy option was not attractive to Yeltsin's main constituencies.

The instinctive Marxist solution to privatization, if it were to be done, was to give an enterprise to the workers who were employed there and then to establish some kind of self-management by those workers. The concept of collective property or even the model of stock ownership used at the Saratov Aviation Works in the Gorbachev period embodied this type of privatization.

Nevertheless, the solution of employee ownership had major flaws. First, if employees were to acquire property at little or no cost, the result would be very inequitable. Workers of the oil industry would become rich, those of textile plants would receive relatively little of value, and teachers and librarians would receive nothing. The disastrous shortcoming of this model from a political point of view was that the radical intellectuals who had provided Yeltsin's core support were almost all employed in institutions whose employees would not benefit.

Second, in the real world, power in employee-owned enterprises would almost surely devolve to top management. Even if they did not sell off assets to friends and relatives, inside managers might not be the most innovative capitalists. Soviet managers had been production engineers whose job performance was judged only by output indicators, and they might not make the transition to the efficient production of consumer-oriented goods. The notion that these plant managers might be retained as assembly plant managers in large corporations was not part of the debate.

The major alternative to employee privatization was the issuing of vouchers to the broad population on a free or virtually free basis and allowing the recipients either to use them to acquire property or to sell them to others. But even here a variety of plans was possible. Citizens could be offered shares in mutual funds, or they could use the vouchers themselves to buy shares in mutual funds or enterprises. The latter program in turn had two major variants, one in which the recipients did not have the right to transfer their shares for a number of years and the other in which they were free to sell their vouchers or give them away immediately.

There were two major arguments for distributing property to the population free or basically free through a voucher system, but, unfortunately, the arguments were inconsistent with each other. The first—and naturally that most frequently used in public—emphasized equity and political factors. All would be treated equally regardless of where they worked; everyone would become a share-owning capitalist. Yeltsin was lyrical on this point in August 1992. With everyone gaining from privatization, it should enjoy widespread political support. In fact, our December 1993 survey (see preface) near the end of the voucher process found support for privatization of large-scale enterprises evenly divided, a much more favorable result than in the past or the future.

The second argument for voucher privatization was proclaimed less loudly because it was politically less appealing. The reformers fully expected the vouchers to flow into the hands of those with financial skills and resources either through their own purchase of vouchers or through the creation of mutual funds. This would create a group of powerful outsiders with financial and economic expertise who could challenge the insiders for control of the large enterprises. Neither the economists in the international economic community nor the young economists associated with Yegor Gaidar doubted the superior ability of those with economic expertise.

The first problem with the argument about restructuring was practical, as Stanley Fischer, soon to be deputy head of the IMF, made quite clear in 1993:

The key question . . . is whether privatization will lead to restructuring . . . [It is argued] that privatization is the one reform that brings immediate benefits to consumers and voters. That is true of the first stage of the process, when vouchers are distributed and consumers are given ownership of firms. However, it is not true at the restructuring stage, when unemployment is likely to grow—and that may help explain why restructuring has been so slow.[23]

"Restructuring" was, in fact, a euphemism for downsizing the labor force and reducing unproductive social expenditures. If the mutual funds or other financial groups began to reduce the number of workers, close down factory social service institutions, and so forth, workers being displaced were not likely to see privatization as an unmitigated good.

Quite apart from practical political objections, major theoretical questions need to be raised about the arguments in favor of the voucher privatization. The core argument for vouchers came, first of all, from the analysis of Friedrich von Hayek:

A "neo-Austrian" economist following the philosophy of Friedrich von Hayek would advocate the immediate marketisation of virtually all state assets. Of course the neo-Austrian would concede that this could result in speculation and incumbent abuse on a large scale, especially in the short term, but would insist that such speculation is at the very heart of the capitalist system. . . . The profits and losses of successful and unsuccessful entrepreneurs are the signals that lead others to compete and follow. . . . On this view it is irrelevant whether those who profit are foreigners, criminals or communists, so long as the signals are observable, thus making competition inevitable.[24]

Anatoly Chubais reports that reading Hayek had an enormous impact on him as a young man,[25] and he was quite cavalier about the criminal background of those who would buy trade and service firms. "We are taking into account the demand from representatives of the 'second economy,'" Chubais told the press in January 1992.[26] Former deputy premier Leonid Abalkin reported that Anatoly Chubais had made a similar argument privately: "[He] said that the task is to create a modest number of real owners. Chubais realized that the owners will mostly be criminally oriented people. But, he said, there are no others. . . . And without real entrepreneurs and owners, Russia will never get out of the hole."[27]

The argument made by the reformers in the United States referred not to Hayek, but to Coase's theorem, an important part of the American literature on property rights. The theorem was named for Ronald Coase by George Stigler based on ideas that Coase had presented less formally. It has been summarized in the following terms: "*If* (a) property rights are well-defined, (b) transactions costs are trivial, and (c) wealth effects can be ignored, *then* externalities are internalized through the self-interested negotiations of the parties involved, resulting in the same allocation of productive resources regardless of who possesses the property rights or liabilities so long as these rights are well specified."[28]

The Coase theorem argued that if its conditions were satisfied, societal conflicts could always be regulated more efficiently through private contracts than through government intervention. A key implication in the Russian case was said to be that the original owner of the property was irrelevant. Control over the property in a market economy inevitably would flow into the hands of the most efficient owners, and government involvement was counterproductive.

The Coase theorem, however, is quite conditional. Robert Inman and Daniel Rubinfeld, for example, correctly emphasize that "transactions costs are trivial" means that "there are no resource costs associated with reaching agreement," "all bargaining agreements are costlessly enforceable," "preferences over bargaining outcomes and the resources of participants are common knowledge," and "bargaining agents perfectly represent the economic interests of their constituents."[29]

Critics of the Coase theorem insist that its applicability in the United States is severely limited because negotiation costs are always impossibly high when millions of people would have to agree on, say, environmental restrictions. They note that these transaction costs had always been the justification for government and that Coase only demonstrated why government is necessary.

But whatever may be said about the United States, Coase's conditions clearly were not met in Russia: property rights were not well defined, bargaining agents had little information and accountability, and the enforcement of agreements was scarcely without cost or even reliable. Winston Bush made the basic point a quarter of a century ago: "The neoclassical theory of marginal productivity implicitly assumes a post-constitutional state in which a completely effective and costless enforcement mechanism against theft has been instituted."[30]

Western and Russian neoliberal economists gave little thought to the possible consequences of privatization and free negotiations among individuals when none of Coase's conditions were met. For this reason, their assumptions were much closer to Hayek's than to Coase's, for Hayek showed little concern about the preconditions for a successful market economy other than that government not be involved. They also did not emphasize the most obvious implication of Coase—and Hayek—that nomenklatura privatization was no problem. If the property rights of the insider owners were strengthened, property would soon flow into the hands of the efficient.

The Privatization Process

Privatization in economic models looked quite different from privatization in practice. First, privatization was technically difficult if it were to be more than the simple transfer of ownership to those who managed the enterprises or worked at them. Any attempt to give the entire population a share of ownership would at best require several years for vouchers to be printed and distributed, for people to decide what to do, and for auctions to be conducted. In the interim, someone would be in control of property and would manage it. If these managers thought they would be expropriated once the privatization process was completed, they had every incentive to divert money and to strip assets in the brief period that they were in control.

In January 1991 Yeltsin created a new institution to handle privatization—the misnamed State Committee for the Management of State Property, usually called the State Committee for Property, or the State Committee for Privatization. In fact, the state committee was not supposed to manage property, but to manage its privatization. It was charged with the responsibility of drafting the rules of privatization, conducting the auctions, and approving privatization arrangements. It also had control of the shares still in the hands of the state, and its leading officials often sat as the state representatives on the boards of large enterprises in which the government retained shares.[31] It had offices in all of the provinces, city, and raion (county) centers.[32]

The head of the committee after October 1991 was a St. Petersburg economist, Anatoly Chubais. Born in 1955, Chubais graduated from the

Leningrad Engineering-Economic Institute and remained there as an instructor in the economics department. He became the leader of a group of young radical economic reformers in Leningrad. In 1990–91 Chubais was selected deputy chairman and then first deputy chairman of the executive committee of the Leningrad soviet. In November 1991 he was appointed chairman of the State Committee for Property in the Gaidar government. As privatization was placed higher on the agenda in June 1992, he was named one of seven deputy premiers, while retaining chairmanship of the State Committee for Property. Almost all other high officials of the state committee had been close friends of Chubais in Leningrad. They generally were called the Chubais clan.[33]

In retrospect, it is striking that while Yeltsin changed personnel incessantly in almost all spheres of political life, he kept Chubais and his closest associates in control of privatization until November 1997, when the process essentially ended. Chubais was close personally to the dominant person on foreign economic questions in the U.S. Treasury Department, Lawrence Summers, and Yeltsin clearly valued this. But Yeltsin also trusted Chubais completely. Chubais was placed in charge of Yeltsin's presidential campaign in 1996, and then in 1998 and 1999 headed one of the central patronage posts in the government, United Energy Systems, which was providing electricity, usually free of charge, to the various regions. Chubais was at the heart of the Yeltsin insider group called the family.

In his October 28, 1991, speech Yeltsin listed privatization as the second goal of the reform, but with language that was seldom to reappear after Russia became independent: "the creation of a healthy mixed economy with a powerful private sector." The first stage was to be "small-scale" privatization in trade, services, industry, and transportation. He thought it could be half completed in three months.

Yeltsin treated large-scale industry as "significantly more complicated" and said that "not a small part of it" will remain state property. In the coming months, however, he said there would be a "mass and quick process" of transforming large enterprises into stock companies, with shares being distributed between the state and the labor collectives. Then the state shares would be sold "to those who desire them at market prices." He emphasized the problem of monopolization, but promised to break up giant enterprises and concerns and asserted that monopolies "will be undermined by small and medium private enterprises which will arise in the first months of privatization."[34]

Yeltsin's discussion of privatization was marked by the same utopi-anism about the speed of the process that was endemic to Soviet discus-sions of the subject during and after the 500-day plan. It was based on the same assumptions that new private firms would be able to produce new products for the market "in the first months of privatization" despite the fact that the money supply was being reduced, inflation was destroying savings accounts, and banks would not lend money to new firms.

Whether it was realized or not, no real entrepreneur in the industrial sphere would be spending any time in the short or even medium term developing new products or new enterprises to compete with the large plants. The way to obtain wealth in that time period was to concentrate all efforts—and all capital—on the acquisition of enterprises that were being privatized. The great struggles would be waged to ensure that the most profitable plants would be privatized, that insider banks would provide "loans" to insiders to acquire shares in them, and that enter-prises that might not survive would be stripped for personal benefit.

The major determinant of wealth, of course, would be the rules for privatization. Yeltsin's speech of October 28, 1991, embodied the basic recommendations of the western economic community about the correct way to privatize—and these recommendations featured the sale of the state shares, not their free distribution. It is not clear whether Yeltsin and the Russian neoliberals were persuaded by this advice or were repeating it for political reasons. In the next ten months, the method of privatizing the large enterprises was to change twice fundamentally—each time in a way making it easier for young outsiders with economic training to acquire wealth.

Small-Scale Privatization

Small-scale privatization began on November 25, 1991, when Yeltsin decreed that trade and consumer service enterprises had to become "juridical persons," independent from state agencies, by the end of the year. A month later, on December 29, he issued another decree requiring the auction of small enterprises during the first three quarters of 1992. The first three quarters of 1992 would be devoted to privatization of enterprises in trade and consumer services, and in the last part of the year the process would extend to construction firms, small food plants, and trucking firms.[35]

Given the speed with which events were moving, it is difficult to know the extent to which different economic policies were being coordinated. Economists were worried about the amount of money in individual bank accounts. Most assumed that people would use the money in their savings accounts to purchase small stores or enterprises and that this would help absorb the monetary overhang and create a new class of private entrepreneurs. The decree of December 29, 1991, issued immediately before price liberalization, seemed timed to make this process possible.

Nevertheless, the Gaidar government deliberately refused either to index savings accounts or to set the interest rate above or even near the level of inflation. Russians did not have checking accounts, and hence their consumption funds and their savings were commingled. No attempt was made to distinguish between savings and consumption funds in calculating money supply, but both were considered part of the money supply to be reduced. Savings bank interest rates were raised only from 2 percent a year to 3 percent on demand deposits in 1992, even though prices rose 3.5-fold in January alone and more than 25-fold by the end of the year. One-year certificates of deposit (CDs) received 7 percent interest and three-year CDs, 10 percent.[36] In early 1993 the interest rate on savings accounts still had increased only to a 20–60 percent annual range, while prices increased 9.4 times in 1993.

The result was disastrous from all points of view, including the war on inflation. People had every incentive to turn all their rubles into real goods or dollars, thus adding to inflationary pressures. In addition, the broad population had no savings to use in the small-scale privatization that was to occur in mid-year. Chubais, as has been seen, talked very favorably about those who had worked in the illegal second economy. Such persons clearly did not keep their money in savings accounts. Perhaps the Gaidar government thought that their business experience would make them better businessmen than the average population and deliberately destroyed the savings accounts of average citizens to facilitate the process. Or perhaps no one was thinking about the interconnections of different policies.

The privatization of small enterprises was carried out by local government through a competitive auction or tenders, with an advantage given to the employees of the enterprise. If one-third of the shareholders in the group making a winning bid were employees, then they received a 30 percent discount and could stretch their payments over three years. Given the extremely rapid inflation and consequent loss of value of the ruble, later payments actually became nominal. By April 1993, 61,810 small enterprises had been privatized, 25 percent of the total.[37]

The process seemed simple, but it had many complexities. First, the privatization of stores and service establishments was usually limited in nature. The rights to use a building in which a store was located and the inventory of a store were privatized, but not the building itself. Moreover, the right to use the building was conditional. When Lev Kruglikov, chairman of the Yaroslavl city soviet, visited Duke University in April 1993, he boasted about the high percentage of privatized trade in his city. He added, however, that if the private owners changed the profile of their store and deprived citizens of crucial goods (for example, if a shoe store began selling vodka) or charged "excessive" prices, then they could be evicted by the city government, which owned the building. Thus both privatization and price liberalization took place within definite limits.

Second, employee privatization did not necessarily mean that the employees actually acquired a store or small business. In St. Petersburg, more than half of the small enterprises were bought by their own workers. Since the employees of an enterprise received beneficial terms, an outsider who wanted to buy the enterprise was well advised to make an agreement with the employees beforehand. The very first auction in St. Petersburg—a hairdresser's shop on Nevsky Prospect near the Hermitage Museum—illustrates this point. The shop was sold for more than 100 million rubles to the hairdressers. Such a price was well beyond their means, but soon a Danish kitchen unit company opened its store on the spot. Clearly the Danish company had been one of the shareholders along with the workers and the one that had put up the money. Yet as long as the workers constituted one-third of the shareholders, the Danish company received the 30 percent discount and the long-term payments that reduced its real cost drastically.[38] The workers were, no doubt, bought out for a fraction of the value of the store.

Nothing is known about the outcome of small-scale privatization except where foreigners were involved. When the "employees" bought their respective enterprises in the provinces or even the living areas of Moscow and St. Petersburg, no one knows which hidden partners they had. Nelson and Kuzes report on the basis of their interviews that many on the privatization committees in the provinces had no idea who the ultimate purchasers were.[39] It is quite likely that those with money from the second economy were prominent among them, for it is precisely from this time that the local population became deeply convinced that "the Mafia" was taking over the economy.[40] If so, this was the mechanism by which it happened.

In addition, of course, if property were especially valuable, the officials of the privatization committee might not conduct a fair auction. The situation in Moscow was the most visible, and a number of scandals were reported, with the favored buyers alleged to be close to Mayor Yury Luzhkov. Those trying to buy key property sometimes even sat on the board of the city committee for property and influenced the outcome.[41] Without question, similar scandals must have occurred elsewhere, but little information is available.

Large-Scale Privatization

In the second phase of privatization, large-scale enterprises were forced to become stock corporations with boards of directors. The state could retain all or most of the shares, but the normal model entailed the collective's (the managers and employees of an enterprise) acquiring 51 percent of the shares and the state's retaining the rest until it sold part of them in voucher sales.

The radical economists subsequently called employee privatization of large enterprises a grave mistake. In fact, the alternative in the near term was to leave power in the hands of the quasi-ministerial holding companies for a few years. During this period, the heads of the holding companies were planning to use the profits of their firms to buy shares in the enterprises under their control. No doubt they were also acquiring debts from the enterprises that could be exchanged for equity. This might have been the best first step in privatization, but obviously those associated with the Yeltsin team, including the radical economists, did not want these Gorbachev officials of quasi-ministerial institutions to have such control of Russian industry for a prolonged period.

The privatization of large-scale enterprises was carried out according to several different models, but all basically assumed that the employees would become the owners. The option chosen in two-thirds of the cases allowed employees to buy shares equal to 51 percent of the share capital (defined as 1.7 times book value) in a closed subscription. The remaining 49 percent of the shares generally were either distributed by voucher or retained by the state. In practice, approximately 30 percent of the shares were said to be distributed by voucher and 20 percent retained by the property fund.[42] Because the number of rubles in the purchase price was fixed and the ruble was rapidly losing its value with inflation, these privatizations essentially meant that employees could acquire at very low cost the enterprise where they worked. Managers surely often took out loans from their insider banks to buy large numbers of shares—and repaid them with rubles of much lesser value. It is likely that this was the typical pattern.

The new enterprises that were "owned" by the collective usually issued no share certificates, and their employees thus had no legal proof or protection of their "ownership." When outsiders bought shares, they often received little if any information about the financial condition of the enterprise and no guarantee that their shares would not be diluted by the issuance of new shares. The problems of exploiting minority shareholders had not ended by 1999, and the majority owners of a leading oil company were shamelessly trying to disenfranchise even foreign owners.[43]

At the same time that Yeltsin announced the details of the insider privatization of the large enterprises, he also decreed that vouchers be distributed in the fourth quarter of 1992. A few months later, on the anniversary of the August 1991 coup, he enthusiastically embraced the idea of voucher privatization in public. "We need millions of owners rather than a handful of millionaires," he proclaimed, and a presidential decree was issued at the time.[44]

In 1991 the radical reformers, including Chubais, had doubts about voucher privatization, but by early 1992 they had become fervent supporters of the idea. Western advisers such as Anders Aslund also changed their position from skepticism to enthusiastic endorsement.[45] To western audiences at least, Chubais was quite explicit at a conference held in June 1992 in his denunciation of insiders' control and the need for "responsible owners," "effective owners," "finding effective management," "a new type of owner."[46] Western advisers were explicit that "large shareholders are essential for effective corporate governance." As a western adviser (Andrei Shleifer) and a Chubais collaborator (Maxim Boycko) phrased it, "Allocating shares to the public [creates] the conditions for effective governance in the future as shares are sold to more efficient investors."[47]

The Chubais team in its western writings implied that the voucher program introduced in August 1992 was the same that Yeltsin had approved in his April 1992 decree. In fact, as Nelson and Kuzes have documented, the two were quite different.[48] The Yeltsin government originally espoused "registered privatization accounts": each citizen would be given a voucher with his or her name on it and would not be able to transfer or sell it for three years. This was the system instituted in the April decree and enacted by the Supreme Soviet in the summer of 1992.

Yeltsin issued the enabling decree on privatization vouchers on August 14, 1992, after the Supreme Soviet recessed, but it differed from the earlier law. The vouchers were issued without names printed on them, and this meant they were transferable. The recipients could sell their vouchers, give them away, or use them to acquire shares in privatized enterprises or mutual funds. Each Russian citizen, adult and child alike, received such a voucher with an original value of 10,000 rubles for the nominal cost of 25 rubles (5 cents at the prevailing exchange rate). The voucher had to be used by the end of 1993, a deadline that was extended to June 30, 1994.[49]

Yeltsin's radical change in the voucher program from that enacted by the legislature was a typical example of the politics of economic reform of the period. Despite continual talk about the great delaying power of the Congress and Supreme Soviet, Yeltsin was able to introduce almost any economic measure that he wanted. In this case he used the rule that he could issue a decree that would come into effect if it were not rejected by the legislature within fourteen days.

Moreover, in this case, as in many others, the legislature actually had no major objection to the final result. Petr Filippov, an economist from St. Petersburg and a close friend of Anatoly Chubais, had been named the chairman of the privatization subcommittee of the Supreme Soviet. Many deputies had a personal interest in the transfer program and the concentration of financial power in Moscow, and they were quite happy to have the program enacted if Yeltsin would issue the decree, allowing the deputies to avoid political responsibility.

The Distribution of Property

Nothing is more difficult to determine and describe than the pattern of actual privatization in Russia. In 1995 official statistics reported that 43 percent of the population was working in state enterprises and institutions, 35 percent in the private sector, and 22 percent in joint property. In 1997 the figures were similar: 43 percent, 37 percent, and 21 percent.[50]

There are, however, vast problems with these statistics. For example, institutions such as the collective farms are included in the private category. The collective farms (*kolkhozy* or *kollektivnye khoziaistva*) never officially were state property in the Soviet period, but in the aftermath of perestroika, they were transformed into entities allegedly based on "real" cooperative or collective property. Few in Moscow believed that anything had changed.

More important, the state retained an average of 20 percent of the shares in the companies it privatized, and hence all privatized enterprises were literally joint. The distinction between an enterprise that is listed as private and one listed as joint property is not clear. The joint category surely included companies like the huge United Energy Systems that were 53 percent state owned and functioned as state enterprises.[51] The real questions arise about firms such as Gazprom, 40 percent of whose shares were owned by the state.

Gazprom was controlled de facto by long-time premier Viktor Chernomyrdin, and it was being forced to provide gas to a wide range of recipients for free. It was private only in the most tenuous or formal sense. Nevertheless, since the West was emphasizing privatization as a major indicator of reform, it seems virtually certain that Gazprom, with its large number of workers and percentage of GDP, was categorized as private to improve the statistical picture.

The Gazprom example was only one among many. Even under Gorbachev, the industrial ministries were being abolished and replaced by "privatized holding companies." When enterprises were taken over by the "collective" (that is, the managers), they usually were dependent on direct government subsidies, "loans" from government-controlled banks, or authorized "postponed" payments for petroleum, natural gas, and other crucial supplies. Thus most enterprises immediately became bankrupt in any meaningful sense of the word, but they were allowed to appear profitable so that they could pay "profit taxes" to local governments.

To help sort out the real meaning of privatization, our various national random sample surveys included questions about the ownership of the enterprise or institution at which the respondent worked. Unfortunately, many Russians probably do not really know the formal form of ownership. In the United States, the term private property applies to corporations such as General Motors that are really collectively owned by their shareholders, but the Russian word for "private"

Table 3-1. *Form of Property of Respondents, 1993, 1995, 1996*
Percent of workers surveyed

Year	Form of property[a]		
	State[b]	Collective	Private
December 1993	58.0	35.3	5.0
December 1995	53.9	37.8	8.3
June 1996	51.7	38.2	10.1

Source: Author's surveys. For an explanation of the survey, see Preface.

a. In 1993 stock, kolkhoz, cooperative, and joint venture categories are merged into the "collective" category used on the 1995 and 1996 questionnaires. Several categories (such as "other" or "difficult to say") are excluded, but together they compose only a few percent of the cases. As a result, figures may not total 100 percent.

b. Includes municipal state property.

(*chastny*) has traditionally referred to enterprises that are owned by a single individual, family, or a very small partnership. The meaning of the Russian words for "stock companies," "firms," and "corporations" is often quite unclear to the typical citizen, all the more so since these enterprises often retain the managers they had when they were state enterprises.

Our 1993 questions about the form of property of the enterprise or organization at which the respondent was employed offered six categories: state, stock, kolkhoz, cooperatives, joint ventures with foreigners, and private. The categories did not work out well, and the 1995 survey offered the following four categories: state property, municipal state property, collective (cooperative, stock company, collective farm), and private. Table 3-1 shows the responses of those who were employed in 1993, 1995, and 1996, with the various state and general (or collective) categories compressed into one of each.

The "state" category in our surveys is larger than in official statistics and probably reflects a tendency of many respondents to count "joint" property as state. The apparent decline in the "state" category may reflect a rise in sophistication about the formal language rather than a change in the real situation.

Naturally, as table 3-2 shows, more younger Russians tended to work in the privatized sector than did older ones. In March 1997 a special study of young people was conducted among those aged seventeen and eighteen, twenty-four and twenty-five, and thirty-one and thirty-two. The seventeen- and eighteen-year-olds had generally not entered the labor force, but 2,076 respondents between the ages of twenty-four and thirty-two were working at the time. (The total sample of this age

Table 3-2. *Form of Property Employing Younger (24- to 32-Year-Old)*
Respondents, 1993, 1995–97
Percent of employees surveyed

	Form of property[a]		
Year	State[b]	Collective	Private
December 1993	54.7	36.1	9.2
December 1995	55.3	33.5	11.3
June 1996	50.1	34.3	15.5
March 1997	52.2	31.8	16.0

Source: Author's surveys.

a. Several categories (such as "other" or "difficult to say") are excluded, but together they compose only a few percent of the responses. As a result, figures may not total 100 percent.

b. Includes municipal state property.

group, including full-time students and those not working, was 2,769 respondents.) The 1993 survey sample included 511 respondents between ages twenty-four and thirty-two who were working; the 1995 sample included 496 of this age who were working; and the 1996 sample, 472.[52]

The small number of twenty-four- to thirty-two-year-olds employed in the 1993, 1995, and 1996 surveys means that the usual warnings about a plus-or-minus percentage point range need to be taken seriously. The general picture, however, is clear: more young people than older said they work in the private sector, but employment in the state sector declined only marginally from 1993 to 1997. Indeed, the figures for twenty-four- to thirty-two-year-olds and the general population in 1996 were very similar.

The greater participation of young people in the private sector is at the expense of employment in the collective ownership category, but the meaning of this is not clear. Table 3-3 increases the mystery. It is unclear why the percentage of state property should be higher in rural areas. It seems likely that less sophisticated rural residents reported the real character of the enterprise that employs them, while those in the larger cities were more cognizant of its formal character.

Either out of a lack of understanding or a desire to deceive, those who are the most enthusiastic in hailing the success of privatization in Russia sometimes shift the categories in reporting what has occurred. They maximize the degree of privatization by including in the private property category any property or enterprise that has undergone the

Table 3-3. *Percentage of Work Force by Size of Place of Residence and Form of Property, June 1996*[a]

	Form of property		
Size of place of residence	State	Collective	Private
1–10,000 (rural)	57.7	36.1	6.2
10,000–199,999	51.0	38.8	10.3
200,000–999,999	47.2	40.9	11.8
1,000,000–2,000,000	54.1	35.4	10.6
2,000,000 + (Moscow–St. Petersburg)	47.9	36.7	15.3

Source: Author's surveys.
a. Percentages may not total 100 as a result of rounding.

slightest change in formal legal status or that was already a collective farm. But when they document the positive results of privatization, they look at the wages only of those working in the private (*chastny*) sector by anyone's definition.

Table 3-4 illustrates the reason why the greatest care must be taken in assessing privatization. Except in trade and consumer services, and to a much more limited degree in construction, the percentage of the population employed in the small-scale private sphere remains very small. The results in agriculture are unstable, probably as a result of a real difference between the formal and informal nature of ownership. The realm where a steady increase in the percentage of the population owning private firms or owning stock in private firms has been occurring is industry and construction.

The differences in the percentages of *chastny* as opposed to collective property in the largest cities—and, indeed, the increase in the percentage of *chastny*—may also signify that the definition of the word *chastny* has colloquially begun to move toward the broader definition found in the West and in the official Russian statistical handbook. At a minimum, Russians would certainly call a foreign firm for which they worked "private" even though it would normally be a publicly owned corporation or a large partnership.

No doubt those who describe their enterprises as private are working in what a westerner would recognize as the reformed sector of the economy, whatever its exact substantive or legal character. The real question is the nature of the collective category. As already mentioned, the American corporation is not, strictly speaking, private property. If the collective sector in Russia is coming to consist of collective firms like

Table 3-4. *Percentage of Work Force by Form of Property and Average Monthly Salary in Different Branches of the Economy, 1993, 1995, 1996*

Branch	Form of property[a]		
	State	Collective	Private
December 1993			
Industry	49.1 (80)	49.7 (85)	1.1 (73)
Construction	32.4 (65)	61.3 (117)	6.3 (103)
Agriculture	32.7 (56)	64.4 (41)	2.9 (43)
Trade	35.0 (68)	38.3 (109)	26.7 (113)
Government, education, science, health, finance	93.1 (55)	5.5 (101)	1.5 (86)
December 1995			
Industry	37.9 (482)	59.7 (521)	2.4 (825)
Construction	44.1 (548)	45.7 (635)	10.2 (1,025)
Agriculture	24.4 (312)	72.0 (294)	3.7 (502)
Trade	30.6 (407)	31.8 (531)	37.6 (855)
Government, education, science, health, finance	91.6 (393)	6.2 (556)	2.3 (761)
December 1996			
Industry	28.5 (549)	67.5 (674)	4.0 (619)
Construction	36.5 (644)	48.2 (736)	15.3 (1,529)
Agriculture	31.9 (344)	64.2 (281)	3.9 (634)
Trade	27.6 (508)	31.6 (648)	40.8 (634)
Government, education, science, health, finance	92.3 (486)	5.3 (712)	2.4 (517)

Source: Author's surveys.

a. For each form of property, the percentage of the total in each branch is given followed by the average salary, in thousands of rubles, in parentheses. Percentages may not total 100 as a result of rounding.

Microsoft, a major change has occurred; if it remains like the old collective farms, not much has happened.

The figures on monthly wages in the various branches shown in table 3-4 suggest a complicated situation. As in the Soviet period, it is better to work in a state enterprise in agriculture than in a collective one, but otherwise salaries in the stock companies and the small-scale private-sector companies are generally higher. However, the enterprises in which privatized salaries are significantly higher often employ relatively small numbers of people. The benefits are not so great when a substantial proportion of the people in the branch work for stockholder or private enterprises, and in the realm of trade, where the private sector is the largest, wages in small private stores are lower than in the shareholder companies.

Table 3-5. *Percentage of Respondents Always or Usually Paid on Time, by Branch of the Economy, 1995–97*[a]

| Branch | Type of Property | | |
	State	General	Private
December 1995			
Industry	47.1	35.1	39.9
Construction	53.6	34.1	72.9
Agriculture	47.6	27.7	31.8
Trade	69.5	83.6	78.8
Government, education,			
science, health, finance	67.1	73.4	71.0
June 1996			
Industry	41.1	34.3	72.2
Construction	46.2	38.9	74.3
Agriculture	23.2	20.3	85.3
Trade	65.5	79.6	79.0
Government, education,			
science, health, finance	54.8	81.4	41.2
March 1997[b]			
Industry	28.7	25.2	45.5
Construction	31.6	25.3	58.9
Agriculture	24.1	34.3	41.4
Trade	48.7	66.6	77.6
Government, education,			
science, health, finance	29.0	83.0	87.0

Source: Author's surveys.
a. Percentages may not total 100 as a result of rounding.
b. Ages 24–32 only.

Table 3-5 further illustrates the complexity of the situation. The stock companies may pay higher wages, but the stock companies in industry and construction did not pay wages on time as often as state enterprises. Thus the creation of such companies allowed businesses for which the government could claim to have no responsibility to pay wages late and ultimately to fire workers.[53] When the government began to promise to pay back wages, it did so only for those employed by the state.

No effort was made in these surveys to estimate the size of the shadow economy. The most wealthy participants in the shadow economy were very unlikely to agree to be interviewed if they fell into the survey sample, and few who made significant amounts of money outside their main job were likely to want to admit it to an interviewer. Hence respondents were simply asked whether and how often they worked in a second job and were not asked how much money they earned in outside work.

Table 3-6. *Percentage of Respondents Involved in Activities to Earn Extra Money, 1993, 1995, 1996*[a]

Frequency of involvement	1993	1995	1996
Never	80.2	77.1	73.7
Seasonal	2.3	4.0	4.1
From time to time	9.6	12.2	14.1
Several times a month	1.3	0.8	1.0
Several times a week	1.1	0.9	1.0
Constantly	5.6	4.9	6.1

Source: Author's surveys.
a. Percentages may not total 100 as a result of rounding.

While the surveys miss the top-level illegal private sector (as, of course, do surveys in the United States and elsewhere), they should accurately indicate whether the mass of the population is engaged in a variety of subsidiary work activities. As table 3-6 shows, they present strong evidence that this was not occurring on a broad scale for the population as a whole. The percentages of those with outside employment are higher among those ages twenty-four to thirty-two, but only quite marginally (see table 3-7).

The only truly important outside economic activity is the private agricultural plot. Well before 1991, Russian urban residents were given the right to have a kitchen garden in the countryside if they did not have a dacha. As conditions became more unsettled in the late 1980s, an increasing number took advantage of the opportunity. One sometimes had the impression that everyone in Russia, including Moscow scholars, became a potato farmer. Urban respondents were asked in the 1993 survey if they grew fruits and vegetables at a dacha or garden, and 65 percent answered "yes"; 72 percent of those were between the ages of thirty-five and sixty. The figure was so high that we decided to economize on space and not ask the question in future surveys, but all the evidence indicates that the figures remained as high in future years or even increased.

The Pattern of Ownership

Did the voucher privatization really change the pattern of ownership of enterprises in a meaningful way? What, if anything, did any change in the pattern of ownership mean? The great justification for voucher pri-

Table 3-7. Percentage of 24-to-32-Year-Old Respondents Involved in
Activities to Earn Extra Money, 1993, 1995–97[a]

Frequency of involvement	1993	1995	1996	1997
Never	76.0	75.1	70.2	63.9
Seasonal	3.0	4.0	3.7	5.6
From time to time	12.6	15.2	17.7	19.7
Several times a month	2.1	1.0	—[b]	2.0
Several times a week	1.7	0.4	1.0	1.3
Constantly	4.7	4.2	6.7	7.4

Source: Author's surveys.
a. Percentages may not total 100 as a result of rounding.
b. Statistically insignificant.

vatization was that it would facilitate the replacement of insider owners, but the western reformers never claimed that this goal was
achieved.

In the fall of 1993 three key figures in the privatization program—
Maxim Boycko, Andrei Shleifer, and Robert Vishny—conceded at an
economics conference that the program had "not worked particularly
well." The paper they presented at the conference was filled with reasons for pessimism, and they were even gloomier in their responses during the question period. "Shleifer indicated that the paper focused on
Russian privatization not because it had been particularly successful,
but because for now it appears to be the only avenue for making
progress in corporate governance."[54] Stanley Fischer's response was
sharp:

> The key question posed by the authors . . . is whether privatization
> will lead to restructuring. . . . They indicate that the privatization
> may have gone too far in the direction of labor management. They
> also argue that restructuring will require nonpolitical control over
> credit allocation, and nonpolitical governance of firms, neither of
> which yet obtains. Apparently, the authors, like other observers,
> do not yet see much in the way of restructuring taking place.[55]

Several westerners surveyed a sample of plants to see if the pattern of
ownership changed after 1993, but their samples seem far from random.
For example, one well-known survey conducted by American advisers
to the State Committee for Property seemed to focus on plants that were
functioning fairly well and that therefore attracted outside interest.
Their 1996 sample included 357 large and medium-sized enterprises,

which constituted 2 percent of all such plants that were privatized and employed 4.6 percent of all employees in such enterprises. In these enterprises, 58 percent of the shares were owned by insiders (18 percent by managers and 40 percent by workers), 32 percent by outsiders, and 9 percent by the state.[56]

These figures for outsider ownership, however, seem too high, and those for state ownership too low. The source of the problem is suggested by the decision made about the heavy industrial city of Volgograd (the former Stalingrad). The city had large machinery and defense enterprises, as well as one of the most important tractor plants in the country. These large plants suffered seriously in the aftermath of reform, and it is doubtful that outsiders would have much interest in purchasing their shares. As a result, the 1996 study selected a margarine factory in Volgograd that was scarcely representative of industrial enterprises in the city. If the purpose of the study was to see how food industry plants and those exporting natural resources were adjusting, the sample was reasonable, but it was misleading if it was meant to show, as Andrei Shleifer said in the introduction, that Russian industry as a whole had entered a new world.

The meaning of outside ownership became more obscure after 1995. As the Russian government moved away from direct subsidies of enterprises, it used an increasingly complex network of indirect subsidies. The foreign trade banks acquired shares not only of oil companies, but also of many other enterprises that seemed to be very poor investment prospects. Profitable exporting firms acquired (or became lead firms in holding companies that acquired) less profitable enterprises in what might seem vertical or horizontal integration. Many oligarchs became part owners of unprofitable newspapers. Gazprom acquired shares in companies in exchange for debt.

In 1995 and 1996 many described these acquisitions as the expansion of the power and wealth of a small group of oligarchs, and hence of the expansion of outsider ownership. Three years later, as most of the banks involved were themselves bankrupt, the only question was whether the oligarchs had business judgment as poor as seemed on the surface, or whether they had been instructed to make these acquisitions so that they could subsidize them out of their own earnings. This book supports the latter interpretation.

However the ownership of these bank-acquired enterprises is seen, the statistic on "outsider ownership" had a different meaning than the economic reformers originally intended. If a bank was forced to acquire unprofitable plants that had no market for their products in the foreseeable future in order to provide their workers with subsidies, this was the opposite of the intentions of the reformers. But if the outsiders controlling the financial institutions had such poor business judgment that they voluntarily acquired unprofitable property that almost surely would bankrupt them, this had even worse implications for the original reform model.

The Real Character of Privatization

Without any question, a great deal of privatization took place in the Soviet Union after 1990, at least formally, but it is unclear what this meant. The Russian economic system fits none of the usual categories of analysis. Much of what was called "state property" was subject to personalized control. Much of what is considered privatized property had little relationship to normal concepts of private property. The "owners" of a major hard-currency producer, Norilsk Nickel, were not allowed to retain enough of its profits to make capital repairs at its copper plant for fifteen years, let alone capital improvements. Tatneft (Tatarstan Oil) had to "barter" its oil to major petrochemical firms in the republic at below-market prices and even then often did not receive payment at the artificially low price and could not pay its workers for three months. This was an enterprise audited by Price Waterhouse and listed on the New York Stock Exchange. Gazprom not only had to send its gas free to many customers, but it had to loan $650 million to Cheliabinsk Tractor Works to pay off its debts even though it would not be able to produce a significant number of tractors in the foreseeable future. Many profitable banks and plants were forced to buy unprofitable ones.

There is a real question how much these large enterprises are privatized and how much they really are still controlled by the state. Their managers or owners were, of course, much freer to misappropriate funds than in well-organized nationalized enterprises. Yet the owners of important pieces of economic property did not have nearly as much independence in decisionmaking as comparable property owners in the West, and the term barter often hid the obligation to fulfill direct state orders. Their "lack of defined property rights" went well beyond the usual meaning of those words. Indeed, the owners often were as susceptible to government removal from the "ownership" of their property as if they were government bureaucrats. The off-budget subsidies meant that all plants were bankrupt and that this could be made formal at any time.

Private property is always a conditional concept. There are a myriad of restrictions on the way that property can be used and sold in the West—restrictions that are embedded in zoning, access, anti-fraud, labor, safety, environmental, and other regulatory laws. Indeed, there are so many restrictions that one can visualize private property in the West as being state-owned and leased to people for their restricted right to use and dispose of in exchange for the payment of a rent called taxes.

In the western conception of private property, however, the various government restrictions on the use of property are relatively impersonal and predictable. They obviously can be modified over time, but the process of change is usually gradual enough to allow owners to adjust or sell. Entrepreneurs, we say, are subject to the law. Although the law is state-made and state-enforced, our language implies that the restrictions are universal, not the product of the discretion of individual state officials. The owners at least own the right to sell their lease. We take for granted that taxes will not be confiscatory and that the restrictions will allow businesses to function and make a profit.

Those who headed the privatization program in Russia claimed that it involved depoliticization. Andrei Shleifer and Maxim Boycko distinguished between managers and politicians in the Soviet Union, and they described the former as largely concerned with value maximization and the latter primarily as the agents of rent-seeking interest groups. They argued against nomenklatura privatization on the ground that "politicians are good at designing subsidy programs, not business plans."[57]

Nothing could be more misleading. It made no sense to distinguish between politicians and managers in the Soviet system. As Zbigniew Brzezinski emphasized at the beginning of the Brezhnev period, the political posts in the Soviet system were occupied by those who had arisen through a bureaucratic, managerial hierarchy.[58] Boris Yeltsin was the typical politician. He worked for eleven years as a successful construction manager before spending nine years in party work dealing with construction. Then he became the equivalent of a state governor. Viktor Chernomyrdin moved back and forth between party and managerial work before becoming minister of the gas industry.

The major flaw in the Shleifer and Boycko argument is that it made no distinction between the different ways in which government can intervene in the economic sphere. As Max Weber correctly emphasized, a government that establishes and enforces impersonal rules and regulations—and that itself largely functions by such rules and regulations—is crucial for a market economy. The process is politicized only if the rules and especially the decisions on how to enforce the rules are too much the product of political pressures.

The Soviet economic system was not really politicized in this sense of the word, but instead was thoroughly bureaucratized. Young scholars in both Russia and the United States often look back at the Soviet Union as if the catch phrase "command economy" actually reflected the reality of the Soviet economic system. No idea is more bizarre to a scholar who studied that system in detail for thirty years. The Soviet economic system was bureaucratic; it lacked competition between producers; and its incentive system encouraged managers to make compromises with quality and with innovation. But it was a system in which the planning process began from below as it does in any bureaucracy. Soviet leaders and economists gave inordinate attention to the creation of incentives and indicators to try to lead managers to optimal decisions and to reward them if they fulfilled the goals set in the indicators.[59] As a result, the economic system had relatively little arbitrary intervention by politicians in the Brezhnev era, but it had the opposite flaw. It was too regularized and too inflexible for a complex modern economy.

The classic literature by western specialists on the Soviet Union demonstrated that the Soviet managers responded quite rationally to a well-integrated incentive system. The incentive system led the managers to behavior that the founders of the incentive system wanted: the maximization of production, even at some cost to quality and efficiency; an emphasis on the expansion of smokestack industry rather than consumers' goods, especially luxury consumer goods; the end of unemployment; and a far more egalitarian distribution of income than in capitalism, especially early capitalism.

The incentive system also had dysfunctional consequences, which were fully discussed in the Soviet press as early as the 1930s.[60] Primary among them were the quality and variety of goods produced, the lead times and inflexibilities in the planning process, and the lack of responsiveness to the customer, both the consumer and other plants. As the economy became more complex and more service-oriented and as the electronics and computer age began, the defects of the system increasingly outweighed its strengths.

The first requirement of economic reform was the introduction of competition into the system and greater flexibility into production and investment decisionmaking. Everyone agreed that this meant a fundamental change in the incentive system for economic actors. The problem for the state was to replace a regularized bureaucratic economic system with one in which the enterprises responded to more impersonal contractual rules and incentives and in which conditions were created for easy entry by newcomers.

In actuality, Yeltsin created a classic politicized economy. An orderly bureaucratized economy was replaced by one ruled through personalistic, patrimonial bureaucracies by top officials without job security who were preoccupied with palace politics and the acquisition of property. Those with successful economic enterprises had no property right in their output, but were forced to give subsidies to others. Those in economic difficulties had to receive subsidies awarded not by some impersonal formula, but through personal favor. The subsidies were made in forms that made them bankrupt. Hence they had no secure property rights of any kind. The line between personal and official was obliterated, and everyone was motivated to concentrate on promoting short-term personal interests and seeking political favor.

The future outcome of this process of privatization is hard to predict. One is reminded of the game of musical chairs in which there are more players than chairs and in which players scramble to find chairs when the music stops. Many who have thought that they had acquired property found that the music started again and that they were on the outside at the end of the next round. Many who seem to be owners today will almost surely find their good fortune to be ephemeral, because some parts of the economy cry out for renationalization.

But, of course, at some point in the future, Russia will leave its time of troubles and begin sustained economic growth. Those in control of many valuable pieces of property at that time will suddenly find that they are real owners and that their property has become profitable. Russia will then begin moving for the first time toward a normal market economy.

One thing is certain. Westerners have too often treated privatization of state property as a panacea and given too little thought to the meaning of the words they use. Few assimilated the idea that secure property rights, which they emphasized as crucial from the first, really meant what it said. The phrase does not mean secure property rights for outsiders with an economic and financial background who would be given secure property rights only after the present owners are bankrupted and expropriated through state actions.

The great paradox of the privatization program was that it was conducted in the name of the Coase theorem, but basically denied all of its assumptions. The Coase theorem implied that once state property was privatized, it eventually would flow to the most efficient producers. But Richard Ericson made a crucial point before voucher privatization was introduced. The thing that was "of absolutely critical importance is the right of exit—the right [of owners] to sell for market capitalized value—which underlies the incentive to use assets for the creation and enhancement of wealth, rather than just its exploitation for current income."[61]

Unless owners have the incentive and opportunity to improve the value of their property through reorganization, investment, redesign of product, and development of new markets, private ownership will provide few benefits. But if the insider-owners had been allowed and even subsidized to improve their property, Coase reassures us that they would, indeed, eventually sell to more efficient owners, either in whole or through stock offerings.

The ugly truth about the Russian privatization program—and it is far uglier than the well-known scandals—is that the neoliberal Russian economic reformers knew that they did not have the managerial skills to be the most efficient owners—that they would lose in the competition Coase described. Hence it was even more necessary for them to engage in grabification than the insiders of the Gorbachev era. The West supported them fully in this effort by opposing transparent subsidy grants and by making bankruptcy of old owners a high priority through a series of mechanisms.

Stanley Fischer, the future first deputy director of the IMF, showed at the Brookings conference in 1993 that he grasped this point when he implied that Yeltsin and those in his government were politicians and driven to rent-seeking like other politicians.[62] Yet Fischer drew no conclusions, at least in public. He explicitly opposed any slowdown in the privatization process. His answer at the conference was not restructuring, but the familiar tightening of credit, macroeconomic stabilization, and liberalization of trade. When he wrote an op-ed in the *New York Times* at this time, he showed none of the doubts he had just expressed semiprivately about privatization. He wrote: "Despite the impression in the West that Russia is sinking, crucial reforms are well under way, especially in the privatization of state enterprises."[63]

Fischer and other westerners should have understood that the crucial difference between the nomenklatura and the politicians in the reform team was that the latter were not limited to traditional types of rent-seeking. The logic of collective action correctly indicated that they had an interest in shaping the fundamental institutions and incentives of the economic system to serve not the collective interests, but their own. They had the ability to do so. Instead, Fischer called for removal of the nomenklatura and their replacement by technically qualified personnel, which is precisely what the old nomenklatura were.

The issue to which the West should have been giving far more attention was the incentives that were being created for the owners of the newly privatized property. The West understood from the experience of eastern Germany that an enormous amount of capital investment was needed to modernize a communist country even of that size. Russia had eight times the population of eastern Germany and did not have a western Germany to support it. The top priority was to create the right incentive structure for massive domestic and foreign investment. Instead, an incentive system was established that made capital investment and capital repair virtually impossible. That was the fatal flaw of Russian economic reform, and the next chapter will suggest why that was so.

FOUR   *Saving and*
         Investment

THE EARLY DISCUSSIONS of economic reform in
eastern Europe and Russia gave little attention to saving and investment.
Most economists said that large-scale investment should be postponed
until institutional change had occurred. Nevertheless, the transition
period was expected to be relatively short, and no major and prolonged
drop in production was anticipated.[1] Investment would, it was thought,
emerge automatically from domestic and foreign sources. As Olivier
Blanchard, an active western participant in the early economic reform
process, stated in 1997, "Given the scope for restructuring, the need for
new capital, the relatively low labour costs by international standards,
and the high level of human capital, one might have expected transition
to be associated with high rates of capital accumulation."[2]

In actuality, as Blanchard documented, this expectation was not met
in most east European countries, and least of all in Russia. According to
official statistics, industrial production in Russia fell to 51 percent of the
1990 level by 1994, while basic capital investment in the productive
sphere fell to 24 percent in the same period.[3] As a World Bank study
emphasized, consumption remained unusually high for a country in
such economic straits, but investment and government expenditure were
unusually low.

Analysts generally believe—indeed, surely too much so—that Russians had ample savings in dollars hidden at home or abroad for the
needed investment, but the statistics are unreliable and vary widely.[4]
Without question, however, domestic savers lacked the incentives, the

94

confidence, or the intermediary mechanisms to invest their savings in the domestic economy. Where analysts disagree is on the reasons domestic investment failed to occur.[5]

Neoliberal reformers have generally given two explanations for insufficient investment in Russia. First they say that the macroeconomic environment was not conducive to investment: inflation, they say, was too high for years, and then the real budgetary deficit absorbed and still absorbs too much potential investment. The second answer, a special favorite of those abroad, is that the mafia and corrupt officials were so strong that they made investment in business unprofitable and even dangerous.

Both arguments are expressed in the assertion that the state has been too "weak," but, unfortunately, the word weak is ambiguous. An article by John Odling-Smee, director of the European II Department of the IMF in November 1998, illustrates the problem. For him, "weak government" primarily meant "insufficient agreement and willingness among the leadership of the country to impose the fiscal discipline to pursue successful reform." Yet Odling-Smee called for more "institution building" at the same time that he said the prime need in Russia was "rapid progress in scaling back the size of the state."[6] Some gained the impression that such a call for a stronger state that reduced its size and role meant that "weak" was a synonym for "antidemocratic"—that is, an appeal for a leader like Augusto Pinochet of Chile, who would impose the IMF policy.

The critics of the neoliberal position fell into two separate camps that had very different perspectives. One, following the lead of Nobel laureate Douglass North, emphasized Russia's lack of what Alan Greenspan called a "capitalist culture."[7] As North put it, even though the formal institutional framework of the communist economy was destroyed, this development was undercut by "the survival of many of the informal constraints."[8] North's Nobel Prize speech was filled with phrases such as "mental models," "belief structures," "collective learning," "path dependence,"[9] and these remnants of the past were often seen as decisive.

A second and different line of criticism is set forth in this book. It does not challenge the proposition that formal rules by themselves may have little effect on behavior. The Soviet Constitution certainly demonstrated that point. Nor does it deny that investment in a modern capitalist society unquestionably rests on a great deal of trust—trust in the safety of bank deposits, in the honesty of stockbrokers and those who issue stock, on the reliable fulfillment of long-term contracts with suppliers and prospective customers, on the security of successful businesses from expropriation by government and others. Indeed, the root of the word *credit* is the Latin word for belief or trust.

In modern society the trust on which investment is based often, in fact, comes to be taken for granted. Professional behavior becomes habitual and automatic for most people instead of being the result of continuous calculation of narrow self-interest. In that sense, a series of informal rules and norms that are crucial for a well-functioning capitalist system are embedded in a capitalist culture.

Nevertheless, the second line of criticism would reverse Douglass North's argument that "Russia had no [informal] norms to provide an hospitable foundation for the establishment of formal rules for such an economy and polity."[10] Rather it would insist that the creation of trust, informal norms, and rules of the game are ultimately based on the confidence created by positive incentives and by the threat of punishment established in the formal rules. The trust is maintained only if laws contain meaningful, enforced incentives and punishment. Trust ultimately is the confidence that a violation of trust by others will lead to severe legal consequences or economic costs for them.

This trust is fragile and can disappear even in a functioning capitalist system. The problem is exemplified by a run on a bank, but it can be seen also in legal violations and corruption virtually anywhere. If people come to think they are the only ones operating by the rules, they will think they are being played for fools. Once an orderly line begins to disintegrate, it quickly degenerates into disorderly pushing and shoving. Large numbers of inherently honest people will change behavior in a rule-breaking direction almost as a matter of honor.

In a market that is just being created, the trust needed for long-term investment often arises from personal ties of friendship (this is frequently the basis for corruption) or, perhaps, kinship or ethnicity (as seen in the traditional role of the Chinese in much of Southeast Asia). Trust in impersonal financial institutions and unknown people rests on the development of confidence in the formal rules, the laws, and the incentive system and on the mechanisms that enforce them. The development of such institutions and especially confidence in them should have been the first task in Russia in 1990, but little effort was devoted to it. Hence it was totally rational for individuals to take an extremely short-term position or, if they could, to send their savings to a safer institutional environment abroad.

Since the development of a well-functioning banking system and stock market normally takes decades, the second group of critics assumes that at early stages of industrialization and marketization government must take a more engaged role in economic life and investment than would be desirable in a well-developed, entrenched capitalist system. This was particularly true in Russia in the second half of the nineteenth century, as Alexander Gerschenkron said,[11] but it was just as true of Russia at the end of the twentieth century.

From this perspective, the problem in Russia in the 1990s was not that the government was weak in the sense of being uninvolved in the economic sphere. The government was directing actions of regions, banks, and enterprises in a very detailed manner. The problem was that it was establishing incentives and taking concrete actions that undercut investment instead of supporting it. Understanding the failure of economic reform in Russia requires looking closely and coldly at the real incentives for savings and investment as they worked in the conditions prevailing in Russia, not the incentives as they were supposed to work in an ideal market.

The Russian Reformers' Assumptions about Investment

The neglect of investment during the 1990s in Russia was peculiar. Olivier Blanchard was right that it seemed obvious that large-scale investment must be a key element in making Russian production more efficient and developing new products. Whatever naive assumptions people may have had in 1989, the enormous investment that western Germany was required to make in eastern Germany should have illuminated the situation for everyone. Even after a decade, the situation in the former East Germany remained so difficult that the local voters turned against Chancellor Helmut Kohl and the Christian Democratic party, voting them out of office. Since Russia had eight times the population of East Germany, it presumably required at least eight times as much investment.

In addition, Boris Yeltsin was a construction engineer who had spent two decades in construction management in enterprises and in the Communist party organs. He then served for ten years as governor (*obkom* first secretary) of one of the most important heavy and defense industry centers. All of his instincts should have led him to emphasize construction and investment. All of his old friends and associates should have been telling him about the disastrous consequences his anti-investment policy was having on the region that he had spent a lifetime building up.

Many elements led to a profound neglect of investment in Russia in the 1990s. They began with Mikhail Gorbachev's belief that the population needed to see the benefits of perestroika before suffering its costs and that high consumption must be maintained. Gorbachev and his advisers did not appreciate that an investment program that sustained and increased production protected consumption better than direct support of consumption at the cost of investment. They did not understand that agricultural reform, after a short transition period, was the best way to raise living standards and to free up export earnings for the purchase of capital goods instead of foodstuffs. Yeltsin and his advisers repeated the same mistakes.

Gorbachev and his advisers defended their decision to maintain consumption at the cost of investment by reference to a long-recognized fact. The Soviet Union historically had a high rate of investment, and much of it went to industries and products that were not appropriate for a country at the Soviet Union's stage of development. If nonproductive investment were reduced, they argued, consumption and even economic growth might be affected only minimally.

Maintaining consumption became even more difficult in 1990. The Politburo was convinced that the Soviet Union's terms of trade with Eastern Europe were unfavorable, and it made an extraordinarily ill-advised decision to put trade with Eastern Europe on a hard currency basis. Eastern Europe had little hard currency at the time, and the Soviet Union was dependent on Eastern Europe for a number of key imports. The trade between the two regions, including exports of consumer goods and medicines to the Soviet Union, dropped precipitously. Oil prices were also falling. As a result, the Soviet Union as a whole had a negative balance of trade of $24.1 billion in 1990. Total Soviet imports fell from $120.7 billion in 1990 to $68.2 billion in 1991 to help correct this situation—from $82.9 billion to $45.6 billion in Russia alone. The Soviet Union had $10.9 billion net credits in 1990 and $12.0 billion in 1991.[12]

At this time the young reform economists associated with Yeltsin became more exposed to neoliberal economics, and they found additional arguments to delay investment. The first was that investment should wait until institutions had changed. Western neoliberal economists had first encountered the problem of investment when communism collapsed in Eastern Europe in 1989. Many westerners called for a new Marshall Plan of investment in those countries, but economists such as Lawrence Summers noted that east-central Europe already had a fairly high rate of investment. "The problem is that given the amount of capital, growth is relatively slow." He drew the following conclusion:

> The answer does not appear to be in simply providing more capital. Rather it seems to require raising the rate of return on the capital investment. . . . If growth is to be accelerated, one needs to create a more productive institutional environment in which investment is made more profitable, and not simply provide increasing amounts of capital. . . . It is that institutional gap, and not a capital gap, that needs to be solved if Central Europe is to have a chance of taking off.[13]

The problem in the Soviet Union was more severe than in Eastern Europe, for it had not had the partial market reforms and administered price adjustments that were introduced in northern Eastern Europe after the 1950s. In addition, young Russian academic economists and westerners without knowledge about the Soviet economy thought the problem was even greater than it was. Western industrialists always talked about the high quality of Soviet managers and the high quality of the technology of their advanced plants, but the neoliberal economists had deeply rooted prejudices about the "nomenklatura" and Soviet technology. For the economists, deindustrialization, whose usual sense was a decline in the percentage of the population employed in industry, often took on a literal meaning: closing industrial plants.

The neoliberal economists believed that if the old enterprises and their managers were hopeless, then large-scale investment should not be devoted to an effort to reconstruct them, especially while they were led by the old managers. Investment should be made by new businessmen or new managers after privatization had occurred. No doubt, the economists believed that the new corporate and financial elite should comprise young persons with economic and financial knowledge like themselves. They believed that a reduction in defense expenditures and investment would allow consumption to be maintained at a reasonably high level during a short period of severe pain produced by the shock therapy.

The neoliberal economists understood that investment would eventually be important for economic growth, but they saw it emerging almost automatically if the proper macroeconomic conditions were created. For this reason, they saw no need to pay special attention to the stimulation of investment in Russia. If property were privatized, prices freed, and monetary stabilization achieved, then potential investors would almost inevitably respond.

This argument, as it applied to Russia, had two obvious flaws. First, the correct conclusion that capital alone would not solve the Russian economic problem did not change the fact that huge amounts of investment were necessary—and necessary quickly. The creation of more efficient plants and of new products would require new machinery and machine tools. If a product proved successful, there would be a need for enormous capital to expand capacity.

This point was made to me in two interviews in 1992. The first was with the chief engineer of the Kharkov Tractor Plant. The plant had long produced large tractors, and Soviet and western economists had long advised it to produce smaller tractors that peasants could use in smaller fields. Now that economic reform was imminent, the plant should obviously follow this advice. The chief engineer expressed a desire to do so, but said it was impossible. The plant received its tractor motors from the Yaroslavl Motor Works, which made motors only for large tractors.

Later in the year, the chief engineer of the Yaroslavl Motor Works was asked whether his plant was beginning to produce smaller tractor motors for the Kharkov Tractor Plant. The answer was that such a change would require new assembly lines and new machine tools, and the plant did not have money to buy this equipment. If plant managers were autonomous and thinking in market terms when making interenterprise loans, as often assumed, the director of the machinery plants could have provided an interenterprise loan to the motor plant. This loan would have led to the production of an item with a market and a reduction in the production of an item with a declining market. But, of course, the managers had no autonomy on interenterprise loans, and the government was not authorizing loans that were associated with new investment.

Even the service sector required great investment. For example, financial institutions needed to be computerized, and the computer industry itself needed to be modernized and expanded. In 1993, 90 percent of all transactions between banks, including the Central Bank clearing houses, were carried out on paper. At least five copies were required, copies that were almost surely made without photocopiers.[14] The banks did not even have checking accounts for deposits.

The notion that all the capital goods plants could be destroyed simultaneously and arise from the rubble with new and more advanced goods simultaneously produced by new and more efficient machinery was little short of insane. It was, however, the implicit assumption underlying policy, for machinery plants were never supported by interenterprise loans and barter arrangements on the same scale as other enterprises.

The second problem with the argument that investment should wait for institutional change rested on Summers' use of the term "institutional gap." The term implied a known set of institutions toward which Russia must move—a set of institutions that came in some kind of package. It implied that the problems to be solved by institutions in the early stages of marketization were the same as those in postindustrial capitalist society, that the same institutions were needed at all stages of development. The belief that investment should be postponed until institutions were ready to use it efficiently was simply another sign of the belief that there was a chasm to an efficient market economy that could be traversed in a single leap.

No neoliberal economist attempted to answer the arguments that Gerschenkron made with respect to Russia in the nineteenth century. What banking institutions would collect savings and make loans in conditions where there was full lack of trust? Why should anyone make a loan to new owners when the top reformers in the Yeltsin regime—and the IMF and western economists as well—were saying that they were incompetent and corrupt and that their plants would be bankrupted in two or three years when the voucher phase of privatization was finished? It was as if industrial development would arise from scratch as in England in the eighteenth century, except that industrialization could not be based on agriculture as it had in England because no agricultural reform was envisaged. It was utterly insane.

The Logic of Crime and Corruption

In the absence of reliable statistics, observers naturally disagree on the amount of crime, "mafia" activity, corruption, and capital flight in Russia, but no one doubts that they are quite substantial. The problem is to understand their significance. The neoliberal reformers see the illegalities as exogenous factors that have harmed if not ruined economic reform. They see them as the product of historical factors: the lack of a capitalist culture, a long-ingrained lack of respect for the government, the absence of a well-established legal tradition, and the high levels of corruption in the communist economic system. As late as September 1999 the U.S. national security adviser, Samuel Berger, was still insisting, "To understand corruption in Russia, we must understand that it is rooted in the legacy of Soviet communism."[15]

The argument is so inconsistent with the basic assumptions of neoliberal economics—or, indeed, of almost any economic theory—that it should inspire the deepest skepticism. The classic neoliberal economists of the past argued that crime and corruption can be the rational response of economic actors to certain sets of incentives. Obviously in any society individual deviance exists among those who are responding to psychological factors instead of economic incentives, but when crime and corruption become widespread, they are certain to be rational responses to the existing incentive system.

Moreover, mafias and corruption can be supportive of economic performance and growth, at least to some extent. Corrupt people want to invest their money where they can make a maximum return, and this is likely to be where they have government protection. Mafias have an interest in the prosperity of their territories so that they can maximize their own return. The real question about economic reform in Russia is why the corruption and mafia activity that arose in Russia did not have this effect.

The Mafia and Investment

As discussed earlier, neoliberal economic theory insists that it is more rational for A to steal corn from B than to trade for it if the two live in an anarchic environment and B is not well armed. The problem of ensuring that A does not steal B's corn goes back to the beginnings of civilization. People originally lived a nomadic life as hunters and gatherers. Civilization began when some groups decided to "invest"—to plant and care for plants and to raise animals so that their hunting and gathering at the end of the season would be easier and more productive. The thought naturally occurred to those who were still nomadic that the fields of the planters and shepherds were the most convenient place to do their own gathering and hunting.

The liberal theory of the origin of the state begins with the need of agricultural peoples to protect themselves and the products of their investment from marauders. One can see the rise of the state in functional terms, but Mancur Olson described the origins of the state with the analogy of a "stationary bandit." A state of anarchy is populated by a large number of roving bandits, but, in Olson's view, the leader of one of those bands understood that if he became stationary and monopolized theft in a particular area, he could become wealthier and lead an easier and more respectable life. The wiser stationary bandits understood that if they promoted growth and regularized their theft (now called taxes) by limiting it to a fixed, finite percentage, they could maximize their long-term economic return.[16]

In historical perspective, the state provided the basis for the rise of civilization and the increase in economic productivity seen over the past 10,000 years. In any briefer perspective, however, the state often failed to provide sufficient protection to economic actors. Indeed, the military force that the state accumulated often posed a direct danger to domestic economic actors or an indirect one through the wars in which it engaged and lost.

When the state is too weak to provide adequate police and military protection to economic actors, the people must provide their own. The essence of feudalism was not only a lord-serf relationship, but also the lord's creation of a military force to protect those in his domain—and, no doubt, also to force peasants into it. The large landlords in Haiti with private police or the tribal militia in Africa are no different in principle. A specialist on mafias, Diego Gambetta, defines them as "agencies that supply protection to illegal markets," but the generalized subtitle of his book on the Sicilian Mafia ("The Business of Private Protection") is more accurate.[17]

Even in a modern capitalist society, some spheres of the economy do not have state-provided police and legal protection and instead are the object of police harassment. This was true of gambling and especially the sale of alcohol in the 1920s. The mafias and gangs of the time were private police who offered protection for these segments of the economy. The same is true of urban gangs of recent decades that protect the illegal drug trade and of the armed political groups calling themselves radical socialists that protect coca agriculture in Colombia.

A mafia is a stationary bandit who functions as a ministate in a small area. Olson would argue that a mafia should be more conducive to economic activity and investment than a state of anarchy, but not as conducive as a state that protects the entire economy over a larger area. It is not surprising that mafias are more often found in less dynamic economies or segments of the economy. If the opportunity for great enrichment increases in an area with economic development, then a stronger stationary band with greater military force—the legal state—will likely act to supplant the smaller and weaker bands.

Nevertheless, mafia protection is more similar to government protection than we like to recognize. In both cases the economic actor has no choice but to accept the protection and pay for it. A person who refuses to pay for mafia protection risks physical injury or worse. Government is more civilized; it simply imprisons those who refuse to pay for its protection. Yet if the mafia and government are basically competitive institutions offering a similar service to economic actors, government has a natural advantage because of its ability to muster superior force—if it chooses to do so.

The Russian gangs and mafias need to be understood in the same terms as western ones. Many see the Russian mafia as a natural continuation of the illegality in the Soviet second economy, but nothing could be further from the truth. As Anatoly Chubais correctly understood, those in the second economy had capital, entrepreneurial instincts, daring, and business skills. Their natural choice would have been to use their funds and skills to become major legitimate businessmen in the new economy—as do their counterparts in the West when conditions change. Joseph Kennedy, the father of President John Kennedy, was driven by a desire for respectability after the end of Prohibition, in which he had enriched himself, and his Soviet counterparts would be no different. If some persons from the second economy did not perceive the wisdom of making a transition to legal economic activity, the new politicians of post–Soviet Russia had every interest to use the full force of the state against them. The new politicians, after all, had a strong interest in monopolizing corruption for themselves.

In the United States, economic activities not protected by the law and, indeed, harassed by it (such as illegal drug sales) are relatively limited now, and so too is the sphere in which gangs serve as the major police force and legal system. If they try to extend their activities into other spheres of the economy or into living areas outside selected poor neighborhoods, the response of the police is harsh. But in Russia there has been insufficient legal protection for any part of the economy, and hence the sphere of mafia protection has been much wider. Large businesses increasingly hired their own private force to protect against independent forces, but the only way to combat the mafia on a mass basis was to build up state institutions as a legal competitor.

Government Corruption and Investment

Government officials and economic actors are usually contrasted, but the individuals working for the government are themselves participants in a labor market. They are presumably motivated by the same calculations of relative benefit as those seeking other employment, but when the government offers more job security, it may be able to attract employees at lower cost. Because this combination of higher security and lower wages is most appealing to the risk-averse, it should lead to a government civil service that is less inclined to take risks by violating the law. Indeed, this is the major reason to create an incentive system that attracts less entrepreneurial and innovative people for government work than work in the private sector.

The incentive system for government employees does not, however, always correspond to our preconceptions. In developing countries, government employment, either military or civilian, may be less secure than that in the traditional agriculture sector, and it may offer much higher rewards. The risk of punishment for illegality may be low, and what we call "conflict of interest" may not even be defined as illegal. Great economic rewards in the urban private sector may be difficult to obtain and may require government assistance. In these circumstances the structure of costs and benefits of government employment should attract those who are not risk-averse but those who are trying to maximize personal economic gain. In short, it may attract those who are primarily motivated by the chance for corruption.

The levels of corruption are generally higher in the early and middle levels of industrialization than in advanced industrial society—not because people are less moral, but because the restraints are less developed. Karl Marx lived in such a period in Europe. He was wrong to see government as the tool of some united bourgeois class, but individual government decisions at that time often did, in fact, result from the subornation of officials by payments from individual members of the bourgeoisie. Marx failed to understand that it would be possible to increase the regulatory role of government in a way that could substantially improve the situation.

Russian neoliberal economists began as Marxists, and they shared Marx's belief that the state played no useful role in a capitalist economy. Yet they rejected Marx's insight into the defects of early capitalism because they did not understand the base of these insights in their own models of individual rationality. They did not comprehend that self-interested "economic men" *should* engage in illegal and corrupt activities if they are profitable. They did not understand that the massive corruption witnessed in Russia flowed logically from their own assumptions, not from defects in the Russian character.

Although many now claim there were especially high levels of corruption in the communist period, the opposite was true. The Soviet economic system made it very difficult to use ill-gotten wealth to acquire property in Russia, and the KGB-protected iron curtain made it very dangerous to have foreign property and foreign bank accounts. Hence the cost-benefit ratio for large-scale corruption was much less favorable than in a normal country at the early and middle stages of capitalist development.[18]

For this reason, the opening of Russia to the world economy, the greater ease in having foreign accounts, and the possibility of emigration, not to mention the opportunity to acquire property at home, would have increased the level of large-scale corruption in Russia sharply, regardless of other factors involved.[19] The problem was exacerbated by a breakdown in discipline within the government apparatus. In the words of Andrei Shleifer and Robert Vishny, two of the leading participants in Russian privatization,

> In the old-time Communist regimes . . . it is always clear who needs to be bribed and by how much. . . . In some African countries, in India, and in postcommunist Russia . . . the sellers of complementary government goods, such as permits and licenses, act independently. Different ministries, agencies, and levels of local government all set their own bribes independently in an attempt to maximize their own revenue. . . . This problem is made much worse in many countries by free entry into the collection of bribes. New government organizations and officials often have the opportunity to create laws and regulations that enable them to become

providers of additional required permits and licenses and charge for them accordingly. Having paid three bribes, the buyer of these inputs learns that he must buy yet another one if he wants his project to proceed.[20]

The analysis of corruption must, however, be pushed further. In particular, why is corruption especially widespread in the early and middle stages of capitalist development? Moisei Ostrogorski and Lewis Namier wrote famous descriptions of the corruption in the relation between king and Parliament in eighteenth-century England that read eerily like Yeltsin's relationship with the Duma.[21] The U.S. bank controversy of the 1820s really was a struggle between politicians over which of them would succeed in having federal money deposited in their personal banks or those of their friends. The generation of the American "takeoff" of the 1850s was called "the plundering generation," while the term "robber baron" was coined in 1867 to describe the major entrepreneurs of the entire period of rapid growth until the end of the century. The corruption in the Pacific Rim countries of the second half of the twentieth century is legendary.

The corruption in the early stages of capitalist industrial development is almost always treated as a factor that retards economic growth.[22] The eradication of corruption, especially that associated with leading politicians, is a perennial demand of the IMF. Nevertheless, the period of widespread corruption is associated with prolonged surges of growth in such a wide range of countries that it cannot be seen wholly in negative terms. In fact, reduction in the scale of the corruption is usually associated with declines in rates of growth.

Large-scale corruption can play an important role in promoting investment and growth at a certain stage of capitalism and even in establishing the constitutional democracy that is so important in protecting a market economy. When people do not trust impersonal financial institutions and when the institutions do not trust potential investors seeking to borrow, a close personal relationship between investors and government, cemented by economic self-interest on both sides, serves many useful functions.

Government investment projects often serve purposes of prestige rather than economic growth, and they are frequently counterproductive. By contrast, private investment by corrupt government officials or joint participation by investors and high government officials in a private investment project should promote economic growth. The government official, especially if he invests himself or participates indirectly in the investment, is motivated to seek the best long-term investment in a way often not captured by the anticorruption literature. Moreover, the project has a better chance of success because the problems of legal protection and informal government assistance are solved.

Clearly high-level corruption is inequitable. If it is carried to an extreme over the long term, it can result in monopoly and its concomitant problems. But to some extent the process is self-correcting. The next ruler and his favorites will want their own projects. As officials age, and as they and their children think more of the future, they develop an interest in a more impersonal system of legal protection precisely because they want to be protected from the next ruler. As society becomes wealthier, more people want to defend interests other than just those of a narrow economic elite and of economic growth alone. The establishment of constitutional democracy to protect property gives greater power to people more concerned with consumption. Not surprisingly, the defense of these other values produces a decline in the rate of growth, but this only demonstrates the close connection between high-level corruption, investment, and growth at the stage that the corruption is most rampant.

From this perspective, the enormous concern about the extent of high-level corruption in Russia in the 1990s is quite misplaced. Given the absence of a functioning banking system, government as an institution and government officials as individuals inevitably had to be key players in the investment process. The real issue was not the corruption, but what the corrupt did with their money. Any defense of corruption assumes that the money will be invested at home. There is every reason for this to occur if the economic incentive system is working properly. An investor with inside knowledge and government protection should receive far higher returns by investing in an emerging market than in a Swiss bank account or even western mutual funds.

The clearest sign that the Russian incentive system was not functioning properly was not that corruption occurred, but that the corrupt did not find it profitable to invest at home. This was true even in the mid 1990s, when westerners saw Russia as a highly profitable emerging market. Corruption should have facilitated investment, but those with inside knowledge saw that capital flight was the most profitable use of their money. The factors in the incentive system that led the corrupt not to invest were the same that influenced potential honest investors. They should have influenced western investors.

Individual Incentives and Investment in Different Economic Situations

Those who insist that the lack of institutions or a weak state has been the cause of poor Russian economic performance have been fundamentally mistaken. It was a remarkable government achievement to keep unemployment so low for so long during a major, long-lasting depression. The system of state-directed subsidies was sophisticated, and the institutional rules were regularized enough to create a fairly well-defined incentive system. The problem was not that government and institutions were absent, but that they created incentives that were counterproductive for economic growth and the collective good. The incentives established by the state did not lead individuals to take a long-term perspective about investment. Instead, economic actors were placed in a game in which the only intelligent strategy was usually to grab.

The problems in investment were not uniform across spheres of the economy. Many Russians who received extra money did, in fact, invest it by buying apartments for their children, remodeling their kitchens, or reconstructing or expanding their dachas. Wealthier Russians often built large houses ("cottages") in the suburbs. All of them were more confident that such investments would retain their value and be less subject to seizure than other types of investment.

Even in the more productive economic spheres, the reasons that investment did not occur varied considerably. Particular incentive structures, consciously or unconsciously, were introduced into different types of economic activity. These include agriculture, new small urban enterprises, medium and large-scale manufacturing plants, and industries that export raw materials in exchange for hard currency. The reasons for the low levels of investment could be quite different in each.

Agriculture and Rural Industry

The one economic sphere that should have had very substantial investment in a country moving toward a normal market economy was agriculture. It had many of the same characteristics as urban apartments and dachas: if land were improved, machinery acquired, and farm buildings constructed, those engaging in the activity were likely to have confidence that they could retain the benefits of their investment. The thorny problems of the free sale of land need not have been raised, for the Chinese system of leasing land for a long period would be sufficient. Instead, disaster occurred: grain production fell by 50 percent as the use of chemical fertilizer fell by nearly 90 percent. Other agricultural products did only marginally better.

The various efforts to reform communist economies before 1989 led to one inexorable conclusion: successful reform of large-scale socialized industry was very difficult, but almost any reasonable agricultural reform brought improvement. Czechoslovakia retained the old collective farms, but allowed managers considerable freedom to make their decisions on the basis of price signals rather than direct orders. Hungary allowed relative autonomy to families or other small subunits within the collective farm. China leased land to peasants. Poland privatized 80 percent of its agricultural land, but this actually was one of the more unsuccessful of the agricultural reforms because severe limitations were placed on the size of the farms.

Gorbachev's first great mistake in economic reform was his failure to introduce any significant type of agricultural reform. The reason was that agricultural reform could not be successful unless anomalies in retail food prices were reduced. Bread in the stores cost less than the peasants were paid for the grain to produce it, and meat was sold in state stores at one-third the price paid to peasants to produce it. Regions were paid different amounts for grain; those with poor land and climate were paid much more than those with good land and climate.[23] Unless these situations were corrected, any marketization of agriculture would have counterproductive results.

Over the years western advocates of decollectivization emphasized the positive effects of individual ownership or control of land on production decisions, but the more knowledgeable understood that agricultural reform would have equally crucial effects on investment decisions. The policy of differential regional prices was designed to equalize conditions for peasants living in different areas, and it had been accompanied by a partial attempt to equalize investment. This was as if too much agricultural investment was directed to areas like northern Maine and too little to areas like Iowa and Illinois.

One purpose of agricultural reform was to ensure that decisionmakers—collective farm managers, if not individual farmers or heads of smaller groups—could acquire the machinery and other equipment they considered most appropriate for their land. In a market economy, those in the most fertile areas in the best climate zones would receive the greatest income, and they would thus have the most money to invest. If investment were concentrated in Iowa instead of being split between Iowa and Maine, the results surely would be much better.

Instead, the Yeltsin government had an unannounced but explicit policy of trying to maintain living standards in the largest cities at the expense of the countryside. The old USSR Ministry of Procurements (sometimes called the Ministry of Grain Products) was retained as Roskhleboprodukt, and wholesale agricultural trade was kept under full state control. Much of the trade was conducted by nonmonetary means, heavily discriminating against the agricultural sector. The Yeltsin regime gave some subsidy to unprofitable northern farms, but did not introduce market prices for the fertile farms in the south. Not surprisingly, the southern farmers, who had a strong interest in real market reform, voted Communist in reaction to that which was introduced.

Urban food prices were officially subsidized in the early years of reform, but controls were quietly kept in place afterward as well. The behavior of Russian food prices in the wake of the August 1998 financial collapse made the policy dramatically clear. The collapse of the currency in Indonesia in 1998 had the expected impact on agricultural prices: the city dwellers could no longer afford to buy as much imported food, and the resulting increase in demand for domestic products meant that food prices rose. The peasant benefited rather than suffered from the financial crisis. In Russia, half of all goods in retail trade were imported. Of retail foodstuffs such as sausage, butter, cheese, canned meat, and macaroni, 30 to 60 percent was imported. Most of the imports were sold in the big cities, where they thus composed an even higher percentage of the trade.[24] In the wake of the financial collapse, urban food prices rose only marginally, however. Obviously they were being controlled.

The Russian reformers shamelessly claimed to be subsidizing agriculture, and many of their western allies were seriously misled. On closer examination, however, the "agricultural subsidies" proved to include subsidies to the food processing industry, such as urban bakeries. The reformers blamed the steady decline in agricultural production on the defects and corruption of the collective farm nomenklatura rather than on the decline in inputs and investment. They pushed the free sale of land as a panacea, but, in fact, the private farm sector failed as badly as the collective farm sector. Prices were just too low for private farmers to survive economically.[25]

The result of policy was dramatically seen in the pattern of regional politics. In the 1890s, the grain-exporting areas of the south had supported free trade, while the north had supported protectionism, a pattern that economic theory would predict.[26] In the 1990s, contrary to the normal logic of foreign economic politics, the fertile rural south was the stronghold of communist support, the so-called Red Belt. Many in the poor farms in the north clung to Yeltsin as the only source of protection against the market. The explanation was not cultural conservatism in the south, but the southern farmers' response to a lack of reform and to a policy that had exploited them to feed the cities, much as Stalin had done in 1929.

Investment in agriculture did not occur because government consciously left the economic actors with too little money to invest. The prices for products required by agriculture (first of all, fuel) rose five times faster than those of agricultural products. The result was a decline in capital investment in the agroindustrial complex in constant rubles from 60 billion (51 billion of which was for agriculture alone) in 1990 to 11 billion (8 billion for agriculture) in 1993 to 8 billion (6 billion) in 1994 and an estimated 6 billion (4 billion) in 1995. Agriculture received 16,000 tractors in 1994 out of 26,700 produced, compared with 143,700 in 1990.[27] Each hectare in agriculture received an average of 99 kilograms of mineral fertilizer in the 1986–90 period, but this fell to 78 in 1991, 43 in 1992, 29 in 1993, and 11 in 1994.[28]

The problems in agriculture also had a major effect on the industries related to agriculture. One of the sad stories in Russian economic reform is that of the Vladimir Tractor Works. In the communist period, it produced a tractor that had some export potential. An economist at the plant with a Moscow University Ph.D., Iosef Bakaleinik, won a scholarship to the Harvard Business School. He worked in a high-paying job at the International Finance Corporation, and he acquired 15 percent of the shares of the plant in the voucher privatization. In May 1994 he became its manager. Despite Bakaleinik's best efforts, his connections, and considerable optimism, however, the decline in production accelerated. The plant had produced 36,000 tractors and 178,000 engines a year in the late 1980s. By 1994 it was down to 16,000 tractors and 45,000 engines, and in the summer of 1996 it produced 10 to 20 percent of capacity. By 1997 Bakaleinik had moved into oil trading. When asked about this by a correspondent from the *Wall Street Journal* in the fall of 1998, he explained simply and correctly: no one in agriculture had any money to buy machinery.[29]

Small Business

The greatest disappointment in Russian economic reform has been the failure of the small business sector to grow as well as expected. The most striking fact about the distribution of old Soviet state enterprises— corporations or assembly plants—was the low number of small enterprises. In October 1991 Yeltsin foresaw the immediate rise of small companies to provide competition for the large corporations with monopoly products and components, but this did not occur. The statistics on the number of small businesses are not accurate,[30] but everyone agrees that far too few have been created, especially industrial businesses or businesses serving industry.

The first reason that the new business sector did not thrive is that it was never a priority of the reformers and government. Unlike China, Russia devoted all its attention to the privatization of existing state enterprises. The government did not focus on creating rules and tax incentives that would encourage small businesses and investment in them. It did not allow the formation of major banks that could make loans to them. As a result, entrepreneurs could more easily maximize profit by trying to acquire an already functioning business in the privatization process than by creating a new one.

The lack of government priority was reflected in a number of problems that were never addressed or corrected. First, Russian citizens had little savings at the beginning of the reform process with which to invest. Despite all the talk about excess money supply ("monetary overhang") from 1989 through 1991, Russia had far too little money in circulation for a society in which almost all investment had come from the state, but in which investment was to be privatized. The government faced the very real problem of increasing the money supply drastically while inducing people to save the extra money rather than spend it. Then the Gaidar government deliberately destroyed savings accounts in early 1992 in an effort to destroy monetary overhang.

Of course, the lack of savings was not a permanent problem. Those engaged in the "second" economy in the Brezhnev era often were engaged in illegal foreign currency exchange, and they obviously did not preserve their wealth in Soviet savings banks. Average citizens also retained a large amount of money in hard currency (usually dollars) or in gold and jewelry that were hidden at home. As Leonid Abalkin emphasized, the "capital flight" into dollars at home was at least as big a problem as that of capital flight abroad.[31]

Moreover, new savings and potential new capital were created in the reform process. Economic reform resulted in extreme inequality in income distribution, creating a stratum of business personnel with ample savings. A certain level of corruption was absolutely inevitable. This meant the accumulation of capital by those with government connections, which, as a rule, would make investment unusually safe and successful.

The question is, why did this money not flow into small-scale business investment of various types? The standard answer was the absence of a reliable legal system, the presence of too much corruption, and the existence of a mafia. Someone who tried to establish a new business had to pay bribes to numerous local officials and police officers. They likely would be visited by those who offered protection for a price and threatened with violence if they did not purchase the protection they offered.

To some extent, this standard explanation is accurate. Yeltsin's high-level tolerance of corruption to make the political and administrative elite dependent on him did not necessarily extend to lower officials, but the culture of corruption was difficult to contain. This was particularly true when Yeltsin gave the regional governors control over the banks that made local subsidies. The selective and personalized nature of the loan-subsidies and the lack of transparency in awarding loans created great discretion for local officials and enormous opportunities for them to seek private rewards for their decisions. Pressure to reduce the government budget created enormous pressure to keep the salaries of local police and officials relatively low. The economic incentives for these officials to supplement their salaries—indeed, even to earn a living wage—with "contributions" from the private sector were extremely strong.

It is likely, however, that the West exaggerates the importance of crime in constraining the small business sector. There is nothing to be said for a state of anarchy in which public and private criminals expropriate all profits. However, if either the state or a powerful mafia establishes control in a region, well-defined payoffs that can be predictably calculated as a cost of business, while not ideal, are not incompatible with a thriving private business sector and investment. One mafia group is unlikely to allow another to operate on its turf.

The real obstacles to the development of a thriving small business sector lay elsewhere. First, a banking system was not established to provide reliable loans to small business at reasonable rates. Originally a number of private banks offered extremely high interest rates to depositors, but they were essentially pyramid schemes. Their collapse and the increase in the interest rates in the state savings banks led citizens to deposit almost all their savings in local branches of the large Moscow banks, most notably Sberbank, the Savings Bank. Sberbank placed its funds at the disposal of the central government instead of lending them locally. As a result, no institutions existed to serve as intermediaries between local savers and business.

Second, the lack of stability in local property rights and the absence of a stable local tax base made the local political elite less interested in controlling local corruption. If local officials had a clear stake in the local community and its long-term prosperity, they would have an interest in promoting prosperity. If they obtained money by legal or illegal means, they would be likely to invest it in the local economy. If criminals began seriously to harm the interests of the local elite, the elite would strive to control or coopt the criminals. In the United States, mafia-like institutions are, after all, quite transitory phenomena that tend to disappear when they no longer serve economic functions.

The primary reason for the problems in the small business sector, however, was the economic depression. The original notion that the imbalance between spheres of the economy could be resolved simply by cutting industrial production and employment and by allowing (or urging) people to move into the services sector was highly schematic. Those without work will obviously do something to try to survive. Of course, many in Russia did not survive as mortality rates soared; some moved into agriculture, farming their private plot. But men selling apples on the street, as in the American depression, or those selling pieces of sugar cane to tourists on the highways in Jamaica do not represent a healthy expansion of the service sector, whatever the statistics on the growth of the service sector may say.

Generally people living on subsidies cannot afford many consumer services that people in the West—or Russians in the Soviet period—take for granted. For example, the amount of dry cleaning declined precipitously in the early 1990s, even in Moscow. The level of trade inevitably declined, and with it the opportunity for potential entrepreneurs to develop stores or shopping malls. But the most crucial failure in the small-enterprise sector was the slow rate of expansion in the professional and business service sphere. Professional services are expensive, and businesses that have no money for investment also have no money to buy services from small business. People did travel to Turkey and Poland to buy cheap goods to sell as peddlers, but they would not invest in small businesses unless they could be persuaded that there were enough customers to make them profitable.

Large Enterprises

Everyone agrees that the most fundamental mistakes were made in the privatization of large enterprises, but analysts totally disagree on which steps were the disastrous ones. It is also clear that the consequences were profound and not easy to correct—and nowhere more profound than in the realm of investment.

A number of scenarios for privatizing large enterprises were quite defensible, including some of those that were used. The mistakes in Russia resulted from the way the different elements in the program were combined. For example, the neoliberal reformers argued that the crucial mistake was the insider privatization that occurred at the beginning of the process. In fact, this argument has no validity whatsoever unless it is combined with a repudiation of rapid privatization. Voucher privatization could not have taken place for several years, and even then there is no evidence that enough outside owners were available at that time who could have served as competent managers. Hence voucher privatization had to be gradual, which would have meant leaving the state and the old managers of the quasi-ministerial companies or enterprises in control. That seems attractive to me, but western and Russian neoliberal reformers both vehemently insisted on rapid privatization.

The same problem is found in the debate on the voucher program. The program has been severely criticized, but primarily for its corruption and favoritism and for its failure to achieve restructuring. In fact, there was much to be said for having a minority public interest in enterprises. Outside shares increased the pressure for transparency, and they gave the public a sense of the value of long-term capital growth. Encouraging the insider-managers to improve their plant and issue initial public offerings was probably the best alternative, but the voucher program by itself was not necessarily a harmful idea.

The disastrous aspect of the voucher program was not its failure to replace insider-owners, but its goal of doing so. The supporters of voucher privatization often referred to the Coase theorem and its implication that the market would lead to property's being transferred to those who could use it most advantageously. If a potential new owner could use a property more profitably than the current owner, then he or she could offer more for the property than it was worth to the current owners to retain it.

In this respect, the Coase theorem actually was quite relevant to the Russian scene, but it had precisely the opposite implication from that postulated by neoliberal economists. Richard Ericson was right when he argued at the beginning of the reform process that the crucial precondition of success was to give managers the incentive and the ability to improve their property and a real prospect to sell it at a profit.[32]

Ericson, like Coase, took for granted that the original owners had secure property rights that they could transfer and that the property had a "market capitalized value." Ericson also reminds us that normal owners seek to sell their property for a maximum price (or at a minimum in the United States to have an initial public offering, or IPO), and they thus have an incentive to make the property as attractive as possible before the sale. As Ericson understood, the implication of the Coase theorem was that the state does not have to assist the market by expropriating the property of allegedly inferior owners and giving it to allegedly superior ones; the market can take care of that. In the interim, however, it was crucial that they have the incentives Ericson rightly said were essential.

This seems a self-evident point, but it was totally ignored in Russia. The reformers, and even more the IMF, spoke of the need for vigorous bankruptcy action, and the voucher system was hailed as a way to change ownership of the large factories without buying out the original owners. Indeed, it is hard to avoid the conclusion that the reformers quietly welcomed—and perhaps even designed—the use of bank loans or nonpayment as the primary means of subsidy in the knowledge that it would bankrupt the plants and in the hope that it would facilitate the transfer of property.

The result was precisely that which Ericson warned against. The insider-owners had no incentive to think about the long-term improvement of their property. They were instead given a strong incentive to exploit their property for current income. Since the depression meant that manufacturing plants usually had little current income, the threat of quick expropriation meant that the insider-owners had every incentive to strip assets as fast as they could.

Neither the westerners nor the Russian reformers understood that Soviet enterprises were much closer to western assembly or production plants than to corporations. This awareness seemed reflected in Stanley Fischer's early argument that the first stage of privatization should occur above the enterprise level, but it was soon lost. Both Soviet and Russian reformers treated plants as corporations and gave little thought to the creation of a real corporate economy in Russia. The idea was not politically feasible at the first stage—neither Yeltsin nor his reformers wanted to strengthen the experienced managers in the quasi-ministerial institutions above the enterprise level—but it was ideal for the second and third stages.

A major reason for the neglect of the corporation was conceptual. Russian radical economists had learned their economics by studying the mathematical economics of Marx's *Das Kapital*, but Marx, like the classical economists such as David Ricardo, had studied the precorporate economies of the mid-nineteenth century. The Russian reformers never really assimilated that the managers of modern western plants are not guided by market forces, but are in a command economy inside the corporation that is as controlled as the plant of the Soviet economy. Western plant managers are *supposed* to be concerned with production—not with finances, marketing, the consumer, and the like—and they can have the background appropriate for that role.

American businessmen universally hailed the quality of the Soviet plant managers and ministerial officials they met during the 1970s and 1980s. The managers of the machinery industry were ranked at the top of the list. The Russian insider-owners were really ideally suited to carry out this type of restructuring in the first stage of economic reform. The process of reconstruction is to a considerable extent a technical one, requiring managers to make judgments about the optimal combination of machinery and workers of different types. In England, enterprises being privatized during Margaret Thatcher's tenure as prime minister underwent reconstruction while they were still state enterprises. If the old Soviet managers had been given to understand that the sell-off price of their enterprise—or its stock value, if they remained owners—

depended on their success in raising the productivity of its labor, they would have had both the incentive and the ability to do so.

An optimal model of economic reform would have involved not the removal of the old-style production managers, but the creation of a corporate structure over them. Whatever the virtues of the young reformers with financial and economic expertise, they did not include the background and knowledge to manage a production plant, let alone to restructure its machinery and work force. If the old managers of production plants had been given the responsibility of restructuring the plant and then had been bought out by a corporate holding company at a price reflecting their success, they could and should have remained as plant managers with various bonus and stock option incentives.

This model would have facilitated the achievement of another crucial goal: the assurance that as many enterprises as possible continued to function in the first years of economic reform. In part this was necessary to maintain incentives for owners to try to improve the performance of their plants. But in larger part it was necessary for the process of restructuring itself. Restructuring requires new machinery, and the process involves a long chain. Unless the chain is maintained—or unless there is a massive influx of technology from abroad—meaningful restructuring cannot occur. Russia, of course, imported primarily consumer goods, not technology.

Resource-Exporting Enterprises and Export Wholesale Trade Firms

Virtually all western and Russian debate on the privatization of large-scale enterprises has dealt with large manufacturing plants, but the most fundamental mistakes were made in the privatization of the industries and the wholesale trading firms that exported raw materials and industrial commodities. Nevertheless, all the alternatives in this realm were so unattractive that it is difficult to avoid the conclusion that these industries and trading firms should have remained nationalized. In my opinion, most of them should be renationalized now.

The fundamental problem with privatization of the resource-exporting industries was the most obvious. These industries generated a huge flow of hard-currency income without any managerial contribution or investment. Exports of natural gas and petroleum were always very large, and the sharp decline in the defense and the machinery industries freed large amounts of ferrous and nonferrous metals for the export market. The decision to cut fertilizer shipments to Russian agriculture by 90 percent had a similar effect on availability of fertilizer for export. Indeed, it is easy to suspect that the desire to keep these items free for the export market was a factor leading insiders high in the government who profited from the trade to oppose an industrial policy and agricultural reform.

Given the exchange rate, the managers of petroleum, natural gas, major metallurgical, and bulk chemical fertilizer plants did not need to improve the performance of their plants, let alone be innovative. Norilsk Nickel engaged in no capital repair from 1985 to 1998. Petroleum production fell, in part because of the need for repair and in part because new fields were not being developed. Since new pipelines and docking facilities were not built, exports of oil and natural gas could not be increased. Even when foreign firms entered into joint ventures with oil firms for exploration and development, the Russian partner never contributed its share of the investment.[33]

The situation with respect to the export-trading firms was even worse. In practice the government limited the access of outsiders to the share auctions in the petroleum and natural gas industries, but outsiders could seek involvement in the wholesale trading firms dealing with such materials, in the banks that were the conduits for the hard currency they generated, or in the government offices issuing licenses or permits for them. Since this work required an ability to manipulate figures instead of technical expertise or managerial skill, it was particularly attractive to outsiders with such a range of skills and inclinations.

The network of wholesale trading firms in the export realm became deeply intertwined with crime and corruption, and hence no question is more difficult—or dangerous—to try to research thoroughly. But the anecdotal evidence and rumors make quite clear that this sphere was often unsavory. The biggest businessman in Ekaterinburg, for example, was Viktor Terniak, who was head of the Euro-Asian Company, a trading company dealing with metals, before he was murdered. The gang activity in Ekaterinburg was concentrated in the area around the huge Urals Machinery Works (Uralmash), and Stephen Handelman was invited to lunch at the plant to meet the representative of the local mafia. Uralmash was controlled by the most successful entrepreneur in Russia in accumulating vouchers, and Handelman reports that everyone in the city was convinced that city government was totally controlled by the mafia.[34]

The apparent connection between Uralmash, a wholesale trading firm, and the mafia was not unique. Many—and perhaps all—top managers in the export spheres created or joined trading firms handling their product in order to try to shelter income from stockholders and government control. These firms had offshore offices, and they were the mechanism that managers could use to divert money abroad for their private use. The managers would also have a relationship—perhaps even a shareholding relationship—with banks that financed trade.

The export of resources was tied to criminal activity in other ways. The sale of petroleum and raw materials at subsidized domestic prices and for IOUs that traded below cost on the market made it profitable to acquire these products at below-world-market prices and to divert them to the export market with documents that were either forged or acquired from corrupt government officials.[35] In addition, it is said that Russia became the major launderer of illegal money in the world. The illegal foreign money could be used to purchase Russian oil or metals, which were then sold quite legally on the world market.

The consequences of these facts were obvious, although seldom discussed in the West. Any intelligent economic actor seeking to maximize profit made every effort to gain access to the flow of hard currency from the export industries. That is where intelligent people would have invested their vouchers if given an opportunity. Even if no corruption were involved, a modest percentage of profits would bring untold riches to the owners of this property.[36] Even a small commission for the wholesale trading firms would involve a great sum of money. Since Yeltsin was being tolerant toward corruption, it was inevitable that those seeking corrupt earnings would also gravitate to the area where the most money was available.

By the same token, intelligent prospective owners should have avoided other industries where the rewards were lower and less certain. Even if worker-owners could be persuaded to change managers (as occurred in the Vladimir Tractor Works), even if manufacturing plants went bankrupt and could be acquired inexpensively, there was no guarantee that a new manager or owner, even one with modern managerial skills, would be more successful. An example is Iosef Bakaleinik, mentioned earlier, who went to work for a petroleum trading firm after the Vladimir Tractor Works failed.

Yeltsin's decision to privatize the natural resource industries and trading firms was, no doubt, motivated by the desire to have the maximum amount of resources to distribute in a paternalistic way to his ever-changing favorites. Nevertheless, he was being heavily pressured to make this decision by the international organizations, and once he did decide to privatize this sector of the economy, for whatever reason, he had few good options.

The size of the wealth and the flow of hard currency in the export industries made it quite inequitable to give these industries either to their managers or, even worse, to speculators who accumulated a sufficient number of extremely inexpensive vouchers. There were also political considerations. If the new owners of the exporting industries were really independent, their wealth would give them enormous resources to influence or even to control the political process. It is inconceivable that the Yeltsin government—or any government—would deliberately create a group with such independence and such power. One way or another, the government was certain to want to retain strong political control over these owners and the resources at their disposal.

If the export industries were to be privatized, a series of measures needed to be adopted. If exchange rates had a distorting effect on the domestic economy, then it was necessary to take measures to ensure that agriculture and the manufacturing sector could survive. Russia should have moved toward domestic market prices for these export products,[37] encouraged investment through depreciation, and then imposed extremely high tax rates on the unearned income from exports. The tax income could have been used to pay for state or local government purchase of the export items and for direct subsidies to other enterprises, as desired.

The problem with this solution was that the international organizations would have objected strenuously. Any subsidies to other industries would have been explicit and would have resulted in large amounts of money being placed on budget, thereby increasing government expenditures. Moreover, the West wanted to buy shares of the exporting industries and would have objected to high tax rates on them.

In addition, for reasons that are not totally clear, the international organizations strongly advocated the privatization of the export industries. They argued that this was a way to balance the budget, but the amount of money to be realized was actually relatively small. Westerners would pay a limited amount for the properties, and the Russian government would lose the income from the property it was selling. When westerners said that Russia was either one of the great investment opportunities of a lifetime or a black hole, they meant they were paying excessively low prices for the assets by normal standards of evaluation unless the enterprises went bankrupt.

Unfortunately, the international organizations and western investors never understood the inevitable corollary of this investment situation, although they often suffered from its consequences. They were seeking very low-priced assets from which they hoped to earn hard currency quickly and make a large capital gain based more on a lessening of risk than on their own contribution. Russians resented this deeply. They saw it as theft, all the more so because, rightly or wrong, they thought government officials were selling assets to westerners for particularly low prices in exchange for some kind of bribe. A deputy premier, Vladimir Filipovich Shumeiko, was widely called Filip Morrisovich Shumeiko as a reflection of the suspicion that Phillip Morris had gained access to Russia too cheaply by corrupting him.

The validity of such suspicions is immaterial. Without question, westerners were seeking to acquire what they thought were inexpensive assets, and it was inevitable that Russians would interpret such activities and those of Russians making the decisions darkly. As a result, Russians developed a sense of morality in which corruption vis-à-vis foreigners or defrauding foreigners was in a very different category from cheating or defrauding Russians. In the minds of many, the major question was simply who would be more skilled in defrauding the other. The insider has a normal advantage in such situations.

If westerners had engaged in out-sourcing arrangements in which they produced, say, tractors for domestic use and pistons for export, they would have created a new enterprise or transformed an old one into a productive operation with substantial employment, training of managerial personnel, and provision of quality products for the domestic market. This is the normal consequence of foreign investment, and Russians, like other foreigners, would generally have been quite satisfied with a substantial western profit.

Off-Budget Subsidies as Predatory Taxation

In discussing the system of off-budget subsidies of the Yeltsin period, this book has focused on those who received the subsidies and the personalistic mechanisms by which they were provided. It has emphasized that they were consumption subsidies, financed by an exploitation of agriculture and a sharp reduction in investment. But, of course, subsidies had to come from specific industrial exporters, banks, and trading firms, and this had a powerful effect on the incentives of the latter.

A cliché in the western history of the Soviet Union was that Lenin made a terrible mistake during the period of war communism (1918–20) in the Civil War by having the Red Army simply requisition grain that it found in the countryside. The result, everyone said, was that the peasants had no incentive to produce. But Lenin recognized this in late 1920 and introduced a tax-in-kind in agriculture. The peasants were assigned a fixed amount of produce to deliver and were allowed to keep whatever production remained after the deliveries were made. When Stalin abolished private agriculture and trade in 1929, he retained the principle of trying to build incentives into the economic system. In a famous 1931 speech, he denounced the practice of "leveling"—of too much egalitarianism.

In essence Yeltsin returned to the system of taxation that the Soviet Union had during the period of war communism, and the system became even more confiscatory as the economic situation became more desperate with the passage of time. If a region decided to introduce some new tax, this would simply have resulted in its receiving fewer loans or less free natural gas and electricity. If an export firm or any other firm generated more profits, it was certain to be required to deliver ("barter") more goods without payment or to purchase an unprofitable factory or make a loan to someone.

It is difficult to imagine another economic system that would have created such powerful incentives for managers not to focus on economic growth or investment. It is difficult to imagine another economic system that would have created such a powerful incentive for the honest and the corrupt alike to send their savings abroad rather than invest at home.

In fact, the system must have given many participants a sense of moral rectitude in corruption. Viktor Chernomyrdin and the oligarchs associated with him in the energy industries have often been criticized in Russia and the West for their corruption. It is, however, difficult not to have some sympathy for them. They had spent their lives in building the Soviet oil and natural gas industry and had every right to be proud of their achievement. Now production had fallen nearly in half because the government refused to allow them to develop new fields or even maintain the old ones.

If Gazprom worked to improve production and sales, it simply would be asked for another $650,000 loan for another plant like the Cheliabinsk Tractor Plant, a plant whose managers were probably largely corrupt. If the government was going to steal from the industry Gazprom's managers had developed, they must have felt a moral right to do so themselves. If they had money abroad, they might have rationalized to themselves it would be available later to invest in Gazprom when an intelligent economic policy was introduced some time in the future.

The West and the System of Off-Budget Subsidies

All westerners have been critical of Boris Yeltsin for his personalistic style of rule based on corruption, and this book also takes that approach. Even if corruption was inevitable and even useful in promoting development, the fruits of corruption needed to be channeled into productive activities that themselves were protected by more regularized legal institutions. This chapter has explained why this did not occur in a series of different economic sectors. Questions remain. One is why the West tolerated and even tacitly encouraged the mechanisms that had the logical consequences that have been described. When United Energy Systems held its annual meeting in 1999, its head, Anatoly Chubais, reported that in 1998 the utility received only about 20 percent of its payments in cash. He did not indicate how much of the remaining 80 percent was received in various kinds of supplies, but large amounts of electricity were essentially provided free to customers. If government departments received the electricity, then their reported deficits were fraudulent; if enterprises received it, then their debts became higher and the property rights of their owners less secure. The story was, as far as I know, not reported in the western press.

Boris Yeltsin was a highly suspicious man, deeply jealous of his political power. He changed personnel incessantly to keep people insecure, but he kept Chubais at the top continually after 1991. Chubais was the person in charge of Yeltsin's 1996 election campaign. It is perfectly obvious that the distribution of free electricity has been one of the forms of economic patronage on which Yeltsin's power rested and that it was a key aspect of the economic system that prevented investment and the marketization of the economy. By placing Chubais in charge of it at a sensitive political time, Yeltsin showed that he trusted him completely. To all intents and purposes, Chubais was a member of the family.

This case is an interesting one for a political scientist studying the mechanisms of political power, but it is even more interesting for a student of international political economy. One would have thought that Chubais—as one of the most trusted members of Yeltsin's political machine, controlling one of Yeltsin's most important instruments of patronage—would have been widely denounced in the West as an element of the unacceptable politicization of the system. Yet the free electricity was hardly reported in the West, except in incorrect stories about free-market barter, and Chubais remained one of the few men with power in the Yeltsin entourage at the end of the 1990s who was hailed in western governments and the business community as a true representative of the free market economy.

By the end of the 1990s a wide range of westerners agreed that Russian economic reform had failed because it did not have secure property rights, because it did not have a well-functioning legal system, because it did not have defined rules and institutions, and because its personnel were not guided by rational-technical norms of behavior. But the West saw Chubais's continued powerful role in the government as a sign that market reform was still alive. There was no other fact that so indicated that the West had the same complete misunderstanding of Russia at the conclusion of the 1990s that it had at the beginning of the decade.

FIVE

The Debate over
Economic Policy,
1991–93

THE COUNTERPRODUCTIVE RESULTS produced in
one sphere of the economy after another by the incentive systems established for the economic actors in Russia are easily explained. The very
assumptions of economic rationality of the reform models clearly
explained many of the most unattractive results that ensued. This is an
important finding for those who still insist that the privatization program, as it was originally established, should have resulted in a flow of
investment and prosperity.

In the second half of the 1990s an increasing number of western
neoliberal reformers began reconsidering the economic strategy that
Russia had introduced in October 1992.[1] Nevertheless, two elements of
the old orthodoxy remained in effect. First, nearly everyone said or
implied that the anarchy produced in Russia by Mikhail Gorbachev
made it impossible for Boris Yeltsin to introduce any state-directed program with price controls. Second, whatever else might have been done,
Russia supposedly did not have the option of adopting the Chinese
model of reform because of the more advanced stage of its economic
development.

These two arguments seem so strange that it is difficult to explain
them on analytical grounds alone. Yeltsin's policies in 1991 and 1992
can, in fact, be seen as the product of political disorder and tactical considerations. Without question, Yeltsin did face extreme administrative
disorder in December 1991, and no coherent economic policy was possible. The program of providing mass subsidies through the factories to

maintain production and consumption in 1992 was brilliant. The IMF program being advanced by Yegor Gaidar would have been an utter catastrophe if implemented fully, and an industrial or manufacturing export strategy would have been just as utopian.

By the end of 1992, however, conditions had changed substantially from the beginning of the year. A functioning state apparatus had been established, and a more coherent program was possible. In fact, in early 1993 Boris Yeltsin overrode the announced policies of his new premier, Viktor Chernomyrdin, and introduced a more selective subsidy program and tighter monetary policy. As a result, industrial production fell sharply in the first five months of 1993. Whatever the virtues of the various programs, Yeltsin could just as easily have enacted a reform similar to the Chinese reform or any part of it—an agricultural reform or a thoroughgoing industrial policy.

The emergence of real policy options naturally provoked a major policy debate within the Russian government. In the fall of 1991 and early 1992, Boris Yeltsin and his young economic advisers had expressed great optimism that radical economic reform would soon produce highly positive results. The Congress had given Yeltsin the emergency powers he demanded in the fall of 1991, and he was ruling much as he wanted. The Congress criticized, but it was only posturing as it waited until the end of 1992.

Yeltsin's emergency powers expired at the end of 1992, and the constitution required him to submit his nominee for premier to the Congress at that time. By then the outcome of Gaidar's program would be clearer, and, by all indications, the dominant groups in Congress hoped to reach an agreement with Yeltsin in which they gave him the strong presidency he wanted in exchange for his "cohabiting" with Congress on economic policy. This was the logic the constitution seemed to dictate.

The public debates took place largely between the radical reformers, who claimed to speak for Yeltsin, and the moderates and conservatives in Congress. In reality, however, the most important debates took place within the Yeltsin team. Even in August and September 1991 a group of economists associated with Yegor Gaidar had argued for a radical monetarist reform and the independence of Russia, while a group led by Oleg Lobov called for an industrial policy and the preservation of the Soviet Union or at least "a common economic space." Lobov's program in 1991 was supported by everyone, including some radicals, with an economic portfolio in Yeltsin's government. It was inconsistent with an independent Russia, however, and Yeltsin chose independence. Those options remained real in late 1992 and 1993, and even more in subsequent years.

All the elements seemed to be in place for a change in policy at the end of 1992. The logic of Yeltsin's desire for power in 1991 had led him to support Gaidar's policy, for it implied the independence of Russia and the destruction of Gorbachev's post of president of the Soviet Union. However, the logic of Yeltsin's electoral strategy as he looked to the 1996 presidential election seemed to lead him in the direction of the Lobov position of 1993. He needed the economic growth it promised.

The selection of Viktor Chernomyrdin as premier in December 1992 seemed to imply a victory for Lobov's position. Then in the late spring and summer of 1993, Lobov himself was appointed first deputy premier and led the battle once more, this time against Gaidar's successor, Boris Fedorov. Yeltsin, however, rejected an industrial policy based on investment in favor of continuing his 1992 policy of monetarism and consumption subsidy. It is difficult to avoid the suspicion that Yeltsin was motivated by the belief that the West would support his desire to suppress the Congress and introduce a more authoritarian new constitution if he continued his economic policy.

Russian Independence and Economic Reform

Yeltsin should not be credited with democratizing Russia; he used the democracy that Gorbachev created and then severely restricted it after he came to power.[2] Yeltsin should not be credited with destroying the power of the Communist party; Gorbachev did that in the first months of 1990, and Yeltsin simply outlawed the party temporarily in 1991 so that its property could be seized. But at the beginning of 1991 no one thought it conceivable that the Soviet Union could be dissolved in the foreseeable future. That was Yeltsin's individual contribution, and to a large extent his alone.

Paradoxically, it is far from certain that Yeltsin was happy with his destruction of the Soviet Union. Officials as different as former defense minister Yevgeny Shaposhnikov and former premier Yegor Gaidar feel that the USSR would still exist if Gorbachev had resigned as president after the August 1991 coup d'état in favor of Yeltsin. Both express regret in their memoirs that this did not occur. But the independence of Russia was the only way that Yeltsin could replace Gorbachev, and he pursued that course of action with great daring, persistence, and even brilliance.

Yeltsin's political achievement in breaking up the Soviet Union was remarkable. It was unprecedented that a country with such a strong bureaucratic structure and powerful army would disintegrate, particularly when the army had not faced meaningful and prolonged opposition in the streets. In the first half of 1991 some in the West thought that Gorbachev would hold the country together with martial law, others that a military coup d'état would preserve the country, and still others that Gorbachev and Yeltsin would come to an agreement. No one seriously thought it would dissolve in the near term. Those who saw irresistible pressure undermining what they called the Russian empire over the long term saw it coming from non-Russians.

The political genius of Boris Yeltsin lay in understanding that he could use the relatively powerless and even superfluous administrative unit of the Russian Republic (RSFSR) as a springboard to power. The closest equivalent to the American state in the Soviet Union had been the oblast or the small republic, but these units had an average population of 2 million people, similar to that of Utah. Twenty-five of the oblasts had been grouped in Ukraine, but more than seventy had been placed in the Russian republic. It was as if half the U.S. states from Virginia northward were subordinated to the national government in Washington D.C. through a superstate government, also located in Washington, D.C.

Intermediate republican governments made sense in areas where large numbers of people used a non-Russian language in addition to Russian, but a huge Russian superstate served no useful function. If it had real power, either the national government or the regional (state) governments would have to be quite weak. The Russians as an ethnic group had little reason to be offended by a weak Russian republic, for they did not need a strong republican government. They controlled the national government and through it all the Soviet republics. Their national identity was linked to the Soviet Union as a whole.

Russians voted 70 percent to 30 percent for the maintenance of the Soviet Union in a March 1991 referendum, and for years larger majorities of Russians told sociologists they thought the break-up of the Soviet Union was more harmful than useful.[3] Yeltsin realized, however, that he could persuade the Russians that *they* had been the ones exploited by "the center" (central government) and that Russian wealth was being siphoned off to ungrateful non-Russians. Yeltsin spoke for their griev-ances, and they gave him strong support. They likely took for granted that the Soviet military and police would keep him in check, while his posturing would help keep the non-Russians within limits.

The First Russian Congress in June 1990 had declared that Russian laws were superior to USSR laws, thus allowing Yeltsin to contribute to the war of laws between the USSR and the republics that was creating administrative chaos. Yeltsin always denied that he favored the break-up of the Soviet Union—a wise position, given Russian public opinion on the subject—but his vision of a federal or confederated system left no power for the Soviet government.

Nevertheless, once Yeltsin received 57 percent of the vote to 17 per-cent for his nearest competitor in the Russian presidential election on June 12, 1991, he moved decisively to take all power from the USSR government. He announced the seizure of all the oil fields, industrial enterprises, and other economic units on Russian soil, as well as all the income they generated. He taunted Gorbachev, expressing regret that this would leave him without tax revenue. For reasons that remain a mystery, Gorbachev did not resist, and top officials of the USSR govern-ment attempted to save the situation with a coup d'état on August 19.

Yeltsin led the resistance to the coup, and when the coup was as inef-fective as Gorbachev himself, Yeltsin emerged with increased legitimacy in a political setting in which no institutions remained to resist him. Gorbachev allowed Yeltsin and his team to have a building in the Kremlin,[4] and he gave Yeltsin a veto on major appointments. After the August 1991 attempted coup d'état, Gorbachev made no meaningful effort to reconstitute a functioning government or to reacquire control over the financial resources that Yeltsin had seized. He did not try to use the army to establish martial law.[5] As a result, power was in Yeltsin's hands. The question throughout the fall of 1991 was what he would do with it.

In the late summer of 1991 Yeltsin relied on two different groups of advisers led by men he had known from Sverdlovsk, where he had worked for thirty years. They disagreed fundamentally about both eco-nomic policy and the independence of Russia. One group, headed by Gennady Burbulis, a social science professor, favored radical economic reform and Russian independence. The other, led by Oleg Lobov and Yury Petrov, who were lower regional (*obkom*) party secretaries when Yeltsin was first secretary, favored an industrial policy and what loosely might be called the Asian economic model. They thought this required maintaining strong ties with the other republics.

Burbulis had been chairman of the Scientific Communism Department of the Urals Polytechnic Institute in Sverdlovsk when he was elected to the USSR Congress of People's Deputies in 1989. He was Yeltsin's liaison in the USSR parliament when Yeltsin moved into the Russian political arena, and he served as Yeltsin's chief political adviser in his 1991 presidential campaign. Burbulis's chief allies were the young intellectuals of the democratic camp; they included a large number of the heads of the more political RSFSR ministries—foreign affairs, internal affairs, justice, and labor, as well as the deputy premier for administering state property (the privatization portfolio).

Burbulis's team did not, however, have much economic expertise. Since the political battle was going to be fought out on the issue of economic reform, Burbulis needed economists who were credible on this issue. He allied himself with a team of young economists led by Yegor Gaidar and Aleksandr Shokhin, both of whom had long been associated with Stanislav Shatalin, the chairman of the commission that drafted the 500-day plan in 1990. In a state dacha in suburban Moscow they began work on a draft economic plan.[6]

The Gaidar team thought that the manufacturing sector other than the defense industry was thoroughly noncompetitive on the world market. Reliance on arms sales was thought to be incompatible with the close relationship with the West that was required for an opening of the economy to the outside world. For these reasons the Burbulis-Gaidar team saw the export of petroleum, natural gas, and raw materials as the only source of the hard currency needed for the equipment to modernize industry.

In their view, the subjecting of the inefficient manufacturing sphere to the harsh discipline of the market would not only force an improvement of its efficiency, but would economize on the fuel and raw materials that were exportable. Domestic market prices for these items, especially petroleum, would minimize their wasteful use inside the Soviet Union, as well as increase the incentives for their production. Gaidar was much taken by the argument of the U.S. economist Mancur Olson that old institutions became so encrusted with interest groups that it was better not to reform them, but to destroy them and let new institutions arise.[7]

Informally, both proponents and opponents of the policy acknowledged that the effect and intention of the Gaidar program would be deindustrialization. The huge state heavy industrial sector and especially the defense industry sector would be drastically reduced in size, and, with nowhere else to go, the redundant work force would stream into the understaffed services sector. Shokhin wrote about how 30 percent of the Italian work force was in the small enterprise and service sector and implied that the unemployment problem in Russia would be easy to solve because of its need for such a sector. The Gaidar economists rejected protectionism, and they saw free trade and a quick end of price controls as a way to subject the inefficient manufacturing sphere to the harsh discipline of the market.

Gaidar's opponents found his team unbearably arrogant. In public at least the Gaidar team tolerated no criticism, and they would not acknowledge the need for compromise not forced by unfortunate political pressure. Indeed, Yeltsin reported in his memoirs that he valued precisely the self-confidence of Burbulis and his team because he wanted to be free to focus on immediate political strategy and tactics.[8]

Oleg Lobov had been a defense industry manager who moved into the party apparatus and was then *obkom* second secretary in the last year of Yeltsin's tenure in Sverdlovsk. He was Yeltsin's candidate for first secretary of the Russian Communist party in 1990 and then became the first deputy premier of the Russian government, Yeltsin's top representative within it. Yury Petrov had also risen out of the defense industry into party work and had served as an *obkom* party secretary from 1977 to 1982 before being brought into the Central Committee apparatus. He returned to Sverdlovsk as *obkom* first secretary to replace Yeltsin in 1985. When Yeltsin fell out with Gorbachev in late 1987, Petrov was exiled to Havana as ambassador to Cuba. In 1991 Yeltsin appointed Petrov head of the presidential administration—chief of the White House staff, in U.S. terms.

Lobov and Petrov were supported by virtually all the top economic officials within the Russian Council of Ministers: the deputy premier and minister of economy (Yevgeny Saburov),[9] the deputy premier for energy (Igor T. Gavrilov), the head of the Higher Council on Economic Reform (Mikhail Bocharov, the founder of Democratic Russia), and the minister of agriculture (Gennady V. Kulik). They drew in a former deputy premier, Grigory Yavlinsky, to draft an economic program and were supported by the premier, Ivan Silaev, who was spending most of his time as the chief of the USSR Committee for the Operational Administration of the Economy.

In the view of this group, Russia had a very sophisticated manufacturing sector and a highly trained labor force, and the two should not be destroyed. Industry might be inefficient, but this only meant it needed to be protected and eased into a market environment slowly. Russia, like the Pacific Rim countries of recent decades, should begin exporting lower-quality manufactured goods at low prices in order to subject manufacturers to foreign competition and give them incentives to improve the quality of their production. Russia could not, as they put it, be Kuwaitized—that is, could not be made to rely totally on the production and export of petroleum and raw materials.

The Lobov-Petrov group wanted insider privatization and was not afraid of movement toward market prices. "Big business" knew that it had a monopoly position in the production of many individual goods and that it could thrive in an inflationary environment. The minister of the economy, Yevgeny Saburov, favored the abolition of the industrial ministries. The industrialists, however, preferred price controls to keep inflation and the price increases of monopoly producers within limits. At a time when the exchange rate bore no relationship to real value, they feared that the freeing of petroleum and other commodity prices might have a harmful effect on the manufacturing sector.

This was the classic infant industry argument—although Soviet industries were infants only as competitors on the world market. Because industry was technologically backward, it was said to need tariff protection until it could reach world levels. The argument could be supported by references to the success of Chinese reform, to the centrality of the manufacturing sector to Russian power, and to the political instability that a shock treatment would produce.

Like Sergei Witte, who engineered the Russian industrialization drive of the 1890s, the Lobov-Petrov team welcomed large-scale foreign investment in Russia. The Lobov-Petrov team assumed, however, that tariffs would protect foreign as well as domestic producers from foreign competition. Indeed, this was the team's answer to the need for capital that Gaidar sought through commodity sales.

The conflict between the two groups of Yeltsin advisers was expressed in macroeconomic terms, but it had the most profound implications for Russia's relations with the non-Russian republics of the Soviet Union. The tightly integrated character of the Soviet economy meant that the Lobov-Petrov position depended on the continued existence of the Union, perhaps in a much looser form. The monopoly suppliers of components were spread throughout the Soviet Union, and economic collapse in the non-Russian republics was certain to reverberate on the manufacturing sector in Russia as well.

The Burbulis-Gaidar economic policy had precisely the opposite implication for the Union. If the Russian export of petroleum, natural gas, and raw materials was to lie at the core of an economic strategy, then the delivery of these products to the non-Russian republics at subsidized prices should be ended because it was extremely costly. If it was desirable to subject the manufacturing sector to harsh market forces quickly, then it might not matter so much if the planned economic ties between the republics were broken. Hence a policy that pursued Russia's full independence from the other republics coincided with the optimal economic policy.

In addition, proponents of the Burbulis position used a series of political arguments to link radical economic reform with independence for Russia. Foreign Minister Andrei Kozyrev asserted that the International Monetary Fund had a precondition: "the presence of a government which enjoys popular support and is ready to conduct tough reform, including unpopular measures at first." Such a government, Kozyrev said, could be formed in Russia only under Boris Yeltsin.[10] Others insisted that only Russia could conduct thoroughgoing economic reform, because many of the other republics were so conservative that they would hold Russia back.[11] A group of young economists that became the core of the Gaidar government argued that Russia had no real choice. The other republics, they said, would not carry out decrees of new superrepublican agencies any better than they carried out those of the old agencies.[12]

Precisely because the two macroeconomic policies had such profound consequences for the structure of political power, the character of the country, and Russian national identity, it is very difficult to judge whether the proponents of the two positions accepted the implications for the Union because of their acceptance of the economic strategy or whether they adopted the economic strategy because of its implications for the Union.

The latter suspicion is particularly strong in the case of the Burbulis-Gaidar team, especially Burbulis. Burbulis had little economic expertise, and he had been a leading adviser to Yeltsin in Yeltsin's fight with Gorbachev over the Union treaty. His policy had long been the political and economic independence of Russia, and at some point he came to the conclusion that it should be achieved by liquidating the USSR. When he chose Gaidar and Shokhin as his leading economists, and as they selected members of their team, willingness to accept the breakup of the Soviet Union was a primary criterion for inclusion. They were instructed "to work out options for action on the supposition that a commonwealth will not be created."[13]

The West was concerned about the repayment of the Soviet debt if the Soviet Union disintegrated or if its economic performance worsened, and U.S. Secretary of the Treasury Nicholas Brady said publicly at a Bangkok G-7 meeting on October 11, 1991, that an interrepublican economic agreement was a condition for substantial western aid.[14] For this reason Yeltsin had to pretend that he favored an economic union, and on October 19, Russia and seven other republics signed a new economic pact. Nevertheless, the issue had already been decided well before the G-7 meeting. Virtually all the industrialists in the Russian cabinet resigned between September 25 and October 9. Clearly the Burbulis position had won.

As already indicated, Yeltsin's main theme in his October 28, 1991, speech was his commitment to radical economic reform, but his subtext was the independence of Russia. Yeltsin began by stating that "in practice, we have been living in a new country for two months," and he casually referred to "the sovereign republics of the former Union." "Russia will proceed from the norms of international law in its relations with the former members of the Union. The economic ties with these states will be based on world prices. . . . If this process is unsuccessful for any reason, Russia will be able to take responsibility as the successor to the USSR on itself."[15] He talked as if the economic agreements recently reached with the non-Russian republics were as nonexistent as the USSR institutions.

On November 6—surely not by coincidence the eve of the anniversary of the Bolshevik revolution—Yeltsin announced his new government. He said he would take over the premiership while remaining president and that Burbulis would become the first deputy premier—in effect his real premier. The idea of Yeltsin's serving as premier was motivated, he later reported, by the desire to circumvent the need to have Burbulis confirmed by the Congress if he were premier.[16] Gaidar became deputy premier, overseeing all the economic ministries and also serving directly as the minister for the economy and finances.

The emphasis on a tight money program played an important role in winning western support. With the central Soviet government deprived of the power of taxation and control over the earnings of nationalized industry, the only way it could acquire significant funds was to print money. But if the Russian government had adopted the monetary orthodoxy that prevailed in the West, then the West could not object if Yeltsin justified the breakup of the Union as a necessary step to stop the "flood of rubles" emanating from the Soviet government and from the non-Russian republics.[17]

The Power Relation of Yeltsin and the Congress

When Russia became independent at the end of 1991, Yeltsin's first task was to build a strong executive branch for the government. The weakness of the Russian Federation within the Soviet Union meant that the quality of personnel its government had attracted was not the best. It had had almost no role in supervising heavy industry and therefore now had few officials in this important sector. Yeltsin could have recruited personnel from the USSR ministries, and did to some extent, but he was suspicious of the USSR "bureaucrats."

By the end of 1992, however, Yeltsin had largely succeeded in constructing an effective executive branch, and his attention turned to his relationship with the legislature. The legislature was structured in a quite peculiar manner. The supreme body was a 1,068-deputy Congress of People's Deputies, which met only twice a year in relatively short sessions. The election of its deputies in 1990, unlike those of the USSR Congress in 1989, had been quite democratic, but most of the deputies were part-time legislators. The Congress in turn elected a large committee from its own deputies, a Supreme Soviet of 256 members. The Supreme Soviet functioned for months as a real legislative body, its deputies serving as full-time legislators.

To gain congressional support for an elected presidency in May 1991, Yeltsin accepted a law on the presidency that created a strong president but not an all-powerful one. As in France, the president was the chief of state and chief executive, but he had to act through a premier. The premier had to be confirmed by the legislature, but not the individual cabinet members. Presidential decrees could be overturned by a majority in the Congress, but, in practice, the president had considerable independence in issuing decrees.

The general weakness of all Russian institutions meant that Yeltsin's efforts to wrest more power from Gorbachev in 1991 served the interests of the Russian legislature as well as Yeltsin's own. No one really believed that the military and the KGB would allow the USSR to disintegrate. Hence Yeltsin's power would always be limited, and the Congress did not fear giving Yeltsin considerable leeway in his actions and granting him various emergency powers.[18]

The Russian Congress also did nothing after the August 1991 failed coup to restrain Yeltsin's seizure of central Soviet institutions. Its leaders even reached a gentlemen's agreement, allowing him to issue decrees that did not correspond to the law if he informally consulted with them. After the August coup Yeltsin also won the right to appoint provincial governors (*glavy administratsii,* heads of administration) until local elections were held, and he removed some of the local leaders most compromised in the coup. In October he was allowed to appoint regional governors for a year and essentially to introduce whatever economic reforms he wanted by presidential decree.

In 1992 and 1993 Yeltsin and his supporters in Russia and the West ascribed all the problems of economic reform to the omnipotence of the Congress and the consequent inability of the executive to take steps that it and the IMF wanted. As Yeltsin himself put it in April 1993, "It is the legislature that is responsible for the hardships associated with reforms."[19] A *Financial Times* editorial echoed the point, "Russia is caught in a war between a reforming government that bears responsibility, but is almost powerless, and a reactionary parliament that possesses power, but bears little responsibility for its use."[20]

This interpretation had almost no relationship to the truth. The emergency legislation gave Yeltsin extraordinary power, which he was exercising in an extremely high-handed manner. His system of off-budget methods of rule left the parliament virtually powerless on economic questions. The formal budget meant almost nothing in light of the various "loans," authorized nonpayments, and tax write-offs, which were the exclusive province of the executive. The chairman of the Budget, Planning, Taxation, and Price Committee of the Supreme Soviet, Aleksandr P. Pochinok, complained bitterly on the eve of the Eighth Congress:

> It is high time to end the wrongful practice of considering credits separately from the budget deficit and thinking that they are not part of the state debt. . . . It is no accident that the very man [Finance Minister Boris Fedorov] who says that the Supreme Soviet is stoking inflation and pumping out money is now asking

for an extra R5 trillion in credit for the Russian Finance Ministry to cover the budget deficit. Yes, this credit is essential . . . to adequately finance the economy. But everything must be included into the budget.[21]

Even those finances on the official budget were not always spent as specified in the budget. Veniamin Sokolov, head of the Chamber of Accounts, said that this was true of at least one-sixth of the budget and probably much more. There was no system of accounting for income and expenditure, and the Ministry of Finance resisted introduction of one so that it could do what it wanted with the budget.[22]

Nevertheless, when legislative leaders complained that the budgets were unrealistic and that the deficit should be honestly recognized, they were calling for an increase in the official deficit. This led to the charge that they were promoting financial irresponsibility. The State Bank was legally forced to print money to cover government-approved expenditures, but officially it was under the control of the Congress. The Congress was thus said to be the cause of inflation.

The Congress was characterized as obstructionist, hard-line, and antidemocratic, but this was wrong. When Yeltsin was elected president, he was succeeded as chairman of the Supreme Soviet by Ruslan Khasbulatov. Khasbulatov was to be demonized, but he was, in fact, a radical economic reformer from Moscow University who had been selected first deputy chairman of the Supreme Soviet as the nominee of Democratic Russia. He was a close ally of Yeltsin. As a Chechen, Khasbulatov was also supported by the non-Russian republics and was deeply committed to a democratic legislature and a diffusion of power from Moscow into the provinces. It was Khasbulatov's resistance to the effort of the "democrats" to establish an extremely authoritarian presidency that led them to charge that he was "antidemocratic" and "conservative."[23]

The congressional leadership and majority always seemed willing to compromise. Yeltsin and Khasbulatov were able to ensure that the Supreme Soviet—the full-time legislative body between congressional sessions—was not as conservative as expected. Any deputy was given the opportunity to receive full-time, paid legislative work in Moscow, if not as a Supreme Soviet deputy, then as a member of one of the committees. The radicals and liberals were usually more interested in a legislative career than the conservatives, and this gave the Supreme Soviet and committees a much more reformist orientation.

At the first Congress, the deputies elected to the Supreme Soviet were more conservative on the average than the other deputies. They scored 4.35 on a scale in which extreme radical was 1 and extreme conservative was 8, while other deputies scored 4.25. But by June 1992, the situation had changed radically. Many Supreme Soviet deputies had left, and another 124 congressional deputies had become full-time legislators, usually working in the committees. If the First Congress roll-call scores are used to ensure comparability, the 244 Supreme Soviet deputies in June 1992 averaged 3.83 in their First Congress voting. The 368 deputies working in the legislature on a full-time basis in June 1992 had an average score of 3.26 in their First Congress voting, and the committee chairmen's score was 3.39.[24]

One fundamental problem did exist in the relationship between Congress and the president. Although the Congress had virtually no power on economic reform questions, it did have one constitutional power that was certain to make any president nervous. By a vote of two-thirds of all its deputies, it could amend the constitution unilaterally on any point, including the power of the president. It could, if it wanted, turn the presidency into a ceremonial post. Clearly it was not stable to have a president who was acting in an extremely authoritarian manner on policy matters toward a legislature that could take all power from him.

For this reason alone, everyone agreed that constitutional change was needed. All agreed that the strange Congress–Supreme Soviet legislature should be replaced by a normal bicameral body, with one house representing population and the other representing the regions. The procedure for amending the constitution inevitably would have to be changed with the disappearance of the Congress. An amendment process along American lines, requiring approval by two-thirds of each house and three-fourths of the regions, would have been quite natural and would have been reassuring to Yeltsin. By all evidence, the Congress was willing to yield on this question if Yeltsin were more accommodating on economic policy.

Yeltsin's Flirtation with the Industrialists

Boris Yeltsin, by all accounts of friend and foe alike, reacted with great prickliness toward superiors, equals, or subordinates who acted with what he considered untoward familiarity. In April 1992 he removed his first deputy, Gennady Burbulis, essentially for this reason. "I won't hide the fact that at a certain point I began to feel an irrational weariness with this man. . . . He overstepped some boundary in our personal relations."[25]

When Yeltsin at the same time raised with Gaidar the question of the resignation of some economic ministers, Gaidar reacted as he did in the fall when his team was offered less than they wanted: Gaidar's ministers resigned all together, a decision that Gaidar announced to the Congress without informing Yeltsin.[26] The tactic worked. The Congress withdrew its motion of no confidence and its resolution calling for the resignation of a number of economic ministers. Yeltsin was angry, and the humiliating manner in which he removed Gaidar's oil minister was his response.[27]

Yeltsin's personality ensured that he would have a strained relationship with the Congress and its leaders. They naturally saw themselves as a coequal branch of government—indeed, the Constitution said "supreme"—and they too reacted to slights. They sometimes chose to clash with Yeltsin on symbolic issues when they would have been wiser to restrain themselves. But any body of democratic politicians was certain to be critical of the economic problems of the first months of 1992. This criticism was still directed at the young reformers in the government, not at Yeltsin himself, but it was certain to irritate him.

By his later testimony, Yeltsin approached the Sixth Congress in April 1992 with the determination "to give it a good horsewhipping." He discovered, however, that he and the Congress were not far apart. He writes of being "forced to mimic [Gaidar's] confidence" and of worrying about the lifting of price controls on energy that was due in April and May. He found, he says, that the ministers who displeased him were the same ministers who displeased the centrist deputies.[28]

In immediate terms, the centrists in the Congress obtained largely what they wanted. Near the end of the Congress, Yeltsin met with the leaders of the different factions, and they found a solution that satisfied them all. Yeltsin agreed informally to replace the Ministry of Industry with five new institutions: a state committee for industrial policy (de facto, a policy-planning staff for the deputy premier for industry) and four branch state committees for the defense industry, metallurgy industry, machinery industry, and energy industry, respectively. They were headed by industrialists, and a new deputy premier for industry had the same background. Although Yeltsin in October 1992 had already promised insider privatization as the first stage, the industrialists and the congressional moderates were also pleased by its introduction in April.

In return for Yeltsin's accommodating decisions on economic structure and personnel at the Sixth Congress in April 1992, the Congress passed amendments to the constitution that strengthened the presidency. It instructed its constitutional commission to engage in further work on the constitution, "taking into account the proposals and comments made by the Russian president."[29] Yeltsin was still expressing his happiness with these changes nearly two years later in his memoirs.[30]

Yeltsin promised the Congress leaders that he would step down as premier, and on June 15, he announced the appointment of Gaidar as acting premier.[31] The acting nature of the appointment deprived the Congress of its right to confirm the premier, but the Congress was patient. Yeltsin's emergency powers expired at the end of the year, and that was the time for the key decisions. The subsequent behavior of the congressional leaders showed that they believed they could make a trade with Yeltsin at the Seventh Congress, scheduled for the end of 1992. They would amend the constitution to make his position more secure, and he would move toward their position on economic reform.

Despite the radicals' characterization of the Congress as hard-line, there were many reasons to think its relationship with Yeltsin might work out. Approximately a third of the Congress deputies were all-out supporters of Yeltsin, and another third were closely associated with Communists of Russia. Yeltsin was always able to reach compromises with those in the center, and in the summer of 1992 they were coalescing in a coalition called Civic Union led by Arkady Volsky, the chairman of the Russian Union of Industrialists and Businessmen. Volsky was eager to work with Yeltsin.

As table 5-1 shows, the economic difficulties of 1992 had been reflected in a sharp drop in Yeltsin's approval ratings. The Russian government structure had been built essentially on the French model, with the premier subordinated to both the president and the legislature. When French president François Mitterrand did not control the National Assembly, he decided to "cohabit" with it—to appoint a premier acceptable to the National Assembly on domestic policy and to concentrate on foreign policy. The drop in Yeltsin's approval ratings suggested the advisability of a similar policy.

A presidential election was not scheduled until 1996, and Gaidar was a convenient scapegoat for the problems of 1992. If Yeltsin had chosen Volsky (or a prominent moderate conservative such as Yury Skokov or Victor Chernomyrdin) and instructed him to develop a coherent eco-

Table 5-1. *Levels of Support for Boris Yeltsin,*
July 1991–September 1993
Percent

Which statement would you choose to describe your attitude toward the Russian president?	7/91	10/91	3/92	9/92	1/93	5/93	9/93
Fully share the views and positions of Yeltsin	29	15	11	5	5	9	6
Need to support him while he leads democratic forces	11	17	9	8	11	10	9
Do not like Yeltsin, but hope he can be useful in future	16	10	4	7	6	6	4
Support him because of lack of other worthy political leaders	15	20	15	15	16	18	13
Liked before, but now have become disenchanted	7	11	18	30	29	18	26
Do not support Yeltsin at all	8	10	13	21	16	20	22
Support anybody but Yeltsin	3	2	5	6	6	5	8
Hard to answer	12	15	26	10	12	14	12
Support (in general)	71	62	39	35	38	43	32
Do not support (in general)	18	23	36	57	51	43	56

Source: "Levels of support for Boris Yel'tsin, July 1991 to September 1993" and "Support for Boris Yel'tsin, 1991–1993," compiled by the All-Russian Center for the Study of Public Opinion, cited in Archie Brown, "The October Crisis of 1993: Context and Implications," *Post-Soviet Affairs*, vol. 9 (July-September 1993), p. 189.

nomic program with a strong industrial policy,[32] it was highly likely that economic conditions would have stabilized by the time of the 1996 election with Yeltsin's getting the credit. If conditions did not stabilize, then Yeltsin had stood above the fray, and there would be a new scapegoat.

Volsky's opponents often described him as a conservative, a hard-liner, or the leader of the pro-inflation faction, but all this was quite wrong. Volsky visited Japan and Korea a half dozen times while refusing invitations to the United States. Civic Union seemed poised to emphasize the Asian model with rapid market reform in the agricultural, service, and small industrial sectors, but to insist that the government provide industrial investment for large-scale industry.[33] Foreign investment would be encouraged, but foreign economic policy would try to incorporate the high-tariff, high-export policy of the Asian countries.

The leading economist of the Russian Union of Industrialists and Businessmen was Yevgeny G. Yasin, who actually had an office several doors from Volsky's. In January 1992 Yasin also became the Russian government's official representative to the Russian Supreme Soviet.[34] When appointed, he supported Gaidar and advocated the freeing of oil prices, although he criticized Gaidar for neglecting the social factor.[35]

In a private interview later in 1992, Yasin was contemptuous of the Chinese model and expressed qualified support for many of Gaidar's policies. The following year he reproached Gaidar, not for his "liberalization of prices and the transition to a strict budget policy," which "was correct," but for weakening his resolve. "We've found ourselves in a narrow track," Yasin said, "and it's only ahead that we can move." The model he put forward was "the Japanese variant of corporative ownership."[36]

The reason that Volsky found Yasin congenial was that he and his industrialists were opposed to one key aspect of the Chinese model—the lack of privatization in the state industrial sector. Volsky and his industrialists wanted privatization as long as the managers received control of the property. Yasin and Volsky were really advocating a mixture of the West German and the Japanese–South Korean models. In the United States, industry is financed in substantial part by the stock market, but in Germany and Japan this function is concentrated far more in investment banks that work under the strong influence of the government or the state bank. Volsky and Yasin wanted Russian banks to be under strict governmental control at first and to be used by the government to direct investment into large-scale privatized industry. They assumed that eventually the government would retreat to the looser leadership exercised by institutions such as the Ministry of International Trade and Industry (MITI) in Japan. They were more than content to have the tight control of inflation found in the Asian countries.

The possibility of cohabitation between Yeltsin and the Congress seemed confirmed when the Fifth Session of the Supreme Soviet opened on September 22, 1992. Yeltsin spoke to the Supreme Soviet on October 7 and gave a speech accurately described by the pro-Yeltsin *Izvestiia*: "Never was the president's criticism of the government so frank and sharp. Never did the president come so close to the parliamentary opposition in many of his positions." *Izvestiia* entitled its article on the subject, "Yeltsin Concludes an Alliance with Civic Union."[37] Yeltsin reports that he had informally promised Yury Skokov, an important defense industry manager long associated with him, that he would appoint him as Gaidar's replacement.[38]

Despite his apparent offer of the premiership to Skokov, Yeltsin still nominated Gaidar as premier when the Seventh Congress opened in December 1992. The nomination required 524 votes for confirmation. The vote, on December 9, was surprisingly close: 467 deputies voted in favor of Gaidar and 486 deputies voted against him. Since the centrists wanted fiscal discipline, they were happy to have Gaidar confirmed as prime minister and to allow Yeltsin to retain his emergency powers if there could be agreement on economic policy. Volsky never attacked Yeltsin directly, and he usually was respectful to Gaidar. The stage seemed set for the familiar private negotiations and concessions. Gaidar might then win on the second ballot, or Yeltsin might offer Skokov as an alternative.

Instead, Yeltsin went back to his dacha on the evening of December 9 "in a complete trance," as depressed as he had been after being denounced at the Moscow party meeting in 1987. Many advisers had recommended dissolution of the Congress and a referendum, but Yeltsin had resisted. On the evening of December 9, however, one of his relatives at the dacha suggested that he ask the people whom they wanted— him or the Congress. It was the first time the idea had been proposed, and he liked it. "That evening," he wrote in his memoirs, "God himself inspired one of the people closest to me with this idea." Yeltsin called several advisers, and they all worked through the night on a speech for the next day.[39]

On December 10, with only two hours' sleep, Yeltsin came to the Congress with a blistering speech. He accused his opponents of "a creeping coup" and charged that they had scheduled the Eighth Congress in April 1993 "to make short work of the government, the president, the reforms, and democracy and thus to make a sharp turn backward." The leaders of the Supreme Soviet, he charged, wanted to become "the absolute rulers of Russia . . . similar to what existed in the recent past when the country was ruled by the Politburo."[40]

Yeltsin called for a referendum so the people could choose between the president and the Congress. He proposed a question that was the epitome of simplicity: "Whom do you trust to get the country out of its economic and political crisis and to regenerate the Russian Federation— the current composition of the Congress and the Supreme Soviet, or the president of Russia?" The referendum was to be held in January 1993, and Gaidar was to remain acting premier until then.

Yeltsin did not have the constitutional right to call a referendum himself, and in his December 10 speech he followed the constitutionally correct path of asking the Congress to authorize a referendum. He left unanswered what he would do if the Congress refused to call a referendum on the question as he phrased it, as it was certain to do.

The congressional leadership responded to Yeltsin's speech of December 10 by calling the defense minister, the two police ministers, and the prosecutor general to the Congress and asking them if they supported the constitution. They all pledged their support, and, if they were to be believed, Yeltsin had lost any ability to introduce a referendum unconstitutionally. On December 12 Yeltsin met with Khasbulatov and the chairman of the Constitutional Commission. They came up with a compromise that seemed to give a victory to the Congress while saving Yeltsin's face.

The congressional resolution agreed to a referendum on April 11, 1993, but on "the basic tenets of the new constitution." Since the Supreme Soviet and the president might well not agree on a mutually acceptable draft, the operative clause seemed to be the following: "In the event of a failure to reach agreement on individual formulations of the draft, they will be put forward for alternative balloting. The draft basic tenets of the new constitution and basic law of the Russian Federation must be sent to the subjects of the Russian Federation."[41]

A referendum on a series of abstract wordings of clauses seemed unlikely to draw the required 50 percent of the population to the polls. But in any case, the subjects of the federation (the regional governments) were unlikely to approve a highly centralized regime, and the stage seemed set for the endless bargaining between center and republics that had characterized Gorbachev's Union Treaty negotiations.

The Congress moved to satisfy the president by prolonging his emergency powers, including his right to appoint governors until the next local elections.[42] However, the Congress won the right to confirm the appointments of the four "force ministers"—the ministers of defense and internal affairs, the chairman of the secret police, and the procurator general.

In addition, the president agreed to consult with the factions to obtain their candidates for premier and to present several of them to the Congress for a "soft rating" vote, which meant that Congress would vote favorably or unfavorably on each candidate in a nonbinding popularity poll. The president would then have the right to nominate one of the three top vote-getters for confirmation by the Congress.

On the surface, the basic problem was not solved. Obviously Gaidar would not receive the most votes in the soft rating vote, and if he was in the top three and was nominated by Yeltsin, he was certain to be rejected once more. Yeltsin put forward six men for a soft rating vote. The three who received the most votes were Yury Skokov (secretary of the Security Council), with 637 favorable votes; Viktor Chernomyrdin (deputy premier for the oil and gas industry), with 621 votes; and Gaidar, with 400.[43]

Despite the fact that Skokov received the most votes and had already been promised the premiership, Yeltsin decided to nominate Chernomyrdin as a compromise candidate. He thought that Gaidar's nomination would produce a major confrontation, and Gaidar and the other democrats preferred Chernomyrdin to Skokov.[44] Chernomyrdin was nominated, and the Congress approved him with 721 votes in favor, 172 against, and 48 abstaining.

The Mystery of Viktor Chernomyrdin

Viktor Chernomyrdin was born in 1938, some twenty years before Yeltsin's young economists. He graduated from an engineering correspondence institute while working at a local refinery and quickly moved into party work dealing with the oil and gas industry. But while Chernomyrdin was engaged in the same type of industry-oriented party work as Yeltsin at the same time, he was at a lower level and returned to industrial management, serving as director of the Orenburg Gas (Helium) Processing Plant from 1973 to 1978.

Then during the drastic increase in oil and gas investment from 1978 to 1982, Chernomyrdin became head of the oil and gas section of the Central Committee, reportedly recommended for the position by Arkady Volsky, who headed the machinery industry department of the Central Committee. From 1982 to 1985 Chernomyrdin served as USSR deputy minister of the gas industry, supervising the extraction of gas in the new Tiumen fields in Siberia. In 1985 he became minister. When the ministry was formally turned into the "concern" Gazprom (Gas Industry), Chernomyrdin became its head. He remained in this post until April 1992, when Yeltsin named him deputy premier for the energy complex.

On the surface Viktor Chernomyrdin was an ideal compromise candidate. He had been a minister in Gorbachev's government beginning in

1985—the head of the natural gas industry—and he seemingly was close to Arkady Volsky, leader of the moderate forces in the Congress. On December 14 Chernomyrdin talked about the need to move to "the next stage" of reform. "The most serious attention," he said, "should be paid mainly to production [with] the main emphasis on our basic, essential industries":

> First of all, the slump in production must be halted, for no reform can go ahead if we destroy industry completely. Therefore, I believe that the reform should now take on a slightly different tone. . . . In this new stage the most serious attention should be paid mainly to production. . . . I believe that we probably should, or rather must, place the main emphasis on our basic, essential industries. . . . Our country must not become one of shopkeepers, given such powerful infrastructure, such richness, such resources. Must we be impoverished with all this? No, our people do not deserve this.[45]

Nevertheless, Chernomyrdin had come out of the natural gas industry, and that industry had a strong self-interest in an economic policy based on energy export. Moreover, in the fall of 1992 Yeltsin had for the first time agreed in principle to the privatization of the natural gas industry. If the insiders were to have control of this incredible wealth, then Chernomyrdin surely would gain access to it, even as premier. His personal interests and those of the branch would coincide. No doubt Gaidar and the other democrats, in preferring Chernomyrdin to Skokov, understood that this would push him in a free-trade direction.

On becoming premier Chernomyrdin indicated he was, indeed, going to carry out the program promised to the Congress. On December 31 he signed a decree introducing price controls on a number of crucial items. A week later Chernomyrdin's friend Viktor Gerashchenko, chairman of the Russian Bank, gave an interview that many took as a Chernomyrdin manifesto. Gerashchenko declared that the liberalization of prices had not produced a restructuring of prices because of the monopoly position of the state enterprises. He said that privatization of large plants might well worsen the situation. He talked about the desirability of a price and wage freeze, the need to raise interest rates in savings banks (the annual rate was between 20 and 60 percent, while prices rose 26-fold in 1992), and the importance of a differentiated investment policy.

After appointing Chernomyrdin premier, Yeltsin gave the key post of deputy premier for finance to Boris Fedorov. Fedorov was a neoliberal economist who, if anything, was more radical than Gaidar in pushing the monetary policy favored by the IMF. In October 1992 Fedorov became the first Russian representative at the World Bank, and when Chernomyrdin's decree on the price control was published on January 6, 1993, Fedorov was in Washington talking with the international economic organizations and representatives of the incoming Clinton administration. When he returned to Moscow on January 12, he declared that the premier's price control decree did not reflect government policy. It was rescinded the next day.[46]

Russia had $20 billion worth of debt coming due in 1993. The same article in *Financial Times* that reported Fedorov's victory over Chernomyrdin noted that Deputy Premier Aleksandr Shokhin, then in charge of foreign economic relations, was negotiating a rescheduling of the Russian international debt. The strong impression was created that the repeal of Chernomyrdin's price control was the condition for the rescheduling of the debt.[47]

The reversal of Chernomyrdin's price decree was a sign that changes would not be forthcoming. A few personnel changes were made, but the core of the government remained the leading deputy premiers—Vladimir Shumeiko, Boris Fedorov, Anatoly Chubais, Aleksandr Shokhin, and Sergei Shakhrai. Their policy was little changed from that of 1992. In the words of a correspondent, "The formation of the new Russian cabinet showed [that] Yeltsin at the present time is not too inclined to take into account the opinion of his premier, in any case in personnel questions. . . . Boris Yeltsin preferred to bet on people who already more than once had proved their personal dedication."[48] By March one of the leaders of Civic Union, Aleksandr Vladislavlev, was calling the situation in the Russian government "absurd," because the new premier "is deprived of the possibility to form a team of like-minded people."[49]

After humiliating his nominal superior, Fedorov continued to act with great self-confidence. He criticized Gaidar for following an expansionist monetary policy and threatened the large-scale dismissal of factory managers.[50] Fedorov spoke repeatedly about the danger of hyperinflation— deliberately exaggerating the danger for political effect, high Russian government officials told the *New York Times*.[51] In fact, as Yeltsin was to boast in April, inflation was declining at the time. Over the next two months Fedorov was to demand the resignation of the chairman of the Russian Bank and to issue decrees sharply reducing credit to the economy and introducing, at least putatively, a real shock therapy.[52]

During the spring Chernomyrdin frequently repeated statements he had made at the time of his appointment. In March he seemed to speak from the heart in criticizing the policy of the previous year. Acknowledging that "of course, there is no investment, no money [and that] as a rule, enterprises have not thought of investment," Chernomyrdin said production had fallen 30 percent since the previous year. He declared, "We had no right to let production rates drop so drastically. We cannot implement reforms if there is no production."[53] In April 1993 he likened Deputy Premier Anatoly Chubais's rapid privatization plan to the rapid collectivization drive of the 1930s.

In April 1993 Yeltsin appointed his old Sverdlovsk subordinate, Oleg Lobov, as first deputy premier and minister of the economy, and Lobov renewed the policy battle of September 1991, only this time against Boris Fedorov. Now, however, Chernomyrdin shifted his position and supported Fedorov against the policy that he himself had proposed only a few months before. In September 1993 Yeltsin supported Fedorov and Chernomyrdin against Lobov as he dissolved the Congress.

The reason for Chernomyrdin's switch in position in the summer of 1993 has never been explained. Perhaps his position before the April 1993 referendum was a tactical step to support Yeltsin in the referendum, or perhaps Yeltsin's response to his victory in that referendum made Chernomyrdin's earlier position untenable. Perhaps most important, a key decision was made in May to limit the privatization of Gazprom to insiders. Chernomyrdin had a strong reason to remain an insider.

The Economic Policy of the April 1993 Referendum

In December 1992 Yeltsin had demanded a referendum, and the Congress agreed to one that did little more than save his face. In his memoirs Yeltsin indicated he had given up on the Congress and was determined to get rid of it. When the Eighth Congress opened on March 10, 1993, Yeltsin threw down the gauntlet by demanding that the Congress take up questions other than those that were on the agenda agreed to in December 1992—questions worded to guarantee his total dominance. The Congress rejected the presidential proposal by a vote of 623 to 382, and on March 12 annulled the compromise that extended his emergency powers. Yeltsin declared temporary presidential rule, but again he failed to get the support of the force ministers. Yeltsin made detailed plans to arrest the Congress deputies if they impeached him, but the Congress did not have enough votes to do so.[54]

Once more the Congress tried a compromise to break the stalemate. A congressional leader, Vladimir Isakov, taunted Yeltsin that general questions were meaningless. He said, "Why not ask in the presidential referendum directly and honestly: People, . . . do you consent to the continuation of *my* course of reforms?"[55] If the issue were put this way, the leaders of the Supreme Soviet—and even many of the president's men[56]—could not believe that the population would support the Yeltsin position. As a consequence, a referendum was scheduled for April 25, with four questions:

—Do you have confidence (trust) in the president of the Russian Federation, Yeltsin?

—Do you approve the socioeconomic policy carried out by the Russian Federation and government since 1992?

—Do you think early presidential elections are necessary in 1993?

—Do you think early elections of deputies are necessary in 1993?[57]

The two questions about elections required an absolute majority of all eligible voters in order to pass, an impossible barrier. The two other questions were only advisory, but they were politically important. The congressional leaders assumed that the question about trust in the president would be approved, while that about his socioeconomic policy would be disapproved. This, they hoped, would both reassure Yeltsin and give the Congress some leverage on economic policy.

In reality Yeltsin very skillfully obscured the nature of his economic program. He acknowledged that mistakes had been made by the government, and he pledged to "correct various facets of strategy:" "the fundamental direction of these corrections . . . unconditionally . . . is a movement toward common sense, or, in political terms, to a more balanced systemic position." He declared, "There will not be a second shock like the one that has taken place, especially in the first half of last year."[58] Chernomyrdin's position seemed to support these words.

As the April 25 referendum approached, Yeltsin became what John Lloyd called a "super-populist."[59] He promised that savings account holders as of January 1, 1992, would be compensated for the inflation that had wiped out their accounts. He stopped a planned increase in the price of gasoline from 40 rubles to 80 rubles and refused to raise the price of coal. In the provinces the Yeltsin-appointed governors claimed that only the president was protecting the people from market forces.

Even though the textile oblast of Ivanovo would suffer the most from a market policy in agriculture and industry, it voted 58.3 percent for Yeltsin's socioeconomic policy.[60] Reportedly the governor of Ivanovo said that only the president was obtaining subsidized cotton for the region.

Leaders in all countries often take populist steps before an election, and the educated population surely interpreted most of Yeltsin's prereferendum program cynically. One action, however, seemed much more serious. On April 15, as has been noted, Oleg Lobov was appointed first deputy premier and minister of the economy. Anyone knowledgeable about Moscow politics knew that Lobov had been the leading opponent of Gaidar in Yeltsin's close entourage in the fall of 1991. Lobov's appointment seemed an attempt to assure the educated public that the "correction" would be serious and that there would not, in fact, be a second wave of shock therapy.

In most respects the results of the referendum were fairly close to what had been anticipated. The voter turnout was 64.5 percent of the total electorate, and Yeltsin received the support of 58.7 percent of those who cast votes. The turnout was somewhat higher than expected and the support figure largely in line with expectations. Of those casting a valid vote, 51.3 percent approved an early presidential election and 69.1 percent an early congressional election, again not unexpected.[61] The great surprise of the election was that Yeltsin's social and economic policy was approved by 53.1 percent of all voters, 54.4 percent of those casting a valid ballot.

The approval of Yeltsin's social and economic policy was an utter disaster for the legislative leaders, for they had no way to explain away the result in a credible manner. They were demoralized and could not think of another move to make. They fell into relative inactivity, confident (or at least hopeful) that Yeltsin would be restrained by a provision in the constitution that he would automatically remove himself from power if he dissolved the Congress.

The Lobov-Fedorov Conflict

After the referendum, Yeltsin moved rapidly to get the constitution he wanted. The draft of his preferred constitution was published on April 30. On May 11 he created a working commission to perfect the constitutional convention, and on May 13 *Izvestiia* reported that he was "forcing" the pace of the constitutional process. On May 21 Yeltsin announced that the constitutional convention would open on June 5.[62] On the surface, the members of the constitutional convention in June were broadly representative of the country's regions and political organizations, but they overwhelmingly supported the president's position.

When the convention opened on June 5, Khasbulatov was placed at the far right end of the table that contained the presiding group, and Valery Zorkin, chairman of the Constitutional Commission, was placed at the far left end. Both expected to be closer to the center and were offended, Yeltsin noted with some satisfaction in his memoirs.[63] Their location was meant to symbolize their political power. In late May Yeltsin's press secretary had publicly said that Yeltsin should not meet with Khasbulatov, chairman of the Supreme Soviet, "because they have different degrees of legitimacy."[64]

On July 13 a draft constitution was approved, with 433 delegates voting yes, 62 no, and 63 abstaining.[65] Yeltsin made some concessions, but the constitution concentrated power overwhelmingly in the hands of the president and made his position as invulnerable as possible from legislative attack.

With the constitutional convention out of the way, Yeltsin moved quickly toward a showdown with the Congress. The minister of state security, Viktor Barannikov, had been investigating corruption high in the government. On July 28 Yeltsin fired him, and even the pro-Yeltsin *Izvestiia* spoke of the "unexpected firing" and of a bomb's exploding.[66] Barannikov had been Yeltsin's candidate to head the secret police in the wake of the August 1991 coup, but, more important, he was a "force minister." If Yeltsin was going to follow the constitution, he had to submit the name of Barannikov's successor to the Congress for confirmation. The removal of Barannikov because he was investigating corruption meant that the Congress was not likely to confirm a successor.

On September 1 Yeltsin went a step further, suspending Vice President Aleksandr Rutskoi temporarily from office for alleged corruption. The charge seems to have been totally fabricated,[67] but again the crucial fact was that, whatever Rutskoi did or did not do, Yeltsin had no constitutional power to remove or to suspend him. At approximately this time Yeltsin reports that he wrote out by hand and signed an edict to dissolve the parliament, but he told no one and locked the edict in his safe.[68]

Throughout the late spring and summer, Yeltsin largely maintained the economic position he adopted during the referendum. He did renege on the promise to compensate people for their lost savings, and he did raise the prices of gasoline and coal.[69] Nevertheless, at the beginning of May, he still spoke of "a socially oriented market economy." More important, he appointed Oleg Soskovets, the last USSR minister of the ferrous industry, as another first deputy premier. Rightly or wrongly, Soskovets was considered a conservative by the radical reformers.[70]

There were many interpretations of the Soskovets appointment,[71] but the most obvious was made by the respected *Izvestiia* economics reporter, Mikhail Berger. The political balance in the cabinet was changing, Berger thought, and the country would be run by a coalition of industrialists as the Congress had hoped at the beginning of the year: Chernomyrdin from the oil and gas industry, Soskovets from the steel industry, and Lobov from the defense industry.[72] Berger might have added that a representative of the kolkhoz chairmen, Aleksandr Zaveriukha, had been named deputy premier for agriculture, and Yury Yarov, the former chairman of the executive committee of the Leningrad Soviet and a Civic Union supporter, was the deputy premier who supervised the regions.

Lobov acted as if his and Soskovets's appointment gave him a mandate to introduce fundamental change. Reportedly Lobov's analytical group had written a memorandum calling for an increased role for the Ministry of the Economy, which had led Chernomyrdin to take the initiative to appoint him.[73] The Ministry of the Economy was the new name for Gosplan (State Planning Committee), the most powerful economic institution in the old system. It remained a huge institution with more than 2,000 specialists and fifteen deputy ministers, four of them first deputy ministers. It had been excluded from policymaking, a new deputy minister reported, because the Gaidar team thought it too reactionary.[74] Its huge staff, however, surely was deeply involved in the planning of the various off-budget loans.

Lobov obviously thought he had a mandate to rebuild the authority of the ministry. He proposed reinstating its former power to issue mandatory orders and called for a major increase in capital investment. The Ministry of the Economy would work out this investment policy, supervise long-term credits for the enterprises, carry out conversion of the defense industry, and subsidize science to stimulate Russian technological innovation.[75] Lobov's opponents claimed he wanted to reestablish the old economic system dominated by Gosplan.[76] His supporters thought he was creating the institution that could conduct an industrial policy—a Russian equivalent of the Japanese MITI.

In reality the appointments left the government deeply divided. Deputy premiers Shumeiko, Chubais, Shakhrai, Fedorov, and Shokhin had the orientation of the Gaidar team, although they ranged from Fedorov's extremely doctrinaire approach on economic policy to Shokhin's willingness to compromise. Fedorov, as before, led the counterattack to Lobov. He categorically opposed Lobov's proposal to increase capital investment, and he began holding press conferences and writing articles to defend his position.[77] He charged that Russia was subsidizing the former republics of the Soviet Union with $17 billion a year by selling goods below cost or on credit,[78] implying that Russia should move to market prices for raw materials and ruthlessly cut off former union republics that could not pay.

After the referendum, Chernomyrdin threw his support to Fedorov. On August 6 he presented the Fedorov program to the cabinet as the government plan.[79] In retrospect, the reversal of Chernomyrdin's position had been signaled by an important agreement that had been signed between the government and the State Bank on May 20.[80] The agreement embodied the bank's and Gerashchenko's acceptance of a tight monetary policy.[81] The State Bank had been used as the scapegoat for financial difficulties, but in September 1993 Yegor Gaidar was to note with satisfaction that the bank's agreement with the government had been carried out.[82]

As the quasi-ministerial holding companies and the central branch banks declined in 1993, the real immediate issue was whether their role would be assumed primarily by the Ministry of the Economy or by the regional governors. Whatever Fedorov's intentions, his policy meant shifting more of the subsidy-making power to the governors. Chernomyrdin probably either knew or sensed that Yeltsin's victory in the referendum meant he would support Fedorov's position.

It is likely, however, that decisions about the privatization of Gazprom were also highly important. Yeltsin had issued a decree in November 1992 on the privatization of Gazprom, but a dispute broke out in the Duma and in the government on how its shares were to be distributed. Consideration was given to distributing shares by region in a way that would make the privatization similar to that of other enterprises, but in May Gazprom was allowed to conduct its auction of shares in a closed manner designed to benefit insiders.[83] Chernomyrdin reportedly received or was allowed to buy a number of shares in the gas industry concern.[84]

On August 29, the day after Chernomyrdin left for his meeting with Vice President Al Gore, Lobov presented a memorandum to Yeltsin on his plan. The next day Yeltsin wrote on the memorandum, "I firmly support the proposals. Please submit a draft edict within ten days."[85] A working group was set up to work out the final version, and the business newspaper, *Kommersant*, reported that Fedorov was supported only by the IMF and the remnants of the Gaidar team in the cabinet.[86]

Once again Yeltsin moved to gain U.S. support for political moves against the Congress by pledging to support the program of the IMF. In April Shokhin had reported that he was trying to have a standby agreement with the IMF signed by October, and this date was key for Yeltsin's timing.[87] On September 7 Yeltsin instructed his press secretary to float a trial balloon that he was thinking of radical action against the Congress. On September 10 *Izvestiia* published the story, attributing it to "sources close to the president."[88] *Kommersant Daily* at this time was reporting strong support in the cabinet for the Lobov plan. Lawrence Summers, undersecretary of the treasury, flew to Moscow for meetings on September 14 and 15. The IMF and the World Bank were delaying a $1.5 billion and a $600 million loan, respectively, the *New York Times* reported, "as a carrot to push Moscow to get its economic house in order."[89]

On September 16 Lobov was replaced as first deputy premier by Yegor Gaidar, and the Lobov plan disappeared.[90] Lobov became executive secretary of the Security Council—a low-profile post until a crisis erupted over Chechnya a year later. On the eve of the Summers visit, President Clinton, when asked whether the United States should be talking with Vice President Rutskoi as well as Yeltsin, answered, "I don't think we should be hedging our bet." As *New York Times* columnist William Safire put it, "The Russian leader—assured that no Clinton bet on him would be hedged—made his move."[91]

The Dissolution of the Congress

Boris Yeltsin moved immediately to disband the Congress and the Supreme Soviet. Appearing on television on September 21, he leveled the same criticisms at these two bodies that he had made in his December 10, 1992, speech to the Seventh Congress and in his March 20, 1993, speech to the Eighth Congress. This time, however, he attacked the constitution itself as contributing to the gridlock. Yeltsin declared that as "the guarantor of the security of [the] state, . . . I am obliged to break this ruinous, vicious circle. . . . [As a consequence], I have approved, by my decree, amendments and addenda to the current Constitution of the Russian Federation."[92]

This time Yeltsin did not use euphemisms. He ended the powers of the deputies and declared that the Congress and the Supreme Soviet no longer performed their functions. He set new elections for December 11–12 for new institutions created by his unilateral "constitutional amendments." These were a new bicameral federal assembly based on the draft of the constitution approved on July 13. The upper house, the Federation Council, was supposed to be a nonelected body, and Yeltsin's decree referred only to elections of the lower house, the State Duma. In his television address Yeltsin said he was in favor of an early presidential election, and he issued an official presidential edict setting a presidential election for June 12, 1993.

At the time that it had approved a presidency in May 1991, the Congress had included in the final version of the constitution—and Yeltsin had accepted—a clause providing that if any branch of government tried to abolish the institutions of another branch, it would by this action forfeit power itself. When Yeltsin rejected the constitution and disbanded the legislature, the legislature invoked this clause of the constitution. According to the constitution, Yeltsin had vacated his own office by his action, and Vice President Rutskoi thereby automatically became president. The Supreme Soviet declared that Rutskoi was, in fact, president and swore him in.

As president, Rutskoi appointed his own minister of defense and minister of internal affairs and ordered the troops to take orders from them. The parliamentary leaders, together with Rutskoi, remained in the White House, and they convened an emergency session of the Congress of People's Deputies. Only 638 deputies attended, almost exactly the same number that had voted for impeachment in March. After they expelled other deputies for support of an unconstitutional action, the Congress voted unanimously to remove Yeltsin from office.

Once again Moscow entered one of those strange periods that had often characterized its politics since 1990. The country had two quite legitimate presidents, depending on whether one construed as the basis for legitimacy the 1991 election or the 1991 constitution under which the president was elected. With television cameras present, Yeltsin's minister of defense, Pavel Grachev, and minister of internal affairs, Viktor

Yerin, ostentatiously strolled with him in public.[93] The military line of command accepted orders from them, not from Rutskoi's ministers, on normal military questions. Yet, as had been the case since the August 1991 coup, neither the military nor the militarized troops of the police were reliable supporters of any political contender. Neither Grachev nor Yerin was willing to call out troops. As a result, all the political leaders were operating on an extraordinarily unstable political base.

On September 24 Yeltsin moved police around the White House and turned off its electricity. The number of congressional deputies who remained in the building dwindled, but when Yeltsin supporters tried to rally supporters in Moscow on September 26, they could get only some 15,000 persons to attend. The Moscow and St. Petersburg city councils, both elected with strong radical majorities in 1990, refused to support Yeltsin's action.

Supporters of the Congress in the square in front of the White House were considerably fewer in number at any one time, but they maintained a constant presence. While these supporters constituted a very mixed group, the persistent ones were usually quite hard-core. They were led by Viktor Anpilov, the head of the most militant Communist group, and General Albert Makashov, an arch-conservative who ran in the 1991 presidential election.

For more than ten days, there was a stalemate. On the surface Yeltsin had the upper hand. He could simply let the rump Congress occupy the building, go about the business of government, hold the election, and have a new legitimate legislature with which to work. Nevertheless, the persistence of the resistance and troops in the center of Moscow was a constant reminder of the limits of his authority. A substantial number of moderate and centrist figures called for a compromise based on simultaneous legislative and presidential elections, and the Patriarch of the Orthodox Church, Aleksei II, attempted to mediate. The heads of administration appointed by Yeltsin largely supported him, but many leaders of soviets throughout the country supported the Congress or called for some reconciliation.

The crisis ended in a way that emphasized the fragility of the support on which both sides rested. On Sunday, October 3, a relatively small group of militants, perhaps a maximum of 2,000 persons, gathered a mile away from the White House in Smolensk Square at 2:00 in the afternoon. They lit bonfires and pelted the security police with stones. Antiriot forces with water hoses and tear gas could easily have dispersed them, but the police were not prepared for even this minor challenge. At 3:35, the demonstrators broke through the barricades, and at 5:00 they seized the building next to the White House that housed the office of the Moscow mayor. Within an hour, Yeltsin declared a state of emergency. Rutskoi appeared on the balcony of the White House and called on the demonstrators to seize the television studio of Ostankino. General Makashov led a relatively small group that did, in fact, seize part, but not all, of the building. A spectacular firefight ensued, but the confrontation ended in a stalemate.

During the night Yeltsin brought Alpha and Vympel, two militarized units of the police into town. Alpha had been a hero of the defense of the White House during the August 1991 coup. At 7:00 in the morning on October 3, tanks of these units shelled the White House. The following day the troops finally stormed the building and brought out the remaining leaders and soldiers supporting the Congress. Even then, however, the issue was much more in doubt than seemed on the surface. At 5:00 in the morning on October 4, the commanders of Alpha and Vympel had refused to obey a presidential order to attack the White House. In hopes of provoking an incident, the president asked the troops at least to appear before the White House as an act of intimidation. When a White House sniper killed an Alpha soldier, Alpha finally attacked.[94]

Yeltsin's Calculations in the Economic Debate

The sequence of Yeltsin's actions from December 1992 through October 1993 fit a well-defined pattern. For whatever reason, Yeltsin emerged from his December 1992 confrontation with the Congress believing that he had been defeated, not that he had reached a compromise such as he envisaged in his October 1992 speech to the Supreme Soviet. He saw the Congress as the enemy, and he was determined to destroy it. Once Yeltsin set his course, he pursued it with steadfast purpose and considerable daring.

The first difficult question is why Yeltsin engaged in the December 1992 confrontation with the Congress and why he was so convinced that he had been defeated. Another puzzle is why Yeltsin did not modify economic policy after either the defeat of the neoliberal reformers in the December 1993 Duma election or the collapse of the ruble in September 1994.

The broad question is why Yeltsin spent a year allowing his attention to be engaged not by questions of economic reform, but by political confrontation with an institution that never was a real challenge to his power and that was eager to compromise. Yeltsin's victory should not distract from the fact that his strategy was quite risky. He did not have reliable military force at his disposal in September 1993, and his chief adversary, Vice President Rutskoi, was an air force general. If Rutskoi had had the support of a single parachute division, as he apparently thought he did, the outcome could have been very different.

One reason Yeltsin was so offended by the Congress surely is that he had a difficult personality and was apt to see slights everywhere, even if none existed. No doubt the young radical intellectuals who were the real target of congressional attacks did everything they could to play on his sensitivities and persuade him that he was being personally attacked. One of the radicals, Yeltsin's press secretary Viacheslav Kostikov, is totally frank in his memoirs that he thought the Communist party and its newspapers should have been abolished. Kostikov reported in his memoirs that he felt men such as Yury Skokov "were very close to the pro-Communist Supreme Soviet." He thought and surely was telling Yeltsin that if Skokov became premier, he would unite with the Congress "and under this or that pretext, Boris Nikolaevich would be removed from power in the next few months."[95] Skokov had headed Yeltsin's 1991 presidential campaign and, by all indications, was quite loyal. His views were similar to those of Arkady Volsky, but, perhaps especially for this reason, the two men were personal rivals.

Yeltsin was suspicious of everyone, and he was fully capable of understanding the efforts of assistants to manipulate him. It is likely that the fundamental reason that Yeltsin chose risky confrontation rather than compromise was precisely that he liked risky confrontation. Yeltsin himself has written about his bouts of depression, and many of Yeltsin's closest associates have testified to this condition.[96] The day-to-day work of a chief executive did not appeal to him and contributed to his depression.

By contrast, a clear-cut struggle for power with a clear-cut victory or defeat invigorated him, and a risky struggle seems to have been the most invigorating of all. On March 18, 1993, Kostikov declared in public that the president had been in "a kind of lethargy," but that the battle with the Congress had shaken him out of it. Kostikov reported that at "Wednesday's Presidential Council session he had seen the president as he had been in 1991."[97] Yeltsin may have been driven to what his personality needed.

Yeltsin's memoirs testify to his great love of volleyball and tennis, and for him the struggle for power also seemed very much a game. When he played volleyball and tennis, he could not bear losing,[98] and he was just as competitive in politics. But by the same token, he felt no more need to destroy a political opponent than a tennis opponent. Kostikov described in his memoirs how "Yeltsin, after having enjoyed victory, loses interest in an opponent and moves to the side."[99]

This had profound implications for economic reform. The pattern of events made clear that Yeltsin was willing to support, at least verbally, any economic reform in 1993—either that which would win him the support of the public in the referendum or that which would win the support of the West in his struggle with the Congress. It did not matter to him that the two policies were inconsistent with each other. Lobov was serious in his policy position—and had the best of the argument— but it is impossible to believe Yeltsin ever was serious about supporting Lobov unless the West refused to support the dissolution of the Congress. Lobov served the purposes of reassuring the Russian moderates during the summer and frightening the West into believing that Yeltsin had a policy alternative if it did not support him.

Unfortunately for the future of economic reform, Yeltsin learned two lessons from the events of 1993. The referendum had shown that the urban population understood that consumption was being subsidized and the rural population that it depended on the government for fuel allotments. The referendum showed that both groups saw Yeltsin as the guarantor of these necessities and would support him in fear that a successor might be a change for the worse.

By the same token, the strong western support for his restriction of democracy both in the March and September crises showed Yeltsin that the West was really interested in the formal economic policy being enunciated, not the real policy. Perhaps the West was extraordinarily naive and did not understand the nature of real policy or thought a market and investment would emerge despite it; perhaps the West was simply responsive to a few domestic exporters who wanted free trade; perhaps it only needed the right rhetoric for domestic U.S. political purposes. But the one point of importance for Yeltsin was that the West was not going to object seriously to the off-budget subsidies that gained him personal support in his elections.

No combination of lessons could have been worse for the Russian economy in the 1990s. Westerners disagree on the nature of the optimal policy in Russia, but surely they can agree on the wholly unsatisfactory character of the policy that was adopted. A state-directed economic policy that distributed hidden subsidies by personal favor rather than by impersonal formulas subverted any possibility for the development of property rights and a rule of law. A policy in which the state did not promote investment, but destroyed the possibility of any significant investment, was disastrous for economic growth. In conjunction, the two policies had to be the worst of all available choices.

SIX   *The Response of*
        the Political System,
        1993–96

THE WEST INSISTED THAT Russia institute democracy along with economic reform, but to a large extent the two concepts were used synonymously. Indeed, the radical economic reformers all called themselves democrats. Democracy was justified as a means of obtaining popular support or toleration of painful economic actions, not as a way of adjusting economic reform to the desires of a majority of a population. The real democrats who had led the fight for democratization from 1988 to 1990 were pushed aside by the radical economists associated with the government.

Democracy should, however, be a self-correcting mechanism. Just as economic theory recognizes that entrepreneurs can make major mistakes and become bankrupt, so democratic theory assumes that political entrepreneurs can learn from their mistakes or that new entrepreneurs will arise. When American political parties stray too far from the mainstream and suffer a major defeat, they normally adjust the image they present at the next election and nominate a candidate with a greater chance of victory.

Russian politics did not show this characteristic in the 1990s. The electoral system introduced in 1993 was carefully designed to produce a small number of broad coalitional parties, but instead thirteen parties, none of them coalitional, made it to the ballot. Yegor Gaidar headed a party (*Vybor Rossii*, Russia's Choice) that expected to receive from 25 to 40 percent of the vote but deliberately adopted a radical posture in order to receive a mandate for radical reform. Instead, Gaidar's program, as an American political scientist might have warned, cut his vote to 15 percent of the total vote in 1993 and to less than 4 percent in the 1995 parliamentary election.

Nevertheless, instead of drawing lessons from Gaidar's experience, Russian politicians did not respond to the incentives of the political system in the 1995, 1996, or 1999 elections. Public opinion surveys about economic reform continued to show a fairly classic bell-shaped curve, with only a small minority of the population wanting the reform model of the IMF and a relatively small minority rejecting marketization completely. Although the Russian politicians had two years to plan for and organize the 1995 Duma election, forty-three parties appeared on the ballot, again none of them a broad coalitional party. As a result of the number of parties, half the votes cast in the party list election were wasted because they went to parties that did not receive the five percent of the vote required for obtaining seats.

Why did an electoral system structured to produce several large centrist parties produce none that attempted to follow the coalitional strategy of an American Republican or Democratic party or a British Conservative or Labour party? Why did the Communist party not move more convincingly into the center, as its counterparts often did in eastern Europe?

Ultimately, Yeltsin is an even greater mystery. His actions in the year before the crisis with the Congress can be explained by his desire to destroy a body that could change his constitutional powers by a two-thirds vote. But why, after the defeat of Yegor Gaidar in the December 1993 election, did Yeltsin not associate himself with a radical change in economic policy as a way of strengthening himself for the 1996 presidential election?

The actions of other political candidates in 1996 are even more peculiar. At the beginning of 1996, Yeltsin was in extremely poor health, and the country was in a depression as bad as the United States experienced in 1932. Most observers thought that Yeltsin would not run, and almost no one thought he could win. Public opinion polls showed that the views of the public were far closer to those of the leader of the Communist party, although the majority of the population did not trust the party. The situation cried for a credible centrist candidate, but none emerged.

There are specific and general answers to these mysteries. The key point, however, is that early democracy has many similarities to early capitalism. Just as the incentives of an abstract capitalist model do not operate in the same manner in early capitalism as they do in modern America, so the incentives of a democratic electoral model often do not function in early democracy in the same way they do in more developed democracies.

The basic problems in early markets and early democracy are much the same. The entrepreneur, economic or political, often has no compelling reason to respond to the incentives the model makers think should be decisive. If economic actors think they can get away with crime or corruption, this is often the most rational strategy. If political leaders believe that they can call off or control the next election, or if other political actors think that they can seize power in a coup, they need not worry about maximizing votes.

In addition, of course, economic and political actors need not limit themselves to playing in the "game" that analysts posit for them. Why, for example, should a politician make it a top priority to be reelected to the legislature or to form a political party if the legislature has little power? Anthony Downs's famous book that explained why politicians tend to move to the center was entitled *An Economic Theory of Democracy*.[1] But in a country such as Russia, political actors following the path of economic rationality will not focus on reelection, but on the acquisition of property and other economic side payments.

Similarly, Downs's model is based on the assumption that the voters will vote for the lesser of two evils. They will engage in strategic voting, not casting a ballot for a third candidate they may prefer if it will help their least-favorite candidate win. That is the reason why politicians should, according to the model, move toward the center and take the voters on their end of the spectrum largely for granted.

Voters can be compelled to choose the lesser of evils in other cases as well, however. The situation in the late 1990s in Turkey illustrated this point. The voters supported Islamic party candidates for the mayor of Istanbul and for the national legislature. The military forced the arrest of the mayor and dismissal of the Islamic premier chosen by the parliament. A new election was called, and the percentage of votes cast for the Islamic candidates fell sharply. Surely many voters believed that the military would again intervene against victorious Islamic candidates, and hence they chose the candidate they considered best among those that the military would accept.

Turkey is not the only authoritarian state in which the choices—the electoral space—in a formal democracy are not defined in the way that democratic theory assumes. Political leaders can be paid economic payments to form small parties to attract votes from other opposition parties. Credible presidential candidates can be subject to various inducements or threats not to run. Prospective opposition candidates may find it impossible to gain campaign funds or access to television, especially in a system in which economic and political actors are dependent on government largesse. The importance of the way that the political space can be structured to shape the outcome is crucial to an understanding of Boris Yeltsin's Russia. That in turn makes the Russian political system in the 1990s an important case study for theorists of democracy.

The 1993 Constitution and Election Law

Boris Yeltsin faced an unusual problem in the fall of 1993. He had abolished the legislature and the constitution that established it. Normally he should have presented his new constitution for approval at a referendum and then held elections for the institutions established by the constitution. Unfortunately, the constitution was controversial, and an election campaign that allowed opponents to focus on its defects might have led to its rejection or to a voter turnout lower than the 50 percent required.

If, however, the election for the legislature were held at the same time as the referendum on the constitution, this would tend both to increase voter turnout and to distract attention from the debate on the constitution. Unfortunately, Yeltsin's abolition of the Congress and the Supreme Soviet meant that there was no legislature to pass an election law and not even a legislature to which deputies could be elected. Yeltsin solved the problem by holding the election to the posts established by the new constitution that was being submitted to the voters at the same time. He enacted the election law himself by decree. This strategy had the further advantage of giving politicians an incentive to approve the constitution so that they would not be elected to a legislature that did not exist.

The legislature was bicameral and was given the name of the French legislature, "the National Assembly." One house was elected by the population and one by the regions—the eighty-nine "subjects of the federation." The house based on population was called the Duma and contained 450 deputies.[2] The body representing the country's eighty-nine regions was called the Federation Council (*Sovet Federatsii*) and had 178 members, two from each region.

"Duma," the name of the weak legislature established by Nikolai II after the Revolution of 1905, was used for the lower house in order to suggest the old relationship between tsar and legislature. Indeed, the first chairman of the Duma, Ivan Rybkin, titled his book "The Fifth Duma" to emphasize continuity with the prerevolutionary institution, and Yeltsin was heard to call himself "tsar Boris."[3]

The Federation Council reflected Yeltsin's desire for an upper house of the legislature that, like the U.S. Senate in the nineteenth century, was not directly elected. While the American state legislatures in the nineteenth century elected full-time senators, Yeltsin wanted the regional governors and the chairmen of the regional legislatures to serve simultaneously as part-time senators. This intention was reflected in the language of the constitution, which spoke of the "selection," not "election," of "members," not "deputies," of the Federation Council.[4]

The constitution established a complex division of powers and responsibilities between the State Duma and the Federation Council. The Federation Council had sole power to confirm members of the Constitutional Court (the Supreme Court, in American terms) and the Prosecutor General (the American attorney general, but much more powerful). The Federation Council alone had to give consent to presidential decrees about martial law or the use of Russian troops outside the boundaries of Russia. It voted on impeachment, and it called new presidential elections in case of the death or disability of the president.

Only the State Duma had the power to confirm the chairman of the government (the premier) and to cast a no-confidence vote. The Duma was also the only body that could pass laws. The Federation Council had the right to approve Duma laws, but if the Duma refused to revise the law in an acceptable manner, it could also overrule the Federation Council veto with a two-thirds vote. Because of the Duma's ability to override a Federation Council veto and its sole authority to confirm the premier or declare no confidence in him, Russian constitutional lawyers could describe the Russian National Assembly as a legislature with a relatively weak upper house.[5]

In reality, of course, Yeltsin had little theoretical interest in the relative strength of the upper and lower houses of parliament or even in the abstract power of the presidency. He was concerned only with a constitution that strengthened the power of Boris Yeltsin and made his position secure. From this perspective, the key fact in executive-legislative relations in the 1990s was the complete central control of regional finances and the personalized nature of the distribution of subsidies. This made the governor and chairman of the regional legislature totally dependent on the president. Yeltsin tolerated a fair amount of regional autonomy on policy questions and did not probe into regional corruption, but he was very insistent on loyalty on questions concerning his own power.

Several provisions of the constitution were crucial for Yeltsin. First, of course, he was eager for key questions such as the decisions on impeachment, martial law, declaration of presidential disability, and confirmation of the chairman of the Constitutional Court to be in the hands of the Federation Council. Second, he did not care whether the Duma could override a Federation Council veto. The crucial provision was that a presidential veto could be overridden only with the concurrence of both houses. Third, the president had extraordinary power to issue decrees on a wide range of subjects. These decrees could be overridden by the legislature, but only by the Duma and Federation Council acting in concert. The latter two provisions meant that, as long as the Federation Council remained loyal, Yeltsin had nearly total control over the Duma.

The law enacted for the Duma elections was a variant of the German election law combining party-list proportional representation with district elections. Half the Duma deputies were to be chosen in a party-list election and distributed by proportional representation among parties that received at least 5 percent of the vote. The other half were elected in districts with more or less equal numbers of voters.[6] Unlike the German system, deputies elected in the districts were added to those elected by party list, not subtracted.

Party-list proportional representation requires voters to choose between parties and, therefore, by definition, it requires parties to be formed. Seats are distributed to those at the top of the party lists in proportion to the votes they received. This should allow major Moscow politicians membership in the Duma without winning a regional election. The district elections, by contrast, would permit regional leaders to be elected, regardless of the place they were given on the party list by Moscow leaders.

The election law was crafted to link the party-list and district elections and to give politicians the incentive to create broad parties. Parties that received less than 5 percent of the votes in the party-list election were denied seats in the Duma in order to ensure that politicians would cooperate in elections. In fact, many top Moscow politicians were not elected in 1995 precisely because they insisted on forming individual parties that did not achieve the 5 percent minimum.

Those on the party lists could simultaneously run in the districts and receive the district mandate if they won in the district. The next lowest person on the party list was moved up and declared elected. This created a powerful incentive for a party to nominate all its strong candidates both on its list and in the districts and also to establish regional organizations to support its district candidates.

The runoff was abolished in the district elections as a further incentive for parties to amalgamate. Runoffs allow a large number of candidates or parties to run in the first round; the various losers can consolidate behind candidates closest to themselves in the runoff. In elections without a runoff, parties with similar views that do not join together before the election split the vote in their part of the political spectrum and may give the opposition an unearned victory. As a result, Russian politicians not only had an incentive to join together at the national level to reach the 5 percent minimum but even to move toward a two-party system that would allow them to win at the district level as well.

Public Opinion and the 1993 Duma Election

In actuality, the Russian election law did not work as its academic drafters intended. Thirteen parties won places on the party list ballot in 1993; none of these was like the broad-based centrist parties found in the West. There was little connection between the party-list election and the district elections.

In 1993 the most prominent party was Russia's Choice. Its list was headed by First Deputy Premier Yegor Gaidar and contained a number of government officials associated with him. Its leaders were convinced that they could win a parliamentary majority and an unambiguous mandate for an explicit shock therapy program. Gaidar raised the price of bread four times on the eve of the election, held up the wages of workers, peasants, and soldiers, and promised even greater pain after the election.

A number of other rapid reform parties on the ballot claimed to be centrist, but, in fact, had platforms as radical as Russia's Choice on economic reform. Indeed, one of these parties, PRES (Party of Russian Unity and Concord), had two of Yeltsin's most radical deputy premiers among its leaders, while another, Yabloko, was headed by the radical drafter of the 500-day plan, Grigory Yavlinsky.[7]

On the other side of the political spectrum were three conservative parties, each with its own peculiarities. The Communist party of the Russian Federation, headed by Gennady Zyuganov, was a genuine party, but it was largely unconnected with either the Russian Communist party formed in 1990 or the Communists of Russia faction of the Russian Congress. Only two of the eighteen members of the Communist Polit- buro of the Russian Republic elected in September 1990 were on its list, and one of them was Zyuganov himself.[8] Several weeks before the elec- tion, 39 percent of the population said that they had never heard of the Communist party, and another 13 percent had no opinion about it. As bizarre as it seems that Russians could claim not to have heard of the Communist party, most voters, in fact, had no idea how to distinguish between the Communist Party of the Russian Federation and the other four Communist parties.

The other two conservative parties actually seemed like government parties. The Agrarian party had a program little different from that of the Communists, but the person occupying the number-three spot on its party list was the deputy premier in charge of agriculture, and numbers five through seven were the chairman of the State Agricultural-Industrial Committee, the first deputy minister of agriculture, and the chairman of the State Committee of the Food Processing Industry.[9] The Liberal Demo- cratic party of Vladimir Zhirinovsky had a fascist program, but Zhiri- novsky in his early career had held a series of minor jobs almost always reserved for KGB agents. Rumors swirled that the KGB or the govern- ment was providing him with money and television time in order to take votes from the Communists. When the Liberal Democrats proved to be one of the strongest supporters of the Chernomyrdin government on key votes over the next five years, these rumors took on great credibility.

The most interesting parties were those that did not form. Not a sin- gle person with significant administrative experience before 1991 formed or headed a party. Russia's Choice, which expected to obtain a percentage of votes similar to that of the American Republican party or the British Conservative party, did not form an alliance with big busi- ness, which is always at the core of a broad conservative party, but rather denounced it as "the nomenklatura." It rejected any of the sym- bolic issues of a conservative party, even patriotism.[10] Most of the cen- trist parties formed were unknown to voters, and only Women of Russia and the Democratic Party of Russia broke the 5-percent threshold. Again, like the Agrarian party, both had close ties to the executive.[11]

On the eve of the 1993 election, leading Russian sociologists and radicals assumed that the radical parties would receive a majority or near majority of the vote and thus receive a mandate to carry out radical economic reform. They read the support given Yeltsin's socioeconomic policy in the April 1993 referendum as support for Yegor Gaidar's socioeconomic policy, not for Yeltsin's policy of off-budget subsidization.[12] Instead, Gaidar's party received only 15 percent of the vote and the other right-wing parties another 19 percent.

It is most unclear why anything else was expected. As seen in chapter 5, Yeltsin's approval ratings fell from the temporary 43 percent positive and 43 percent negative level of May 1993 to 32 percent positive and 56 percent negative in September, slightly more negative than in January 1993. Our December 1993 survey found a very similar result—36 percent approval and 53 percent disapproval.

The reasons for the doubts about Yeltsin and his policy could be found in any statistical handbook. By December 1993 Russia was in a major depression that Yegor Gaidar and Boris Yeltsin had said in October 1991 would not occur. Precise measurement of the economic decline may be difficult, but precision was not really necessary. Economic conditions had become quite difficult for large numbers of people, especially outside of Moscow and St. Petersburg. In our survey only 3 percent of the respondents said that the economic and financial situation of their family had improved a lot in the previous year, and 13 percent said that it had improved a little. Another 24 percent said that it remained unchanged, but 23 percent said that it had worsened a little and 34 percent that it had worsened a lot.

The fact that the population as a whole was quite unhappy with the course of economic reform and the breakup of the Soviet Union did not mean that the majority rejected economic reform altogether. The majority of the Russian electorate wanted gradual reform, not the rapid reform advocated by Yegor Gaidar or a total rejection of the market. On specific questions of economic reform, they repeatedly took a middle option— regulated foreign investment and regulated sale of land instead of free investment and free sale, price controls rather than the setting of prices.

Our surveys showed a decline in support for radical economic reform from 1993 to 1996, but a rise in support for gradual reform rather than in opposition to reform. A leading public opinion firm, VTsIOM (All-

Table 6-1. Attitude toward Transition to the Market, 1990–96
Percent[a]

Date of poll	Type of transition favored			
	Rapid	Gradual	Oppose transition	Don't know
Mid-1990	19	40	15	24
End 1991	30	40	14	16
End 1992	18	49	13	20
Mid-1993	16	46	13	25
December 1993	14	44	18	24
December 1995	7	45	23	26
June 1996	7	53	17	24

Source: Mid-1990 through mid-1993: Matthew Wyman, "Figure 7.1: Support for Transition to a Market Economy, 1990–93," Public Opinion in Postcommunist Russia (St. Martin's, 1997), p. 176; December 1993 through June 1996: author's surveys (see preface for an explanation of the polling).
a. Percentages may not total 100 as a result of rounding.

Russia Institute of Public Opinion), began polling before 1993 and used a question virtually identical to ours; table 6-1 includes the results of its early surveys with our own. VTsIOM's results often exaggerated the support for strong reform,[13] but even its figures showed a bell-shaped curve with most respondents in the center.

As table 6-2 shows, more specific questions elicited answers reflecting a more sophisticated pattern of Russian attitudes toward economic reform. Housing privatization was widely supported, but there was great reluctance to discard the collective farm system. Russians of all ages and places, even young people from Moscow and St. Petersburg, strongly supported tariffs against both industrial and agricultural imports, but also were quite supportive of foreign investment as long as it was controlled by the state.

The campaign posture of the politicians in 1993 and 1995 demonstrated that the vast majority saw public opinion in similar terms. Most claimed that they were centrist, including politicians who clearly were not. They obviously thought that this claim was the correct electoral strategy. Similarly, during both the April 1993 referendum and the 1996 presidential election, Yeltsin moved strongly to the center, promising subsidies to everyone and pledging to change policy in a moderate direction. The question is why the political parties did not do this as well.

The 1995 Duma Election

There is an easy answer to any anomaly in the 1993 Duma election. Politicians had only two months to organize parties and nominate can-

Table 6-2. *Attitudes toward Different Types of Privatization, 1993*
Percent[a]

Response	Types of property		
	Big enterprises	Trade	Housing
Completely support	17.5	22.0	40.9
Support somewhat	20.8	21.6	22.7
Oppose somewhat	14.4	13.5	12.2
Completely oppose	21.7	26.0	9.4
Don't know	25.7	17.0	14.8
Attitude toward private farming			
Private farms should quickly replace collective and state farms			8.8
Private farms should gradually replace collective and state farms			14.1
Private farms should coexist with collective and state farms			58.0
Private farms should be banned or strictly restricted			9.1
Don't know			10.0
Attitude toward the free sale and purchase of land by individuals			
Favor without restrictions			14.4
Favor with restrictions			36.3
Do not support			39.4
Don't know			9.9
Attitude toward foreign investment in Russia			
Completely support			13.0
Support, but under strict state control			42.5
Useful, but on the whole does more harm than good			12.0
Completely oppose			17.5
Don't know			15.0

Source: Author's surveys (see preface).

a. Percentages may not total 100 as a result of rounding.

didates and then only one month to campaign. However, politicians had two years to prepare for the 1995 election, and when the Duma convened in January 1994, its leaders were determined to strengthen the party system. Those parties that elected deputies from their party lists were officially recognized as factions—groupings within the legislature that controlled committee assignments and the ordering of speakers during session. Deputies who had been elected as independents could either become members of these factions or form new factions if they could persuade thirty-five deputies to join.[14] Powerful incentives were created for deputies to become members of factions. The leaders of the old Supreme Soviet had been the committee chairmen, but the executive committee of the Duma was deliberately composed of the faction leaders, and the faction leaders had a key role in choosing the committee chairmen.

The economic situation certainly should have stimulated party formation. Russian statistics on gross domestic product are dependent on dubious reporting from below, the impossibility of measuring a subsistence service sector,[15] major distortions by high-priced foreign currency items and an inappropriate exchange rate, prices that are distorted by subsidies and nonpayment "barter," and outright central manipulation. Officially experts of the State Statistical Agency raise the reported statistics by an unreported amount to compensate for unreported goods and services, and then the IMF adjusts them upward again on the dubious assumption that the Russian experts for some reason make underestimations. In measuring trends over time, the huge second (service) economy of the Soviet period is totally ignored. However, the statistics on industrial, agricultural, food, and medical production in table 2-2 show clearly why the opposition should have coalesced to be effective.

Nevertheless, forty-three parties qualified for the ballot in 1995, again none of them the typical broad-based centrist party of the West. Once more the connection between the party list and the district elections was minimal. Many political scientists suggest that durable parties tend to arise out of the legislature. However, not a single new faction in the 1993 Duma became the base for a new party in the 1995 election.

The turnover of the deputies between the 1993 and 1995 dumas was almost as high as that between the 1990 Congress and the Duma elected in 1993. In part, this resulted from the failure of some old parties to receive 5 percent of the vote, but the successful parties also had placed relatively few members of the Duma at the top of their list, especially if the Liberal Democrats are excluded (see table 6-3).

Whatever the base of new parties in 1995, there seemed to be extremely strong incentives for at least two broad political parties to

Table 6-3. *Turnover of Party List Deputies, Second Duma (1995), Compared with the First Duma (1993)*

Party or faction	Elected in 1995	1995 deputies elected to Duma in 1993	1995 deputies elected to partial terms in Duma, 1993–95
Communist party	99	16	3
Liberal Democratic party	50	26	0
Our Home Is Russia	45	4	0
Yabloko	31	13	2

Source: Ivan Rybkin, *Piataia rossisskaia gosudarstvennaia duma* (Fifth Russian state duma) (Moscow: Izdanie gosudarstvenoi dumy, 1995); *Rossiiskaia gazeta*, January 6, 1996.

Table 6-4. *Answers to Selected Questions, 1993 and 1995*
Percent[a]

	1993	1995
"Do you approve of B. N. Yeltsin's activity as president of Russia?"		
Completely approve	11.0	3.0
Generally approve	25.1	12.8
Generally disapprove	26.5	28.9
Completely disapprove	26.8	44.1
Don't know	10.6	11.2
"What do you think of the transition to a market economy in Russia?"		
Should be rapid	13.8	6.5
Should be gradual	44.0	44.9
Should be no reform	18.1	22.6
Don't know	24.2	26.0
"Do you support the privatization of big enterprises?"		
Absolutely yes	17.5	6.3
Probably yes	20.8	14.0
Probably no	14.4	18.1
Absolutely no	21.7	35.2
Don't know	25.7	26.4
"Is the West pursuing the goal of weakening Russia with its economic advice?"		
Absolutely yes	28.1	35.6
Probably yes	24.2	23.7
Probably no	14.4	13.6
Absolutely no	11.2	6.9
Don't know	22.1	20.2
"Should the government of Russia reduce its expenditures on defense?"		
Reduce quickly	8.0	5.0
Reduce gradually	23.5	16.7
Maintain level	34.1	30.4
Increase	20.1	31.7
Don't know	14.3	16.2

Source: Author's surveys (see preface).

a. Percentages may not total 100 as a result of rounding.

form, both to the left of Gaidar's Russia Choice and the existing government of Viktor Chernomyrdin. The economy had continued to decline, and by December 1995 the population had become disillusioned about the voucher program and the nationalization of large enterprises. As table 6-4 illustrates, all these developments were reflected in an evolution of public attitudes in a conservative direction on a variety of questions.

In the 1995 Duma election, half of the forty-three parties were virtually unknown, and hence the election results are difficult to classify precisely. Yeltsin's supporters tried to paint the results as favorably as possi-

Table 6-5. Votes for Parties of Different Ideological Persuasion, 1993 and 1995

Parties	Percentages		Total votes	
	1993	1995	1993	1995
Left-wing[a]	20.4	35.5	10,958,920	22,296,000
"Nationalists"[b]	22.9	18.3	12,318,562	14,210,000
Right-wing (Reform)[c]	34.2	24.5	18,374,104	16,601,000
Centrist	16.3	14.5	8,784,433	9,860,000
Miscellaneous	1.9	4.4	1,047,714	2,999,000
Against all	4.2	2.8	2,267,973	1,918,000
Total	99.9[d]	100.0	53,751,696	67,994,200

Source: Biulleten' tsentral'noi izbiratel'noi komissii rossiiskoi federatsii (Bulletin of the central election committee of the Russian federation), no. 1, 1994, pp. 38, 67; "Dannye protokolov no. 2" (Protocol figures no. 2), Rossiiskaia gazeta, January 24, 1996 (special edition), p. 2.

a. "Left-wing" included the Communist and Agrarian parties in 1993 and, in addition, the parties of Viktor Anpilov, Aleksandr Rutskoi, and Nikolai Ryzhkov in 1995.

b. "Nationalists" included the Liberal Democrats in 1993 and, in addition, the parties of Aleksandr Lebed, Stanislav Govorukhin, My Fatherland, For the Motherland, and the National-Republican party in 1995.

c. The "right-wing" parties include Russia's Choice (renamed Russia's Democratic Choice in 1995), Yabloko, PRES, and RDDR in 1993 and, in addition, Our Home Is Russia, Boris Fedorov's Forward Russia, Common Cause, Party of Economic Freedom, and the Christian Democrats in 1995.

d. Percentages may not total 100 as a result of rounding.

ble by listing some parties as "democratic" or "reform" that presented themselves as left-wing. They also listed the seemingly frivolous Beer-Lovers party as "democratic" or "reform," likely a sign that it was a Yeltsin-sponsored party. Yet the "centrist" category in table 6-5 is over-stated by some 4 percentage points at most. The pattern of votes in table 6-5 makes it absolutely clear that the voters were ready to vote for a change in policy.

The most obvious point about table 6-5 is that the left-wing parties received a much higher percentage of the vote in 1995 than in 1993. The right-wing and centrist parties together won 50.5 percent in 1993 and 39.0 percent in 1995. The change in the percentage of party vote is, however, not the statistic of note. In 1993 only 53.8 million valid votes were cast in the party list election.[16] In 1995, by contrast, the number of valid ballots rose to 68.0 million—an increase of 26 percent.[17] As a consequence, a larger number of actual votes lay behind each percentage point of support received by each party in 1995. Thus it masks the size of the gain of the Communists simply to say that they increased their proportion of the valid vote from 12.4 percent to 22.4 percent. It is more relevant to say that support for the Communists went from 6.7 to 14.4 million votes and the support for the left oppositional parties from 11.0 to 22.3 million.

Even these figures minimize the swing toward the center and the left. The "government party" in 1995 was Our Home Is Russia, which was headed by Premier Viktor Chernomyrdin. It promised to continue the privatization, tight money, and free trade that had caused such discontent in the past. Yet it distanced itself from the radicals and portrayed itself as a center-right party—the party of stability, order, and continuity.

In 1993 Gaidar's Russia's Choice was unquestionably radical, while PRES was headed by two very radical deputy premiers in the government. Russia's Choice and PRES combined received 22.2 percent of the vote in 1993, but only 4.3 percent in 1995. If Yabloko and Our Home Is Russia are considered only semiradical in 1995, the four remaining radical parties on the 1995 ballot received a total of only 7.9 percent of the vote.

Since only four parties reached the 5-percent minimum required for seats in the Duma, each party with the minimum received twice the percentage of seats that they received in votes in the party-list election. Once the district seats were included, opposition deputies had more than 60 percent of the Duma seats if Zhirinovsky's Liberal Democrats are counted as an opposition party. But since the Liberal Democrats were really a government party and voted as such on key issues, the Duma was much more evenly divided than seemed on the surface.

The Reasons Meaningful Parties Did Not Form

The timing of the 1993 election was abnormal. Normally the Duma elections were to be held every four years, six months before the presidential election. The purpose of this timing was to allow the Duma election to be a sounding board for issues and candidates for the forthcoming presidential election. The 1995 election was, therefore, an important trial run for the more significant election in June 1996. Since few analysts in late 1995 thought that Yeltsin would be a viable candidate in 1996, prospective presidential candidates had every reason to begin organizing in 1995 to position themselves for 1996.

From this perspective, the crucial fact about the 1995 election was not the forty-three parties on the ballot but, except for the Communists, the absence of the kind of large party that would provide a platform for a strong presidential candidate in 1996. Even the Communists did not move to the center as convincingly as their counterparts in eastern Europe. Although the evolution in public opinion and in voting behavior showed the potential for a major political breakthrough, no major politicians tried to form a credible centrist party. Almost all the governors avoided any formal involvement with parties.

The situation was little better in 1999. The ballot did contain twenty-eight parties, but the population gave sixteen of them less than 1 percent of the vote and another four less than 2.5 percent of the vote. Only 3.3 percent of the votes were cast against all parties. A serious right-center party was created by Moscow mayor Yury Luzhkov, St. Petersburg mayor Vladimir A. Yakovlev, and former premier Yevgeny Primakov, but the state media directed devastating fire against it and it only received 13.3 percent. A new party linked with new premier Vladimir Putin received the most votes among the non-Communists (23.3 percent), but it had absolutely no program other than support for a war in Chechnya that clearly was launched for electoral purposes alone.[18]

The district election choices were less focused. Each district had 9.9 candidates, the average winner received 33.6 percent of the vote, and 11.5 percent of the voters cast a ballot against all candidates. These figures included a number of fairly noncompetitive elections in ethnic districts. The situation in the areas that should be more democratic was truly discouraging. The districts in Moscow, St. Petersburg, and the region (oblast) surrounding each averaged 12.1 candidates. In the average district, the winner received 26.4 percent of the vote, while 15.2 percent of the votes were cast against all candidates. The figures were little better in the other districts centering on the regional capitals: 11.5 candidates, with the winner receiving 29.4 percent and 12.4 percent being cast against all.[19] All in all, only 33 percent of the deputies elected in 1995 were reelected in 1999.

At one level, the failure of meaningful parties to develop in Russia from 1989 through 1999 is not unprecedented. The United States had no serious national protoparties until the mid-1790s, a dozen years after the end of the Revolutionary War. Its real mass parties were not created until fifty years after the Revolution. In Africa, the same scholars who thirty years earlier stated that "political parties are the most crucial political structures shaping the new African polities," now hardly include the word party in their index. They write about "personal politics" in which "politicians [are] operating largely without the aid of effective institutions and in a manner that discredits the institutions that exist."[20]

Many early national leaders are like Boris Yeltsin in being suspicious of political parties. Richard Hofstadter asserted in his classic study of party formation in the United States that early American leaders held "the root idea . . . that parties are evil."[21] Alexis de Tocqueville in the 1830s likewise wrote that "parties are an evil inherent in free governments."[22] When parties do arise in early democracy, they always tend to be very personalistic.[23]

There are, however, more basic reasons that politicians and parties do not respond to the political incentive system in expected ways in the early stages of democracy. The great economist Joseph Schumpeter was one of the first to insist without qualification that politicians are not people seeking to enact programs, but rational actors trying to get elected by taking whatever actions would maximize their votes. He did not model the implications of this insight in various institutional situations, but he was aware that in many situations, politicians do not behave in the expected way.

> If a physicist observes that the same mechanism works differently at different times and in different places, he concludes that its functioning depends on conditions extraneous to it. We cannot but arrive at the same conclusion. And it is as easy to see what these conditions are as it was to see what the conditions were under which the classical doctrine of democracy might be expected to fit reality to an acceptable degree. . . . Democracy thrives in social patterns that display certain characteristics and it might well be doubted whether there is any sense in asking how it would fare in others that lack those characteristics.[24]

Some of the factors that Schumpeter emphasized were subsumed under the term "political culture" by later political scientists. The first of his preconditions was that "the human material of politics . . . should be of sufficiently high quality. . . . [There must be] a social stratum, itself a product of a severely selective process, that takes to politics as a matter of course."[25]

The second condition was that "the effective range of political decision should not be extended too far." This involves "Democratic Self-Control," his fourth condition.

> Electorates and parliaments must be on an intellectual and moral level high enough to be proof against the offerings of the crook and the crank. . . . The voters outside of parliament must respect the division of labor between themselves and the politicians they

elect. . . . They must understand that, once they have elected an individual, political action is his business and not theirs.[26]

Although an economist, Schumpeter had an understanding, seldom found in modern economists, of the importance of "appropriate institutional devices." He saw that being a successful politician, like being a successful corporation president, requires a learning experience, a stable institutional framework in which to learn the rules of the game, and an administrative structure that is a repository of professional expertise but that also creates the confidence that it is worthwhile to think seriously about policy because policies will be carried out. The stratum of professional politicians must arise through "a severely selective process." There must be "a well-trained bureaucracy of good standing and tradition, endowed with a strong sense of duty and a no less strong *esprit de corps*. . . . It must also be strong enough to guide and, if need be, to instruct the politicians who head the ministries."[27]

In today's United States, for example, college graduates who want to go into politics must work within a well-defined system of institutions, rules, and incentives, and they must follow one of several well-defined paths. By contrast, no firm organizations exist at the early stage of democratization within which ambitious young politicians may try to work their way upward. Few rules exist to restrain them, and the incentive system leads them to "maximize profit," either by seeking to get quickly to the top or by using politics for maximum financial gain. Small wonder that the first parties tend to be very personalistic and ephemeral.

Many of the major political scientists of the past half century shared Schumpeter's belief that democracy must rest on a strong institutional base. The French political scientist Maurice Duverger emphasized that the bases of effective mass parties were large societal institutions— churches, trade unions, business and agrarian interest groups, and urban political machines. They became part of the coalition on which broad-based political parties were formed, and they were the mobilizing and fund-giving institutions that permitted such parties to function. "There must be a fairly large number of cases of political parties created by groups of intellectuals," Duverger said. "It is, however, very rare for such a party to enlist sufficient popular support for it to be successful in countries with universal suffrage."[28]

V. O. Key, commonly considered the top American political scientist of the postwar period, saw interest group representatives as members of a common "leadership echelon." He even surmised that "the pluralistic interactions among leadership echelons may occur, and may be tolerable, precisely because leadership clusters can command only a relatively small following among the masses."[29]

The same point was made indirectly by the highly influential literature of the 1980s on the transition to democracy. Based largely on the experience of southern Europe and Latin America of that period, it insisted that the key step toward a stable democracy in these countries was a "pact among elites." The key unspoken assumption was that a pact was not possible until a number of solid elite groups had formed that could make a pact.

Russian democracy had none of these characteristics. The pro-Yeltsin reformers came from the intelligentsia and opposed the members of all other elite groups—big business ("the nomenklatura"), the military, agrarian groups, the police, the Orthodox Church, the "bureaucrats." Westerners attempting to promote democracy also counseled against alliance with these groups on the ground that they were too "conservative." Instead, they encouraged the formation of small groups of intellectuals—"civil society"—that Duverger correctly cautioned are seldom effective in early democracy.[30]

Most important of all, however, democratic theory assumes the absence of an authoritarian ruler, except perhaps as an obstacle to be overthrown. This is a key flaw of modern democratic theory, for early democracy almost always begins with an authoritarian leader or military that has a major impact on the political process. This was true of England in the eighteenth century, of France in much of the nineteenth century, of Germany under Otto Bismarck, and of virtually all third world countries at some point in the postwar period. The rulers of the semiauthoritarian or authoritarian democracies are able to shape election rules, control campaign finances and the media, and affect the incentives of potential candidates in powerful ways.

In this comparative perspective, Yeltsin was a typical authoritarian ruler of early democracy. An excellent analogy to the role of Yeltsin in Russia is found in the role of the king in eighteenth-century Britain. Lewis Namier insisted that the political parties of that time were not like modern parties. Parliament in midcentury was dominated by "the Government party," which "owed its large majority in the House of Commons to the patronage of the Crown." Through the use of appointments, grants, and rewards, the king ensured the loyalty of enough members of parliament to maintain his effective control, and he was greatly aided by the distortions in the electoral system embodied in the phrase "rotten boroughs." Indeed, even the opposition was compelled to rally around the heir apparent who became their patron.[31]

An earlier student of British politics, Moisei Ostrogorski, described the corruption of the eighteenth century in the crassest of terms:

> In the beginning . . . the post [of Patronage Secretary] was created for the corruption of members in the criminal sense of the word. Ministers bought their majority by payment of actual cash; they had a window in the House itself where members came to be paid for their votes after the division. The First Lord of the Treasury, having too much to do, created, in 1714, the office of political secretary to the Treasury to aid him in these financial operations.[32]

The fact that Yeltsin had overwhelming power in relation to the Duma did not mean, however, that he had no interest in the elections to the Duma, especially the 1995 election. It did mean, however, that his attention was more focused on the implications of the Duma elections for the presidential election. Yeltsin was delighted to have the opportunity to learn about the popular response to issues, but he did not want a strong rival to be legitimated by success in the Duma election.

After his election as president in 1991, Yeltsin strove mightily and successfully to break down the emerging party system and to maintain the Manichean good-and-evil imagery of the election of 1990. The "party system" that Yeltsin emphasized was based on a single criterion: were they for or against the augmentation of presidential power? Those who were in favor of increasing Yeltsin's power were called democrats or reformers, and those who were opposed were called communists. When the majority of the Congress swung into opposition to the president, Yeltsin's men denied the democratic character of the 1990 election, despite all the evidence to the contrary. Indeed, the Congress had originally elected Yeltsin chairman and even gave him the two-thirds vote necessary to create an elected presidency.

In 1999 a communist newspaper claimed that the preparation for the forthcoming 1999 Duma election was marked by active intervention of Yeltsin forces, bribing candidates to form and not form parties depending on Yeltsin's interest.[33] It would not be surprising if we were to discover in the future that Yeltsin and his presidential staff had a similar role in party formation in the 1993 and 1995 elections. Yeltsin's first priority in 1993 was to create parties that would support the constitution and be loyal to him. The presence of so many top officials loyal to him at the top of almost all party lists achieved this goal, as did Zhirinovsky's support of the constitution.

Yeltsin's first priority in 1995 was to ensure that no credible alternative to himself emerged on the right and central part of the spectrum on the eve of the 1996 presidential election. The formation of a strong centrist party would have been a great danger, as would have been a strong performance by Viktor Chernomyrdin, Aleksandr Lebed, or Grigory Yavlinsky. The multiplicity of parties lessened the chance that any one party would do well, and, at a minimum, Yeltsin and his men did not discourage this development. It is very probable that they encouraged it, providing financial inducements or promises of jobs.

Yeltsin's second priority in 1993 and 1995 was to give dissatisfied voters many alternatives to voting Communist. Once a doubtful voter crossed the line and voted Communist in a legislative election, it would be easier for him or her to vote Communist in the presidential election. Once a voter found a reason to reject the Communists in the legislative election, perhaps he or she would remember those reasons in the presidential election. The large number of parties and the support for the Liberal Democrats served Yeltsin's purpose.

Yeltsin and the Presidential Election

Boris Yeltsin was not on the ballot in the 1993 and 1995 Duma elections, and he deliberately refused to associate himself with any party. In part this simply reflected his long-time desire to stand above all parties as the personal representative of the whole people. In addition, both Russia's Choice in 1993 and Our Home Is Russia in 1995 had a program and a style far removed from the populism that Yeltsin always embraced at election time. He must have been horrified or amused about their strategy and must have seen the results as confirmation of the wisdom of his own approach.

At the end of 1995 almost everyone took for granted that Yeltsin would not survive until the presidential election, would not be healthy enough to run, or would choose not to run out of fear of defeat. In the summer of 1994, his health deteriorated seriously, and he began disappearing for long periods of time. A stroke cut short his visit to China, and then, in September 1994, he was too comatose to get off the air-

Table 6-6. *Evaluation of Boris Yeltsin and the Communist Party,*
December 1993 and December 1995[a]

	1993	1995
"Do you approve of B. N. Yeltsin's activity as the president of Russia?"		
Completely approve	11.0	3.0
Generally approve	25.1	12.8
Generally disapprove	26.5	28.9
Completely disapprove	26.8	44.1
Don't know	10.6	11.2
"How do you evaluate the Communist Party of Russia?"		
Have not heard of party	38.7	10.7
Completely positive	11.1	22.4
Generally positive	7.8	12.0
Generally negative	7.0	10.1
Completely negative	23.0	26.5
Don't know	13.0	18.4

Source: Author's surveys (see preface).
a. Percentages may not total 100 as a result of rounding.

plane at Shannon Airport to greet the Irish prime minister.[34] In both
cases it was considered less damaging to tell reporters that he was
drunk than to report the serious health problem involved.[35] Yeltsin had
a serious heart attack in June 1995 and another in October. He was
totally out of public view from late October 1995 until the end of
December. As late as February 1996, Anders Aslund, one of the
strongest supporters of radical economic reform over the years, wrote
an op-ed in the *New York Times* entitled "Almost Anyone Is Better than
Yeltsin."[36]

Because of doubts about his health or his record or both, the public
had an extremely negative attitude toward Yeltsin. The deterioration in
his ratings from December 1993 to December 1995 found in our surveys is shown in table 6-6. However other polling agencies phrased the
question, they all found similar results.

The opposition figure who consistently received the greatest support
in the polls was Gennady Zyuganov of the Communist party. The Communist party was evaluated negatively, but its negative ratings were not
nearly as high as Yeltsin's. Not only had it received twice as many votes
as any other party in 1995 (and more than twice as many as it had
received in 1993), but also its positive ratings had increased.

The data from our 1995 survey showed clearly that some 30 to 35
percent of the likely voters would vote relatively happily for Zyuganov

in a runoff with Yeltsin, and some 25 to 30 percent for Yeltsin. Most of the rest were negative toward both: nearly 70 percent of those who were negative toward the Communists in our 1995 survey or who were undecided about them were also negative toward Yeltsin. A third of those whom Zyuganov needed to pick up between the first and second rounds expressed an intention to vote for Zhirinovsky in 1995.

The same conclusion emerges from analysis of the policy views of those who had a negative, more negative than positive, or undecided attitude toward the Communists. Many in this group had an entirely negative opinion of privatization of large enterprises or of the sale of land, even if regulated. Zyuganov needed to win only one-half of this group alone to defeat Yeltsin.

Nevertheless, Yeltsin won the election handily. Excluding those who chose the odd option "against all" on the Russian ballot, Yeltsin defeated Zyuganov by a 36.4 percent to 33.0 percent margin in the first round and by a 57.2 percent to 42.8 percent margin in the runoff. Yeltsin won even though he suffered his third major heart attack in a year immediately after the first round of the election and totally disappeared from view in the last two weeks before the runoff.

Yeltsin's victory in 1996 was his greatest achievement after the breakup of the Soviet Union. Our 1996 survey predicted the results of the two election rounds almost perfectly if likely nonvoters are excluded.[37] Nevertheless, only 24 percent of the likely voters in the survey thought that Russia was on the correct course, while 51 percent thought it was on an incorrect course. Public opinion on specific questions of economic reform and nationality policy remained virtually unchanged from the end of 1995 and was much closer to the Communist party's position than to Yeltsin's.[38]

In the wake of the election, Yeltsin's supporters described him as more ineffectual during the campaign than did his opponents. Each group of supporters claimed to have produced victory despite Yeltsin and his other advisers. Nevertheless, the basic campaign strategy surely was Yeltsin's. Yeltsin was by far the greatest Russian politician of the post-Brezhnev period. His ability to appeal to Russian public opinion was always flawless, and he never erred in his judgment of his political opponents. The themes of his 1996 campaign followed those of earlier campaigns and included key elements that each of his chief advising groups strongly opposed. The notion that Yeltsin conducted his 1996 campaign without any sense of what he was doing is contrary to both the evidence and the logic of the campaign. But the question still remains—how did he achieve the victory?

The Possibility of Electoral Fraud

Virtually all countries in the third world have elections. Some are not unlike the old Soviet elections, with nearly 100 percent of the vote cast for the official candidate. In others, the official candidate receives a huge advantage through his or her domination of television and organizational methods. In still other cases, the election may be competitive and even fair in many senses of the word, but the vote count is fraudulent.

Charges of fraud in vote counting have often been made by both sides in Russian elections. Widespread charges were leveled against the government in the 1993 election, with the most credible involving the level of turnout or support for the constitution. But Yeltsin forces also charged that the Communist rural officials overcounted their vote in the countryside in 1995.

Such vote fraud is one obvious potential explanation for Yeltsin's 1996 victory. Michael McFaul has noted the great similarity in the vote for Yeltsin in the four elections in which he was formally or informally on the ballot: the 1991 presidential election, the April 1993 referendum on approval of the president, the December 1993 referendum on the constitution, and the 1996 presidential election (see table 6-7). McFaul attributed the similarity in these votes to the stability in the bipolar distribution of votes, but, of course, there is another hypothesis. Several persons working for the Yeltsin team in 1996 reported anonymously that they had been asked to project how many votes each region should cast for Yeltsin and then had been astonished to see how closely their "quotas" were met. They then were thanked publicly on television for their contribution to the victory.

Without doubt, there were two areas where strong suspicions can be raised. The most obvious problem is the vote reported for Yeltsin and Zyuganov in the central and southern republics of European Russia, most of them with a predominantly Muslim population. In most regions the respective vote for Yeltsin and Zyuganov between the first round and the runoff usually increased in a reasonable way, but in the republics listed in table 6-8, the vote for Zyuganov actually declined between the first and second round in some types of district, especially

Table 6-7. *Support for Yeltsin and Opposition, 1991, 1993, 1996*
Percent

Election	For reform (Yeltsin)	For opposition
June 1991 presidential election	58.6	36.0
April 1993 referendum on trust in Yeltsin	58.7	39.3
December 1993 referendum on constitution	58.4	41.6
July 1996 presidential election	53.8	40.3

Source: Michael McFaul, *Russia's Presidential Election: The End of Polarized Politics* (Stanford, Calif.: Hoover Institution, 1997), p. 8.

in rural areas.[39] In some republics—such as Tatarstan and Dagestan— the difference was spectacular.

The second reason for suspicion is the vote in small towns and rural areas. One of the most consistent results in surveys and voting in Russia since 1989 was the strong correlation between the size of community in which a people live and their attitudes and voting behavior. The results in table 6-9 are representative.

Nevertheless, the actual vote reported for Yeltsin and Zyuganov in electoral districts showed that Yeltsin did surprisingly well in the rural areas and especially the small towns. He lost the districts in which more than half the population lived in rural areas, but only by a 53 percent to 43 percent margin (see table 6-10). In the districts that were at least 75 percent urban, however, the size of the "urban" town or settlement in the district had almost no significant effect on the size of the Yeltsin victory, except in the very largest cities. By all accounts, the small towns were suffering greatly, and in our surveys their inhabitants were very negative about the course of events. The official reports that they voted for Yeltsin by such substantial margins obviously raise questions.

The basic problem with any hypothesis that fraud in vote counting was decisive, however, is the result of public opinion surveys. As indicated earlier, our surveys predicted the votes perfectly if likely nonvoters were excluded, and they overpredicted Yeltsin's victory if likely nonvoters were included. I have worked with my scholarly survey group for five years, and I absolutely do not believe that any sample problem or falsification explains Yeltsin's "victory" in our survey. Other surveys showed a larger Yeltsin victory. Except for isolated cases such as the rural results in the republics of Dagestan and Tatarstan, it is extremely difficult to believe that election fraud accounted for more than a few percentage points of Yeltsin's victory.

Table 6-8. *Percentage of Vote for Yeltsin and Zyuganov in First and Second Rounds of 1996 Election in Selected Republics, by Population of Largest Settlement in Electoral District*

Population of largest settlement	First round		Second round	
	Yeltsin	Zyuganov	Yeltsin	Zyuganov
Bashkortostan				
Under 10,000	35.6	49.8	53.8	43.9
10,000–199,999	30.4	46.5	46.3	49.5
200,000–999,999	28.4	47.4	47.6	47.9
Ufa	42.7	28.5	60.0	35.0
Mordovia				
Under 10,000	25.5	56.5	49.9	48.0
10,000–199,999	24.8	53.1	47.4	50.1
Saransk	24.7	45.3	45.2	49.9
Tatarstan				
Under 10,000	33.1	51.9	68.3	29.6
10,000–199,999	32.3	47.3	63.5	33.1
200,000–999,999	28.1	40.3	51.0	43.4
Kazan	62.3	17.8	68.8	27.0
Kabardino-Balkaria				
Under 10,000	46.1	40.9	65.8	32.9
10,000–199,999	42.4	38.0	65.9	32.3
Nalchik	39.9	39.0	58.9	37.9
Kalmykia				
Under 10,000	61.6	26.5	70.4	27.5
Yelista	45.7	35.8	64.2	33.5
North Osetia				
Under 10,000	13.9	73.8	39.1	59.1
10,000–199,999	14.3	78.8	41.0	58.2
Ordzhonikidze	26.3	52.1	50.0	46.7
Dagestan				
Under 10,000	30.3	65.9	51.4	48.0
10,000–199,999	37.9	54.4	58.9	40.0
Makhachkala	27.9	61.7	60.3	38.3

Source: Jerry F. Hough, "Political Geography of European Russia: Republics and Oblasts," *Post-Soviet Geography and Economics*, vol. 39 (February 1998), pp. 69–72.

Yeltsin's Occupation of the Political Center

Given people's negative views of the economy and Yeltsin's low approval ratings, how then did Yeltsin win? The easiest hypothesis is that the Russian electorate was highly polarized and that the 1993 referendum showed that the majority was on Yeltsin's side. In this view, often

Table 6-9. *Attitudes about Economic Reform, by Size of Settlement in Which Respondent Lived, June 1996*
Percent

Size of settlement	Russia is on correct path		Big enterprises should be privatized		Land should be privatized			Foreign investment should be allowed	
	Yes	No	Yes	No	Yes	Limited	No	Yes	No
Rural	14	58	17	55	11	34	44	42	38
1,000–49,999	22	49	20	56	15	46	32	56	31
50,000–199,999	19	52	22	54	17	39	30	50	33
200,000–999,999	26	44	26	51	15	47	27	61	28
1,000,000+	38	35	31	47	25	45	21	68	20

Source: Jerry F. Hough, "Political Geography of European Russia: Republics and Oblasts," *Post-Soviet Geography and Economics*, vol. 39 (February 1998), pp. 69–72.

expressed in the West, Russians might be quite unhappy, but they saw a clear choice between reform and opposition to reform. Michael McFaul has expressed this thesis clearly:

After flirting early in the campaign with a sub-optimal strategy of acting more like his opponents, Yel'tsin realized that he could win reelection only by first establishing himself as the only leader capable of uniting all of Russia's reformist forces, and then convincing Russian voters that he was the lesser of two evils. . . . When politics are polarized, all ideological differences, class divisions and/or ethnic identities are subsumed by two broad categories: reform or anti-reform, *status quo* or *status quo ante*. . . . Russia's polarized electorate constitutes the one variable that has remained relatively constant throughout that country's recent electoral history. One major issue has divided the country into two camps for the last eight years: those for 'reform,' however defined, and those against.[40]

There are, however, many problems with this interpretation. Public opinion polls did not show that public opinion was polarized, and Yeltsin's strategy in 1996, as in 1993, involved movement to the center, not to the reform side. Obviously by definition, voters who are given a choice between two candidates in a presidential race—Yeltsin and Zyuganov or Bill Clinton and Robert Dole—have to make a choice. When Russians were given this choice in 1996, a majority chose Yeltsin. Nevertheless, this no more demonstrates that Russian public opinion

Table 6-10. *Percentage of Vote for Yeltsin and Zyuganov, by Percentage of Urban Population in Electoral District and Size of District's Largest Town and City, 1996 Presidential Election, Second Round of Voting*

Largest town or city	Percentage Urban							
	Less than 25		25–49		50–74		More than 75	
	Yeltsin	Zyuganov	Yeltsin	Zyuganov	Yeltsin	Zyuganov	Yeltsin	Zyuganov
Rural	42.8	54.0	43.5	52.2	60.5	34.0	54.2	40.2
1,000–9,999	42.8	53.4	41.2	54.8	50.1	45.0	59.1	34.2
10,000–24,999	37.1	59.3	39.4	56.9	46.4	48.8	54.8	39.2
25,000–49,999	...	...	41.6	55.1	47.7	47.9	54.0	40.4
50,000–199,999	...	...	...	...	51.6	43.5	54.8	39.8
200,000–999,999	...	...	...	...	...	...	56.7	37.1
1,000,000–2,000,000	...	...	...	...	...	...	64.5	30.2
St. Petersburg–Moscow	...	...	...	...	...	...	76.9	18.8

Source: The author obtained a computerized database of all the votes by electoral district and added the information on the population of the largest town in the district. The same data, but in percentage terms, are found in *Vybory prezidenta rossiiskoi federatsii 1996: Elektor'naia statistika* (1996 elections for president of the Russian federation: Electoral statistics) (Moscow: Ves mir, 1996), pp. 198–279.

was polarized than the Clinton victory demonstrates the polarization of American opinion.

Once an election has narrowed to two candidates, most voters must choose between the lesser of evils. This fact underlies the famous electoral model of Anthony Downs. Downs insists for this reason that the rational candidate can, except for gestures on symbolic issues, tend to take for granted the voters on his or her part of the political spectrum and move to the center to compete for the median voter. The Downs model does, in fact, correspond fairly substantially to the strategy that Yeltsin followed.

The radicals always called themselves the strongest supporters of Yeltsin's reform, thereby implying that he was a strong supporter of their reforms. After the 1995 election this was an impression that Yeltsin needed to change, and he did so vigorously. In the first months of 1996, he replaced the foreign minister, the first deputy premier, the deputy premier for nationality questions, his chief of staff, and the chairman of the State Committee for Property—all radical academics in 1990. Their replacements were more conservative in one way or another.

Yeltsin's policy seemed to flow in the directions suggested by the new appointments. He pledged an end to the policy of delaying wage payments as a way of controlling money supply, saying the Ministry of the Economy was responsible for the delays. He criticized the dismissed first deputy premier, Anatoly Chubais, for having "sold off our major enterprises for a song." Major privatization was suspended and to some extent reversed, and a policy of higher tariffs was introduced in the face of IMF objection.[41] Yeltsin said, "Those who do not lament the disintegration of the union do not have a heart," and he signed a treaty of union with Belarus and one of economic integration with Kazakhstan, Kyrgyzstan, and Belarus.[42] He took a very nationalistic position in the face of Chechen terrorism in January.

This is the early strategy that McFaul calls suboptimal and incompatible with the goal of uniting the reform group around him. Nevertheless, Yeltsin actually followed this strategy during the first three months of 1996, precisely at the time when he had to—and did—establish himself as the only candidate on the reform side of the spectrum. Moreover, it was a strategy he never abandoned at any point during the campaign after April 1.

The change in early April involved little more than widening the election team to bring in media experts and Yeltsin's most trusted economic patronage lieutenant, Anatoly Chubais, to coordinate fund-raising and distribution. The conservative Oleg Soskovets had been the head of the Yeltsin campaign in early 1996, but on March 23 he was replaced by a broad-based campaign council. Anatoly Chubais, the man with the best connections with the new banks and the international economic institutions, was made responsible for the raising and distribution of campaign funds. The head of Russian State Television was removed for negative reporting, and Igor Malashchenko, the head of the "independent" television network, NTV, was put in charge of the media campaign in what Yeltsin's former aide, Aleksandr Korzhakov, called "the height of cynicism."[43] Not surprisingly, the coverage of the campaign on NTV suddenly became quite pro-Yeltsin.

The liberals took the broadening of the campaign team as a sign that Yeltsin had abandoned his drift to the center and had embraced their reform position. But this interpretation only showed, as Downs would have predicted, that the liberals were grasping for any excuse to support Yeltsin. The council remained broad-based and continued to include all the old conservatives. Moreover, Yeltsin's basic campaign themes did not change.

When Yeltsin made his first campaign trip in early April, it replicated his campaign in the referendum of April 1993. He promised to maintain the *kurs* (course or policy) of reform. The liberals could—and did—interpret this as a continuation of neoliberal reform, while others just as logically could treat it as a pledge to maintain the subsidy policy of the previous four years. Indeed, Yeltsin now promised greater benefits for nearly every conceivable group—higher scholarships for students, payment of back wages for everyone, a rise in the minimum wage, higher pensions.

In early April Yeltsin signed decrees that provided a loan to the pension fund to pay all arrears by the end of the month and to restore savings that had been lost in the inflation of 1992 and 1993.[44] A decree established twenty-five-year interest-free mortgages for private houses. He appealed to young people by promising an expensive all-volunteer army by 2000, and he issued decrees giving soldiers who served in Chechnya preference at health resorts and in admission to military schools.[45] He promised to restore a tax break for failing companies and to give agriculture a special subsidy.[46] Commercial electric rates in the countryside were lowered by 50 percent.[47] The cabinet decided to reverse some of the loans-for-shares privatizing deals by repaying the loans from banks and retaining the shares the government was using as collateral.[48]

But the most striking feature of Yeltsin's performance was his personal promises to individuals wherever he campaigned. A village priest in the south was promised the funds to restore his church.[49] In Yaroslavl Yeltsin promised a Tatar leader $50,000 for a Muslim cultural center, a convent $100,000 to cover costs, and a woman installation of her telephone. All in all, in the words of Alessandra Stanley of the *New York Times*, Yeltsin had added "a new level of pageantry and reckless largesse to his populism."[50]

Yeltsin also never abandoned the nationalist themes of the first three months of the year. The red Soviet flag was restored as one of the country's flags, although a star replaced the hammer and sickle in the corner. At the annual holiday celebrating victory in World War II, Yeltsin spoke from Lenin's Mausoleum and emphasized the new flag as "a living link between the generations."[51] "By, quite literally, again raising high the red banner," Chrystia Freeland wrote, "Mr. Yeltsin has abandoned the effort to forge a new post-communist and post-imperial Russian identity."[52]

In short, as Downs would have predicted, the liberal part of the Russian spectrum accepted the relatively minor symbolic gestures offered by Yeltsin and supported him strongly against Zyuganov, whose election they genuinely feared. Yeltsin aimed his message at those in the center and on the left part of the spectrum, and, as table 6-11 shows, was extraordinarily successful.

Table 6-11 divides the electorate into four equal groups by their attitudes toward economic reform. A scale was constructed on the basis of ten questions. A respondent who favored gradual reform on each question received a score of 200 and one who answered "completely oppose" on all a score of 500. Hence the "pro-reform" group in table 6-11 is not limited to those who wanted radical reform, but includes those generally consistent in taking the gradual reform position on all questions.

Table 6-11 includes not only percentages, but also the actual number of respondents in each group. The 2,450 survey respondents are the exact number who would have voted if the turnout of those in the sample corresponded actually to the actual turnout in the election. This technique illuminates the meaning of the percentage figures more clearly.

In the hypothetical electorate of table 6-11, the victorious candidate needed a minimum of 1,226 respondents, and Yeltsin received only 556

Table 6-11. *Percentage of Support for Yeltsin and Zyuganov, by Attitude toward Economic Reform*[a]

Political orientation	Is Russia on correct course?			Intend to vote in runoff for	
	Yes	No	Do not know	Yeltsin	Zyuganov
Proreform	58	18	24	91.8	8.2
Score: 100–275				(556)	(51)
Moderate conservative	25	41	34	70.3	29.7
Score: 280–345				(435)	(187)
Conservative	12	61	27	46.8	53.2
Score: 350–400				(291)	(332)
Archconservative	4	83	14	20.1	79.9
Score: 405–500				(119)	(479)
Total				57.2	42.8
				(1,401)	(1,049)

Source: Survey (see preface). For the detailed methodology of its construction, see Jerry F. Hough and Susan Goodrich Lehmann, "The Mystery of Opponents of Economic Reform among the Yeltsin Voters," in Matthew Wyman, Stephen White, and Sarah Oates, eds., *Elections and Voters in Post-Communist Russia* (Cheltenham, U.K.: Edgar Elgar, 1998), pp. 201–08.

a. Number surveyed in parentheses. Percentages may not total 100 as a result of rounding.

votes—45 percent of this minimum—from the proreform group, even loosely defined.

The conservatives and archconservatives in the sample in table 6-11 were quite conservative, but Yeltsin did surprisingly well among them. If public opinion had really been polarized—that is, if Zyuganov had received the same percentage among the archconservatives as Yeltsin received among the proreform group and the same percentage among the conservatives as Yeltsin received among the moderate conservatives—Yeltsin would have received 1,225 votes, exactly half of the total. The mystery is deepened by the fact that the pro-Yeltsin conservatives and archconservatives were quite similar in their social background and social attitudes to the Zyuganov voters.[53]

From the perspective of the Downs model, the obvious explanation for Yeltsin's success is that Zyuganov failed to move significantly to the center and hence that Yeltsin was able to win even though he was far from the center in his enunciated economic reform. To some extent this was true. Zyuganov was not a natural media candidate, and, although his major speeches on television were quite moderate, he felt that he had to take some actions to solidify his position on the left—for example, repudiate the break-up of the Soviet Union—that suggested he was closer to the extreme end of the spectrum than he actually was.

Nevertheless, the 1996 election reminds us of an important corollary to the Downs model. What is crucial in the Downs model is not the actual position of the candidates on the political spectrum, but their position as perceived by the voter. In the United States, the purpose of negative campaigning is to convince the voter that the opposing candidate is far removed from the center. This sometimes succeeds, but in a free election both candidates have a chance to define and defend themselves. Indeed, in the United States, reporters often help the voters position the candidates by focusing on this question in their articles.

Russia in 1996 was very different. The election campaign featured the most thoroughgoing negative advertising, but no corrective was possible. Every Yeltsin speech strongly emphasized the Communist threat. Except for the three American advisers working closely with Tatiana Diachenko, Yeltsin's daughter, almost all Yeltsin advisers, especially on the democratic side, opposed a strongly negative campaign against the Communists. Their focus groups had convinced them that negative advertising in Russia would be counterproductive.[54] Yeltsin always believed in describing the political struggle as a Manichean one between good (himself) and evil (the Communists), and he overrode the view of his liberal campaign advisers.

Officially there were strict limits on campaign spending, but Yeltsin's team acted as if they did not exist. Yeltsin spent lavishly on polling, advertising, focus groups, and direct mailings. The three American consultants alone were paid $250,000 plus all expenses and had an unlimited budget for polling.[55] There was supposed to be no radio, television, or billboard advertising before May 15, but Yeltsin took advantage of the Victory Day celebration in early May to send a direct letter to all World War II veterans. On May 30, millions of copies of an extreme anti-Communist pamphlet, *Ne Dai Bog* (God forbid), were distributed throughout Russia. Zyuganov was compared with Hitler as a hate-monger.[56] Television documentaries suggested that Zyuganov would tear down the churches and expropriate people's private agricultural plots, steps never taken even by Stalin after 1930.

But unlike the situation in the United States, Zyuganov had little opportunity to try to correct the popular perception of the position he was being assigned on the spectrum. His campaign funds were far too small for an effective advertising campaign, and television took a strongly anti-Communist position and covered his campaign in an extremely tendentious manner. Instead of discussing Zyuganov's attempts to move to the center, television gave great attention to extremists in the Communist party, implying that they spoke for Zyuganov. Little attention was given to his moderate statements.

The nature of the television reporting was apparent on Zyuganov's first campaign trip to Siberia. On this trip he told his audience, among other things, that both he and Stalin had great respect for the Russian Orthodox Church. Those watching both state-controlled and "independent" NTV television never knew that Zyuganov went to Siberia or said anything, for the trip was not covered.[57] Candidates other than Yeltsin were even more invisible on television. This disparity between the campaign on the hustings and the campaign that the viewer saw on television remained strong until the end.

Intimidation

Given the population's suspicion of the Communists and Yeltsin's ability to define the political spectrum, the result of the runoff election for president is perhaps not surprising. The real surprise was the result in the first-round election. Given the economic depression and the negative attitude of the population toward Yeltsin and the Communists, the Downs model and democratic theory in general would have predicted that attractive centrist candidates would have appeared to challenge both of them.

Michael McFaul's argument that Yeltsin prevented the rise of competing candidates from the center and right by moving to the right at the beginning of April 1996 neglects the obvious fact that such challenges had to be prevented in the first months of that year. This was when it appeared Yeltsin could not win and when analysts such as Aslund were writing articles suggesting that anyone would be better than Yeltsin. By April 1 public opinion polls showed that Yeltsin was the only real alternative to Zyuganov, barring a sudden shift of opinion.

Yeltsin essentially prevented the rise of any challenger from the right or center in the first months of 1996 and afterward by ruthless organizational measures. Serious potential centrist candidates were almost totally denied access to television, and they found it impossible to raise money. Rumors circulated that anyone who thought of making contributions to them would be visited by tax collectors threatening audits. The sociologists linked to the president reported results in February and March in such a way as to minimize the chance that other candidates on the right could be seen as credible.[58]

In fact, except for Chernomyrdin, who showed few political skills, none of the opposing candidates who surfaced seemed credible as president. Grigory Yavlinsky and Vladimir Zhirinovsky did not have the experience for the job, quite aside from their views. Zyuganov had been a Communist party official all his life, but he had never held the post of party first secretary of a county, city, or region that would have allowed him to rise toward the top in the Soviet system. Aleksandr Lebed was a capable and decisive division commander, but he was only forty-six years old and had never had the broad responsibility of being commander of a military district, deputy minister of defense, or minister. Nevertheless, Russia had many governors with solid administrative and political experience in the Soviet system who had served as capable political bosses in the new system. None ever hinted he would run for president.

Yeltsin's appointment of Oleg Soskovets, the first deputy premier, as his campaign manager in early 1996 was not a mistake, but a key decision. As first deputy premier, Soskovets was in charge of day-to-day administrative decisions in the executive branch. In October 1994 he was chairman of the Commission on Inter-Enterprise Debt and probably still held this post in 1996.[59] A campaign manager in charge of approving interenterprise and interregional debt was not one to be ignored by the enterprises or the regions. When the question arose of whether Soskovets would step down as first deputy premier, Yeltsin answered with scorn that when the chairman of the State Committee for Property, Sergei Beliaev, stepped down to head the campaign of Chernomyrdin's party, the "regional administrations lost all interest in him."[60] Soskovets surely was warning the governors of the consequences for the funding they sought if they advanced themselves as candidates or let someone else gain major support in their region.

Yeltsin's closest confidant, Aleksandr Korzhakov, played the role of chief intimidator. On April 16 he had a conversation with Chernomyrdin that he reported verbatim in his memoirs.[61] Korzhakov was frank in telling Chernomyrdin how he had intimidated others. He had told the Communists, he said, "We will not give up power to you" even if you win. He suggested to the Communists that they agree on a postponement of the election. He had told Yeltsin, he said, to replace Pavel Grachev with Igor Rodionov as minister of defense because Grachev would count the soldiers' votes honestly and "Rodionov will peacefully bring Yeltsin 90 percent of the vote in the army." "I was a member of the Electoral Commission, and I know how this is done."[62] Korzhakov made these points to intimidate Chernomyrdin, for he accused him of disloyalty to Yeltsin, citing evidence that Chernomyrdin knew had to come from surveillance.

The opposing candidates themselves were summoned and told that since they could not raise money, they should cut a deal with Yeltsin. Sviatoslav Fedorov apparently was concerned about subsidies to his eye surgery clinics, but the most interesting negotiations took place with Aleksandr Lebed. McFaul claims that a deal was made with Lebed in March when he was offered the post of minister of defense, but Korzhakov reports only a conversation in which Lebed was told to cooperate but offered only the head of the Paratroop Corps.[63] Korzhakov's report seems more credible, but Yeltsin came back to Lebed at the end of the campaign.

Once Yeltsin had made it impossible for meaningful non-Communist candidates to arise and win support, he began using intimidation against the Communists. For the first time, he began threatening prison. Once he even threatened the arrest of former premier Nikolai Ryzhkov, a thoroughly decent man, and another time he spoke of the same fate for university presidents who permitted Communists to organize on campus.

In early May, Korzhakov gave an interview to the London *Observer* in which he openly advocated postponing the election. He said that a Communist victory would produce civil war, and he was supported by the commander of the Moscow Military District, the key district in any coup. Yeltsin told the press that the election would be held, but he said that Korzhakov was not alone in thinking that civil war would ensue from a Communist victory.[64]

It was an extraordinarily cynical claim, for civil war could emerge from a Communist victory only if Yeltsin forces refused to hand over power. Another time Korzhakov also told the radicals he would not permit the Communists to come to power, and it was not until May that a law was even passed on the timing and mechanism of a transfer of power. When the Yeltsin forces then began emphasizing the theme of the need for stability in the last weeks of the campaign,[65] the message was not one of stability in economic policy, but of Yeltsin's remaining in power in a stable, constitutional manner rather than by other means.

In the weeks before the election, Yeltsin forces made an unexpected and shrewd decision to deal with General Lebed. Money was poured into Lebed's campaign either from Yeltsin's funds or from those encouraged by the Yeltsin campaign. It was no longer feared that Lebed might defeat Yeltsin, but it was hoped that he would attract anti-Yeltsin votes that might otherwise go to the Communists. On the Friday before the election, Yeltsin even hinted that Lebed would be his successor, saying that his successor was in the race and "I know such a man," a Lebed slogan.[66]

Clearly Yeltsin believed that it was crucial to provide disenchanted voters with an alternative to the Communists. As in 1995, he calculated that it was crucial to prevent voters from crossing the psychological divide to vote for the Communists even once. In addition, he was determined to win the first round, for the regional officials were going to be making a judgment about who would be in a position to punish or reward them after the election. If Zyuganov won the first round, even marginally, this might affect their behavior.

But Lebed also served as another intimidating element in the runoff. Yeltsin's power had never rested on a solid military or police base, and his threats not to turn over power in case of a Communist victory depended on his ability to mobilize enough force to suppress Communist demonstrations. For the first time, the alliance with Lebed made Yeltsin's threats credible, all the more so if Lebed believed he was the chosen successor.

The Rational Voter Model

Some political scientists have developed a truly radical conception of how the electorate decides to vote. They suggest that the voters weigh a variety of factors—the quality of the candidates, their programs, the needs of the country (for example, the primacy of foreign or domestic policy), and the nature of political conditions. In this view, the voters or at least the swing voters then emerge with a rational choice that balances these considerations.[67]

Clearly this is a theory that only the most self-confident social scientist could advance in the face of certain scorn from virtually all colleagues, but it may even be valid. From this perspective, the Yeltsin victory was the product of a combination of factors, many of them already discussed. He did move to the center more convincingly than Zyuganov. He was a very experienced leader of historic proportions, while Zyuganov had never led a region, an enterprise, or a ministry. Zyuganov may have been frightening not because he seemed Stalin-like, but because it was unclear whether he could control his fractious party, let alone a huge country.

There were, however, two other factors that should have entered the calculations of a rational Russian voter, and they may well have been quite important. One is "program" in the concrete sense of the word. Even in the American context, the phrase "move to the center" is too vague. American candidates do not say they are 4.9 on a scale from 0 to 10 while their opponent is 5.5 or even 7.5. Instead, they take positions on concrete issues and must do so in a way that convinces people that they are simultaneously standing on principle, are moderate, and will make pragmatic (but not unprincipled) compromises. The architect of President Clinton's "movement to the center" has discussed the process in a very sophisticated manner as "triangulation."[68]

In Russia, "program" had a more precise meaning: what steps should be taken to end the depression? Yeltsin's opponents usually talked vaguely. Reform should be more gradual; "correctives" should be introduced; the population should receive more social protection. These arguments would have seemed compelling if the Gaidar-Chubais policy had been in place, but, of course, it was not.

As this book documents, Yeltsin's economic reform had been gradual, and correctives had been introduced in the policy that Gaidar had announced. Consumption was being subsidized. People might complain about late wages, but they were aware that they were being paid for not working. The Communists were calling for a more equitable policy toward agriculture, and people knew this implied that Yeltsin had kept down food prices by nonmarket means. They knew that their cities were receiving electricity and natural gas and that the costs of rent and utilities had not been raised very much.

Yeltsin's opponents were not saying how their gradualism or social protection would be different from his. If they had enthusiastically embraced an industrial investment policy, if they had wrapped it in Russian nationalism by saying that the country needed to go back to the successful Russian program of the 1890s and early 1900s, they might have sounded convincing. This they failed to do, and voters had genuine reason to wonder how they would change course from the subsidies of the Yeltsin era and whether Yeltsin's opponents themselves knew what they would do.

A second factor was impossible to discuss publicly—Yeltsin's health. It often was said that Yeltsin won because he campaigned vigorously or, at least, seemed to be doing so on television. No doubt this had some impact, but few can have thought he would be a healthy president. If the people were convinced that Yeltsin's reelection meant four years of moribund leadership, they might have reacted to him with the complete rejection they manifested in 1998 and 1999.

But if the people thought that Yeltsin was likely to die within the year, their rational calculation changed radically. Why should they offend a leader whom they had strongly supported since the late 1980s? Why should they take the chance that he or his men really would attempt to retain power by force or that Lebed would take advantage of the situation to conduct a military coup? Why should they elect a Zyuganov, whom they mistrusted, when a post-Yeltsin election might have attractive new candidates? The rational choice was to give one more vote to Yeltsin and then to wait—perhaps only a few months— until they might have a chance to vote in a real presidential election with a range of strong candidates. They did not suspect that the United States would persuade Yeltsin to have a heart operation and that this would keep him alive.

SEVEN

*The Collapse of
the Ponzi Game*

WESTERN SUPPORTERS OF Boris Yeltsin and his
economic reform focused on inflation as the key indicator of success. If
inflation were controlled, they asserted, investors would gain confidence
and foreign investment would surge. The economy would turn around
and begin to boom. If foreign money stimulated growth, the results
would be ideal for both Russia and foreign investors. But, of course, if
foreign investment were simply used to maintain consumption, then the
level of Russian debt service would continue to rise with no increase in
the ability to pay. Misplaced optimism would be drawing short-term
investment money into a pyramid scheme, and short-term investment
money can exit very quickly in the modern world.

Inflation declined sharply after July 1993, reaching 5 percent a
month in December 1993. After a blip in late 1994, it quickly declined
again to a few percent a month through 1996 and most of 1997. Since
the policies that produced the price stabilization in 1995 and 1996 took
effect just before and during volatile election campaigns in both years—
a very unusual pattern in third world countries—some saw unorthodox
political methods as an explanation and a model to be used elsewhere.[1]

In reality inflation was not hard to control because so many prices
were negotiated by the government in "barter" arrangements and
because many sellers knew they would not be paid in any case. The
Russian government was actually engaged in the familiar practice of
maintaining consumption on the eve of elections, but its tight control of
the economy meant the policy did not have the usual inflationary

effects. Investment continued to be suppressed, and new foreign money was used to import consumer goods and to finance the various off-budget subsidies.

Unfortunately, the techniques of starving investment and using foreign investment to subsidize consumption could not be used forever, especially in tandem. The absence of investment was certain to affect the level of production in the future, while a steady increase in the level of foreign debt meant a steady increase in interest payments and a reduction in the amount of money available to subsidize consumption. A growing economy can afford growing debt, but a declining economy reaches its debt limit fairly quickly.

The obvious solution for Russia was to change economic policy after the July 3, 1996, presidential election—a frequent postelection strategy in third world countries and elsewhere. If investment were emphasized and consumption restricted, economic growth would build popular support for the reform forces by the time of the next election. Unfortunately, this did not occur. Yeltsin made major changes in personnel in the government in August 1996, but the new appointees represented the same mix of views as before. This ensured that the same policy would continue after the election. In fact, the level of barter and nonpayments increased as the policy of off-budget subsidies of consumption continued.

The IMF made no change in its policy advice, either. The options of a state-sponsored investment policy to stimulate economic growth, tariffs to stop consumer imports, and a sharp devaluation of the ruble to serve the same purpose continued to be denounced. Now the IMF emphasized greater tax collection as the needed solution. Those accused of tax arrears were the oligarchs in the oil and natural gas industry, who were forced to provide their product free to domestic users and who had little cash for the tax collector. Although the point was never recognized in newspaper editorials, presumably the IMF really was demanding that the free and subsidized barter deliveries be ended or reduced. It was continuing to assume that this macroeconomic adjustment would elicit large-scale investment.[2]

But how were local governments and the military to pay for the fuel they needed for the winter if budgetary expenditures were not increased to cover these expenditures? If the manufacturing sector were forced to pay for materials and energy it could not afford, why would entrepreneurs want to invest in it? If the export industries were forced to pay more taxes without additional income, why should western investors find them attractive? Indeed, why would the value of the stocks not collapse? These questions were never answered.

The Asian monetary crisis and the fall in oil prices precipitated the final collapse. Even before this, however, Ariel Cohen had noted in May 1997 that Russia faced a looming financial crisis as a result of its "profligate borrowing." The bonds were "a Ponzi scheme" designed to pay the interest of old debt, he said; Russia had "no viable revenue base"; tax collection was "near collapse"; and "Russian municipal debt does not appear to be sufficiently collateralized."[3] In July 1997 John Thornhill of the *Financial Times* warned about the "pitfalls in the paperchase"—that is, the western rush to buy Russian government and nongovernment bonds. He reported that "the most glaring doubts . . . concern the solvency of the government itself."[4]

The Developing Financial Crisis and the 1995 IMF Loan

At least judging by reports in the American press, 1994 had begun very well for Russia. After the 1993 election, the leaders of the Duma decided to adopt a nonconfrontational posture toward Yeltsin, and the Duma chairman and former Communist leader Ivan Rybkin moved in a moderate and then pro-Yeltsin direction. Inflation was slowly declining, and the value of the ruble vis-à-vis the dollar was declining less rapidly than inflation. The ruble was stabilized at around 1,200 to the dollar from mid-1993 to February 1994. Not accidentally, this was the period of the confrontation with the Congress and then the 1993 election.

The stable ruble allowed Yeltsin supporters in the West to claim the economic reform was working and to support the suppression of the Congress. But the success was a sham. If a plant's production was worth 12 billion rubles in mid-1993, this converted into $10 million at the current exchange rate; if production remained at the same level but its value rose to 24 billion rubles because inflation doubled, its real value had not changed, but now its dollar value was $20 million. A person such as Lawrence Summers could pronounce reform a success by proclaiming that dollar incomes—but, carefully, only dollar incomes—had increased.[5]

Industrial production dropped 19 percent in the first five months of 1994, but real income was said to have risen. Table 2-2 shows just what this meant. "Market economists largely agree," the *Wall Street Journal* reported, that "reports of falling industrial production are no cause for alarm, but a sign of economic health. . . . Wasteful industrial production is in decline."[6] The rise in consumption in the face of declining industrial production was the sign not of a healthy transition to a service economy, however, but of a continuation of the old policy of subsidizing consumption at the expense of investment. Indeed, the much heralded increase in the percentage of the private service sector in Russian GDP reflected in substantial part an increase in banking activity—banking activity that was private in name only and that did not involve consumer or real business loans, but subsidy loans that would not be repaid.

The first indication of serious financial problems occurred in the second half of 1994. After February 1994 the ruble had been allowed to fall gradually to 2,200 to the U.S. dollar in August. After a short respite, it fell to 2,500, where it was stabilized from September 21 to October 6 with some $2 billion of Central Bank money.[7] The problem was that Russia was beginning to encounter problems with the service of its foreign debt. It had been financing a substantial part of its imports with foreign loans, and the interest payments were growing. In early October 1994, Minister of the Economy Aleksandr Shokhin went to the IMF annual meeting in Madrid to say that Russia had a debt service of $13 to $16 billion over the next three years and could afford to pay less than half of it. The IMF tried to create $24 billion of special drawing rights from which Russia would have the unconditional right to borrow, but the developing nations voted as a bloc and, with their 30 percent of the vote in the IMF, defeated the move.[8]

The next day Russian financial officials stopped supporting the ruble. By October 10 it had fallen from 2,500 to 3,081, and the next day— Black Tuesday—to 3,926. The timing of the end of support for the ruble was a clear signal to the West. Yeltsin reinforced this signal with the appointment of a relative conservative as minister of state property (privatization) and then in December with the launching of the war in Chechnya. The Moscow media—and the western commentators who followed their lead—were filled with stories about the rising influence, even the power, of a new conservative "Politburo" under Yeltsin's security chief, Aleksandr Korzhakov, that allegedly was strengthening its hold on Yeltsin and Russia. In the words of Michael McFaul, "The Security Council is the government. . . . The situation couldn't be worse."[9]

A young economist who had entered the government several years earlier, Deputy Finance Minister Sergei Aleksashenko, was blunt about the conclusion that the West was supposed to draw. "If the West does not provide the money, the whole reformist wing of the government loses its influence and its importance." A few days later, Aleksashenko increased the political stakes: if the IMF did not relax its conditions, "'fascists and communists' would take control of the government."[10] When the IMF loan did come through, Aleksashenko resigned to become deputy chairman of the Central Bank.[11]

When the ruble bounced back above 3,000 after Black Tuesday, some suggested that foreign reserves had simply been mismanaged, and the Central Bank chairman was removed as a scapegoat. But the ruble soon began sliding again. It passed the 4,000 level on January 26, 1995, and dropped to 5,130 at the beginning of May 1995. It then was stabilized, returning to the 4,500 level by the end of June and remaining essentially in a band between 4,400 and 4,600 for the rest of the year.[12] The Clinton administration did not want a collapse of the Yeltsin regime on the eve of the American election, and the IMF began negotiating a new loan.

The IMF had several fundamental concerns. First, inflation had been declining, but the government deficit continued to be large. The off-budget subsidies kept budget expenditures down, but the tax write-offs naturally had a negative effect on tax revenue. The IMF began emphasizing the need for better tax collection as the key to reducing the deficit.

Second, the IMF began to worry more seriously about the stability of the Russian banking system. Since 1991 many banks had been making loans that were nonperforming or whose value had been destroyed by inflation. Originally bank resources were replenished with direct subsidies from the budget, but this policy was long decried by the IMF. In response the Russian government reduced direct subsidies, but it increased indirect ones through bank loans that could not be repaid. These in turn undermined the stability of the banking system.

The outstanding bank loans to industry, agriculture, and other sectors of the economy soared from 5 trillion rubles at the beginning of 1993 to 70 trillion at the end of 1994.[13] Only part of the increase reflected inflation, and any knowledgeable observer had to suspect that most of the loans would never be repaid. The reduction in the rate of inflation meant that the value of the loans would not depreciate nearly as fast as in the past, and westerners naturally worried about the level of bank reserves that stood behind them.

Third, the IMF was pressuring the Russian government to sell assets in order to obtain money to balance the budget. In fact, the net extra income that could be obtained for the budget by asset sales was small. Only the export industries were likely to attract significant investment interest, and Russia was already receiving hard currency income from its ownership of these properties. It would lose this income if it sold the assets. The IMF presumably was responding to the desire of western investors when it pushed asset sales.

On March 10, 1995, an IMF delegation, ostentatiously led by the head of the IMF, Michel Camdessus, arrived in Moscow to sign an agreement pledging $6.5 billion over a three-year period. It was the largest loan in IMF history and was to cover one-half of the Russian deficit.[14] As always was the case from 1992 onward, the top officials of the Yeltsin government responded positively to all the IMF concerns, received the money, and then either reneged on their promises or subverted them to their own benefit.[15]

The Loans-for-Shares Program

In early March 1995, the Russian government, surely as part of its negotiations with the IMF, announced its intention to sell some of its assets. On March 30 the Russian cabinet approved a plan for a consortium of seven (or perhaps nine) Russian banks to loan the government some R20 trillion ($4 billion at the official exchange rate) to help cover the 1995 deficit.[16] This was to become known as the "loans-for-shares" program. It provided that the government would put up enterprise shares it owned as collateral for the loans. If the government did not repay the loans, and no one expected it would, the shares would become the property of the banks. The government deficit would be covered, and the banks' balance sheets would be strengthened as the shares increased in value.

Michael Bernstam and Alvin Rabushka believe that the plan was a complete surprise to the IMF and even to the Russian government,[17] but it was approved by the cabinet only a few weeks after the IMF decision. The author of the program, Vladimir Potanin of Oneximbank, was very close to Vice Premier Anatoly Chubais, the deputy premier for finances at the time. At a minimum, the proponents of the plan surely told the Americans that the primary purpose of the program was to strengthen the banking system and balance the budget as the IMF wanted.

Western defenders of the loans-for-shares plan saw it as reflecting "a belief in the permanence of Russia's economic reform effort."[18] The

Russian banks had grown enough in stature to take on an investment role. They would acquire shares, make loans to the enterprises, assist in their restructuring, and then sell the shares at a higher price, surely to foreigners. The Russian banks themselves naturally did not emphasize this last possibility at home. Instead, they said, there was so little capital in Russia that they had a virtual duty to acquire large blocks of shares to prevent foreigners from buying them at too low a price.[19]

In the original plan, the loans-for-shares program was to be concluded between the government and a consortium of banks, but in mid-May, the government instead announced an intention to have competitive bidding. The number of shares, the interest rate, and the duration of loans would be fixed, and the winning bank would be the one to "bid" the largest loan.[20] This competition was formally enacted at the end of August.[21] It was alleged that the bank consortium had collapsed because it could not raise the required $1.8 billion.

In fact, the auctions were conducted as if the consortium were still in place. Different banks were used to conduct the auctions of different companies and received underwriting expenses for their efforts. Each bank then won its own auction in a way that strongly suggested the process was rigged. The large banks also purchased shares in a large number of domestic manufacturing enterprises and in leading Moscow newspapers and television networks.

The auction of 5 percent of the shares of Lukoil, the premier Russian petroleum company, was typical. In September Atlantic Richfield had purchased convertible bonds of Lukoil worth 5.6 percent of the shares of the company for $250 million.[22] When the government put up 5 percent of the Lukoil shares to obtain loans in November, it used Imperial Bank as its agent in conducting the auction, with the minimum bid put at only $35 million. Imperial Bank was largely owned by Gazprom and Lukoil, and it submitted the winning bid in the December auction: $35,100,000, only $100,000 above the minimum.

Despite the claim that foreigners were being barred from the bidding to prevent a foreign takeover of the Russian oil industry, the Lex comment column in the *Financial Times* noted correctly that everyone assumed that banks would eventually sell the shares on the stock market and that foreigners would buy them. The question, therefore, was not whether foreigners would own part of the Russian oil industry, but who would receive the price the foreigners were willing to pay, the government or the banks.[23] At the end of March 1996, a block of 3.3 percent of Lukoil stock of unknown origin was sold on the secondary market to a private western investor for $130 million, nearly six times the price paid four months earlier.[24]

Many other members of the original bank consortium also obtained valuable properties in a similar process. Menatep got 45 percent of Yukos oil company for $159 million. Oneximbank paid $170 million to buy 51 percent of Norilsk Nickel, which produced 20 percent of the world's nickel and 40 percent of the world's platinum and which had revenues of $3 billion in 1995.[25] An affiliate of Oneximbank obtained 51 percent of Sidanko petroleum, the fourth-largest producer, for $135 million, just $5 million over the minimum.[26]

These auctions were unseemly even on the surface, but the reality was far worse. The banks were essentially bankrupt and did not have any funds to loan the government. The government had been depositing its funds in a range of banks, but now it apparently concentrated them in the seven foreign trade banks that would be making loans to the government.[27] In essence, the banks would be loaning the government the interest on the government's own funds—or even those very funds. With creative accounting the government would be able to double-count its deposits and the loans in reporting to the IMF.[28]

Not surprisingly, Russian banks that had been frozen out complained bitterly. Three losing banks—Inkombank, Rossiiskii Kredit, and Alfa Bank—issued a public statement claiming that Menatep had less than ten percent of the $1.1 billion it pledged to the government and that it was going to use the money of the Ministry of Finances.[29] Indeed, two months later Chrystia Freeland reported what she called a "bizarre deal" with Menatep: the bank was given a package of shares in six oil companies in a reverse loans-for-shares deal in which the government took $2.5 million of Menatep's shares in return.[30] All the banks were issuing stock, and it may be that the government often was the buyer.

Rossiiskii Kredit, the country's fourth-largest bank, soon received justice. In December 1995 it was allowed to issue three-month bonds on western credit markets to borrow $33.3 million at just below an 11 percent annualized rate. Since Russian banks had not been able to borrow abroad since bank defaults in August, the Ministry of Finances issued government-backed bonds as collateral for the Rossiiskii Kredit paper. Rossiiskii Kredit was to use the foreign loan to invest in Russian government securities that would yield 80 percent in dollar terms.[31] A naive observer might wonder why the Ministry of Finance did not sell government securities directly on the European market for 11 percent instead of to Rossiiskii Kredit for 80 percent. Then in early 1996, Rossiiskii Kredit raised a further $28.7 million, this time at 9.6 percent interest, but again fully collateralized by government bonds.[32] The government had found one more way to launder the money it was providing the banks to make their subsidy loans.

The Fictional "Financial Oligarchs"

The various machinations of the loans-for-shares program were the great melodrama of Russian political theater of the mid-1990s. Supposedly the men who headed the auction banks were great financial "oligarchs," seizing Russia's assets and becoming the country's dominant political figures. U.S. newspapers were filled with juicy details about power, scandals, and corruption. These men were seen as the J. P. Morgans and the Rockefellers putting together the great Russian fortunes, men with the power that Lenin had attributed to the financial oligarchy in his *Imperialism—The Highest Stage of Capitalism.*

It was, indeed, classic melodrama, but in the traditional sense of the word—a fictional morality play. The banks involved were either the traditional foreign trade banks or new foreign trade banks associated with leading members of the government.[33] The lack of transparency and the legal bank dividends greatly facilitated corruption, but most of the money was going to subsidize consumption. With direct subsidies being reduced, the rate of inflation declining, the ruble exchange rate stabilizing, and an increasing percentage of export revenues going to debt service, new methods were needed to finance the subsidy loans. One method was the sale to the banks of short-term government bonds. A second method was the acquisition of oil property and its revenue by the banks. The third was the use of stories about powerful private oligarchs to legitimate the acquisition of private dollars from abroad. As private institutions they would be able to go bankrupt, while their creditors had no legal recourse.

The most important aspect of the banks' acquisition of enterprise shares was given little attention in the West—their acquisition of many domestic manufacturing enterprises. Inkombank, for example, established a machinery industry sector headed by former premier Ivan Silaev. It had been making loans to the Magnitogorsk Metallurgy Combine, and now it took on the "lion's share" in a new "financial-industrial group (FPG)" centered on Magnitogorsk.[34] Oneximbank began signing agreements with regional administrations to conduct their international settlements and help their local banks.[35] A range of banks made large loans to regions and local governments, although at least officially with Ministry of Finance guarantees.[36]

Various banks purchased shares in the food industry, but in such a way as to divide the market rather than to compete. They thus became virtually monopoly purchasers of certain types of crops from certain regions. Inkombank's firm, for example, bought 70 percent of the sugar beets produced in the Stavropol region.[37] This facilitated payment of below-market prices to Russian farms for their produce. Regional banks became part of a new institution that proliferated—the industrial-financial complex. This usually included the bank, an export plant that earned hard currency, and domestic manufacturers that required subsidies. The oligarchs also acquired television networks and networks that were losing money.

The press was told that these purchases reflected the great power of the financial oligarchs in charge of the banks and their desire to broaden their control over the country. In fact, the foreign trade banks were already engaged in what should have been a highly profitable business. Aside from their purchases in the oil industries, they were entering spheres of the economy that were not profitable and not likely to be so for some time.

Unless the oligarchs are seen as playing a selfless role, they surely were being dragged unwillingly into economic activities they would have preferred to avoid. They were being forced to take money from their foreign trade and oil businesses to help finance their losing firms. Then, just like the Congress of People's Deputies in 1992 and 1993, they and the heads of the oil and gas companies were used by "reformers" such as Chubais and especially Boris Nemtsov as scapegoats for the economic difficulties in 1997 and 1998.

The foreign trade banks also were being used to make "loans" to other banks that did not have foreign trade earnings. On January 1, 1995, the debt on the interbank credit market totaled 24.6 trillion rubles, 741 billion rubles of which was overdue. However, interest was paid on all but 167 billion of it. By July 1, 2.6 trillion was overdue, and interest was not being paid on 789 billion worth of the loans. On Black Thursday, August 24, 1995, 150 banks had not been able to close the limits of their positions, and the banking system became illiquid.[38]

The Central Bank restored the liquidity of the banks by purchasing 1.5 trillion rubles in government bonds from the banks and by providing credit of 300 billion to three banks.[39] The three banks to which credit was granted were Inkombank, Most-Bank, and Stolichny Savings Bank, three of the largest Moscow banks in the financial oligarchy. Presumably they were among the victims of default. Their resources were being diverted by the government to prop up the weakest institutions in the system, and the August crisis indicated that this particular game had reached its limit.

In addition, the banks were serving another function that few in the West have yet acknowledged. If the great financial oligarchs of Russia were so optimistic about Russia's future that they were buying manufacturing industries, then the logical implication was that westerners should follow their lead. If the financial oligarchs were so rich and powerful that they could force the government to sell them shares for low prices, then surely the West should have the confidence to buy the paper that the banks were offering. Indeed, when westerners began buying government short-term bonds offering very lucrative interest rates, they trusted the Russian banks so much that they used them to ensure against a devaluation of the ruble with forward-currency contracts.

When the Russian financial pyramid collapsed and the ruble with it in the summer of 1998, almost all of the "great" banks were declared bankrupt and disappeared. The only survivors were the banks associated with Mayor Yury Luzhkov of Moscow, and only a fool would bet that they would survive if he fell. Westerners were left with the worthless paper of the banks and the worthless insurance the banks had offered against devaluation. The banks were really state banks, but westerners had accepted them as private and thus were left with no claim against the government to get their money back. It was one of the classic confidence games in the history of international economic relations, and the melodrama about powerful oligarchs was a key part of it.

Bringing in the Foreigners

In the last few years of perestroika, Gorbachev and his associates treated foreign aid as a panacea that would save Soviet reform. The media of the Yeltsin era strongly reinforced this myth in an effort to convince Russian voters that western support for Yeltsin was crucial. The argument seems to have reflected genuine belief. In the early 1990s Chubais told a Russian businessman about "the queue of foreign investors lining up to buy Russian industry."[40] The reformers seemed to have no sense of the huge amount of money required for reconstruction of East Germany, a country with one-eighth the population of Russia. They entertained hopes for a number of different kinds of investment, but actually did little to attract it other than mislead investors.

Direct investments are by far the most desirable form of investment for any emerging country. Even before the Asian and Russian crises of 1997 and 1998, it was recognized that foreign investment in stock markets and bonds could be withdrawn at any moment. This is most likely to happen at moments of domestic panic when the withdrawal will do the most harm. Investment in an industrial plant, by contrast, is far less likely to be abandoned. In addition, direct investment is a highly effective form of technical assistance in training large numbers of managers and workers.

The problem with large-scale direct foreign investment in the early stages of market capitalism is that it almost always depends on some kind of tariff protection. This did not exist in Russia. IBM built a plant to assemble computers, but the Yeltsin government gave insiders the right to import computers without tariffs and taxes. IBM, which had to pay taxes, could not compete. The lack of a protectionist policy meant pharmaceutical companies feared that they would be undercut by inexpensive imports from Turkey and India. They therefore did not invest. In 1999 it was not a coincidence that Russia established a tariff on luxury imported cars at the same time that Ford Motor Company decided to invest in a plant in Russia near St. Petersburg.

Similarly, the Russian starvation of domestic investment also made effective joint ventures with foreigners impossible. For example, in 1993 Amoco won the rights to explore oil fields in Siberia with a Russian oil company, with financing to be split 50-50. Because the oil company was forced to distribute oil free to so many domestic customers, it had no money for investment, and Amoco found itself responsible for all costs. It cut staff and eventually closed out the operation altogether.[41]

The exact amount of direct foreign investment in Russia is difficult to determine, but Russia clearly received relatively little in the 1990s. The great hopes for foreign investment in Russia in the mid-1990s centered on the stock market. Portfolio investment was only $300 million in 1993, but it was beginning to rise rapidly in 1994.[42] Again it is difficult to be certain about the scale of the investment, for the statistics cited could refer to new investment by westerners, to reinvestment, or to the current value of stocks held by westerners, which in turn could be expressed either in dollars or in rubles. Offshore Russian money being returned to Russia was counted as foreign.

In the spring of 1996, Citibank estimated the value of the Russian stock market at $12.8 billion (see table 7-1). In the twelve months from March 7, 1996, to March 7, 1997, the value of Templeton Russia, one of the leading American mutual funds buying Russian stocks, was up 174 percent as foreigners became more confident about the results of the June 1996 presidential election. In October 1997, however, Russian domestic investment funds managed only around $24 million worth of stock, and foreign funds about $3 billion.[43] Foreigners almost totally dominated the trading on the stock exchange.

The reason for the difference between the Citibank $12 billion figure in 1996 and the much lower figure of 1997 is not clear, especially given the foreign domination of trading. Presumably, however, the Citibank figure included insider Russian holdings, most of which were never traded and often were even semifictitious. It may even have included state shares in publicly owned plants.

In any case, three facts are clear about foreign investment in the Russian stock market. First, from any perspective, it was quite small in absolute terms, especially in comparison with the tens of billions of new dollars that were needed each year for sustained growth.

Second, the mid-1990s were a period of great American enthusiasm about emerging markets. According to the Institute of International Finance, the amount of American investment in these markets rose from $57 billion in 1990 to $255 billion in 1996.[44] This enthusiasm extended to Russia as well, and hence movement on the Russian market was closely correlated with movement on the Thai and Mexican markets in 1995.[45]

If this enthusiasm continued and Russia was simply recognized as a legitimate emerging market and included in the group of countries represented in diversified emerging markets funds, huge amounts of money could be drawn in from investors not focusing on Russia alone. But by the same token, if investors became disillusioned about emerging markets in general and withdrew their money from the general mutual funds, Russian stocks would be sold along with the rest.

There was ample enthusiasm about Russia itself specifically. In the fall of 1994, Morgan Grenfell forecast a 500 percent rise in dollar terms

Table 7-1. *Market Value of Stock Markets and Daily Turnover of Emerging Markets, 1996*
Billions of dollars

Country	GNP 1994	Daily foreign exchange turnover	Market value
Brazil	536.3	4.5	166.5
Russia	392.5	.5	12.8
Mexico	368.7	1.2	96.1
South Korea	366.5	1.75	179.3
India	278.7	1.0	124.9
Indonesia	167.6	3.5	77.1
Turkey	149.0	1.1	27.1
Thailand	129.9	5.0	149.3
Saudi Arabia	126.6	.25	n.a.
Hong Kong	126.3	2.5	355.0
South Africa	125.2	6.0	306.0

Source: Citibank. Philip Gawith and Conner Middleman, "Exotic but Not for Faint Hearts," *Financial Times*, May 15, 1996.
n.a. Not available

in the Russian stock market by 1996.[46] The same year, Mark Mobius, president of Templeton Emerging Markets, predicted that in the next two decades Russia's capital markets could be as big as America's. He thought Russia might have as much as 20 percent of the weighting in his fund within ten years, as against 15 percent for Hong Kong and China.[47] A long article in the *Wall Street Journal* in September 1996, entitled "A Mistrustful West Finds It Hard to Grasp Real Change in Russia," focused on the question, "Why does the West have it wrong?" The result was well described by James Libera of Libera's Closed-End Country Fund Report: "There has been a mania going on. . . . It's like a momentum play. . . . When you have a small, illiquid market like Russia, it doesn't take much to drive it up."[48]

Third, it was abundantly clear that the Russian policy of off-budget subsidies made leading Russian companies difficult to evaluate and dangerous to buy. For example, Lukoil was Russia's premier oil company, and it was reputed to be the most open and forthcoming to foreign investors. A careful reader of the *Wall Street Journal* in mid-1996 should, however, have had a most uneasy feeling. On May 9 the newspaper carried a Lukoil report that 1995 pretax profit fell 58 percent, to $82.8 million, from 1994. Revenue fell 43 percent. But on May 20 the newspaper reported that Lukoil had revised its 1995 earnings. Net income had actually jumped 69 percent, to $528 million. Pretax income had more than tripled, from $246 million to $814 million, and revenue was up 90 percent, to $6.5 billion. On August 30, 1996, the *Wall Street Journal* reported that the company said it had earned $261 million for all its units in 1995 and that the holding company had earned $13 million. The company provided no previous-year figures, but promised to revise its accounting to meet western standards.[49] Lukoil often was not paid for its product and had not paid all its taxes, but no outsider knows how these various nonpayments were or were not reflected in its various income statements.

Another favorite stock was United Energy Systems, a company owned 51 percent by the state. It generated 70 percent and transmitted 100 percent of the electricity in Russia. In March 1997 it had risen 160 percent in value since the beginning of the year, but was still trading at 2.5 times earnings.[50] However, it had substantial tax and pension arrears, and more and more customers were not paying their bills.[51] By 1998 only 20 percent of customers were paying cash.

The Volga Auto Works in Togliatti (AvtoVAZ) produced 70 percent of all cars in Russia. The company lost $442 million in 1995 and owed $500 million in back taxes. Its total debt was 13 trillion rubles, including 1 trillion to the pension fund, 2 trillion to the federal government, and 2.5 trillion to Vneshekonombank. Nevertheless, the stock rose from $1.60 to $16 during the year.[52]

The more basic questions flowed, however, from the phenomena discussed earlier in this chapter. If the Russian economy and finances were on a favorable path, the various problems with arrears would be solved. The great companies would survive, and they would be the blue chips of the future. But if the government were engaged in a pyramid game from which it could not extract itself, then it inevitably would be driven to seek money wherever it could. The "privatized" firms that really were state enterprises and that earned foreign currency abroad were a certain target, and this would affect the value of their stocks. Moreover, if the ruble collapsed because of the pyramid scheme, then the dollar value of the stocks would be correspondingly affected even if their ruble value did not decline.

The final type of investment attracted from abroad was that which went into Russian government and "private" bonds. In a country such as the United States, government bonds are a traditional—indeed, a very safe—component of bank reserves. Moreover, the purchase of government bonds directly by the population or indirectly through the use of its deposits by banks absorbs purchasing power and domestic investment funds. The issuing of government bonds is, therefore, often recommended as an anti-inflationary measure, and it was one of the first suggestions made by the IMF in 1994 and 1995.

The sale of Russian government bonds began in May 1993, and the amount sold grew rapidly in 1994. Their cumulative value rose from 420 billion rubles at the end of the first quarter of 1994 to 2.4 trillion in the second quarter to 6.2 trillion in the third quarter and 11.5 trillion in the fourth quarter.[53] Almost all were short-term bonds—*gosudarstvennye kratkosrochnye obligatsii* or GKOs (known as Gekkos by foreigners). "Short-term" meant very short-term: at first they were from less than a week to three months in duration, but gradually more GKOs had a six-month or even one-year term. The Russian government was also issuing longer-term bonds, but they were not bought.

At the time of the IMF loan in early 1995, a Central Bank official reported that Russian internal debt was only 12 percent of gross domestic product (GDP), as opposed to 50 to 100 percent for many developed countries. This, in his words, was "colossally low" and should be raised.[54] The IMF apparently agreed. The vast majority of government bonds were bought by Russian banks, officially to strengthen bank reserves.

At first the bonds were treated as a domestic anti-inflation measure, and until mid-1996 only 10 percent of the bonds could officially be bought by nonresidents. The reason, however, was very disturbing. In the wake of the August 1995 bank crisis, the government began selling the bonds at implied interest rates that far exceeded the rate of inflation.[55] Moreover, the interest was tax-free. The yields on six-month GKOs reached 212 percent just before the 1996 election, and those on three-month GKOs 180 percent.[56] The GKOs were the most important source of profit for the banks in 1996.[57] The government was reluctant to have foreigners or private Russians buy the bonds because it did not want to pay them these extravagant interest rates.

The very high rates were attributed to political uncertainty and the fear of a Communist victory, but in the last months before the election it was highly probable that Yeltsin would win, and the Russian stock market was soaring. Indeed, after Yeltsin's victory, the interest rates fell only to 144 percent for six-month bonds and to 129 percent for three-month bonds.[58]

The *Wall Street Journal* reported in early 1996, "Outside interest [in GKOs] has been piqued by secondary-market yields averaging 80 percent to 90 percent and a relatively stable ruble."[59] The reference to the secondary market indicated that some—perhaps a considerable amount of the GKOs being sold to the banks—were finding their way to foreigners. As the foreign currency needs of the Russian government increased, the desire of foreigners to purchase Russian paper more directly was impossible to resist.

The Russian government debt expanded very rapidly. In 1996 alone, the government tripled its borrowing through bonds, and public debt rose from 16 percent of the national economy to 26 percent.[60] The problem was not only the foreign debt of the federal government. All the talk about regions that were independent of the center, about powerful financial oligarchs, and about privatized banks and enterprises led western investors to treat these units as independent and to provide them with loans or to purchase their stocks and loans. Thus cities and regions were also able to sell bonds abroad, as did, in different ways, the major Russian banks and Russian enterprises, especially those in the energy industry. Russian companies had foreign borrowings of $6.8 billion in 1997 and an additional $5.2 billion in the first eight months of 1998.[61] Aleksandr Lebed in September 1998 put the total Russian debt at $210 billion—$155 billion state, $30 billion commercial banks, and $25 billion private enterprises.[62] Unfortunately, none of these institutions were independent of the central government, and, worse, they all were either still dependent on the central government for their subsidies or were required to use their resources to subsidize other enterprises. When the central government had no resources to help the regions, banks, and enterprises to repay their foreign currency debts, the latter had no resources of their own.

By such traditional measures as the percentage of foreign loans to level of GDP or percentage of debt service to export earnings, Russia did, in fact, appear to be in good shape. This was, indeed, one of the arguments used by analysts to advocate foreign investment in Russia from 1995 through 1997 and by bond rating agencies such as Moody's to rate Russian foreign bonds as secure as Mexican ones.

But as the chairman of the Central Bank told a meeting of the collegium of the Ministry of Finances in February 1998, there were other much more worrisome indicators: "Although the state debt is extremely moderate in relation to GDP . . . it is extremely high in terms of its burden on the federal budget—the debt repayments and interest payments. Without a reduction in the tempo by which the state debt is rising and a change in its structure, the federal budget will be hard pressed to support all other (social, military, etc.) programs."[63]

The Beginning of the Collapse

All signs pointed to yet another financial crisis after the 1996 presidential election. Financial discipline clearly was weakened more than usual during the first half of the year. Huge sums were said to have been diverted to the Yeltsin campaign or stolen from the Yeltsin campaign and sent abroad, including a World Bank loan of $500 million to support the coal industry.[64] Tax collection was kept to a minimum to allow enterprises to pay wages and wage arrears. At the same time the government increased direct subsidies (including one to the pension fund to cover a $779 million shortfall),[65] and Yeltsin made campaign promises that, if carried out, would have increased the deficit enormously. As early as July 1996, a *New York Times* correspondent who described these phenomena rather fully reported, "Economists all seem to agree that some kind of collapse of the teetering banking system is imminent."[66]

On July 22, 1996, the IMF postponed the monthly payment of its three-year loan to Russia because of insufficient tax collection.[67] A *New York Times* editorial called the step "a polite warning to Mr. Yeltsin."[68] Nevertheless, on August 21 the IMF pronounced its satisfaction with July tax collections and released the funds. The IMF had reportedly relaxed its conditions to do so,[69] but it remained dissatisfied. At the end of October it once more held up two monthly payments until tax payments improved. The Russian government, in response, reported that tax collection in November was 1.4 times the October level and promised in November and December that it would be 90 to 95 percent of projections.[70] A new bankruptcy law was passed, and Yeltsin announced that he would reestablish the state monopoly of vodka. The IMF unfroze the loan on December 14.

Nevertheless, fundamental problems remained. If the economy did not turn around quickly, the borrowing would, as Arkady Volsky of the Russian Association of Businessmen and Entrepreneurs warned, simply create a "debt trap."[71] The debt could not rise indefinitely if it were being used only for financing consumption and ever-larger debt interest payments. The domestic debt continued to rise. On February 1, 1998, the summary overdue (*prosrochennaia*) debt of enterprises of industry, construction, agriculture, and transportation was 724.5 billion rubles.[72] The bulk of the debt was owed either to banks whose sole assets were the GKOs or to major suppliers that did not have money to pay their taxes as a consequence. These were precisely the firms that also had acquired foreign debt or whose stocks were held by foreigners.

Wage arrears for government and private employees remained around 40 billion rubles in the last months of 1997, but rose to 48 billion in February 1998, 50 billion in March, 52 billion in April, and 55 billion in May. Most of these were the "private" companies that were not paying all their taxes. If they were forced to pay more taxes, they would have even less for wages. Of course, if they simply laid off workers, that would reduce the wage and pension taxes they owed, but such a move would scarcely help the government to acquire revenues.[73]

As the emerging markets in general began to decline after the Asian crisis, the Russian stock market suffered also. By October 1997 it had declined 40 percent, but then on October 27, the New York Stock Exchange plummeted. If people did not have confidence in the Hong Kong and New York markets, why should they have confidence in Moscow stocks? The next day the Moscow exchange dropped 19 percent.

Although the immediate stimuli of the Russian financial crisis were events in Asia, the Russian problem went much deeper. First, the price of oil declined and with it the amount of foreign currency that Russia earned from its export. The price of Russian crude oil dropped from more than $18 a barrel in 1997 to $11 in mid-March 1998.[74] Second, the foreign debt kept rising, and with it Russian interest payments. Increasingly the Russians were borrowing to service and recycle old debt. Because Russia's debt was very short term, it was continually driven back to the market even if interest rates rose. The very rise in interest rates signaled risk to investors and led them to want to withdraw or to demand a higher return.

The need to attract foreign capital inevitably drove down the rates on the GKOs because the government could not afford to pay above-market rates on bonds to foreigners. The top official of the Ministry of Finances dealing with this question reported in early 1997 that the rates had dropped to what he considered a normal level—one-and-a-half times the rate of inflation. But an unspoken question remained: if the rates dropped to a more normal level and the commercial banks had been depending on the extra income, would they not soon be in financial difficulties?

In October 1997 Russian interest rates, adjusted for inflation, were around 10 percent. They rose steadily to nearly 40 percent in January and February 1998, declined to the 20–30 percent levels over the next three months, and then rose precipitously to 55 percent in a month's time.[75] Since the debt comprised very short-term zero-coupon bonds, refinancing was a constant concern, and the increase in interest rates— and their very high absolute level—reflected rising investor reluctance to reinvest when their bonds became due.

By January 1998 *Kommersant Daily* was describing the situation in desperate terms. Foreigners were pulling their money out, and one of the longest-playing insiders, Boris Jordan, was using words such as "catastrophic." By March 1, 1998, the central reserves had fallen to $15.0 billion, $4.8 billion in gold and $10.2 in hard currency.[76] The Central Bank kept raising interest rate payments on new GKOs to increase their attractiveness, but foreigners still refused to purchase them because the forward dollar market was frozen and they could not hedge their bond investments.

The Political Response

Yeltsin's closest associate in early 1996, Aleksandr Korzhakov, feared that the vigorous campaigning urged on Yeltsin during the 1996 presidential election would kill him, and his memoirs contain an alarmed memorandum from physicians that support this judgment.[77] In fact, Yeltsin suffered a serious heart attack almost immediately after the first round of the election. His inauguration had to be cut short, and he did not have the strength to make an inaugural address.

Western heart specialists were to say that Yeltsin had an excellent chance of returning to normal after a heart operation, but a skeptic noticed that the operation was postponed until the very day of the American presidential election. The thought occurred that the Americans were not quite as optimistic as they stated and did not want an untoward event to disturb the American policymakers or population on the eve of the election.

Obviously, Yeltsin was not in any condition to rule the country in any detailed manner. This did not mean, however, that he did not retain great power. He continued to use his old technique of creating a divided cabinet, but now his purpose was different. In the past he had fostered competition between a Fedorov and a Lobov so he could choose between them to serve his strategic and tactical political goals. Now he put opposing personnel in key positions for protective purposes. Basically he insisted that no major policy change be initiated without the agreement of the divided officials. Since this was impossible, existing policy was locked in place.

When Chernomyrdin announced his new cabinet after Yeltsin's inauguration, the leading banker associated with Anatoly Chubais, Vladimir Potanin, was named first deputy premier for economic policy and privatization. The other new first deputy premier, who answered for industry, Aleksei Bolshakov, was no favorite of the neoliberal reformers. Oleg Lobov remained a deputy premier, while Yeltsin's long-time personal aide, Viktor Iliushin, became deputy premier for social policy.[78]

Potanin's appointment was itself a dramatic endorsement of the bank-centered subsidy system of previous years. Potanin was director of Oneximbank and chairman of the original consortium in the loans-for-shares program, its purported author. One of Oneximbank's most dubious acquisitions had been a 38 percent share of Norilsk Nickel. Two days before Potanin's appointment, Norilsk Nickel was given tax breaks worth almost $1 billion. As an analyst at CS First Boston noted, "The question remains: where does the budget plan to get all its money if such [important export] companies as Norilsk Nickel cannot pay their taxes?"[79]

Yeltsin's heart operation in November 1996 was called a success, but in December he was said to have developed pneumonia. He returned to prominence only in March 1997. A *Washington Post* subheadline proclaimed, "Newly Robust Leader Reasserts Power," but the article itself reported, "Sources say he still spends no more than two or three hours a day in his Kremlin office. Although he has seemed animated and cogent, the loss of more than 50 pounds gives him a gaunt appearance and makes him look a decade older than his 66 years."[80]

In March 1997 Anatoly Chubais returned as first deputy premier in charge of economic policy. Boris Nemtsov was brought into the cabinet as deputy premier for social policy, and he pledged a drastic marketization of housing. In actuality, however, little happened. Both men scapegoated the oil and gas oligarchs—in essence, their great rival within the government, Viktor Chernomyrdin—for all economic difficulties and especially for tax arrears. It was all high drama, but its effect and likely its purpose were to divert attention from the financial developments of far greater importance.

As the financial crisis worsened in the fall of 1997, Yeltsin himself began using the reform economists as scapegoats. Anatoly Chubais and his key subordinates in the State Property Committee had signed a contract for a book on the history of privatization for $90,000 each. Since the publishing firm was owned by Potanin, who had been favored by Chubais in the loans-for-shares deals, the critics of the two men wondered aloud whether bribery was involved.

The book scandal gave Yeltsin an opportunity to punish Chubais publicly. He fired three Chubais protégés and removed Chubais himself as finance minister. The latter post was given to Mikhail Zadornov, an associate of Grigory Yavlinsky. Zadornov was a neoliberal economist, but the Yavlinsky group was the political archenemy of the Gaidar-Chubais group. Although Chubais remained first deputy premier in charge of economic policy, Zadornov reported directly to Chernomyrdin.[81] The other key first deputy premier, Boris Nemtsov, was also removed as minister of energy, although his protégé from Nizhnii Novgorod, Sergei Kiriyenko, replaced him.

In December 1997 Yeltsin began to attack the government as a whole, especially for delays in paying wages. He had scheduled a television speech on the subject, but had to cancel it because of what was called an acute viral infection. When he returned on January 19, he sharply criticized the government's failure to pay back wages.[82] A month later he repeated the criticism and said if the government does not solve the problem, "We will have a new government."

The word "government" in Russian jargon had always meant Chernomyrdin. The press gave credence to those who thought it was a bluff, rather than to Yeltsin's aides who assured them that Yeltsin was serious.[83] When Chernomyrdin came to the United States for his regular meeting with Vice President Gore in early March 1998, the *New York Times* headline referred to Chernomyrdin as "Hero to the U.S."[84] The *Washington Post* proclaimed "Gore Carves Unique Post with U.S.-Russia Collaboration."[85]

However, on March 23 Viktor Chernomyrdin was removed and the rest of the cabinet with him. The *New York Times* correctly reported that politically active Russians were engaged in a "frenzied search for a rationale" and were "torn between crediting the byzantine world of back-room intrigue or the byzantine thinking of their president."[86] In fact, Yeltsin was down to his last scapegoat and had been signaling his intentions for months. In addition, Chernomyrdin was a real danger. Yeltsin's speech was described as "still slow after much illness, and his movements stiff and labored." If Yeltsin were to be removed for health reasons, Chernomyrdin would automatically become president. That outcome seemed eminently satisfactory to both a large part of the Russian elite and the Americans, and Yeltsin had a strong interest in having a less credible figure in the direct line of succession.

When Yeltsin dismissed the cabinet, he stated that he himself would assume the duties of premier until a permanent one was appointed.[87] Told that the constitution did not permit this, he announced on March 24 the appointment of Sergei Kiriyenko, the unknown thirty-five-year-old protégé of Nemtsov who had been minister of energy for four months, as acting premier. On March 27 Yeltsin nominated Kiriyenko as permanent premier, calling him a "technocrat."

Kiriyenko was anything but a technocrat. He was a shipbuilding engineer who was a Komsomol secretary in the huge Krasnoe Sormovo plant in Gorkii (later called Nizhnii Novgorod), one that produced submarines among other items. As Gorbachev began his reform, Kiriyenko was one of the young Komsomol leaders who managed either to "privatize" some Komsomol assets or to use the organization as a façade for business activities. He became second secretary of the Gorkii regional Komsomol committee. As discussed in chapter 2, Kiriyenko had become head of the bank dealing with the local oil refinery and the pension fund and had been a chief Nemtsov lieutenant for managing the regional off-budget subsidy system.

The opposition forces in the Duma proclaimed that Kiriyenko was completely unqualified for the post of premier, which, of course, was true. They denounced his intention to pursue the old economic policy, which, of course, was their right. But after rejecting Kiriyenko two times, the Duma confirmed him when Yeltsin nominated him a third time. Many in Moscow sneered at the weakness of the Communists in surrendering to Yeltsin, but Kiriyenko satisfied the opposition for the same reason he was attractive to Yeltsin: he was not a credible president. For the opposition, this meant that if Yeltsin died, Kiriyenko, unlike someone such as Chernomyrdin, would not be a meaningful candidate in the subsequent presidential election and could not use the machinery of government to support himself. Kiriyenko as acting president would be a more or less neutral interim leader.

The Final Collapse

Despite the drop in oil prices, Russia was still running a trade surplus in 1998, but by July 1998 its current account deficit was depleting reserves at the rate of $6 billion a year.[88] This in itself was not a healthy development since it had reserves of only about $12 billion. Moreover, the government continually had to roll over the debt (that is, get new loans to pay those coming due).

Major turmoil began in the last week of May 1998. On June 3 Russia was able to sell a $1.25 billion sovereign Eurobond, but it had to pay almost double the interest rate it had paid previously—753 basis points more than the ten-year U.S. bond. Moreover, the *Financial Times* reported that it was unclear how much new money was involved.[89] On June 10 Standard & Poor's downrated Russia's sovereign rating by one notch to B plus.[90]

On June 17 Chubais was given the job of coordinating relations with the IMF, and the next day, the IMF postponed the latest $670 million tranche. Anders Aslund reported a growing divergence of views between the United States and the IMF, and he argued that the IMF was "overly pessimistic."[91] On the same day, Russia successfully floated a $2.5 billion, thirty-year Eurobond.[92] It was heavily oversubscribed. Russia also obtained some secret loans from western banks at a rate below the domestic rate.[93]

On July 7 alone, the yield on the GKOs rose from 90 percentage points to 113, and the next day the market almost ceased to function.[94] The IMF acted on July 13. It promised an additional $11.2 billion in 1998, with the World Bank and Japan providing an extra $1.4 billion. Together with existing commitments, this meant $22.6 billion in international financial support by the end of 1999. Of this amount $4.8 billion was released immediately. The Russians as usual promised to increase tax collection. Russia's federal budget deficit would fall from 6.8 percent of GDP to 5.6 percent in 1998, they said, and the government would run a budget surplus of 3 percent of GDP in 1999.

Boris Nemtsov, with the extreme arrogance that had marked the Yeltsin reformers from the beginning, told Chrystia Freeland that a "geopolitical calculus" left the West with no choice: "For the West it would be absolutely undesirable to have a financial collapse of Russia, a financial and political collapse. . . . I think they behaved absolutely predictably." But Nemtsov also had a second, very different explanation.

Freeland reported that the U.S. Treasury "swung the deal for Russia," and Nemtsov explained, "[The Treasury team] are Chubais's friends. . . . This is one of those rare occasions when personal relations to a large extent determine the taking of large political decisions."[95]

As part of the agreement with the IMF, the Russian government swapped $6.4 billion of GKOs for foreign currency bonds and announced it would no longer issue short-term bonds of less than a year's duration. Nevertheless, the debt swap added 40 percent to the total stock of outstanding foreign currency debt. The title of the *Financial Times* report included the words "exchange gamble" because of a recognition that "the response means that Russia may be tempted to repeat the exercise as a way of further restructuring its domestic bond market."[96] A week previously the restructured Soviet-era paper known as Prins already was selling at 43 cents on the dollar, and a huge new supply was not likely to increase its value. In fact, it fell to 36 cents on the dollar. Every Wednesday the finance ministry had to redeem $10 billion in government bonds.[97]

The likelihood of a favorable western response decreased still further as news—or rumors—circulated about what had happened with the July IMF money. The *Wall Street Journal* concluded flatly that when Russia received the emergency grant of $4.8 billion in July 1998, "The Russian central bank spent nearly all the IMF money bankrolling capital flight." Michael Mussa, the IMF's chief economist, who disagreed with the policy of his superiors and the U.S. Treasury Department, reportedly called the Russian government a "bunch of criminals."[98]

As short-term bonds became due every week and had to be refinanced, the rates that had to be offered reflected the perception of high risk. By late August the ruble could no longer be defended. On August 22 Yeltsin announced the return of Viktor Chernomyrdin to the premiership to replace Kiriyenko, a sign that the situation was becoming desperate. On August 25 the currency fell 9 percent before the Central Bank suspended trading twice and supported the ruble. The Russian banks themselves were reportedly dumping any rubles or ruble-denominated instruments for dollars. A long-time Russian observer of the economy, Mikhail Berger, defended them, saying that they had no choice. "There are no GKOs, there are no bonds that are worth anything."[99] On August 27 the Central Bank stopped supporting the ruble and suspended payment on some debt. It was no longer possible—and would not be for some time—to obtain dollars at banks and even for Americans to send dollars to other Americans in Moscow through the banking system.

The speed of the financial collapse was breathtaking. The Russian RTS stock index had declined from 411 at the beginning of the year to the mid-130s in the week before the IMF loan, but rose to 193 on July 20.[100] It then fell back to 143 by July 20 and had reached 101 by August 13 and 66 by the end of the month. On September 18 it stood at 50. The price of Vimpel on the New York Stock Exchange fell from 51 on July 15 to 9 by the end of August and to 6 on September 18. Many had talked about a devaluation of the ruble by some 20 percent, but it fell from 6 rubles to the dollar in July to 14 in October and 20 in December. By the spring of 1999, it was around 24.

The Aftermath of the Collapse

Viktor Chernomyrdin had little credibility after serving as premier for more than five years and pursuing a policy different from what he had promised the Congress when he was confirmed in December 1992. His new promises inevitably were unconvincing. The Duma refused to confirm him. This time Yeltsin chose not to have a confrontation with the Duma, but nominated Yevgeny Primakov as premier. Primakov, like Yeltsin, had been a candidate member of the Politburo in the Gorbachev period, but he was one of only a small group of Gorbachev associates whom Yeltsin trusted. Yeltsin had put him in charge of foreign intelligence in 1991 and then in early 1996 had named him foreign minister.

Primakov's tenure as premier was to last for little more than half a year, and it had a most peculiar character. When he came to power, he named a leading Communist, Yury Masliukov, as the first deputy premier in charge of the economy. Masliukov proclaimed an industrial policy. He had been chairman of Gosplan under Gorbachev and also a candidate member of the Politburo. A leading member of the Agrarian party, Gennady Kulik, was named deputy premier for agriculture. A large group of economists with whom Primakov had been associated in the Academy of Sciences argued for a more expansionist money supply, and most thought they spoke for Primakov.

But Yeltsin retained his neoliberal minister of finance, Mikhail Zadornov. Again the cabinet was irreconcilably divided. With Primakov's approval or without, Zadornov continued a tight monetary policy. The collapse in the ruble and the end of an inflow of foreign money meant a major decline in the import of consumer goods. The 1998 grain harvest had fallen to the 1995 level, 48 million tons, and living standards declined approximately 25 percent. With the government, despite the announced policy of Masliukov, still refusing to introduce a pro-investment industrial policy, the Primakov government actually introduced a policy as close to shock therapy as had ever been seen in Yeltsin's Russia.

By April and May, Russian authorities were reporting an increase in industrial production. Some claimed that the decline in the exchange rate of the ruble had been so pronounced as to constitute an effective tariff against imports and to promote an import-substitution program. These were usually the same people who in the previous summer had insisted that the collapse of the ruble would be a disaster for Russia, and, in fact, the Russian government in September 1999 claimed only investment had stopped falling.[101]

This was a period when oil prices rose from the $11 level toward $25 and when the prices of other commodities firmed. According to the international rating agency Fitch IBCA, a $1 rise in the price of oil meant a $2 billion increase in revenues for the energy section, and gross domestic product was $230 billion. These figures imply that a $14 increase in oil prices should raise the value of production by $28 billion.[102] The rise in announced industrial production was surprisingly small in light of these improvements, and basically the Russian economy in the spring of 1999 seemed to be suffering from all its old ills. Many basic items were being distributed free by barter, and agriculture and manufacturing seemed stagnant.

The real change after August 1998 involved the end of hope of foreign loans or investment. A year after the collapse Fitch IBCA reported a sovereign foreign currency debt of nearly $160 billion, 7.7 times the annual federal cash revenue in 1998, "by far the highest of any rated sovereign."[103] The debates about IMF assistance focused on loans that never left Washington, but that were used only to roll over old IMF loans. A scandal about the Russian flow of money through American banks threatened even this assistance.

EIGHT   *Institutions,*
Market Reform,
and Democracy

At the beginning of the 1990s, many explicitly or implicitly assumed that new market institutions would arise almost automatically if the institutions of the old communist system were destroyed. By the end of the decade, virtually everyone recognized that the early assumptions had been too optimistic. They drew the lesson that the state and legal system are more important for a well-functioning market than they appreciated at the beginning of the decade. They turned to the insight of Douglass North that markets are not some inherent part of the state of nature and that institutions are a crucial foundation for markets. "Institutions are the humanly devised constraints that structure human interaction. They are made up of formal constraints (rules, laws, constitutions), informal constraints (norms of behavior, conventions, and self-imposed codes of conduct), and their enforcement characteristics. Together they define the incentive structure of societies and specifically economies."[1]

Unfortunately, the universal new recognition of the importance of "institutions" only means the word is so vague that any meaning can be imputed to it. For some it means a military dictator such as Augusto Pinochet who will impose the IMF's program, while for others it implies a government-directed industrial policy such as that found in the Pacific Rim countries. For still others, strengthening institutions means protecting legality and property rights in some vague and ill-defined manner. Almost no one focuses on North's reference to "incentive structure" and draws the conclusion that the fundamental task of a reformer is to try to modify it to produce desirable behavior.

Those who want to say that the West and its model had no responsibility for developments in Russia have been attracted to North's "informal constraints," to his use of phrases such as "mental models" and "belief structures" in his Nobel Prize speech, and to his assertion that even though "the formal institutional framework" of the communist economy was destroyed, this development was undercut by "the survival of many of the informal constraints" of the old communist system.[2] Such persons tend to use the absence of institutions and the corruption endogenous to Russian society as an excuse for the failure of reform. The conclusion, as Stanley Fischer of the IMF argued in September 1999, is that the West probably had little influence on Russia.[3]

There are three fundamental problems with this position. First, as noted in previous chapters, Yeltsin was a construction engineer with twenty years of experience in construction administration. He came from the industrial center of Sverdlovsk, where he had made major contributions to its industrial development. The political and administrative elite comprised other engineers like himself, and they clearly wanted an industrial policy to support insider-owners. Without unwavering western support for Russian neoliberal economists, it is inconceivable that either Yeltsin's instincts or domestic Russian political forces would have produced the policy that resulted.

Second, everyone was totally aware in the 1980s and the early 1990s that Russia had no cultural and institutional preparation for capitalism. In fact, western advocates of radical reform explicitly referred to the lack of institutional preparation as the reason that the old institutions had to be utterly destroyed and that the transition to a market had to be rapid.[4] But if, in fact, the communist system and Russian culture were incompatible with a rapid transition to a normal market economy, and if new institutions would not rise automatically, then the West should have advocated a different policy and made its assistance conditional on its adoption.

Third, classical economics was developed by men such as Adam Smith and David Ricardo in the very early stages of capitalism when their societies had little capitalist culture and few of the governmental institutional restraints that we take for granted at the end of the twentieth century. The economists of the early nineteenth century were right in insisting on the primacy of self-interest and incentives as motivating forces for economic actors at that time. It was precisely the destruction of old institutions and the failure of the new capitalist informal restraints to have developed that made self-interest so crucial a factor at this stage. It was this that made "formal constraints . . . and their enforcement characteristics" so important. As the giants of contemporary neoliberal economic thought realize, rational self-interest can—and sometimes should—lead people to crime, corruption, the creation of a mafia, and capital flight.

Capitalism without enforceable restraints—pure laissez-faire capitalism—is "Klondike capitalism": the capitalism of the gun and the claim-jumper. That is the rational response of rational economic actors when enforceable restraints do not exist. Early capitalism often has this character. Thomas Hobbes was not that wrong in suggesting that life in England in the 1680s was "poor, nasty, brutish, and short," and not simply because of the civil war. Karl Marx was not that wrong about the defects in German capitalism before 1850. Indeed, Douglass North himself equates "laissez faire" and "anarchy."

Without question, Russia in the 1990s featured a great deal of illegality and corruption. Nevertheless, the central thesis of this book is that the importance of illegality and corruption as an exogenous force in the Russian economy has been greatly exaggerated. The utter scandal is that so much of the "corruption" in Russia has been legal and has been the logical consequence of the policy that has been advocated by the West. Yeltsin's Russia had well-defined institutions in the sense of rules of the game enforced by the state—and enforced rather strictly. Firms that essentially remained state enterprises were "privatized" so that state officials could receive dividends and sell their shares to foreigners. Firms with profits were forced by the government to give them as subsidies to other enterprises and local government. Most subsidies were given through "loans" or deferred payments so that the insider-owners would be bankrupted and lose their property rights. As long as the Russian government formally agreed to say publicly what was required to conform to IMF policy, the West did not seem to care if even the most widely read "reform" newspapers such as *Izvestiia* and *Kommersant Daily*, let alone the left-wing press, reported that the words were fraudulent.

The problem in Russia in the 1990s has not been the dead hand of old Russian or communist culture, values, and institutions. Russia is like the western Europe of Adam Smith, Ricardo, and Marx, when the destruction of old cultures and institutions threw economic actors back on their "naked self-interest" (Marx's phrase)—and very short-term self-interest at that. Russians were given no incentives to follow their long-term interests, let alone those that would lead to the collective public good. The central problem was not the capital flight of the corrupt, but the fact that the corrupt and noncorrupt alike had an incentive to take a very short-range perspective and to send their capital abroad.

Thus the Russian experience did not refute the insights and models developed by the classical economists in early European capitalism, but reaffirmed their accuracy. The Russian reform demonstrated that its authors were right that Russians were normal, rational economic men. Unfortunately, it demonstrated the point by creating an incentive system that led rational actors to the kind of behavior that was incompatible with economic growth.

The central problem with the economic system is that the rules and incentives did not promote economic growth. The rules and incentives were not the impersonal ones inherent in the western economic model, but instead they flowed from the needs and instincts of a personalistic, premodern ruler. Russians responded well to the actual incentives created for them, but neither the Russian economic reformers of the 1990s nor their supporters in the West ever showed any awareness of this fact.

For this reason the pattern of Russian economic reform provides a powerful impetus for both political scientists and economists to rethink their institutional theories. These lessons must also be absorbed in Russia if it is to move toward the creation of a normal market and real democracy. Vague talk about the need for institutions and a legal system, let alone a vague demand for an end to corruption, is no more useful than the earlier insistence that Russia jump to the other side of the chasm in a single leap.

Drafters of tax legislation in the West are keenly aware that the tiniest provision, the smallest misstep in language affects behavior profoundly as economic actors play games with the tax code or seek loopholes. A comparative study of reform in Latin America found that "fairly precise differences in the rules for political competition appear to make big differences in the behavior of politicians. . . . As a result, differences between authoritarian and democratic systems appear relatively insignificant."[5] That sense of the major impact of incentives and the need to craft them carefully must be even more important when even broader economic reform is introduced. This is true not only of Russia, but of other nonmarket or semimarket economies as well.

Conceptualizing Russia in Developmental Terms

We in the West have had enormous difficulty in thinking about Russia. The supporters of Yeltsin and the IMF program moved with embarrassing speed to say that Russia had a normal market economy and a democracy, and many continued to describe Russia in these terms long after it was clear that they had little relevance to the Russian scene. At first both political scientists and economists tended to see Russia in terms of Latin America of the 1980s. The economists explicitly took "the Washington consensus" developed by the international community of economists working with Latin America in the 1980s and applied it in eastern Europe and then Russia. The political science theory of democratization in Russia and Eastern Europe in the 1980s and 1990s was also based almost entirely on the experience of southern Europe and Latin America of the 1970s and 1980s.

As conditions deteriorated, observers grasped for other images. The old neo-Marxist descriptions of the managers of the means of production (the nomenklatura) continued to be applied to them after they became insider-owner capitalists. Russia's capitalists, it was said, were against capitalism, and they were the main cause of the failure of capitalist reform![6] Then Lenin's and Stalin's image of an all-powerful financial oligarchy (government is subordinate to Wall Street) was applied to those who actually were Yeltsin's patrimonial agents in distributing subsidies through banks that were only formally privatized. When all else failed, Russia simply was described as an inherently corrupt society because of the alleged corruption of the Soviet period. Often these images were combined in an utterly inconsistent manner.[7]

All this was highly misleading. The analogy with the large Latin American countries in the 1980s and 1990s is particularly dangerous. These countries were actually comparable to southern Europe in their economic and political development. Their capitalism was relatively advanced. They had been through a number of cycles of attempted and failed democratization, through which their elites had accumulated a great deal of experience with democracy and semidemocracy. The American literature on the transition to democracy in Latin America in the 1970s described it as a pact among these elites, and at a minimum Latin America certainly had solid elite groups.

Russians in the 1980s, however, had no memories of the country's earlier attempts at democratization and capitalism, and economic reformers did not even study the highly successful Russian industrialization program of the 1890s and early 1900s. Most dictatorships in the early and middle stages of capitalism feature quasi-democratic institutions without much power, but with real political competition. Such dictatorships often develop a limited, almost semiconstitutional nature. England, we say, became liberal before it became democratic. The Communists in Russia, by contrast, did not tolerate any organized opposition, and they explicitly rejected the legitimacy of political restraints on the representatives of the proletariat—that is, themselves.

Our conceptualization of Russia must be based on the experience of Europe, the United States, and Latin America in the eighteenth, nineteenth, and early twentieth centuries. Lewis Namier described the relationship of eighteenth-century British kings and the House of Commons as we would describe Yeltsin's relationship to the Russian legislature.[8] The politics of the United States before the Civil War centered on the acquisition of property by dubious means, the seeking of deposits of government money for personal banks created for the purpose, and the obtaining of subsidies for canals and then railroads. This was fifty years before the era of the robber barons and their corrupt links with government.

The introduction of universal white male suffrage and real democracy in the United States during the 1820s and 1830s led to a period of political chaos, in which no president was even renominated from 1844 to 1860 and the party system disintegrated. This contributed mightily to the Civil War.[9] The introduction of universal suffrage in Italy after World War I quickly led to Mussolini's coming to power and, more slowly, to Hitler's victory in Germany and civil war in Spain. Democracy would have produced a fundamentalist Islamic regime in Algeria in the 1990s had not the army intervened. Small wonder that early democracy usually has the limited character of Germany under Bismarck, Turkey and Indonesia during this century, Russia from 1906 to 1917, Nigeria today, and the United States for the first fifty years after the revolution. Boris Yeltsin is a typical authoritarian ruler in early semidemocracy and should not be criticized for this fact, but for the economic policy he chose to follow as a limited authoritarian ruler.

The foremost problem for understanding of Russia for supporters and critics of Yeltsin alike is that we all take for granted a modern society—what Max Weber called a "rational-technical society." We take for granted that laws exist and have meaning, that bureaucracies function more or less effectively, and that government and bureaucracy should be damned for being too impersonal rather than the opposite.[10] Adam Smith's phrase "invisible hand" does not mean anarchy (the absence of a hand), but predictable, impersonal rules, laws, and incentives with a powerful impact on economic actors, but without continual arbitrary and personal intervention by government officials. These must be created.

Compare our expectations about Russia in the 1990s with our assumptions about the collapse of the quite effective preindustrial polities and economies—"civilizations"—about which Arnold Toynbee wrote. The pharaohs, Roman emperors, and Mayan rulers all created well-functioning, state-dominated systems of rules, regulations, and incentives, but Toynbee would have considered it bizarre to expect that their collapse would automatically give rise to a new and better set of market-oriented rules and incentives. So would we. But we somehow think that rational-technical rules and laws are inherent in the state of nature in modern society and that the collapse of communist civilization should automatically have a different result than that of the Inca civilization.

In fact, a rational-technical society was never inherent in the state of nature. Max Weber treated all polities before industrial society—all of Toynbee's "civilizations"—as patriarchal and patrimonial in their political systems. He considered the rise of rational-technical capitalism such an aberration for human psychology that he was driven to explain it as the product of a strange and inconsistent Calvinist religion.[11] Russia under Yeltsin has much in common with these early premodern polities. Yegor Gaidar caught this when he complained about the palace politics of the Yeltsin regime. Russian reporters catch it when they use words like "clans," "court favorites," or "the family," and Yeltsin encouraged it when he called people such as Aleksandr Korzhakov and the young neoliberal reformers his "children."

Similarly, Russia has been much closer to the traditional subsistence premodern economy without investment than we have been able to assimilate. The line between "private" and "state" property is quite blurred, and both have much in common with Max Weber's conception of patrimonial bureaucracy, in which officials expropriate their "salaries" on an irregular basis from those they administer. Subsidies are not granted on the basis of impersonal formulas, but on a personal, ad hoc basis. The problem in Russia is neither the lack of government involvement in the economy, nor "a weak state," but the governing of the economy through the all-too-visible hand of individual government officials rather than through a more invisible hand. Indeed, a very substantial number of people, including many in the city, avoid hunger only by growing their potatoes and vegetables on their own garden plot.

All observers of Russia agree that the first crucial task in Russia is to establish impersonal rules and incentives that lead economic actors to behavior that is beneficial to society, not harmful to it. The second crucial task is to institutionalize these incentives—that is, to give economic actors the confidence that the incentives have meaning in the present and will continue to have such meaning in the future so that they can take a long-term view.

The government is a key part of the guarantee of the predictability on which modern capitalism rests. Indeed, at the most basic level, a modern market is an artificial construct that is *created* by government and enforced by it—even a badly functioning market such as in Russia or Zaire. Capitalism is not a synonym for markets. After all, markets in the sense of bazaars have existed since Biblical times and before. Capitalism also is not synonymous with private ownership of the means of production, for premodern privatized agriculture is not capitalist in nature. The nomadic shepherds of Biblical times owned their own flocks. As the word itself implies, capitalism is a system for accumulating and using large sums of capital over the long term.

The key differences between the market of the bazaar and the market of modern capitalism are two. The modern capitalist market needs much larger long-term investment and a longer-term perspective on the part of economic actors than the market of the bazaar. In a bazaar, like a flea market, an exchange or purchase is usually made on the spot, and the seller may not even worry about a reputation for reliability for future sales.

A well-functioning market is dependent on an exogenous enforcement agency that has the force to control any private armies (mafias, gangs, enterprise security forces, and the like) and demonstrations in the streets against unpopular economic actions. It must have the desire and the ability to protect economic actors against theft, to enforce contracts, and to regulate banking institutions. The modern state also engages in a wide variety of other regulatory actions that are broadly popular. In these senses, Russia needs a strong state.

While the state is necessary to create and protect a market, it can also be a great threat to property and economic growth. Mancur Olson saw the state as a "stationary bandit" that finds it more profitable to extract money through regular taxation than through traditional banditry, and he argued that this gives a far-sighted ruler the incentive to promote economic growth in order to increase tax collection. We do not object strenuously to the type of dictatorship found in Jordan or to the semidictatorship found in Turkey, which generally protect John Locke's "life, liberty, and property."

Unfortunately, many rulers have seen it to be in their interest to maximize short-term profits through a predatory policy, and Olson was unable to explain why one ruler decides to adopt a short-term policy and another a long-term one. This indeterminacy in the policy of dictatorial rulers led Olson to argue that democracy is necessary because the broad population has a long-term interest in growth.[12] Olson fails to mention, however, that democracies in countries in the early and middle stages of industrialization—such as the Philippines, India, and Latin America before the 1970s—often emphasized consumption and protection rather than growth. Indeed, as Yeltsin continued his policies of subsidies and toleration of corruption, many Russian supporters of radical market reform quietly moved to the belief that democracy has been counterproductive.

A democratic political system has many similarities with a market. It is supposed to provide incentives that, like Adam Smith's "invisible hand" in the economy, lead politicians to be responsive to the public. Indeed, the election law introduced in Russia was carefully drafted to have even more precise consequences: the formation of several centrist parties for the legislative elections and the attraction of centrist candidates for the 1996 presidential elections. The formal rules did not have the projected effect in either the 1993, 1995, or 1999 Duma elections or in the 1996 or 2000 presidential elections.

The abstract democratic model in Russia failed to produce the predicted results for the same reasons that the abstract economic model failed to do so. Political actors, like economic actors, respond to the real incentives that they encounter, not the incentive structure of some abstract model, and the real incentives for both political and economic actors were shaped decisively by the political leader.

Nevertheless, general talk about the need for a strong state or strict enforcement of the laws to institutionalize impersonal rules encounters Mancur Olson's problem of ensuring that the dictator takes a long-term view. In fact, historically the early state has precisely the same characteristics as the economy. Just as economic actors find it economically rational to steal, so political officials have an interest in demanding bribes and calling off the next election or conducting a coup. There are, in fact, countries that have "Klondike politics," in which officials usually do precisely these things. Indeed, it is the personalized, patrimonial character of the state that creates personalized and patrimonial rules in the economy. Government leaders often have an interest in resisting an institutionalization of rules that will restrict their political power and advantages in gaining wealth. People like Yeltsin and Chubais are familiar figures during a preinstitutionalized stage of development.

Unless dictators operate under self-imposed constraints, introduce a certain amount of predictability, create incentive systems conducive to economic growth, and begin to organize bureaucracies and legal structures, they can have an economic policy even more predatory or populist than Yeltsin's. If the market is to function well, the state must operate in a fairly predictable way with a well-structured bureaucracy.[13] Written constitutions, unfortunately, often impose little restraint on rulers, and political scientists have made little progress in specifying why and how meaningful constitutional restraints develop.

It is not that crucial whether Russia has a democracy, a semidemocracy, or a dictatorship. What is crucial is that it have the right type of whatever form of government it has. All recognize that it is crucial to institute impersonal rules that guide the actions of economic actors in socially desirable directions. However, the political sphere needs the same kind of impersonal rules and incentives, and the processes of establishing them in the political and economic spheres are closely related. The creation of a "rational-technical" economy and a "rational-technical" polity must go together.

We need to understand that Russia has reached the present point in history by a very atypical path. The development of modern constitutional democracy usually begins with the establishment of constitutional government—of formal and informal restraints on the ruler's ability to interfere with John Locke's "life, liberty, and property." Government—even dictatorial government—becomes more bureaucratized, more regularized, more responsive to a plurality of elites rather than simply to the military or the landed aristocracy. The process, however, often is not as linear as it was in England.

From this perspective, Russian history is extraordinarily atypical. The introduction of the provincial zemstvos in the 1870s and then the liberalization and creation of the Duma after the Revolution of 1905 seemed to represent a "normal" European pattern. The tsar seemed to be evolving toward constitutional monarchy as had England after 1688 and Germany after 1848. That the attempt at democratization in March 1917 ended in dictatorship was also quite normal. The nature of the dictatorship established in November 1917 was not typical, however. The communist dictators explicitly rejected the legitimacy of the limitations on government power that usually are key elements in the development of constitutional democracy at this stage.

As a result, the Russian population entered the democratization of the 1980s with an extraordinarily high level of education and experience with participatory institutions, but it had a political elite and intelligentsia with none of the usual experience with a limited, liberal dictatorship or with the semidemocracy of a Turkey or Jordan today. No doubt, the failure of the population, thus far, to support a demagogue at the polls is testimony to the former phenomenon, and the failure to establish a more regularized political and economic system is testimony to the latter. The tragedy of the Yeltsin experience was not that he was authoritarian, but that he instituted personalistic, patrimonial rule rather than the normal authoritarian system of more impersonal rules and laws.

In a sense, however, this was to be expected in a country with Russia's unusual pattern of development. Neither Gorbachev nor Yeltsin had any sense of the strange combination in constitutional democracy of majority rule and of limitations on the majority that would have developed in a normal limited government. Gorbachev had an almost anarchistic definition of democracy in which the use of any force is illegitimate, even to enforce the law. Yeltsin not only seemed incapable of the normal bargaining that occurs in a limited dictatorship among institutionalized elites, but he never accepted the legitimacy of such elites. It was the West's duty to emphasize the need for constitutional government, but instead it encouraged Yeltsin in his personalistic definition of democracy.

Getting from Here to There

But if the crucial requirement in Russia is the creation of a "rational-technical society" in which public and private units act on the basis of impersonal rules and laws rather than personalistic considerations, no one has a firm grasp of how this is to be done. Social scientists have never really explained how the corruption and chaos of early markets is transformed into the more stable markets we know, or why early democracy that is so subject to coup d'états evolves into modern democracy that seldom has them. Rational actor analysts have done much to explain the behavior of people acting within a particular framework of incentives, but they have been much less successful in explaining why one framework is established and not another.

Even less do analysts know how to advise other countries how to make the transition. Clearly the process takes decades, and clearly the transition is characterized by distasteful measures and activities that may be necessary, but that are difficult to recommend. The process of institutionalizing market and democratic institutions is the subject of another book that will follow this one, and this concluding section will focus only on several general points that are important to keep in mind in thinking about Russia.

Embracing Russian Capitalists and the Coase Theorem

The first crucial prerequisite for successful economic reform in Russia is to recognize that capitalists are indispensable to capitalism. The Russian capitalist class should be supported instead of being the subject of continuous and sustained attack. The most remarkable and bizarre development in western thought about Russia in the 1990s was that capitalism in its neoliberal vision was glorified inordinately by the same people who saw Russian capitalists in Marxist terms as evil parasites. The Russian capitalist class was supposed to be against reform—that is, to be against capitalism.

Despite the rhetoric of the Russian revolution, the people who actually carried out the revolution and destroyed the Soviet state were the bureaucrats, the members of the nomenklatura. They did not defend the presumed interests of their institutions, but persistently followed their individual interests in acquiring and defending their property.[14]

Instead of throttling reform, the bureaucrats took advantage of vague legislation, such as the Law on Enterprises of 1987, to maximize their own personal interests at the expense of the interests of society. The danger was not that those employed in the control agencies prevented managers from being independent, but that they themselves displayed independence by "privatizing" taxation of those making private profit legally or illegally.

In October 1991 Yeltsin announced that those who conducted the capitalist revolution in Russia would become its first capitalists. Small-scale property would be subject to sale so that a range of people could enter the petit-bourgeoisie, but the insiders would acquire control in the privatization of large economic units, the real means of production. Those associated with the Chubais team reported that anything more was hardly conceivable in the fall of 1991. Power was soon taken from the quasi-ministerial institutions that came to dominate the Russian economy from late 1991 through the first part of 1993, but even their officials had the opportunity to acquire important positions at the enterprise level.

The transfer of property to insider-owners was an intelligent decision to the extent that privatization of large industry was to be undertaken. Westerners always had a high opinion of the quality of the Soviet heavy industrial managers they had met. These men did not have any experience with the market, and clearly they needed to hire staff members who understood finance, marketing, advertising, and the like. Nevertheless, they were engineers with production experience, and there was no other group in Russian society that was remotely as qualified to restructure industry. At a minimum, they ultimately should have become the plant managers within a larger corporate or banking-corporate structure.

The West and those supported by the West in the Yeltsin government, however, quickly adopted a policy of expropriating the property of the new Russian capitalist class. The United States financed a voucher program to achieve this goal. Westerners protested open subsidies, but not the practice of making subsidies through loans, which had the inevitable and foreseeable consequence of bankrupting the capitalist owners. The western economists continually pushed for a more vigorous application of the bankruptcy laws. The very people who supported this policy most strongly were those who said that secure property rights in Russia were the first precondition for successful reform!

The expressed reason for this policy was the belief that the production managers of the old regime—nay, the nomenklatura—were too hidebound to respond to the incentives of a market economy and to restructure industry. In this view, only young academic economists and former Komsomol (Young Communist League) secretaries, neither of whom knew anything about industry and little about markets except from academic models, had the necessary skills to transform Russian industry.

In fact, the Komsomol officials of the 1980s were the group most often described by specialists on the Soviet Union as incompetent political hacks. For example, the future premier, Sergei Kiriyenko, was to be inordinately praised as a technocrat. In 1990 he was a twenty-eight-year-old second secretary of the Gorkii (Nizhnii Novgorod) regional committee of the Komsomol, a position he had attained after serving as Komsomol secretary at a local defense plant. Three years later Nemtsov selected him as head of one of the key banks in Nizhnii Novgorod to assist him in the politically determined distribution of subsidies. This was the type of person to whom state intervention was supposed to transfer the property of the insider-owners.

The American democratization program was an arm of the economic policy, and it defined democrats as those intellectuals who supported radical economic reform and supported Yeltsin, not as those who tried to move to the center of the political spectrum in the manner of American politicians. The young procapitalist radicals were strongly advised not to associate with Russian capitalists, whom we would call Big Business, but to damn them as conservative and procommunist. The reform parties were expected to become large conservative parties like the Republican party in the United States and the Christian-Democratic party in Germany, but not to have the alliance with big business or the right-wing or nationalist symbolic issues that all major conservative parties have. By all appearances, aid was made dependent on their taking this position.[15]

The ideology of this policy was the Coase theorem. Neoliberal reformers particularly emphasized the implication of the theorem that, without state intervention, property would naturally flow into the hands of those who could use it most effectively. That is, in the name of the Coase theorem and a neoliberal model that said property inevitably would flow into the correct hands if the government were not involved, the West supported active state intervention to take property away from the capitalists who understood industry and give it to these young economists and Komsomol secretaries.

The reader of the previous paragraphs must suspect that they are satire or at least gross exaggeration. Unfortunately, they are the literal truth. Unfortunately, the consequences of the policy were precisely those that the neoliberal model would predict. The establishment of well-functioning markets is a public good, and the economic reformers in charge of creating institutions had no individual self-interest in creating a public good. Instead, they had an interest in setting up institutions that would enrich themselves personally, and this they did while the IMF made their rent-seeking a condition of aid.

The capitalist insider-owners, deprived of "the incentive to use assets for the creation and enhancement of wealth," in Richard Ericson's words, followed their rational self-interest. As Ericson predicted, they engaged in the "exploitation [of property] for current income."[16] The policy was doubly foolish, for Yeltsin was determined to subsidize large city consumption to maintain his political base—a goal that the American government approved. This meant he would limit the amount of unemployment that could be imposed on their workers, and the policy of making the insider-owners insecure in their property rights could accomplish nothing positive.

No doubt the new Russian capitalists—the insider-owners—have various serious flaws. They have little experience with capitalism, and they often have sought government subsidies, tariffs, and other kinds of assistance. But Marx was also right that the capitalists of his time had flaws and that they tried to subordinate government to themselves through individual corruption, if not united class action. The muckrakers were right about the robber barons in the United States and the corruption of that time. Today American capitalists all have lobbyists in Washington, D.C., and most give political contributions to politicians. Both steps are an attempt to use the state to further their economic goals. In capitalism, capitalists seek to maximize profit, and the use of government is one obvious way to try to do so.

Russia and the West should, in fact, wholeheartedly accept the argument from the Coase theorem that property in Russia eventually will flow to those who can use it most productively. The implication is that we need not worry about the insider-owners. They should be supported in a variety of ways and with a variety of investment funds to improve the performance of their property. Only as the property becomes attractive will the most competent owners buy out the insider-owners. The insider-owners should be reassured that they will, in fact, have an opportunity to sell out at a major profit if they improve performance. There is every reason to think that they will sell stock to raise capital and enrich themselves as Bill Gates and the many developers of American Internet firms have done in recent years.

Instead of emphasizing the need to bankrupt the members of the Russian capitalist class (except in the case of small or new businesses that fail), Russia should be emphasizing the sanctity of their property rights. It should be proclaiming that it will apply the bankruptcy laws to significant enterprises only in the rarest of cases. Those large enterprises that have been bankrupted or lie idle should usually be returned to their former insider-owners—if not to the old managers, then to their younger chief deputies. Old loans should be written off, and new loans should be given only for long-term investment or for short-term operating expenses in which repayment from cash sales is absolutely certain. Subsidies should come in the form of outright grants or state orders.

Officials have a particularly strong interest to use the state to grab property when the property produces immediate windfall profits. For this reason, it is important to renationalize the industries producing raw materials for export and the trading firms engaged in this activity. Because of the depression, most manufacturing plants are not in this category and can be left privatized to those who will rebuild them. It is quite likely that the young economists who have been trying to use government to try to expropriate the Russian capitalist class for their own benefit will not win in a true Coaseian competition. They simply do not have the skills. But this is precisely why the West should not have been supporting them.

Gradual Reform as a Response to Information Problems

The literature of economics and political science of the past four decades has emphasized the problems of insufficient information and of information cost, both in economics and in politics. Customers will not always seek the lowest prices in the market, nor will entrepreneurs always follow a strategy of maximizing profit, for the information costs may simply be too high to follow this strategy. Transaction costs often are too high for the kind of free negotiation that Ronald Coase has shown is theoretically best; hence state intervention is a more efficient alternative. The same argument has been made in the political realm. For example, political parties are said to be crucial to reduce information costs for the voter and to facilitate participation.

Rational actors must adjust to the amount of information at their disposal and weigh the costs of acquiring more. When they do not know, they usually do not have the luxury of waiting for complete information, and they court disaster if they try blindly to maximize on the basis of some abstract ideological model. In the words of Herbert Simon and James March, they must "satisfice."[17]

The information problem is a crucial argument in favor of gradual reform. No one can be certain about the effects even of simple macroeconomic monetary policies;[18] even the effects of changes in the U.S. tax code or banking regulations are not clear until they are thoroughly explored by lawyers and business people trying to enrich themselves. The United States continually adjusts its rules, regulations, and tax codes in response to unexpected behavior and problems. The consequences of radical structural changes in a little-understood foreign economy are even more obscure, and the possibility of serious mistakes is quite high.

The crucial lesson to be relearned by westerners and to be learned by Russian reformers is that mistakes are not irreversible. For example, it is wrong to say, as is often done, that Gorbachev should have considered the Chinese reform, but that now it is too late.[19] No complete reform of any country should ever be totally introduced in another, but many aspects of the Chinese reform are still quite appropriate today. Thus Russian economic reform should have begun in agriculture in 1986, and it is still not too late today. Indeed, it remains the most immediate priority.

Similarly, privatization of the resource-exporting industries was a major mistake, but they can be renationalized. Now that it is clear that investment will not occur automatically, steps can be taken to make it happen. As Gerschenkron correctly pointed out in his discussion of the Russia of Nikolai II, the government can promote investment in different ways, at first directly more than indirectly, and can gradually pull back as economic actors gain confidence and financial institutions are created.

For many, gradual reform simply means introducing the ideal measures of the neoliberal model gradually. The economists of the international economic community have become so accustomed to dealing with the third world, with poorly functioning markets and distorting governmental intervention, that they proclaim almost automatically that government's role must always be reduced. They use language like "a strong state," but they simply mean a state that controls popular desires for social welfare measures and protection. They automatically condemn an industrial policy on the grounds that governments cannot choose winners better than the market—without realizing that this argument is not even relevant to the argument that in early capitalism government must play a crucial role in investment because of the lack of trust in impersonal financial institutions.

A number of very serious compromises are necessary. Of course, property rights must be strengthened, but this is incompatible with universal privatization and continual talk of bankruptcy. Of course, there must be a real banking system in which banks make real loans for real economic purposes. But until the economy begins to function adequately, this means an end to the use of the banking system for covert subsidization of consumption. And this means that the IMF must free the Russian government from the need for constant deceit in the way that it provides subsidies.

Of course, there must be a concerted effort to attract foreign investment, but this will occur only when foreign investment in the manufacturing sector is protected by high tariffs. Paradoxically, the renationalization of the energy sector in conjunction with open subsidies of, say, urban heating plants in other parts of the budget might well create the transparency that encourages foreign investment in a formally nationalized sector more than in one more formally privatized.

The first stages may require various compromises that can later be phased out. Agricultural reform is an excellent example. Even accepting that the free sale and purchase of land is the basis of the most efficient agriculture, nothing would be more disastrous in Russia than the kind of privatization usually called "land reform." If land were simply distributed to the peasants, more than half would be acquired by persons too old or unqualified to work it. The countryside, however, is not limited to old peasants. There are many people who have college or secondary specialized agricultural education and great administrative experience within the collective farms. These highly trained individuals would make first-class private farmers, as would many of the well-educated and skilled "mechanizers" (tractor and combine drivers).

Agricultural reform must be introduced in stages so that productive incentives are phased in properly. First, agriculture needs to be monetarized, with the collective farm managers free to produce what they think most profitable for the market. The prices must be determined by the marketplace, and the farms should not have to compete with subsidized foreign imports, either those financed by foreign credit or those received by "barter" from the former union republics. The farms must be advanced credit so that they can purchase farm machinery, fertilizers, and pesticides.

Second, the collective farms must be divided into parcels of land or types of activity (chicken broiler units or pig farms), with each placed under the supervision of a qualified specialist-farmer. The land should be leased to these specialist-farmers, who should pay rent to the collective farm or be required to hire the older or unqualified peasants on a subsidized basis as a form of rent.

These leases should be long-term, but after a period in which the system has worked smoothly, the specialist-farmers should be given the right to sell the leases to others who will engage in agriculture. Eventually they should be able to buy out the lease. As in China, the collective farm should take on industrial and related activities on a market basis.

The reason that neither Gorbachev nor Yeltsin introduced agricultural reform was a fear that the immediate result would be increased food prices and lower living standards in the major cities. The August 1998 financial crisis only increased the fear of a surge in food prices in the face of the disastrous 1998 and 1999 harvests. The government needs to consider a solution such as that adopted at first by China: the government would purchase a fixed amount of food at low prices and distribute it through a system of rationing at highly subsidized prices to meet the minimum needs of the poor. Then the farms would be free to sell the rest at market prices.

This example in agriculture is the kind of approach that must be used in many spheres. Of course, such sequencing and such thought about less-than-perfect measures requires some knowledge of the specific economic situation. It is understandable that neoliberal economists might not have an interest in such a strategy because they do not know enough to conduct it. Those who determine policy for the international economic institutions could consider teams in which knowledgeable area specialists, knowledgeable sector specialists, and neoliberal economists are brought together.

But whatever gradual reforms are undertaken, three points must be understood. First, "gradual economic reform" has no more reality than the most abstract neoliberal model. Advocacy of the former is no more useful than of the latter. Concrete measures must be taken, often quite well-defined concrete measures. When they are introduced, this often must be done quite quickly and decisively. The question is the nature of those concrete measures and their sequencing.

Second, the desired outcome must be understood, and that is neither pure democracy nor pure capitalism. The optimal outcome would be a constitutional democracy with checks and balances, not a Rousseauian president empowered to express "the general will" of an atomistic civil society because he won a plebiscite. It would be capitalism with corporations, with a myriad of regulations, with a strong welfare state—a mixed economy. The capitalism and constitutional democracy valued in the West are both based on a culture in which gradualism, pragmatism, and responsiveness to the public—the "middle" American—are enshrined as key values.

Third, "gradual" must be understood not to mean just a year or two. Westerners need to regain some sense of the sweep of their own history and of the gradual character even of radical change. China has taken twenty years to make its great changes, and it is still far from a modern mixed economy. Fifty years passed between the American Revolution and mass democracy, and then the democracy comprised only white males. Another ten years were required for the rise of mass parties. The New Deal took thirty years to be instituted. The creation of modern markets and democracies took much longer. Tariffs arose to protect infant industries, but even more the frightened newcomers to factories and the cities before all political parties embraced, although only in words, free trade. These processes took decades—often more than the remaining lifetime of any adult who is currently suggesting change to the Russian government.

Tolerating the Hard-to-Tolerate

One can comfortably argue that the gas industry should be renationalized, for this industry is nationalized in France and Germany. The staged reform of agriculture proposed above, including temporary partial rationing, is certainly within the realm of reason. China demonstrated that. It is even quite thinkable to reverse our attitude toward the insider-owners and to support their inclusion in the major proreform political parties.

Other changes are going to require difficult changes in attitudes. Western democracy rested on major organizations—trade unions, churches, corporations, and large interest groups. Duverger noted that successful parties can almost never be formed by intellectuals.[20] But the Russian Orthodox Church, the Russian Association of Businessmen and Entrepreneurs, any legitimate trade union, and large subsidized enterprises all have characteristics that are somewhat unseemly at best. Any Russian nationalism, which at least in mild form must surely be part of any successful democratic movement, surely will be anti-IMF and partly anti-American.

The Americans involved in the democratization programs in Russia received their definition of democracy from the antiorganization movements of the 1960s, and they are much attracted to small-scale "civil society" organizations of intellectuals. Their answer to democratization is to create small personalistic civil society groups and personalistic political parties of intellectuals. They—and, to be frank, all Americans—find it most comfortable to deal with those who speak fluent English and who are pro-American. To support large and often alien organizations that are the political enemies of our friends is not easy. At a minimum, such political enemies should be brought to the United States en masse on short-term visits.

Still other changes are going to be almost impossible to recommend officially. Most American historians would quietly admit that the city bosses performed very important functions before the Progressive Era began to limit their power and change their role. It seems highly probable that Russia at the current stage would profit from having similar city bosses performing similar functions and that this would be a key stage in the development of Russian democracy. It would be useful to include in American technical assistance programs historians who could explain how Tammany Hall was organized and functioned in the nineteenth century, but this is virtually impossible to do.

The phenomenon of corruption is even more difficult to handle. No one can advocate corruption, and neoliberal economists and progressive political liberals alike join in saying that corruption is not only immoral, but also harmful to economic growth and democracy.[21]

It would be wonderful if this were really accurate.

Historians know that the last third of the nineteenth century was a period of great economic growth for the United States and that it set the stage for the next century of unmatched American power. No one would acknowledge that corruption might have been necessary or at least useful for American economic growth and the consolidation of elite support for the basic American democratic system. Historians remain children of the Progressive Era and see only inferior U.S. presidents. Ulysses S. Grant, one of America's finer presidents on his record in a difficult period, is ranked a failure or near-failure because of corruption in his administration. The same is true in the treatment of Pacific Rim Asian countries in the second half of the twentieth century where corruption, rapid economic growth, and gradual movement toward democracy also coexisted.

There are two reasons that corruption—the right kind of corruption—can play an important and useful role in economic and political development. First, the trust necessary for financial institutions that provide long-term investment is normally absent in the early stages of capitalism. Government can provide the necessary funds and guarantees, but individual government officials who share in the profits of the investments have a better incentive to seek out the most profitable investment than does a ruler interested in political support or an ill-informed government department subject only to broad political pressure. Projects in which specific government officials and specific entrepreneurs cooperate in financing and protecting investment projects that they consider economically optimal are likely to be highly advantageous for growth. This type of arrangement is associated with periods of rapid growth.

Most scholarly discussion of the relationship of government, corruption, and economic growth is highly unsophisticated. Andrei Shleifer, for example, talks only about bribes to government officials, not their participation in investment projects, which actually is more lucrative to them.[22] Even so, he does not ask what the government officials do with bribe money, but takes for granted that it does not flow into domestic investment. In other discussions, it is totally forgotten that government comprises individual officials with individual self-interest. Government is treated as a collective unit without the knowledge or self-interest to promote advantageous investment, subject only to pressure group activity to maximize consumption. This is not true of individual officials investing at home.

The second possible benefit of corruption is in developing support for constitutional government. The development of constitutional democracy is a real mystery in the collective choice literature. As Mancur Olson has shown, mass participation in collective action seldom is rational on an individual basis if the purpose is to promote a public good, and the establishment of optimal political and economic institutions is the ultimate public good. Participation in a revolution against a ruler who controls the means of force seems the ultimate in individual irrationality.[23]

Since control of the government machinery can be so economically lucrative, and since the broader public finds it difficult to organize against a tyrant, one would expect to find predatory rulers and a struggle for political power that centers on those capable of military coups. In fact, this is precisely what one usually finds at the early stages of economic development.

Why does society normally evolve toward political systems based on more impersonal rules and more regularized political succession? Why does it become "constitutional" and then democratic? The answer is likely to be found in the close corrupt relationship of early government, the military, and the economy.

In agricultural society, the owners may feel that castles, moats, and knights can provide them as much protection as can be achieved, but this is not the case with urban and industrial property. If leading state officials acquire such property, they or their children may easily lose it when political power shifts to others. Hence they develop an interest in institutionalizing the sanctity of property vis-à-vis government in the future. As government officials and military officers become involved in economic investment, usually through what westerners would call corruption, they acquire an interest in the protection of the property rights of their children and other family members against the next ruler. The clearest recent example was Indonesia, as the health of long-time leader General Suharto declined.

In addition, the children of rich government officials and military officers, like those of gangsters and drug bosses in the United States, move into other occupations and other elites. They intermarry with members of other elites. The so-called pacts among elites that scholars see underlying constitutional democracy in Latin America are not treaties among isolated warlords, but informal agreements among groups that are interconnected by family ties. It is very difficult for the military or government to fire on a student demonstration in which their sons are marching or to expropriate an economic elite whose members are married to their daughters and are the fathers of their grandchildren.

This analysis has implications that are unsettling for those in the policy community. First, of course, it explains the need for enormous patience. The model suggests that Indonesia had to wait thirty years for General Suharto to pass from the scene and that we should have encouraged him and his family to accumulate large sums of money to invest at home. It suggests that today it would be wrong to expropriate his family or even to have a democracy that might elect populists who would demand that this be done. Instead, the model suggests that the priority at the beginning of the twenty-first century is to establish a constitutional semidemocracy in Indonesia that protects property rights and that integrates the children and grandchildren of past and present military officers into all the most respectable elites. This process may take another half century before western constitutional democracy is established. This timing corresponds to the experience of the West.

Nevertheless, members of the policy community have to find any model unsatisfactory that promises good results only decades after they themselves have passed from the scene and that demands unattractive concrete measures in the interim. For the West to praise General Suharto as an ideal ruler and for the IMF to include the right kind of corruption in its conditions for aid is unthinkable. It cannot say that if China and the Soviet Union wanted a prosperous transition to capitalism, China was not ready for democracy in 1989 or that Gorbachev should have used force to maintain the Soviet Union.

In fact, of course, the West lived with General Suharto, and it certainly can tell dictators that demonstrations, such as that in Tiananmen Square, should be dispersed before they become so large that bloodbaths are required to suppress them. It can, as the Bush administration did when Gorbachev imposed an oil boycott on Lithuania in 1990, signal its views by changing its policy on Kashmir to show its fear of the breakup of large multiethnic countries.[24] The shelling of the Russian parliament in 1993 would not have been necessary if Russian police had had modern crowd-control techniques.

Similarly, we must quietly understand that democratization usually is a troubled process. A range of countries in Latin America and in southern Europe, and even Japan, introduced democracy first in the nineteenth century and had a series of failed or partial democracies before they evolved, as they have now, toward more stable western-type democracies. Even in the United States, the introduction of mass democracy in the 1830s contributed heavily to the political disorder that produced the Civil War, and the great wave of emigration at the end of the century was handled in part by limiting the rights of new immigrants and other poor people to vote.[25] It was not until the 1920s that women were given the vote and not until the 1960s that all blacks were enfranchised. The process often takes from 150 to 200 years. The apparent movement, at last, of Japan and Mexico toward fuller democracy in the past decade illustrates the length of the process.

The Russian "democratic" political system had the same problems. Whether Russia is democratic or not, Russia first needs to establish a constitutional regime in both its politics and its economics. It needs institutionalized rules that give rational political and economic actors a reason to engage in long-term planning. It needs economic and political incentives that give these actors a reason to take actions that promote investment, economic growth, and a politically free society. We do not demand pure democracy today in Turkey, Algeria, and Saudi Arabia, and we should be emphasizing constitutional government in Russia.

Clearly corruption must be criticized, for otherwise the children of the elite may not understand what the movement to respectability requires. But if the process by which the institutions needed for modern "capitalism" (mixed economy) and "democracy" (constitutional democracy) are created is not fit to be described in a civics textbook for the young or in directives by the IMF, we can at least use language that is not incompatible with it and that points in the right direction.

The West certainly needs to look seriously at the history of its own political and economic development and draw the necessary conclusions. It needs to focus on avoiding a repetition of the really serious mistakes in western history—World War I, the rise of Lenin and Hitler, and so forth—not on the avoidance of the "mistakes" like the robber barons and Tammany Hall that caused no great harm and may have been useful. It can speak of the priority of avoiding capital flight and the need for investment. It can talk about the close relations between banks, government, and business in Japan as no longer appropriate in 2000 in a way that recognizes it may have been less objectionable in the past. In the political sphere, it can emphasize the value of constitutional democracy and checks and balances, not unrestrained democracy and elected rulers.

Ultimately, however, the main lesson of Russia is the need to be cautious and humble in intervening in the domestic affairs of developing countries. The West involved itself very deeply in the Russian reform process. It supported one group of reformers rather than another simply because that group of rent-seekers learned how to use the right kind of economic language. The language of these reformers had no relationship to the real policy they were following, but either out of ignorance or fear of political embarrassment, western governments accepted the language as genuine. They even told their own investors to put billions of dollars into what was a pyramid scheme, a con game.

The Russian experience demonstrates once more that western scholars, especially the economists in the international economic institutions, do not understand the complex character of constitutional democracy and a mixed market economy, let alone how to make the transition to one. It demonstrates how easy it is to be misled—"conned" is actually the better word—by those who learn how to use the right language out of the neoliberal model and democratic theory to obtain support for the worst kind of rent-seeking and for authoritarianism.

Russia some day will leave the Yeltsin era. Some new ruler will adopt a policy that promotes economic growth. Russia will realize that the chasm between socialism and capitalism is not a crack in the ground; it is the Grand Canyon. It will understand that the result of trying to jump it in a single leap is disaster: it must be crossed by tortuous and indirect mule trails. Indeed, the foundations of capitalism must be built slowly with the loads of many mules. Americans can hope that the process will be associated with a more regularized political system and a foreign policy that is not too different from that which Yeltsin followed.

Given Americans' lack of knowledge about the development process and the difficulty of tolerating the hard-to-tolerate, it is perhaps best in any case to back away from close involvement. We can wish the Russian reform process well as we do the Chinese. Westerners can organize exchanges and visits to allow Russians to gain a better sense of western reality. Americans can and should worry about controls on nuclear weapons. But if westerners do not pretend that they have the answers or that the few billions they can provide are a panacea, the Russians will be thrown back on their own resources. Self-reliance has been the secret of all major industrialization drives.

This is an important point not only for policy toward Russia. Events in India, Indonesia, Pakistan, Algeria, and other countries underscore that the major countries in Asia at the end of the twentieth century are at stages of development similar to that of Europe at the beginning of the century and that this can have not only domestic but also foreign policy consequences. Africa is at a still earlier stage, lacking the educated populations of Russia, but the uneducated and frightened populations of which earlier political philosophers warned.

Most of all, westerners should not become euphoric about the political effects of a global economy. Exposure to the world economy was a crucial element in arousing fears and anxieties among semieducated populations in Europe that were exploited by the great populist leaders of the twentieth century. As early as 1774, a tax on tea imported from India destabilized Boston. It would be good to think that those in Asia and Africa will not be subject to the same political forces in the twenty-first century as those that devastated Europe in the twentieth century. But this is a goal, not a certainty, and the lessons of Russia of the 1990s about institutions, incentives, and the institutionalization of both can be ignored only at the risk of far greater dangers in the twenty-first century.

Notes

Preface

1. See, for example, Mikhail Guboglo's three-volume *Razvivaiushchiisia elektorat Rossii* (The developing electorate of Russia) (Moscow: Institute of Ethnology and Anthropology, 1996), which discusses the 1993 and 1995 elections in the republics. One volume is his monograph; the other two are edited volumes including works by scholars in the republics. Another example is S. V. Tumanov and others, *Kul'turnye miry molodykh rossiian: tri zhiznennykh situatsii* (The cultural world of Russian youth: three life situations)(Moscow: Izdatel'stvo Moskovskogo universiteta, 2000).

2. For a comprehensive discussion of fraud by other polling agencies in this election, see Vladimir Shliapentokh, "Review: The 1993 Russian Election Polls," *Public Opinion Quarterly*, vol. 58, no. 4 (Winter 1994), pp. 579–602.

3. Ideally we would have liked surveys in each oblast, but with the money available, we could not offer enough per respondent to persuade all regional sociologists to participate.

4. For an example of what can be done, see Susan Goodrich Lehmann's table on the impact of place of birth and age of migration to the city on attitudes toward transition to a market economy, based on approximately 20,000 respondents, in Jerry F. Hough, Evelyn Davidheiser, and Susan Goodrich Lehmann, *The 1996 Russian Presidential Election* (Brookings, 1996), p. 6.

5. Jerry F. Hough, "The Russian Election of 1993: Public Attitudes toward Economic Reform and Democratization," *Post-Soviet Affairs*, vol. 10, no. 1 (1994), pp. 1–37.

6. For a fuller methodology of this study, see Tumanov, *Kul'turnye miry molodykh rossiian*, pp. 8–13.

7. For data out of this survey as well as the others, see Jerry F. Hough, "The

Political Geography of European Russia: Republics and Oblasts," *Post-Soviet Geography and Economics*, vol. 39, no. 2 (1998), pp. 63–95; and Susan Goodrich Lehmann, "Inter-Ethnic Conflict in the Republics of Russia in Light of Religious Revival," *Post-Soviet Geography and Economics*, vol. 39, no. 8 (1998), pp. 461–93.

Chapter One

1. "K s'ezdu narodnykh deputatov" (To the Congress of People's Deputies), *Rossiiskaia gazeta*, October 29, 1991, p. 1.

2. Ibid., p. 2.

3. The words are those of the first deputy minister of the economy (Gosplan), Andrei Nechaev, the de facto minister of the economy. *Rossiiskie vesti*, no. 27 (November 16, 1991), p. 3.

4. Anders Aslund, *How Russia Became a Market Economy* (Brookings, 1995), pp. 3–4. Aslund first proposed this argument in "Russia's Success Story," *Foreign Affairs*, vol. 73, no. 5 (September–October 1994), pp. 58–71.

5. Stanley Fischer, Ratna Sahay, and Carlos A. Vegh, "Stabilization and Growth in Transition Economies: The Early Experience," *Journal of Economic Perspectives*, vol. 10, no. 2 (Spring 1996), p. 64.

6. For Aslund's optimism even after the June 1998 IMF loans, see his "Russia's Financial Crisis: Causes and Possible Remedies," *Post-Soviet Geography and Economics*, vol. 39, no. 6 (June 1998), pp. 325–27.

7. Douglass C. North, "The Process of Economic Change" (Helsinki: UNU World Institute for Development Economics Research, 1997), p. 3.

8. For efforts to probe behind the earlier façade, see Jerry F. Hough, *The Soviet Prefects: The Local Party Organs in Industrial Decision-Making* (Harvard University Press, 1969), and Jerry F. Hough and Merle Fainsod, *How the Soviet Union Is Governed* (Harvard University Press, 1979), especially chapters 11–14.

9. Olivier Blanchard, *The Economics of Post-Communist Transition* (Oxford University Press, 1997), p. 13.

10. Stanislaw Gomulka, "Output: Causes of the Decline and the Recovery," in Peter Boone, Stanislaw Gomulka, and Richard Layard, eds., *Emerging from Communism: Lessons from Russia, China, and Eastern Europe* (MIT Press, 1998), p. 13.

11. Maxim Boycko, Andrei Shleifer, and Robert Vishny, *Privatizing Russia* (MIT Press, 1995), p. 9.

12. Alan Greenspan, "The Embrace of Free Markets" (Washington: Woodrow Wilson International Center for Scholars, 1997), p. 2. Greenspan was generally following Douglass North's argument.

13. Douglass C. North, "The Contribution of the New Institutional Economics to an Understanding of the Transition Problem" (Helsinki: UNU World Institute for Development Economics Research, 1997), p. 16.

14. The term IMF is used for ease of expression and conventionality; the policy originated in the Treasury Department, and its primary architect was Lawrence Summers.

15. For a strong argument that a well-functioning bureaucracy is a prerequisite of stable democracy, see Joseph Schumpeter, *Capitalism, Socialism, and Democracy* (Harper, 1942), pp. 293–94.

16. Barrington Moore, *Terror and Progress USSR: Some Sources of Change and Stability in the Soviet Dictatorship* (Harvard University Press, 1954), pp. 187–88. Max Weber, *Economy and Society: An Outline of Interpretive Sociology*, edited by Guenther Roth and Claus Wittich (New York: Bedminster, 1968), vol. 3, pp. 956–1005.

17. Yeltsin's closest aide in the first half of the 1990s, Aleksandr Korzhakov, uses the phrase "the autumn of the patriarch" in describing Yeltsin's decline. Aleksandr Korzhakov, *Boris Yeltsin: Ot rassveta do zakata* (Boris Yeltsin: From dawn to sunset) (Moscow: Interbuk, 1997), p. 387. The same point is made in the constant use of terms such as clan or the family in Russian discourse. See the discussion in George W. Breslauer, "Boris Yel'tsin as Patriarch," *Post-Soviet Affairs*, vol. 15, no. 2 (April-June 1999), pp. 186–200.

18. Weber, *Economy and Society*, vol. 3, pp. 1006–69.

19. See, for example, Jerry Hough, "On the Road to Paradise Again? Keeping Hopes for Russia Realistic," *Brookings Review*, vol. 11, no. 1 (Winter 1993), pp. 12–17, much of which material appears in chapter 2 of this volume. See also Jerry F. Hough, Evelyn Davidheiser, and Susan Goodrich Lehmann, "Boris Yeltsin and Economic Reform," in Hough, Davidheiser, and Lehmann, *The 1996 Russian Presidential Election* (Brookings, 1996), pp. 14–26.

20. Douglass C. North, "Epilogue: Economic Performance through Time," in Lee J. Alston, Thrainn Eggertsson, and Douglass C. North, eds., *Empirical Studies in Institutional Change* (Cambridge: Cambridge University Press, 1996), pp. 342–43.

21. Lawrence Summers, "Comments and Discussion," *Brookings Papers on Economic Activity, 1: 1992*, p. 112. There were, of course, exceptions among economists. See, for example, the prescient 1991 article by Peter Murrell, "Evolution in Economics and in the Economic Reform of the Centrally Planned Economies," in Christopher Clague and Gordon C. Rausser, eds., *The Emergence of Market Economies in Eastern Europe* (Cambridge, Mass.: Blackwell, 1992), pp. 35–53. William Nordhaus in April 1992 at a Brookings conference also explicitly called for an industrial policy. See "Comments and Discussion," *Brookings Papers on Economic Activity, 1: 1992*, p. 123.

22. Lawrence Summers, "The Next Decade in Central and Eastern Europe," in Clague and Rausser, *The Emergence of Market Economies in Eastern Europe*, p. 32.

23. John Williamson, "The Process of Policy Reform in Latin America," in John Williamson, ed., *Latin American Adjustment: How Much Has Happened*

(Washington: Institute for International Economics, 1990), pp. 358–59. The phrase was used repeatedly by Joseph Stiglitz, chief economist of the World Bank after 1996, in his criticism of IMF policy. See, for example, Joseph E. Stiglitz, "More Instruments and Broader Goals: Moving toward the Post-Washington Consensus," WIDER Annual Lecture 2, UNU World Institute for Development Economics Research (Helsinki: UNU/WIDER, 1998). For later Stiglitz criticisms, see his "Whither Reform? Ten Years of the Transition" (World Bank, April 28–30, 1999).

24. Stanley Fischer and Alan Gelb, *Issues in Socialist Economy Reform* (Washington: World Bank, 1990).

25. Williamson, "The Process of Policy Reform in Latin America," p. 360.

26. Stanley Fischer, "What Washington Means by Policy Reform," in Williamson, ed., *Latin American Adjustment*, pp. 27–28.

27. Williamson, "The Progress of Policy Reform in Latin America," pp. 378, 380.

28. Summers, "The Next Decade in Central and Eastern Europe."

29. Dennis C. Mueller, *Public Choice II* (Cambridge: Cambridge University Press, 1989), pp. 9–10. Mueller presents the game matrix that demonstrates this point. He rests his analysis on Winston C. Bush, "Individual Welfare in Anarchy," in Gordon Tullock, ed., *Explorations in the Theory of Anarchy* (Blacksburg, Va.: Center for the Study of Public Choice, 1972), pp. 5–18.

30. Gordon Tullock, "Corruption and Anarchy," in Gordon Tullock, ed., *Further Explorations in the Theory of Anarchy* (Blacksburg, Va.: University Publications, 1974), pp. 66–67.

31. Stanley Fischer, "Comments and Discussion," *Brookings Papers on Economic Activity, 2: 1993*, p. 183.

32. Maria Rozhkova, "'Noril'skii nikel' na polgoda lishilsia kryshi" ("Norilsk Nickel" didn't have a roof for a half year), *Kommersant Daily*, January 23, 1998, p. 9.

33. Gretchen Morgenson, "On the Seamier Side of the Bull Market," *New York Times*, July 11, 1999, section III, p. 1.

34. Eileen Daspin, "The Cheater Principle," *Wall Street Journal*, August 25, 2000, p. W1.

35. Alexander Gerschenkron, *Economic Backwardness in Historical Perspective: A Book of Essays* (Harvard University Press, 1962), pp. 19–22.

36. Ibid.

37. Ibid.

38. Ibid.

Chapter Two

1. Richard E. Ericson, "Economics," in Timothy J. Colton and Robert Legvold, eds., *After the Soviet Union: From Empire to Nations* (W. W. Norton, 1992), p. 58.

2. Douglass C. North, "The Process of Economic Change" (Helsinki: UNU World Institute for Development Economics Research, 1997), p. 3.

3. Anders Aslund, *How Russia Became a Market Economy* (Brookings, 1995), pp. 141, 150, 159, 167. See also Barry W. Ickes and Randi Ryterman, "Roadblock to Economic Reform: Inter-Enterprise Debt and the Transition to Markets," *Post-Soviet Affairs*, vol. 9, no. 3 (July-September 1993), pp. 231–32.

4. John Lloyd, "Battle over Russia's Runaway Central Bank," *Financial Times*, January 22, 1992, p. 2.

5. Ivan Elistratov and Sergei Chubaev, "Boris Yeltsin: I vse-taki liudi ne teriaiut nadezhdy" (Boris Yeltsin: And still people don't lose hope), *Izvestiia*, January 17, 1992, p. 1.

6. *Izvestiia*, February 21, 1992, p. 1.

7. Boris Yeltsin, *The Struggle for Russia* (Random House, 1994), pp. 166–67.

8. "K s'ezdu narodnykh deputatov" (To the Congress of People's Deputies), *Rossiiskaia gazeta*, October 28, 1991, p. 1.

9. Mikhail Berger, "Budushchee prineset nam novye tseny i zabytye tovary—schitaet Yegor Gaidar" (The future will bring us new prices and forgotten goods—thinks Yegor Gaidar), *Izvestiia*, January 3, 1992, p. 2.

10. Leyla Boulton, "Russia's New Economy Chief Warns West on Aid," *Financial Times*, January 10, 1992, p. 2. These were not the same rubles that existed in 1998 when the ruble fell from 6 rubles to the dollar to 24 to the dollar. In 1998 three zeroes were taken off all ruble notes.

11. Leonid Abalkin, *Ne ispol'zovannyi shans: Poltora goda v pravitel'stve* (The wasted chance: A year and a half in the government) (Moscow: Politizdat, 1991), pp. 55–57.

12. "Deputy Minister Nechayev on Price Controls," *Paris Liberation*, January 3, 1992, pp. 8–9, in Foreign Broadcast Information Service (hereafter FBIS), *Daily Report: Russia*, January 7, 1992, p. 45.

13. B. Rakitsky, "Polozhenie naseleniia Rossii: Sotsial'naia nadlomlennost' pri 'pryzhke v rynok'" (The state of the Russian population: Social fracture during the leap into the market), *Voprosy ekonomiki*, no. 4(April 1993), p. 53.

14. "Gaydar Answers Questions," Moscow Russian Television Network, January 24, 1992, in FBIS-*Daily Report: Russia*, January 27, 1992, p. 41.

15. *Rossiia v tsifrakh, 1998: Kratkii statisticheskii sbornik* (Russia in numbers, 1998: short statistical collection) (Moscow: Goskomstat Rossii, 1998), p. 162.

16. Calculated from *Rossiiskaia federatsiia v 1992 gody: Statisticheskii ezhegodnik* (The Russian federation in 1992: statistical yearbook) (Moscow: Respublikanskii informatsionno-izdatel'skii tsentr, 1993), pp. 121, 367; and *Rossiia v tsifrakh, 1998*, p. 43.

17. Robert H. Bates, *Markets and States in Tropical Africa: The Political Basis of Agricultural Policy* (University of California Press, 1981) describes the political logic that leads to subsidization of the city. Stephen K. Wegren, *Agricul-*

ture and the State in Soviet and Post-Soviet Russia (University of Pittsburgh Press, 1998) describes the situation in Russia.

18. The classic description of this was William Taubman, *Governing Soviet Cities: Bureaucratic Politics and Urban Development in the USSR* (New York: Praeger, 1973). See also Jerry F. Hough, *The Soviet Prefects: The Local Party Organs in Industrial Decision-Making* (Harvard University Press, 1969), chapter 11.

19. The information for this and the preceding paragraph came from interviews with the head of the Yaroslavl Pharmaceutical Office, the head of the city health department, and the head of Pharmindustriia (the head of the pharmaceutical industry in Russia).

20. "Khasbulatov Addresses Presidium," Moscow Mayak Radio Network, January 13, 1992, in FBIS-*Daily Report: Russia*, January 14, 1992, pp. 45–46.

21. "Programma uglubleniia ekonomicheskikh reform pravitel'stva Rossiiskoi federatsii" (The program of deepening economic reforms of the Russian federation government), *Voprosy ekonomiki*, no. 8 (August 1992), p. 24.

22. "Pochinok Speaks on State Budget," Moscow Russian Television Network, February 26, 1993, in FBIS—Daily Report: Russia, March 1, 1993, pp. 39–40.

23. Hedrick Smith, *The New Russians* (Random House, 1990), p. 256.

24. The Kharkov plant that had produced the computers for the SS-18 rocket was a part of Rosobshchemash, its director reported in an interview.

25. Maxim Boycko, Andrei Shleifer, and Robert Vishny, *Privatizing Russia* (MIT Press, 1995), pp. 57–58, 81.

26. Paul L. Joskow, Richard Schmalensee, and Natalia Tsukanova, "Competition Policy in Russia during and after Privatization," *Brookings Papers on Economic Activity: Microeconomics, 1994* (Brookings, 1994), pp. 327–30. The quotation is from p. 330. Also see Steven L. Solnick, *Stealing the State: Control and Collapse in Soviet Institutions* (Harvard University Press, 1998), p. 229.

27. Stephen Fortescue, "The Restructuring of Soviet Industrial Ministries since 1985," in Anders Aslund, ed., *Market Socialism or the Restoration of Capitalism* (Cambridge: Cambridge University Press, 1992), pp. 121–41.

28. Interview with the head of the Tractor and Agricultural Machinery Department of the Ministry of Industry.

29. At times the two ministries had been combined, and the location of the offices of the "separate" ministers showed that they still worked in a highly coordinated manner. The Ministry of the Automobile Industry was really a Ministry of the Truck Industry, and not only were the two ministries dependent on similar suppliers, but they both produced items for the mobility of troops and weapons for the defense industry.

30. Maria Rozhkova, "'Roslesprom' ostalsia bez 'nachinko'" ("Roslesprom" is left without the "filling"), *Kommersant Daily*, January 14, 1998, p. 11.

31. Irina Poliakova, "'Rostekstil' pomozhet svoim Vladimirskim aktsioneram" ("Rostekstil" will help its Vladimir shareholders), *Kommersant Daily*, January 13, 1998, p. 11.

32. Joel S. Hellman, "Breaking the Bank: Bureaucrats and the Creation of Markets in a Transitional Economy" (Ph.D. dissertation, Columbia University, 1993), pp. 145–46, 151–52, 193–217.

33. Stephen Handelman, *Comrade Criminal: Russia's New Mafiya* (Yale University Press, 1995), pp. 135, 142–43.

34. *Argumenty i fakty*, no. 3 (January 20–26, 1990), p. 8.

35. Hellman, "Breaking the Bank," p. 154.

36. Hellman found that commercial banks at which he interviewed paid an average of 8 to 10 percent in 1990 and 12 to 15 percent in 1991. Ibid., p. 181.

37. A. V. Ksenofontov, "'Eleksbank': Korotko o sebe" (Eleksbank: briefly about ourselves) *Den'gi i kredit* (Money and credit), no. 3 (March 1992), p. 48.

38. Ickes and Ryterman, "Roadblock to Economic Reform," p. 232.

39. Aslund, *How Russia Became a Market Economy*, pp. 188, 195.

40. N. E. Sokolinskaia, "Bankovskie riski" (Bank risks), *Den'gi i kredit*, no. 12 (1993), p. 25.

41. A. N. Anisimov and others, *Upravlenie liberalizatsionno-privatizatsionnymi preobrazovanniami* (Directing liberalization-privatization transitions) (Moscow: KUbK, 1997), p. 216. The total direct credits of the Central Bank were 38 percent of GDP in 1992 and 19 percent in 1993.

42. V. Gerashchenko, "Rabota Tsentral'nogo banka Rossii" (Activities of the Central Bank of Russia), *Rossiiskii ekonomicheskii zhurnal*, no. 9 (1994), pp. 10, 12.

43. E. Batizi, "Kommercheskie banki—upolnomochennye pravitel'stvennye agenty" (Commercial banks—authorized government representatives), *Rossiiskii ekonomicheskii zhurnal*, no. 8 (1994), p. 32.

44. Michael S. Bernstam and Alvin Rabushka, *Fixing Russia's Banks: A Proposal for Growth* (Stanford, Calif.: Hoover Institution Press, 1998), p. 34.

45. M. P. Berezina and Iu. S. Krupnov, "Mezhbankovskie raschety: Analiz praktiki" (Intrabank payments: Analysis of the practice), *Den'gi i kredit*, no. 4 (April 1993), p. 21.

46. Batizi, "Kommercheskie banki," p. 32.

47. As will be discussed, Stephen Handelman reports that the "best businessman" in Ekaterinburg was the head of European-Asian Company, who traded in metals. He was subsequently murdered. Handelman, *Comrade Criminal*, pp. 75–78.

48. Rose Brady, *Kapitalizm: Russia's Struggle to Free Its Economy* (Yale University Press, 1999), p. 138.

49. This paragraph is based largely on Aleksei Mukhin, *Estestvennye monopolii v Rossii* (Natural monopolies in Russia) (Moscow: SPIK-Tsentr, 1998), pp. 22–53.

50. V. I. Bukato and Iu. I Lvov, *Banki i bankovskie operatsii v Rossii* (Banks and bank operations in Russia) (Moscow: Finansy i Statistika, 1996), p. 207.

51. Maksim Poliakov, "Nastupili novye vremena" (Different times have come), *Kommersant Daily*, April 14, 1995, p. 5.

52. "Evropeiskii bank interesuetsia aktsiiami Uralpromstroibanka" (A European bank takes interest in Uralpromstroibank shares), *Kommersant Daily*, March 10, 1995, p. 5.

53. "Bank pristupil k realizatsii aktsii piatoi emissii (Bank begins realizing fifth emission shares), *Kommersant Daily*, February 1, 1995, p. 5.

54. Maksim Akimov, "Kapital banka budet uvelichen v 14 raz" (Bank's capital to be increased 14-fold), *Kommersant Daily*, March 24, 1995, p. 5.

55. Elena Stanova, "Chrezmernyi konservatizm mozhet sozdat' dlia banka problemy (Excessive conservatism could create problems for bank), *Kommersant Daily*, March 4, 1995, p. 6.

56. Often the party apparatus and the ministries were treated as part of the united nomenklatura, but, in fact, anyone who read the articles and speeches of the regional party officials knew they detested the ministries. See Jerry F. Hough, "The Party Apparatchiki," in H. Gordon Skilling and Franklyn Griffiths, eds., *Interest Groups in Soviet Politics* (Princeton University Press, 1971), p. 70; and Jerry F. Hough, *Soviet Leadership in Transition* (Brookings, 1980), pp. 65–68.

57. S. Iu. Yevseev, "Bankovskie sistemy rossiiskikh regionov: Sovremennye tendentsii razvitiia" (The banking systems of the Russian regions: Current trends of growth), in Anatoliy I. Arkhipov, ed., *Gosudarstvo i investitsii: Aktual'nye problemy makroekonomicheskoi politiki* (Government and investment: Actual problems of macroeconomic policy) (Moscow: Institut Ekonomiki, 1998), p. 22.

58. David Hoffman, "Yeltsin Chooses 'Technocrat,' 35, as New Premier," *Washington Post*, March 28, 1998, p. A22.

59. Mukhin, *Estestvennye monopolii v Rossii*, p. 58.

60. The director of Uralmash (Urals Machinery Works) told Hedrick Smith that the plant had a profit of $125 million, but a tax of only $13 million. However, it was required to provide the government with a "deduction" of $83 million. Smith, *The New Russians*, pp. 254–55. Officially the *otchislenie* came from profits, but the artificiality of the price system made profits or losses the result not of managerial skill, but of the accident of whether prices happened to benefit or hurt the plant.

61. Jeffrey D. Sachs and Katharina Pistor, "Introduction: Progress, Pitfalls, Scenarios, and Lost Opportunities," in Jeffrey D. Sachs and Katharina Pistor, *The Rule of Law and Economic Reform in Russia* (Boulder, Colo.: Westview, 1997), pp. 9–10. It is clear that money was not expended as the donors intended, but it is likely that much was distributed for various off-budget purposes instead of going to personal corruption. American agricultural aid, for example, went

through the Menatep Bank at the insistence of the Russians, and it seems quite possible that the money remained there to be distributed as subsidies.

62. "Documentation Quality Criticized," TASS, January 24, 1992, in FBIS-*Daily Report: Russia,* January 27, 1992, pp. 46–47.

63. Betsy McKay, "Yeltsin to Step Up Tax Collection, an Issue in Budget," *Wall Street Journal,* October 14, 1996, p. 14. This was the same Zadornov who was to become minister of finance in the fall of 1997.

64. Chrystia Freeland, "Russia Warned It Must Tighten Its Purse Strings," *Financial Times,* June 5, 1998, p. 2.

65. The problem was not the lack of a tax apparatus. Boris Fedorov reported that the State Tax Service had a staff of 200,000, which he claimed was more per 100,000 of population than in any developed country. Boris Fedorov, "Mozhno li v Rossii sobrat' nalogi?" (Can taxes be collected in Russia?), *Rossiiskie vesti,* November 26, 1996.

66. Anisimov and others, *Upravlenie liberalizatsionno-privatizatsionnymi preobrazovanniami,* p. 211.

67. Claudia Rosett, "Big Gas Firm Proves a Liability for Yeltsin," *Wall Street Journal,* March 5, 1996, p. A11.

68. Betsy McKay, "Investors Flock to Gazprom's Offering, Russian Firm's First Sale to Foreigners," *Wall Street Journal,* October 7, 1996, p. A19.

69. Eric Magnussion, "Russia Must Clarify the Ambiguity Surrounding Gazprom's Status," *Financial Times,* July 16, 1998, p. 30.

70. Viacheslav Goncharov, "Shalchterskaia karta vnov' stala kozyrnoi" (The coalminer card has become an ace once again), *Rossiiskaia gazeta,* December 5, 1996, p. 1.

71. Igor Semenenko, "Chubais Strengthens Grip on UES," *Moscow Times,* June 26, 1999, as cited in David Johnson's Russia List, no. 3362, June 26 1999. This started early. In February 1994 only half of electricity payments were in cash, and only one-quarter in the summer of 1994. David Woodruff, *Money Unmade: Barter and the Fate of Russian Capitalism* (Cornell University Press, 1999), pp. 119–20. All of chapter 4 of Woodruff's book gives an excellent description of the rise of nonpayments at this time, but he often sees independent regional actions where I see a deliberate central policy to replace overt subsidies and continued strong central control.

72. David Hoffman, "Goods Replace Rubles in Russia's Vast Web of Trade," *Washington Post,* January 31, 1997, p. A15.

73. Edward L. Andrews, "How to Make Big Rubles? Investing Comrades' Debt," *New York Times,* October 14, 1997, p. 14; Lyuba Pronina, "Moscow Gets Ready for Big Freeze," *Moscow Tribune,* October 7, 1998.

74. Subsidies came in many forms: loans to enterprises, nonpayment of bills of various suppliers, differentials in the way that allocated budgetary expenditures were sequestered, the percentage of local taxes that could be retained by

the locality, low food prices mislabeled agricultural subsidies. Since the largest amount of taxes was collected in the largest cities, the tax transfer form of subsidy favored other regions. Scholars looking at tax transfers alone incorrectly concluded that the big cities were being subsidized less than other regions. See Daniel Treisman, "Fiscal Redistribution in a Fragile Federation: Moscow and the Regions in 1994," *British Journal of Political Science*, vol. 28 (January 1998), pp. 185–222. Daniel Treisman, "Deciphering Russia's Federal Finance: Fiscal Appeasement in 1995 and 1996," *Europe-Asia Studies*, vol. 50, no. 5 (1998), pp. 893–906.

75. Charles Clover and John Thornhill, "Gazprom Chief Threatens Tax Revolt," *Financial Times*, June 15, 1998, p. 3.

76. Carol Matlack, "The High Cost of Easy Money," *Business Week*, December 7, 1998, pp. 110–12. Galina Pechilina, "'Tatneft' ne khochet byt' doinoi korovoi" (Tatneft does not want to be a cash cow), *Komersant Daily*, January 28, 1998, p. 10.

77. For example, Oneksimbank bought the two most important shipyards in St. Petersburg. Mikhail Golubev, "Oneksimbank poka ne budet 'slivat' peterburgskie verfi" (Oneksimbank will not yet merge St. Petersburg shipyards), *Kommersant Daily*, March 5, 1998, p. 10.

78. Rozhkova, "'Roslesprom' ostalsia bez 'nachinko,'" p. 11.

79. Andrei Fedorov and Kirill Gorskii, "Volzhskii avtomobil'ni zavod podnimaet tseny" (Volga automobile plant is raising prices), *Kommersant Daily*, January 31, 1998, p. 4.

80. German Galkin and Dmitrii Zorkov, "Rukovoditelei ChTZ na raboty privezli spetsnazovtsy" (The directors of ChTZ were brought to work by members of Spetsnaz), *Kommersant Daily*, February 20, 1998, p. 7, and February 27, 1998, p. 9.

81. Alfred Kokh, *The Selling of the Soviet Empire: Politics and Economics of Russia's Privatization—Revelations of the Principal Insider* (New York: S. P. I. Books, 1998).

82. Sachs and Pistor, "Introduction: Progress, Pitfalls, Scenarios, and Lost Opportunities," p. 9.

83. Brady, *Kapitalizm*, p. 30.

Chapter Three

1. The collective farm managers in communist Czechoslovakia and the state oil firms in many countries have responded more or less well to market incentives. In Poland, the state enterprises had responded in like manner after stabilization was completed. Margaret Thatcher assumed that the restructuring and downsizing of state enterprises had to be done before privatization, and the sharp increases in productivity were achieved while they were still state enterprises. Indeed, Sir Alan Walters recommended the Thatcher model in 1992. Alan

Walters, "The Transition to a Market Economy," in Christopher Clague and Gordon C. Rausser, eds., *The Emergence of Market Economies in Eastern Europe* (Oxford: Blackwell, 1992), pp. 102–03.

2. Anders Aslund, *How Russia Became a Market Economy* (Brookings, 1995), p. 223.

3. Ibid., pp. 224–25.

4. Igor Filatotchev, Trevor Buck, and Mike Wright, "Privatisation and Buy-Outs in the USSR," *Soviet Studies*, vol. 44, no. 2 (1992), pp. 276–78.

5. Hedrick Smith, *The New Russians* (Random House, 1990), p. 271.

6. The author, it turned out, was an unknowing part of one such operation. A plant manager agreed to do a sociological survey for us for dollars. We were later told that he had actually paid for the survey with the plant's *beznalichnye* funds. It seems quite possible that the hard currency we provided did not reach the enterprise account, but that the plant was repaid in rubles.

7. Philip Hanson, "Property Rights in the New Phase of Reforms," *Soviet Economy*, vol. 6 (April-June 1990), pp. 95–124.

8. Smith, *The New Russians*, p. 256.

9. Kathryn Hendley, "Legal Development and Privatization in Russia: A Case Study," *Soviet Economy*, vol. 8 (April-June 1992), pp. 130–40; Peter B. Maggs, "Taking the 'Poison Pill': A Commentary on a Case Study," *Soviet Economy*, vol. 8 (April-June 1992), pp. 158–63; Simon Johnson and Heidi Kroll, "Managerial Strategies for Spontaneous Privatization," *Soviet Economy*, vol. 7 (October-December 1991), pp. 281–316.

10. Lev Timofeyev, *Russia's Secret Rulers* (Knopf, 1992), p. 117. The letter "kh" in Russian is pronounced like the German "h," and hence the pronunciation of the two words was more similar than might seem to an American.

11. Yegor Gaidar, *Dni porazhenii i pobed* (Days of defeats and victories) (Moscow: Vagrius, 1996), p. 80.

12. Yevgeny Shaposhnikov, *Vybor* (The Choice), 2d ed. revised and expanded (Moscow: Nezavisimoe izdatel'stvo PIK, 1995), p. 69.

13. S. Sokolov, "Zoloto partii: Dan prikaz emu na zapad" (The party's gold: It has been ordered west), *Komsomol'skaia pravda*, October 31, 1991, p. 2. See Timofeyev, *Russia's Secret Rulers*, pp. 117–18, for the assertion that this was a Central Committee decision, but the original article does not actually say so.

14. "'Kapital,' tom poslednii? O finansovykh i inykh sekretnykh partdokumentakh" ("Das Kapital": The last volume? Concerning financial and other secret party documents), *Ogonek*, November 9–16, 1991, p. 4.

15. S. Sokolov, "Kuptsy nevidimogo fronta" (Merchants of the invisible front), *Komsomol'skaia pravda*, December 7, 1991, p. 2.

16. Such a document about the sale of raion (borough) buildings in Moscow was also published in "'Kapital,' tom poslednii?" and treated as a sign of corruption by the Moscow first secretary, pp. 4–5. However, the raions were being amalgamated, and the party had extra buildings. Timothy J. Colton, *Moscow: Govern-*

ing the Socialist Metropolis (Harvard University Press, 1995), p. 645. The first secretary was only asking higher officials for the authority to dispose of them.

17. This is described for the Komsomol by Steven L. Solnick, *Stealing the State: Control and Collapse in Soviet Institutions* (Harvard University Press, 1998).

18. Stephen Handelman, *Comrade Criminal: Russia's New Mafiya* (Yale University Press, 1995), p. 91.

19. Peter Murrell, "Evolution in Economics and in the Economic Reform of the Centrally Planned Economies," in Christopher Clague and Gordon C. Rausser, eds., *The Emergence of Market Economies in Eastern Europe* (Cambridge, Mass.: Blackwell, 1992), pp. 35–53.

20. S. Razin, "Ne priachte vashi denezhki po bankam i uglam" (Don't hide your money in jars and corners), *Komsomol'skaia pravda*, July 5, 1991, p. 1.

21. See the discussion in Jerry F. Hough, *Democratization and Revolution in the USSR, 1985–1991* (Brookings, 1997), pp. 422–43.

22. Maxim Boycko, Andrei Shleifer, and Robert Vishny, *Privatizing Russia* (MIT Press, 1995), pp. 11–12.

23. Stanley Fischer, in "Comments and Discussion," *Brookings Papers on Economic Activity, 2: 1993*, pp. 182–83.

24. Filatotchev, Buck, and Wright, "Privatisation and Buy-Outs in the USSR," pp. 279–80

25. "Sale of the Century," *Economist,* April 8, 1995, p. 5, as quoted and discussed in Hilary Beth Appel, "Mass Privatization in Post-Communist States: Ideas, Interests, and Economic Regime Change" (Ph.D. dissertation, University of Pennsylvania, 1998), p. 190.

26. Vladimir Orlov, "Gosudarstvo idet s molotka," *Moskovskie novosti*, no. 2 (January 12, 1992), p. 14. Quoted in Lynn D. Nelson and Irina Y. Kuzes, *Radical Reform in Yeltsin's Russia: Political, Economic, and Social Dimension* (Armonk, N.Y.: M. E. Sharpe, 1995), p. 46.

27. Quoted in Nelson and Kuzes, *Radical Reform in Yeltsin's Russia*, pp. 53–54.

28. William Mitchell and Michael Munger, "Economic Models of Interest Groups: An Introductory Survey," *American Journal of Political Science*, vol. 35 (May 1991), p. 532. The italics are in the original. George J. Stigler, *Memoirs of an Unregulated Economist* (Basic Books, 1988), pp. 73–80.

29. Robert P. Inman and Daniel L. Rubinfeld, "The Political Economy of Federalism," in Dennis C. Mueller, *Perspectives on Public Choice: A Handbook* (Cambridge: Cambridge University Press, 1997), p. 76.

30. Winston C. Bush, "The Hobbesian Jungle or Orderly Anarchy," in Arthur T. Denzau and Robert J. Mackay, *Essays on Unorthodox Economic Strategies: Anarchy, Politics, and Population* (Blacksburg, Va.: University Publications, 1976), p 34.

31. Lynn D. Nelson and Irina Y. Kuzes, *Property to the People: The Struggle*

for Radical Economic Reform in Russia (Armonk, N.Y.: M. E. Sharpe, 1994), p. 126. A leading privatization official reports that by 1997 most shares were transferred to the Ministry of the Economy, the old Gosplan. Alfred Kokh, *The Selling of the Soviet Empire: Politics and Economics of Russia's Privatization—Revelations of the Principal Insider* (New York: S. P. I. Books, 1998), p. 81.

32. Anatoly Chubais and Maria Vishnevskaya, "Main Issues of Privatisation in Russia," in Anders Aslund and Richard Layard, eds., *Changing the Economic System in Russia* (St. Martin's, 1993), pp. 89–90.

33. See Janine R. Wedel, *Collision and Collusion: The Strange Case of Western Aid to Eastern Europe, 1989–1998* (St. Martin's, 1998), pp. 121–23, 129–31.

34. "K s'ezdu narodnykim deputatov" (To the Congress of People's Deputies), *Rossiiskaia gazeta*, October 29, 1991, pp. 1–2. Westerners often claimed that insider privatization was the result of Yeltsin's need to compromise with the Congress of People's Deputies in April 1992, but as this speech indicates, the basic decision was already made in October 1991.

35. Nelson and Kuzes, *Radical Reform in Yeltsin's Russia*, pp. 43–44.

36. "Savings Bank Introduces Higher Interest Rates," Moscow Mayak Radio Network, January 5, 1992, in FBIS-*Daily Report: Russia*, January 6, 1992, p. 36. For a later sharp criticism of the government's refusal to raise rates, see Jeffrey Sachs and David Lipton, "Remaining Steps to a Market-Based Monetary System in Russia," in Aslund and Layard, eds., *Changing the Economic System in Russia*, pp. 138–40.

37. Anatoly B. Chubais and Maria D. Vishnevskaya, "Privatization in Russia: An Overview," in Anders Aslund, ed., *Economic Transformation in Russia* (St. Martin's, 1994), p. 94.

38. Tuomo Summanen, *Privatization in Russia: Experiences, Problems, and Opportunities* (Helsinki: Ministry of Trade and Industry, 1995), pp. 20–21.

39. Nelson and Kuzes, *Property to the People*, pp. 50–51.

40. The range of literature on the subject is discussed in Joseph R. Blasi, Maya Kroumova, and Douglas Kruse, *Kremlin Capitalism: The Privatization of the Russian Economy* (Cornell University Press, 1997), pp. 114–21.

41. Handelman, *Comrade Criminal*, pp. 147–48. See Yury Shchekochikhin, "Strakh," *Literaturnaia gazeta*, June 10, 1992, p. 11, for accusations of Luzhkov's involvement while he was still deputy mayor.

42. Katharina Pistor and Joel Turkewitz, "Coping with Hydra—State Ownership after Privatization: A Comparative Study of the Czech Republic, Hungary, and Russia," in Roman Frydman, Cheryl W. Gray, and Andrzej Rapaczynski, eds., *Corporate Governance in Central Europe and Russia: Insiders and the State* (Budapest: Central European University Press, 1996), vol. 2, p. 205. For the peculiarities of privatization in the defense industry, see Clifford G. Gaddy, *The Price of the Past: Russia's Struggle with the Legacy of a Militarized Economy* (Brookings, 1996), pp. 76–84, 178–79.

43. Floyd Norris, "The Russian Way of Corporate Governance," *New York Times*, April 5, 1999, p. A20.

44. Aslund, *How Russia Became a Market Economy*, p. 235.

45. See Nelson and Kuzes, *Radical Reform in Yeltsin's Russia*, p. 47. Gaidar confirms these early doubts in his memoirs.

46. Gaidar, *Dni porazhenii i pobed*, p. 92. Anatoly Chubais and Maria Vishnevskaya, "Main Issues of Privatisation in Russia," and Maxim Boycko and Andrei Shleifer, "The Voucher Program for Russia," in Aslund and Layard, *Changing the Economic System in Russia*, pp. ix, 89–111.

47. Andrei Shleifer and Maxim Boycko, "The Politics of Russian Privatization," in Olivier Blanchard and others, ed., *Post-Communist Reform: Pain and Progress* (MIT Press, 1993), p. 51. In other writings, however, Shleifer and Boycko claimed that, unlike other economists, they were not really interested in corporate governance, but in the destruction of the state. Andrei Shleifer and Robert W. Vishny, *The Grabbing Hand: Government Pathologies and Their Cures* (Harvard University Press, 1998), p. 11. Maxim Boycko, Andrei Shleifer, and Robert W. Vishny, "Privatizing Russia," *Brookings Papers on Economic Activity, 2: 1993*, p. 189.

48. Nelson and Kuzes, *Radical Reform in Yeltsin's Russia*, pp. 48–51.

49. By early December 1993, 29 percent of the respondents in our study still had not decided what to do with their vouchers. Of those who had made a decision, 17 percent had invested it in the enterprise where they or a member of their family worked, 8 percent in another enterprise, and 36 percent in a mutual fund. A quarter of the respondents had sold the voucher, and 14 percent had given it away. Kokh, *The Selling of the Soviet Empire*, p. 34.

50. Joint property—property with some degree of foreign ownership—is primarily a feature of oil, gas, and electric firms with heavy state ownership and strong state control. Actually, 0.7 percent was reported to be working in social organizations and 0.7 percent in joint ventures with foreigners. The former has been included in the state category and the latter in the private. *Rossiia v tsifrakh: Kratkii statisticheskii sbornik* (Russia in numbers: Short statistical collection) (Moscow: Goskomstat, 1999), p. 80.

51. When the board of directors of United Energy Systems, the giant electrical utility, tried to change its head, Boris Brevnov, a protégé of first deputy premier Boris Nemtsov, it was reminded that the 53 percent state-ownership of shares meant the state appointed the director. "Russia's Potential to Become a Major Player in Electricity Market." Chrystia Freeland, "Bid to Oust Russian Power Reformer," *Financial Times*, January 29, 1998, p. 2.

52. The total number of respondents in this age group was 637 in 1993, 655 in 1995, and 637 in 1996.

53. Indeed, when the government was to promise to pay back wages, it never included those in the "stock company" sector, even if, by all meaningful indicators, they were state or semistate enterprises.

54. Boycko, Shleifer, and Vishny, "Privatizing Russia," p. 189.

55. Fischer, "Comments and Discussion," pp. 182–83.

56. Blasi, Kroumova, and Kruse, *Kremlin Capitalism*, pp. 54, 193, 210.

57. Boycko, Shleifer, and Vishny, *Privatizing Russia*, p. 59.

58. Zbigniew Brzezinski, "Victory of the Clerks: What Khrushchev's Ouster Means," *New Republic*, vol. 151 (November 14, 1964), pp. 15–18.

59. Peter A. Hauslohner, "Managing the Soviet Labor Market: Politics and Policymaking under Brezhnev" (Ph.D. dissertation, University of Michigan, 1984).

60. See David Granick, *Management of the Industrial Firm in the USSR: A Study in Soviet Economic Planning* (Columbia University Press, 1954), which was based on press accounts from the 1930s, and Joseph Berliner, *Factory and Manager in the USSR* (Harvard University Press, 1957), based on interviews with former managers from the same period.

61. Richard E. Ericson, "Economics," in Timothy J. Colton and Robert Legvold, *After the Soviet Union: From Empire to Nations* (W. W. Norton, 1992), p. 64.

62. Fischer, in "Comments and Discussion," *Brookings Papers on Economic Activity, 2: 1993*, p. 184.

63. Stanley Fischer, "$1.6 Billion: Just a Start," *New York Times*, April 6, 1993, p. A23.

Chapter Four

1. Stanislaw Gomulka, "Output: Causes of the Decline and the Recovery," in Peter Boone, Stanislaw Gomulka, and Richard Layard, eds., *Emerging from Communism: Lessons from Russia, China, and Eastern Europe* (MIT Press, 1998), p. 13.

2. Olivier Blanchard, *The Economics of Post-Communist Transition* (Oxford: Oxford University Press, 1997), p. 13.

3. *Rossiia v tsifrakh 1998: Kratkii statisticheskii sbornik* (Russia in numbers: Short statistical collection) (Moscow: Goskomstat, 1998), pp. 162, 331.

4. The serious figures on hidden domestic dollar savings and capital flow abroad are calculated from the discrepancies in the official statistics on exports, imports, and currency flows. However, there can be explanations for the discrepancies other than hidden savings at home or abroad—for example, unreported consumption or errors in one of the foreign commerce statistics.

5. For a statement of the differences from a neoliberal Russian participant, see A. Illarionov, "Nashi raznoglasiia" (Our disagreements), *Voprosy ekonomiki* (Questions of economics), no. 5 (May 1994), pp. 21–28.

6. John Odling-Smee, "Other Voices—What Went Wrong in Russia?" *Wall Street Journal Europe's Central European Economic Review*, October 26, 1998. Quoted in David Johnson's Russia List, no. 2498, December 1, 1998.

7. Alan Greenspan, "The Embrace of Free Markets" (Washington: Woodrow Wilson International Center for Scholars, 1997), p. 2.

8. Douglass C. North, "The Contribution of the New Institutional Economics to an Understanding of the Transition Problem (Helsinki: UNU World Institute for Development Economics Research, 1997), p. 16.

9. Douglass C. North, "Epilogue: Economic Performance Through Time," in Lee J. Alston, Thrainn Eggertsson, and Douglass C. North, eds., *Empirical Studies in Institutional Change* (Cambridge: Cambridge University Press, 1996), pp. 348–49.

10. Ibid.

11. Alexander Gerschenkron, *Economic Backwardness in Historical Perspective: A Book of Essays* (Harvard University Press, 1962).

12. Stanley Fischer, "Stabilization and Economic Reform in Russia," *Brookings Papers on Economic Activity, 1: 1992*, p. 82.

13. Lawrence Summers, "The Next Decade in Central and Eastern Europe," in Christopher Clague and Gordon C. Rausser, eds., *The Emergence of Market Economies in Eastern Europe* (Oxford: Blackwell, 1992), pp. 31–32.

14. M. P. Berezina and Iu. S. Krupnov, *Mezhbankovskie raschety* (Intrabank payments) (Moscow: Finstatinform, 1993), pp. 39, 42–43.

15. Samuel R. Berger, "Getting the New Russia on Its Feet: Our Assistance Is Making the American People More Secure," *Washington Post*, September 5, 1999, p. B7.

16. Mancur Olson, "Dictatorship, Democracy, and Development," *American Political Science Review*, vol. 87 (September 1993), pp. 572–73.

17. Diego Gambetta, "Comment on 'Corruption and Development,'" in Boris Pleskovic and Joseph E. Stiglitz, eds., *Annual World Bank Conference on Development Economics 1997* (Washington: The World Bank, 1998), p. 58; Diego Gambetta, *The Sicilian Mafia: The Business of Private Protection* (Harvard University Press, 1993).

18. This was true not only in Russia. A whole literature on corruption arose in the 1960s because of the perception that communist Vietcong administered villages more honestly than the South Vietnamese government. See James C. Scott, *Comparative Political Corruption* (Englewood Cliffs, N.J.: Prentice-Hall, 1973), p. ix.

19. The problem of corruption is not limited to Russia among former communist states. See Hilary Appel, "Corruption, Democratization, and Economic Reform: Lessons from the Czech Case," paper presented to the Annual Meeting of the American Political Science Association in Boston, September 3–6, 1998.

20. Andrei Shleifer and Robert W. Vishny, *The Grabbing Hand: Government Pathologies and Their Cures* (Harvard University Press, 1998), pp. 97–98. Shleifer had been Larry Summers' research assistant at Harvard and was said to be quite close to him. Carla Anne Robbins and Steve Liesman, "How an Aid Pro-

gram Vital to New Economy of Russia Collapsed," *Wall Street Journal*, August 13, 1997, pp. 1, 6. When Shleifer discussed the privatization program in which he himself was involved, he was always optimistic and showed little awareness of the logic of the steps he had advocated. See, for example, Maxim Boycko, Andrei Shleifer, and Robert Vishny, *Privatizing Russia* (MIT Press, 1995), p. 9. A later example is his lyrical description of privatization in the foreword to Joseph R. Blasi, Maya Kroumova, and Douglas Kruse, *Kremlin Capitalism: The Privatization of the Russian Economy* (Cornell University Press, 1997), pp. ix–x.

21. Moisei Ia. Ostrogorski, *Democracy and the Organization of Political Parties*, vol. I: *England*, edited and abridged by Seymour Martin Lipset (Garden City, N.Y.: Anchor Books, 1964), p. 71; Lewis B. Namier, *England in the Age of the American Revolution* (London: Macmillan, 1930), pp. 61–65.

22. For a summary article with an extensive bibliography, see Susan Rose-Ackerman, "Corruption and Development," in Pleskovic and Stiglitz, eds., *Annual World Bank Conference on Development Economics 1997*, pp. 35–57.

23. See Jonathan Schiffer, "Soviet Territorial Pricing and Emerging Republican Politics," *Journal of Soviet Nationalities*, vol. 1 (Fall 1990), pp. 67–111.

24. *Narodnoe khoziaistvo RSFSR v 1990 g.: Statisticheskii ezhegodnik* (National economy of the RSFSR in 1990: Statistical yearbook) (Moscow: Goskomstat, 1990), pp. 597–98, 749.

25. Some statistics indicated that a very high percentage of many crops came from the private sector. However, these percentages, first of all, reflected the impact of the decline of production in state and collective sector. Second, the vast majority of the private production came from peasant private plots and urban garden plots, not private farmers, and it was consumed by the producers. The technology was not much more sophisticated than the shovel.

26. Evelyn Davidheiser, "The World Economy and Mobilizational Dictatorship: Russia's Transition, 1846–1917," Ph.D. dissertation, Duke University, 1990.

27. V. Nazarenko, "Agroreforma i antikrizisnye zadachi gosudarstva" (Agrarian reform and the anticrisis goals of the government), *Rossiiskii ekonomicheskii zhurnal*, no. 11 (1995), pp. 47–48.

28. Ibid., p. 48.

29. Steve Liesman and Andrew Higgins, "The Crunch Points How Russia Staggered from There to Here," *Wall Street Journal*, September 23, 1998, p. 12. See Rose Brady, *Kapitalizm: Russia's Struggle to Free Its Economy* (Yale University Press, 1999), pp. 81–91, 116–26, 170–76, 224–25.

30. The problems lie in two opposite directions. Many people do not incorporate their businesses to avoid tax collection, while many businesses that are registered have essentially become inactive.

31. Leonid Abalkin, "Begstvo kapitala: priroda, formy, metody bor'by" (Capital flight: its nature, forms, and methods of struggle against it), *Voprosy ekonomiki*, no. 7 (July 1998), pp. 39–41.

32. Richard E. Ericson, "Economics," in Timothy J. Colton and Robert Legvold, eds., *After the Soviet Union: From Empire to Nations* (W. W. Norton, 1992), p. 64.

33. Michael Gordon, "The Gusher That Wasn't in Russia," *New York Times*, September 5, 1997, p. D2.

34. Stephen Handelman, *Comrade Criminal: Russia's New Mafiya* (Yale University Press, 1995), pp. 22, 88–89. The money-laundering scandal involving the Bank of New York in 1999 led to the publication of a great deal of detail about the formation of trading companies in which central and regional officials were also deeply involved. See, for example, Michael Wines, "Yeltsin Son-in-Law at Center of Rich Network of Influence," *New York Times*, October 7, 1999, pp. 1, 6, which describes the trading firms associated with the Siberian Oil Firm in Omsk.

35. Estonia became a major exporter of nonferrous metallurgy.

36. For a discussion of Vagit Alekperov, head of Lukoil, and his wealth, see Chrystia Freeland and Robert Corzine, "Wanted: Capitalists to Share Russia's Riches," *Financial Times*, January 6, 1995, p. 2.

37. The real problem with market prices was the supply of products to former non-Russian republics of the Soviet Union. If the international community wanted to marketize the Russian economy, it needed to provide aid to the non-Russian republics to purchase the energy, timber, and other products they needed, but little or no thought was given to this option.

Chapter Five

1. Richard Layard, one of the most fervent supporters of radical reform, had moved to the position that "we cannot yet prove that . . . a more gradual evolution would have been a mistake." Richard Layard, "Why So Much Pain? An Overview," in Peter Boone, Stanislaw Gomulka, and Richard Layard, eds., *Emerging from Communism: Lessons from Russia, China, and Eastern Europe* (MIT Press, 1998), p. 5; and Joseph R. Blasi, Maya Kroumova, and Douglas Kruse, *Kremlin Capitalism: The Privatization of the Russian Economy* (Cornell University Press, 1997), pp. 173–76.

2. This section is based largely on Jerry F. Hough, *Democratization and Revolution in the USSR, 1985–1991* (Brookings, 1997), pp. 449–89.

3. See Jerry F. Hough and Susan Goodrich Lehmann, "The Mystery of Opponents of Economic Reform among the Yeltsin Voters," in Matthew Wyman, Stephen White, and Sarah Oates, *Elections and Voters in Post-Communist Russia* (Cheltenham, UK: Edward Elgar, 1998), pp. 223–24; and Hough, *Democratization and Revolution in the USSR*, p. 406.

4. Aleksandr Korzhakov, *Boris Yel'tsin: Ot rassveta do zakata* (Boris Yeltsin: From dawn to sunset) (Moscow: Interbuk, 1997), p. 115.

5. He did strongly suggest to Defense Minister Yevgeny Shaposhnikov that he conduct a military coup. Yevgeny Shaposhnikov, *Vybor* (The Choice), 2d ed., revised and expanded (Moscow: Nezavisimoe izdatel'stvo PIK, 1995), pp. 137–38.

6. *Rossiiskie vesti*, no. 31 (December 14, 1991), p. 8.

7. This position is found in Mancur Olson, *The Rise and Decline of Nations: Economic Growth, Stagflation, and Social Rigidities* (Yale University Press, 1982). It is explicitly cited with approval in Yegor Gaidar, *Ekonomicheskie reformy i ierarkhicheskie struktury* (Economic reforms and hierarchical structures) (Moscow: Nauka, 1990), pp. 192–95.

8. Boris Yeltsin, *The Struggle for Russia* (Random House, 1994), pp. 151, 156–57.

9. For the characterization of Saburov as a strong supporter for privatization, but more cautious on rapid price liberalization, see Anders Aslund, *How Russia Became a Market Economy* (Brookings, 1995), pp. 71, 227.

10. *Nezavisimaia gazeta*, October 12, 1991, p. 2.

11. *Izvestiia*, September 25, 1991, pp. 1-2.

12. *Nezavisimaia gazeta*, September 28, 1991, p. 4.

13. *Nezavisimaia gazeta*, January 22, 1992, p. l.

14. For the sequence of events see Francis X. Clines, "Soviet Republics Agree to Create an Economic Union," *New York Times*, October 12, 1991, p. 1; Steven Greenhouse, "The Soviet Market Makeover Will Mean Erasing Seventy Years," *New York Times*, October 13, 1991, p. 12; Francis X. Clines, "Delay in Election Urged by Yeltsin," *New York Times*, October 17, 1991, p. A3; and Francis X. Clines, "Eight Soviet Republics Sign Economic Pact," *New York Times*, October 19, 1991, p. A3. For coverage of Brady's interview, see James Steingold, "Brady Says Soviet Pact on Union Is the Key to Aid," *New York Times*, October 15, 1994, p. A3. For more information on the cabinet resignation, see Hough, *Democratization and Revolution in the USSR*, pp. 464–67.

15. "K s"ezdu narodnykh deputatov" (To the Congress of People's Deputies), *Rossiiskaia gazeta*, October 29, 1991.

16. Yeltsin, *The Struggle for Russia*, p. 157.

17. The way in which these arguments directed at the West played out in December is nicely described in Serge Schmemann, "Yeltsin to Finance Soviet Payroll to Avert Bankruptcy," *New York Times*, December 1, 1991, p. 1; and Serge Schmemann, "The Soviet Shell," *New York Times*, December 2, 1991, pp. 1, 10.

18. Ruslan Khasbulatov, who was the top official in the Congress after Yeltsin's election as president, was an active supporter of Yeltsin's grab of USSR powers and property, but he has testified that he never expected the USSR to break up.

19. "Yeltsin Holds News Conference in Kremlin," Ostankino Television First Channel Network (Moscow), April 14, 1993, in FBIS-*Daily Report: Russia*, April 15, 1993, pp. 12–13.

20. These words are from "The Choice over Russia," an editorial in *Financial Times*, March 17, 1993, p. 17. As the notes in this book indicate, they bear little relationship to the analysis presented by the Moscow correspondents of the newspaper.

21. "Pochinok Speaks on State Budget," Moscow Russian Television Network, February 26, 1993, in FBIS-*Daily Report: Russia*, March 1, 1993, pp. 39–40. Pochinok finally gave up and joined the executive branch, where he could have some influence. He became deputy minister of finances and a close ally of Chubais.

22. Stephen Fidler, "£6bn of Russia's Budget Misspent," *Financial Times*, June 9, 1998, p. 2. For a defense of Sokolov, see Peter Reddaway, "IMF Funding for Russia Would Not Solve the Country's Problems," *Financial Times*, July 8, 1998, p. 8.

23. Hough, *Democratization and Revolution in the USSR*, pp. 335, 339, 407, 470–74.

24. Ibid., pp. 336–37.

25. Yeltsin, *The Struggle for Russia*, pp. 159–60.

26. Ibid., p. 166.

27. Ibid., pp. 166–67.

28. Ibid., p. 165.

29. "Postanovlenie s"ezda narodnykh deputatov rossiiskoy federatsii" (Resolution of the Congress of People's Deputies of the Russian Federation), *Rossiiskaia gazeta*, April 23, 1992, p. 1.

30. Yeltsin, *The Struggle for Russia*, p. 166.

31. In his memoirs, Yeltsin indicated that the timing was linked with the IMF decisions on stabilization of the ruble, and other Russian politicians could understand that motivation. Ibid., pp. 173–74.

32. Volsky and Skokov had very similar views, but their personal relations were very poor, no doubt because both were appealing to the same social-economic base.

33. "Volsky Advocates Chinese Economic Model," *Milan Il Giornale*, October 18, 1992, in FBIS-*Daily Report: Russia*, October 22, 1992, p. 33.

34. This ability to work with both Gaidar and Volsky was to stand Yasin in good stead in November 1994, when he was named to replace Aleksandr Shokhin as minister of the economy.

35. B. Prokhvatilov, "Tseny podnimutsia v dva-tri raza" (Prices will increase two- or three-fold), *Komsomol'skaia pravda*, March 18, 1992, p. 2.

36. "Victor Chernomyrdin's One Hundred Days," *New Times*, no. 14 (April 1993), pp. 19–21.

37. Valery Vyzhutovich, "Yel'tsin zakliuchaet soyuz s 'grazhdanskim soyuzom'" (Yeltsin concludes an alliance with "Civic Union"), *Izvestiia*, October 8, 1992, p. 2.

38. Yeltsin, *The Struggle for Russia*, p. 176.

39. Ibid., pp. 193–94.

40. "Obrashchenie prezidenta B. N. Yel'tsina k grazhdanam Rossii i ko vsei izbirateliam" (President B. N. Yeltsin's address to the citizens of Russia and to all voters), *Rossiiskaia gazeta*, December 11, 1992; Radio Rossii, December 10, 1992, in FBIS-*Daily Report—Supplement*, December 10, 1992, pp. 1–2.

41. "Postanovlenie VII s"ezda narodnykh deputatov rossiiskoi federatsii o stabilizatsii konstitutsionnogo stroia rossiiskoi federatsii" (Resolution of the VII Congress of People's Deputies of the Russian Federation regarding the stabilization of the constitutional system of the Russian Federation), *Rossiiskaia gazeta*, December 15, 1992, p. 1.

42. Radio Rossii (Moscow), December 12, 1992, in FBIS-*Daily Report— Supplement Central Eurasia*, December 14, 1992, pp. 4–5; *Rossiiskaia gazeta*, December 15, 1992.

43. *Rossiiskaia gazeta*, December 15, 1992.

44. Yeltsin, *The Struggle for Russia*, pp. 197–201. See Yegor Gaidar, *Dni porazhenii i pobed* (Days of defeats and victories) (Moscow: Vagrius, 1996), pp. 234–35.

45. Ostankino television, December 14, 1992, in FBIS-*Daily Report: Russia,* December 15, 1992, p. 23.

46. Mikhail Berger, "Postanovlenie o regulirovanii tsen ne otrazahaet obshchego kursa pravitel'stva" (The decree on price controls does not reflect the general government policy), *Izvestiia*, January 13, 1993, p. 1; Mikhail Berger, "Pravitel'stvo Rossii peresmatrivaet reshenie o regulirovanii tsen" (Russian government revises decision on price controls), *Izvestiia*, January 19, 1993, p. 1.

47. George Graham and Leyla Boulton, "Row with Ukraine Hits Debt Rescheduling," *Financial Times*, January 14, 1993, p. 2.

48. Boris Krasnikov, "GS dumaet o posleel'tsinskoi Rossii (GS is thinking about post-Yeltsin Russia), *Nezavisimaia gazeta*, January 5, 1993, p. 2.

49. "Relations between Yeltsin, Rutskoy Viewed," Interfax, March 1, 1993, in FBIS-*Daily Report: Russia*, March 2, 1993, p. 24.

50. John Lloyd, "Russian Managers Given Warning," *Financial Times*, January 19, 1993, p. 2.

51. Steven Erlanger, "Russian Leaders Said to Have Exaggerated Inflation," *New York Times*, March 3, 1993, p. A9.

52. Leyla Boulton, "Reformers Play Last Economic Card," *Financial Times*, March 24, 1993, p. 2; and John Lloyd, "Fyodorov Proposes Another Dose of Shock Therapy," *Financial Times*, March 26, 1993, p. 2.

53. "Chernomyrdin Interviewed on Political Situation," Moscow Russian Television Network, March 12, 1993, in FBIS-*Daily Report: Russia*, March 15, 1993, pp. 58–59.

54. Korzhakov, *Boris Yel'tsin*, pp. 158–60.

55. Vladimir Isakov, "Protivostoianie" (Resistance), *Sovetskaia Rossiia*, March 16, 1993, p. 1. Emphasis in original.

56. See the testimony of Mikhail Berger in *Finansovye izvestiia*, April 24–29, 1993, p. 1.

57. The votes on all four questions discussed in ensuing paragraphs, as well as the regional breakdowns on all four, are found in Ralph S. Clem and Peter R. Craumer, "The Geography of the April 25 (1993) Russian Referendum," *Post-Soviet Geography*, vol. 34 (October 1993), p. 482.

58. Moscow Russian Television Network, April 16, 1993, in FBIS-*Daily Report: Russia*, April 19. 1993, p. 24; Ostankino Television First Channel Network (Moscow), April 14, 1993, in FBIS-*Daily Report: Russia*, April 15, 1993, pp. 12–15.

59. John Lloyd, "West Drawn into Russian Maelstrom," *Financial Times*, April 3–4, 1993, p. 3.

60. Clem and Craumer, "The Geography of the April 25 (1993) Russian Referendum," pp. 484–85.

61. The electoral commission included the invalid ballots in the total when it reported that less than 50 percent voted for a presidential election. However, the actual vote was 34.0 million for such an election and 32.4 million against, and the number of invalid ballots was suspiciously high.

62. "Konstitutsiia rossiiskoi federatsii [osnovnoi zakon]" (Constitution of the Russian Federation [fundamental law]), *Izvestiia*, April 30, 1993, p. 3; Vasilii Kononenko, "Krizis vlasti v Rossii smeshchaetsia v konstitutsionnoe prostranstvo" (The power crisis in Russia shifts into constitutional realm), *Izvestiia*, May 13, 1993, pp. 1, 2; "Prezident prinial reshenie sozvat' konstitutsionnoe soveshchanie 5 iunia" (President has made decision to call constitutional convention on June 5), *Izvestiia*, May 22, 1993, p. 1.

63. Yeltsin, *The Struggle for Russia*, p. 9.

64. Sergei Chugaev, "R. Khasbulatov ishchet podkhody k B. Yeltsinu" (R. Khasbulatov seeks approaches to B. Yeltsin), *Izvestiia*, May 21, 1993, p. 1.

65. ITAR-TASS, "Konstitutsionnoe soveshchanie odobrilo proekt novoi konstitutsii" (Constitutional convention has approved draft of new constitution), *Izvestiia*, July 13, 1993, p. 1. The constitution was published in *Izvestiia*, July 16, 1993, pp. 3–6.

66. Andre Illesh and Valerii Rudnev, "Viktor Barannikov nastupil na grabli. Kto sleduiushchiu?" (Viktor Barannikov stepped on the rake. Who is next?), *Izvestiia*, July 29, 1993, p. 1.

67. Obviously, the conservatives made this charge, but even the pro-Yeltsin *Izvestiia* published two articles by its former New York correspondent, Aleksandr Shalnev, raising the gravest questions about the authenticity of the documents implicating Rutskoi. *Izvestiia*, August 27, 1993, p. 2.

68. "Yeltsin Interviewed on Failed Coup Attempt," ARD Television Network (Hamburg), November 12, 1993, in FBIS-*Daily Report: Russia*, November 15, 1993, pp. 11–13.

69. Mikhail Berger, "Eshche odin trudnyi shag na puti k rynki—otpushcheny tseny na nefteprodukty" (Another difficult step on the way to the market— prices on oil products freed), *Izvestiia*, May 26, 1993, p. 1; and Sergei Leskov, "Svobodnye tseny na ugol'mogut ukepit' ili vzorvat' economiku Rossii" (Free prices for coal can strengthen or undermine the economy of Russia), *Izvestiia*, June 23, 1993, p. 1. The price of coal was particularly important. It was the only fuel whose price had not been raised since 1992, and a ton of coal was priced at less than a Snickers candy bar.

70. Soskovets was closely associated with the security group around Aleksandr Korzhakov and certainly was conservative in that sense. However, his personal interest lay in a policy of privatizing metallurgy and exporting metals, perhaps not always legally. This made his interests in foreign economic policy similar to those of the oil and natural gas industries.

71. Most focused on the hypothesis that he was a counterweight to Chernomyrdin or Lobov. For an article that lists all hypotheses, see Valery Konovalov, "Oleg Soskovets schitaet, chto reforma idet uspeshno i ee nuzhno razvivat" (Oleg Soskovets thinks that the reform is going well and should be developed), *Izvestiia*, May 13, 1993, p. 2.

72. Mikhail Berger, "Ministerstvo ekonomiki pretenduet na rol' gosplana" (Ministry of Economics aspires to role of Gosplan), *Izvestiia*, May 5, 1993, p. 1.

73. Petr Akopov, "Tret'ia popytka" (The third attempt), *Rossiiskie vesti*, April 23, 1993, p. 2.

74. Yuri Makartsev, "Denezhnyi tromb rossiyskoi ekonomiki" (Monetary bloodclot of the Russian economy), *Rabochaia gazeta*, August 20, 1993, p. 9. See *Rabochaia tribuna*, September 17, 1993. This deputy minister was Valentin Fedorov, the former radical governor of Sakhalin.

75. Lobov's plan was leaked to the pro-Fedorov *Izvestiia* and published in Aleksandr Livshits, "Ministerskii plan 'spasenie ekonomiki' mozhet postavit' krest na reformakh" (Ministry's plan to "save the economy" may put a cross on the reforms), *Izvestiia*, August 4, 1993, and "Proekt programmy vykhoda iz krizisa bol'she napominaet skorospeluiu otpisku" (Draft of the program to come out of crisis is more reminiscent of a premature copout), *Izvestiia*, August 6, 1993.

76. Irina Demchenko, "Ministerstvo ekonomiki sobiraetsia podmenit' soboi pravitel'stvo, a v perspektive—i prezidenta" (The ministry of economics intends to take over the government, and in the future—the president), *Izvestiia*, May 18, 1993, p. 2.

77. Boris Fedorov, "Finansovaia politika Rossii posle referenduma" (Russia's financial policy after the referendum), *Izvestiia*, May 8, 1993, p. 4; and Mikhail Berger, "Rossiia mozhet ne poluchit' spetsial'no dlia nee izobretennyi kredit

MVF" (Russia may not receive the IMF credit especially created for her), *Izvestiia*, May 19, 1993, p. 2

78. Boris Fedorov, "Blizhaishie dve nedeli—vremia politicheskogo vybora" (The next two weeks—the time of political decision), *Segodnia*, August 24, 1993.

79. Mikhail Berger, "Raznoglasiia v pravitel'stve po povodu ekonomicheskoi politiki" (Disagreements within the government about economic policy), *Izvestiia*, September 4, 1993, pp. 1–2.

80. Sergei Mitin, "Soglashenie tsentrobanka i pravitel'syva uskorit khod ekonomicheskii reform" (Agreement between the Central Bank and the government will speed up economic reforms), *Finansovye Izvestiia*, May 15–21, 1993, p. 1.

81. Aleksandr Bekker, "Tvorcheskie plany Viktora Gerashchenko" (Viktor Gerashchenko's creative plans), *Izvestiia*, January 25, 1994, p. 2.

82. P. Vasil'ev, "S chem vernulsia Gaidar?" (What did Gaidar return with?), *Argumenty i fakty*, no. 38 (September 1993), p. 17.

83. Aleksei A. Mukhin, *Estestvennye monopolii v Rossii* (Natural monopolies in Russia) (Moscow: SPIK-Tsentr, 1998), pp. 2, 7–9.

84. Most corruption, by its nature, is impossible to document other than through rumors. The U.S. intelligence agencies, however, picked up a good deal of information on Chernomyrdin, but it was not made public. James Risen, "Gore Rejected C.I.A. Evidence of Russian Corruption," *New York Times*, November 23, 1998, p. A8.

85. Mikhail Berger, "Raznoglasiia v pravitel'stve po povodu ekonomicheskoi politiki" (Disagreements within the government about economic policy), *Izvestiia*, September 4, 1993, pp. 1–2.

86. Vladislav Borodulin, "Konflikt vokrug minekonomiki obostril pravitel'stvennyi krizis" (The government crisis has heightened the conflict around the ministry of economics), *Kommersant Daily*, September 10, 1993, p. 2.

87. Leyla Boulton, "High Hopes in Russia of IMF Accord," *Financial Times*, April 7, 1993, p. 3.

88. Iurii Orlik, "Chego mozhno ozhidat' ot sentiabr'skogo nastupleniia rossiskogo prezidenta?" (What can be expected from the Russian president's September offensive?), *Izvestiia*, September 10, 1993. Kostikov reports in his memoirs that he was the source of the leak and that Yeltsin had instructed him to make it. Viacheslav Kostikov, *Roman s prezidentom: Zapiski press-sekretaria* (Moscow: Vagrius, 1997), pp. 218–19.

89. Steven Greenhouse, "I.M.F. Delays $1.5 Billion Loan to Russia Because Reform Is Stalled," *New York Times*, September 20, 1993, p. A3.

90. It is not clear how much power Gaidar had and how much he was a symbol for foreigners. It was later reported that he was banned from budgetary decisions as of November, when he began leading the campaign of Russia's Choice. Aleksandr Bekker, "Chisto sovetskoe pravitel'stvo" (A purely soviet govern-

ment), *Segodnia*, January 18, 1994, p. 1. The policy was presumably being implemented by Fedorov as minister of finances.

91. William Safire, "Yeltsin Planned His Coup," *New York Times*, September 23, 1993, p. A27.

92. "Yeltsin Disbands Parliament, Calls Elections to 'Federal Assembly,'" Ostankino Television, September 21, 1993, in FIBS-*Daily Report: Russia*, September 22, 1993, pp. 1–3.

93. Serge Schmemann, "Showdown in Moscow; Yeltsin Supported by Security Chiefs in Political Fight," *New York Times*, September 23, 1993, p. A1.

94. Yeltsin, *The Struggle for Russia*, pp. 11–14.

95. Kostikov, *Roman s prezidentom*, p. 158. For his view on the Communist party, see pp. 141–43, 168.

96. Korzhakov, *Boris Yel'tsin*, pp. 203, 316, 359. Yegor Gaidar writes of Yeltsin's "long periods of passivity and depression" in *Dni porazhenii i pobed*, p. 106. Yeltsin, *The Struggle for Russia*, pp. 3, 15–16, 149, 205.

97. "Yeltsin May Take 'More Resolute Steps,'" Interfax, March 18, 1993, in FBIS-*Daily Report: Russia*, March 18, 1993, p. 22.

98. Korzhakov, *Boris Yel'tsin*, p. 61.

99. Kostikov, *Roman s prezidentom*, p. 168.

Chapter Six

1. Anthony Downs, *An Economic Theory of Democracy* (Harper, 1957).

2. To be more precise, the districts were based on the number of eligible voters (essentially adults) rather than population, while party list election, like all proportional representation, divides seats among actual voters, not the population.

3 Ivan P. Rybkin, *Piataia rossiisskaia gosudarstvennaia Duma* (The fifth Russian state duma) (Moscow: Izvestiia, 1994).

4. Since Yeltsin had abolished most of the regional legislatures along with the national one, most regions did not have a chairman of the legislature to send to Moscow. Hence in the 1993 election, but not thereafter, Yeltsin had to have the Federation Council elected as well as the Duma.

5. Iu. V. Kudriavtsev, ed., *Kommentarii k konstitutsii rossiiskoi federatsii* (Commentary on the constitution of the Russian Federation) (Moscow: Fond pravovaia kultura, 1996), pp. 397–98.

6. Each region, even national districts and republics with small populations, received at least one deputy, and this introduced considerable variance into the number of people in the election districts.

7. Aleksandr Shokhin, Gaidar's chief collaborator in economic reform, and Sergei Shakhrai, Yeltsin's chief legal specialist and a fervent centralizer, were among the leaders of PRES. Yabloko (which means "apple" in Russian) was

named for its three founders, Grigory Yavlinsky, Yuri Boldyrev, and Vladimir Lukin.

8. Evelyn Davidheiser, "Right and Left in the Hard Opposition," in Timothy J. Colton and Jerry F. Hough, eds., *Growing Pains: Russian Democracy and the Election of 1993* (Brookings, 1998), p. 183.

9. "Kandidaty i deputaty gosudarstvennoi dumy" (Candidates and deputies to the state duma), *Rossiiskaia gazeta*, November 12, 1993.

10. Hillary Appel, "Mass Privatization in Post-Communist States: Ideas, Interests, and Economic Regime Change" (Ph.D. dissertation, University of Pennsylvania, 1998), pp. 190–95.

11. For example, the Women's party had Yeltsin's top adviser on women's issues, Ekaterina Filippovna Lakhova, who had known him since his Sverdlovsk days, as the number-two person on its list. "Kandidaty i deputaty gosudarstvennoi dumy."

12. A. Sobianin, E. Gel'man, and O Kaiunov, "Politicheskii klimat v Rossii v 1991–1993 gg." (The political climate in Russia in 1991–1993), *Mirovaia ekonomika i mezhdunarodnye otnosheniia* (World economy and international affairs), no. 9 (1993), pp. 20–32.

13. See Matthew Wyman, *Public Opinion in Postcommunist Russia* (St. Martin's, 1997), figure 7.3, p. 180. The apparent rise in the total opposition to reform from mid-1993 to late 1993 shown in figure 7.3 of Wyman's book almost surely reflected sampling defects in the VTsIOM study in the earlier period. For example, in mid-1993 VTsIOM found only 17 to 18 percent of rural respondents totally opposing the transition to the market, while we found 28 percent doing so in December. The VTsIOM figures do not seem credible.

14. Moshe Haspel, "The Party's Just Begun: Party Formation in the Russian Parliament," Ph.D. dissertation, Emory University, 1998, pp. 49, 51–52.

15. If the women in a village are housewives, they contribute nothing to GDP statistics. If they specialize—some cook, some care for children, some garden, some clean—all their activity should be part of measured GDP. In an economy that declines to near subsistence, such mutual help expands the service economy but is scarcely a sign of economic health.

16. The figures are from *Biulleten' tsentral'noi izbiratel'noi komissii rossiiskoi federatsii* (Bulletin of the central election committee of the Russian federation), no. 1 (1994), pp. 38, 67. In 1993, 57.7 million persons were said to have cast a vote in the referendum on the constitution, and 56.4 million a valid vote in the referendum. This difference between the 56.4 million valid votes in the referendum and the 53.8 million in the party list vote led to unproven allegations of fraud. However, local officials were under severe pressure to report high turnout on the referendum, while they may have been more than eager to find a reason to find something to invalidate a party list ballot cast for the "wrong" party.

17. "Dannye protokolov no. 2" (Protocol figures no. 2), *Rossiiskaia gazeta*, January 24, 1996 (special edition), p. 2.

18. *Rossiiskaia gazeta*, December 31, 1999, p. 18.

19. The list of candidates and their vote was published in *Rossiiskaia gazeta*, January 6, 2000.

20. James S. Coleman and Carl G. Rosberg Jr., *Political Parties and National Integration in Tropical Africa* (University of California Press, 1964), p. v; Robert H. Jackson and Carl G. Rosberg, *Personal Rule in Black Africa: Prince, Autocrat, Prophet, Tyrant* (University of California Press, 1982), pp. ix–x, 1. See also David E. Apter and Carl G. Rosberg, eds., *Political Development and the New Realism in Sub-Saharan Africa* (University Press of Virginia, 1994), which has two references to political parties and party systems in its index. See p. 337.

21. Richard Hofstadter, *The Idea of a Party System: The Rise of Legal Opposition in the United States, 1780–1840* (University of California Press, 1969), p. 9. The first two chapters deal with this theme.

22. Alexis de Tocqueville, *Democracy in America*, trans. George Lawrence (Random House, 1966), p. 160.

23. Giovanni Sartori, *Parties and Party Systems: A Framework for Analysis* (New York: Cambridge University Press, 1976), vol. 1, p. 82. The literature of party formation in Asia and Africa in the 1960s emphasized the personalistic character of parties, and the literature twenty-five years later was very similar in its conclusions: "It is perhaps misleading to say that every party needs a leader, when often the leader precedes the party." Vicky Randall, ed., *Political Parties in the Third World* (London: Sage Publications, 1988), p. 175.

24. Joseph A. Schumpeter, *Capitalism, Socialism, and Democracy*, 3d ed. (Harper, 1975), pp. 289–90.

25. Ibid., pp. 289–94.

26. Ibid., pp. 294–95.

27. Ibid., p. 293.

28. Ibid., pp. 289–95; Maurice Duverger, *Political Parties: Their Organization and Activity in the Modern State* (London: Methuen, 1954), p. xxxi.

29. V. O. Key Jr., *Public Opinion and American Democracy* (Knopf, 1961), pp. 530, 537.

30. In fact, in the nineteenth century, "civil society" really meant "civilized society," a society with laws, what Max Weber called "rational-technical society." Karl Marx and Frederick Engels, *The German Ideology*, Part One (New York: International Publishers, 1970), p. 57 and C. J. Arthur's introduction on pp. 5–6.

31. Lewis B. Namier, *England in the Age of the American Revolution* (London: Macmillan, 1930), pp. 61–65.

32. Moisei Ia. Ostrogorski, *Democracy and the Organization of Political Parties*, vol. I: *England*, edited and abridged by Seymour Martin Lipset (Garden City, N. Y.: Anchor Books, 1964), p. 71.

33. Aleksandr Peresvet, "The Electorate's Votes Will Flow by the 'Pipe,'" *Rossiya*, July 9, 1999, in David Johnson's Russia List, no. 3399, July 19, 1999.

34. Aleksandr Korzhakov, *Boris Yel'tsin: Ot rassveta do zakata* (Boris Yeltsin: From dawn to sunset) (Moscow: Interbuk, 1997), pp. 203, 209–11.

35. Fred Hiatt, "Ex-Aides Raise Questions about Yeltsin's Drinking," *Washington Post*, October 8, 1994, p. 21.

36. Anders Aslund, "Almost Anyone Is Better than Yeltsin," *New York Times*, February 13, 1996, p. 21.

37. See Jerry F. Hough and Susan Goodrich Lehmann, "The Mystery of Opponents of Economic Reform among Yeltsin Voters," in Matthew Wyman, Stephen White, and Sarah Oates, eds., *Elections and Voters in Post-Communist Russia* (Cheltenham: Edward Elgar, 1998), pp. 205–07.

38. For poll results, see Hough and Lehmann, "The Mystery of Opponents of Economic Reform among Yeltsin Voters," pp. 201–04, 208, 220–24.

39. Table 6-8 lists only percentages, but the actual figures show the same decline.

40. Michael McFaul, "Russia's 1996 Presidential Elections," *Post-Soviet Affairs*, vol. 12 (October-November 1996), pp. 320, 322, 344. A somewhat expanded version of this article was published as Michael McFaul, *Russia's 1996 Presidential Election: The End of Polarized Politics* (Stanford: Hoover Institution, 1997). The title of the book is misleading. It contains the same hypothesis as the article, but hypothesizes that the 1996 election will be the last polarized one.

41. David Hoffman, "Pre-Election Pause in Privatization," *Washington Post*, March 30, 1996, p. 12; Steve Liesman, "Some Russian Officials Are Moving to Reverse Business Privatization," *Wall Street Journal*, March 20, 1996, p. 1; Michael R. Gordon, "Russian Aide Calls for Higher Tariff, Reneging on Vow," *New York Times*, March 2, 1996, p. A1; Michael R. Gordon, "Yeltsin Picks Soviet-Era Aide to Guide Russian Economy," *New York Times*, January 26, 1996, pp. A1, 3.

42. Michael R. Gordon, "Russia Agrees to Closer Links with Three Ex-Soviet Lands," *New York Times*, March 30, 1996, p. 4.

43. Korzhakov, *Boris Yel'tsin*, p. 326. NTV was always as independent as the major banks were private. Just as different banks were the patrimonies of different key palace figures, so too was television.

44. John Thornhill, "Yeltsin Woos Votes with Savings Pledge," *Financial Times*, April 9, 1996, p. 2. See Andrei Zapeklyi, Aleksei Mukhin, and Nikita Tiukov, *Rossiia: Prezidentskaia kampaniia—1996* (Russia: Presidential campaign—1996) (Moscow: SPIK-Tsentr, 1996), p. 19, which emphasizes "paternalism as the ideological basis of the campaign."

45. Michael R. Gordon, "With Voting Near, Yeltsin Promotes Five Top Generals," *New York Times*, June 15, 1996, p. 5.

46. Alessandra Stanley, "Spendthrift Candidate Yeltsin: Miles to Go. Promises to Keep?" *New York Times*, May 4, 1996, p. 1.

47. Chrystia Freeland and Dmitry Volkov, "Yeltsin Flies the Red Flag Again in Search of Votes," *Financial Times*, April 17, 1996, p. 28.

48. Chrystia Freeland, "Moscow to Buy Back Some Sell-Off Shares," *Financial Times*, April 19, 1996, p. 2.

49. Freeland and Volkov, "Yeltsin Flies the Red Flag Again in Search of Votes," p. 28.

50. Stanley, "Spendthrift Candidate Yeltsin."

51. Freeland and Volkov, "Yeltsin Flies the Red Flag Again in Search of Votes," p. 28; Chrystia Freeland, "Yeltsin Drafts Lenin on to Campaign Team," *Financial Times*, May 10, 1996, p. 2.

52. Chrystia Freeland, "Red Flag Flies over Rival Russian Camps," *Financial Times*, May 29, 1996, p. 2.

53. The characteristics of these groups are explored in Hough and Lehmann, "The Mystery of Economic Reform among Yeltsin Voters," pp. 209–19.

54. Michael Kramer, "Rescuing Boris," *Time*, July 15, 1996, p. 30. This article, which contained the version of the election of the American advisers close to the conservative Yeltsin advisers, reported that this internal battle raged throughout March. Alessandra Stanley of the *New York Times* also reported in mid-May that "almost everyone except Mr. Yeltsin"—certainly including Anatoly Chubais—still thought that the anticommunist theme should be handled gently. Stanley's sources were overwhelmingly in the Chubais group, and her article indicates that the advice of that faction had not changed. Alessandra Stanley, "With Campaign Staff in Disarray, Yeltsin Depends on Perks of Office," *New York Times*, May 13, 1996, p. 1. The *Time* article was severely criticized by those close to the Chubais faction for exaggerating the role of an unimportant group of self-promoting Americans, but the article holds up quite well in retrospect and is an important historical source.

55. Kramer, "Rescuing Boris," p. 33. The amount of money actually spent by the Yeltsin campaign is unknown, but Aleksandr Korzhakov charges that tens of millions were stolen and sent abroad. Korzhakov, *Boris Yel'tsin*, p. 10. Even if this figure is exaggerated, the fact that it could be seen as a credible fraction of the total expenditures is ample testimony to the size of the latter.

56. John Thornhill and Chrystia Freeland, "Yeltsin Pledges Boost to Market Economy," *Financial Times*, May 31, 1996, p. 2.

57. Alessandra Stanley, "Better Unread than Read: Russia's Press Edits Out a Communist," *New York Times*, March 31, 1996, section IV, p. 1; Lee Hockstader, "Russian Media Stack the Deck for Yeltsin: Fearing Return to State Control, Press Ignores Communist Candidate," *Washington Post*, April 3, 1996, p. 1.

58. Jerry F. Hough, Evelyn Davidheiser, and Susan G. Lehmann, *The 1996 Russian Presidential Election* (Brookings, 1996), pp. 79–82.

59. John Lloyd and Dmitri Volkov, "Kremlin Impotent over Large-Scale Managerial Fraud," *Financial Times*, October 6, 1994, p. 2

60. Korzhakov, *Boris Yel'tsin*, p. 321.

61. Ibid., pp. 362–86. These are remarkable memoirs. Korzhakov was the aide closest to Yeltsin on a personal level, and his description of the unattractive sides of Yeltsin's personality, life, and drinking created a scandal. But they are also substantively fascinating on Korzhakov's own role, including the clear indication that he conducted electronic surveillance of other leaders for Yeltsin. His report of the conversation with Chernomyrdin could have come only from a recording of the conversation. The real purpose of Korzhakov's book probably was to inform members of the elite that he had retained copies of the surveillance he had done for Yeltsin.

62. Ibid., pp. 367–70.

63. McFaul, *Russia's 1996 Presidential Election*, p. 330. Korzhakov, *Boris Yel'tsin*, p. 363.

64. Michael Specter, "Aide to Yeltsin Calls for Delay in June Election," *New York Times*, May 6 1996, p. 1; Michael Specter, "The World: The Catch Phrase Is 'Civil War,'" *New York Times*, May 12, 1996, section IV, p. 5.

65. McFaul, *Russia's 1996 Presidential Election*, pp. 27–30.

66. Alessandra Stanley, "Russian Campaign Ends but TV Films Are Telling Voters of Communist Horrors," *New York Times*, June 15, 1996, p. 5.

67 Samuel L. Popkin, *The Reasoning Voter: Communication and Persuasion in Presidential Campaigns*, 2d ed. (University of Chicago Press, 1994), pp. 7, 212–15.

68. Dick Morris, *Behind the Oval Office*, 2d ed. (Los Angeles: Renaissance, 1999), pp. 80–81, 339–40.

Chapter Seven

1. Daniel S. Treisman, "Fighting Inflation in a Transitional Regime: Russia's Anomalous Stabilization," *World Politics*, vol. 50 (January 1998), pp. 235–65.

2. In fact, a Russian economic journal published large excerpts from the written IMF memorandum, and that which was published did not really reflect the actual problems in Russia but seemed written for the home office in Washington.

3. Ariel Cohen, "Russia's Borrowing Spree: A Looming Financial Crisis," Heritage Foundation Executive Memorandum no. 481 (May 28, 1997), pp. 1–4. Indeed, the same point was made in a very paradoxical defense of IMF policy written by Stanley Fischer, deputy head of the IMF, in October 1998. After saying that the IMF policy was completely correct, he chastised the business community for being taken in. The high interest rates, he said, were a clear signal of the high risk. Stanley Fischer, "Lessons from a Crisis," *Economist*, October 3, 1998, pp. 23–24, 27.

4. John Thornhill, "Pitfall in the Paperchase," *Financial Times*, July 1, 1997, p. 23.

5. Steven Greenhouse, "IMF Delays $1.5 Billion Loan to Russia Because Reform Is Stalled," *New York Times*, September 20, 1993, p. A3.

6. Claudia Rosett, "Figures Never Lie, but They Seldom Tell the Truth about Russian Economy," *Wall Street Journal*, July 1, 1994, p. A10.

7. Claudia Rosett, "Ruble Falls 6% against the Dollar as Month-Long Drop Speeds Up," *Wall Street Journal*, October 11, 1994, p. A15; and Adi Ignatius and Claudia Rosett, "Ruble Stages 21.5% Decline against Dollar," *Wall Street Journal*, October 12, 1994, pp. A2 and A10.

8. David Wessel, "Developing Nations Exert Power, Blocking IMF Aid Plan for Russia," *Wall Street Journal*, October 4, 1994, p. A15; "Russia Seeks Reduction in Debt-Service Payments," *Wall Street Journal*, October 5, 1994, p. A12.

9. Chrystia Freeland, "Yeltsin Resurrects Soviet-Style Politburo," *Financial Times*, January 12, 1995, p. 2.

10. John Thornhill, "Russia's Day of Reckoning," *Financial Times*, January 18, 1995, p. 21; Chrystia Freeland, "Markets Hammer the Rouble," *Financial Times*, January 24, 1995, p. 2.

11. Chloe Arnold, "Big Rubles for Country's Biggest Banker," *Moscow Times*, September 30, 1998, p. 1.

12. The value of the ruble against the dollar is published on the first page of every issue of *Izvestiia*.

13. Lev Makarevich, "Gosudarstvo pytaetsia vosstanovit' zhestkii kontrol' nad bankami" (The government is trying to reestablish firm control over banks), *Finansovye izvestiia*, January 26, 1995, p. III.

14. Steve Liesman and Neela Banerjee, "Russia and the IMF to Sign Loan Pact of $6.25 Billion amid Doubt on Reform," *Wall Street Journal*, March 10, 1995, p. A10; John Thornhill, "IMF Chief Backs $6.5 Billion Aid for Russia," *Financial Times*, March 11–12, 1995, p. 2.

15. The game started with a Yeltsin decree in January said to be the result of IMF pressure. John Thornhill, "Moscow Reformers Score Oil Victory," *Financial Times*, January 6, 1995, p. 2.

16. Financial Department, "Kommercheskie banki nashli svoego samogo bol'shogo zaemshchika" (Commercial banks have found their biggest borrower), *Kommersant Daily*, April 1, 1995, p. 6. Although figures such as eight and nine banks were often cited, *Kommersant Daily* could only identify five: Oneximbank, Menatep, Inkombank, Imperial, and Stolichny.

17. Michael S. Bernstam and Alvin Rabushka, *Fixing Russia's Banks: A Proposal for Growth* (Stanford: Hoover Institution Press, 1998), p. 59.

18. Neela Banerjee, "Russia Taking Privatization to the Bank," *Wall Street Journal*, April 20, 1995, p. A8.

19. Ibid.; Gregory White, "Russian Banks Seeking to Thwart Bids by Foreigners to Buy 'Cheap,'" *Wall Street Journal,* April 13, 1995, p. A11.

20. "Russia to Allow Bids by Foreigners for State Shares," *Wall Street Journal,* May 15, 1995, p. A18.

21. Chrystia Freeland, "Yeltsin Approves State Asset Plan," *Financial Times,* September 5, 1995, p. 2.

22. Nicholas Denton and Chrystia Freeland, "Russian Oil Group Raises $320 Million in Share Offer," *Financial Times,* September 20, 1995, p. 29. In fact, although the shares were owned by the government, the money was used to pay off Lukoil's back taxes, and hence was a subsidy to Lukoil if one believed that the taxes had any meaning. For such a criticism, see Steve Liesman, "Bond Deal in Russia Draws Criticism of Government's Special Arrangement," *Wall Street Journal,* September 11, 1995, p. A11c. In reality, of course, the transaction illustrated the meaninglessness of the concept of tax arrears.

23. John Thornhill, "Russian Group Secures 5% of Oil Giant," *Financial Times,* December 8, 1995, p. 2; and The Lex Column, "Cranking Up GEC," *Financial Times,* December 8, 1995, p. 16.

24. Robert Corzine and Nicholas Denton, "ARCO Pays $90m to Lift Lukoil Stake," *Financial Times,* March 30–March 31, 1996, p. 9.

25. Chrystia Freeland, "Russia's Red Barons May Derail Sell-Off," *Financial Times,* February 23, 1996, p. 2.

26. Thornhill, "Russian Group Secures 5% of Oil Giant," p. 2; John Thornhill, "Russian Bank Wins Control of Oil Giant," *Financial Times,* December 9, 1995, p. 2.

27. Presumably this had been one of the causes of the bank liquidity crisis in August 1995 that caused a number of banks to default and fail a week before Yeltsin signed the August 31 degree on asset sales. Chrystia Freeland and John Thornhill, "Russian Banks Face Liquidity Crisis," *Financial Times,* August 25, 1995, p. 2; Chrystia Freeland, "Russian Banking Sector Faces Shakeout," *Financial Times,* August 26, 1995, p. 2; Chrystia Freeland, "Russia Acts to Avert Banking Crisis," *Financial Times,* August 26, 1995, p. 18.

28. See Bernstam and Rabushka, *Fixing Russia's Banks,* pp. 59–61.

29. Chrystia Freeland, "Banks Battle over Russian Privatisation," *Financial Times,* November 28, 1995, p. 2.

30. Chrystia Freeland, "Russian Oil Shares Sold Off for a Song," *Financial Times,* January 27, 1996, p. 2.

31. Antonia Sharpe and Graham Bowley, "Russian Bank Taps Western Market," *Financial Times,* December 27, 1995, p. 11.

32. Antonia Sharpe and John Thornhill, "International Capital Markets: Russian bank cuts cost of issuance," *Financial Times,* January 16, 1996, p. 30.

33. For example, the most prominent of the banks, Oneximbank, was created only in 1993 but, as has been seen, became a leading "authorized" bank

handling all money collected from customs. Its head, Vladimir O. Potanin, was closely associated with Anatoly Chubais. Chubais was Yeltsin's most trusted lieutenant throughout the 1990s in distributing economic subsidies to maintain Yeltsin's political control. From 1995 onward he really was a member of what was known as "the family," the most personal insiders.

34. Mikhail Loginov and Yaroslav Skvortsov, "Ivan Silaev: Iz gossotsializma v goskapitalizm" (Ivan Silaev: From state socialism to state capitalism), *Kommersant Daily*, February 2, 1995, p. 5.

35. Iurii Kalashnov, "Kazhdomy regionu—svoi eksportno-importnyy bank (To each region, its own export-import bank), *Kommersant Daily*, March 7, 1995, p. 6.

36. Rose Brady, *Kapitalizm: Russia's Struggle to Free Its Economy* (Yale University Press, 1999), p. 138.

37. I. Khramova and P. Verkhaym, "Rynochnye struktury prodovolstvennogo kompleksa Rossii v usloviakh perekhodnoi ekonomiki" (Market structures of Russia's food industry in the conditions of the transition economy), *Voprosy ekonomiki*, no. 8 (1997), p. 117.

38. Iu. S. Krupnov, "O mezhbankovskom kreditnom rynke" (On the intrabank credit market), *Finansy*, no. 1 (1997), pp. 9–10.

39. Ibid., p. 10.

40. Brady, *Kapitalizm*, p. 171

41. Michael R. Gordon, "The Gusher That Wasn't in Russia: Expected Oil Bonanza Fails to Materialize," *New York Times*, September 5, 1997, p. D1.

42. Gregory L. White, "Russia's Stock Market Enjoys a Boom as Foreign Institutional Investors Arrive," *Wall Street Journal*, September 8, 1994, p. A15.

43. Edmund L. Andrews, "Capitalism with a Vengeance," *New York Times*, October 5, 1997, section III, p. 11.

44. Jonathan Fuerbringer, "Emerging Bond Markets Suffering Reversal," *New York Times*, April 23, 1997, p. 15.

45. John Thornhill, "Emerging Markets: Investors in Russia Look for Political Stability," *Financial Times*, January 16, 1996, p. 24. Thornhill evaluated this in strong terms: "no matter how absurd that may seem."

46. John Thornhill, "Foreign Speculators Raise the Stakes," *Financial Times*, October 10, 1994, p. 19; and John Thornhill, "Finance and Family: From Russia with Confidence," *Financial Times*, October 15, 1994, p. v.

47. John Thornhill, "Templeton Predicts Strong Growth in Russian Markets," *Financial Times*, October 5, 1994, p. 25.

48. Steve Liesman, "A Mistrustful West Finds It Hard to Grasp Real Change in Russia," *Wall Street Journal*, September 26, 1996, p. A1.

49. "LUKoil's Financial Results Slide," *Wall Street Journal*, May 9, 1996, p. A14; "LUKoil Clarifies Profit Report," *Wall Street Journal*, May 20, 1996, p. A14; "LUKoil Totes Up Its Earnings," *Wall Street Journal*, August 30, 1996, p. A6.

50. Nick Ravo, "Bravery Is Paying Off for Investors in Russia," *New York Times*, March 16, 1997, section III, p. 7.

51. David Hoffman, "Russian Officials Open Anti-Monopoly Drive: Powerful Energy Companies Targeted," *Washington Post*, April 12, 1997, p. 19.

52. Grigory Napolov, first deputy minister of industry, "Industrial Setup Not Hopeless," Russian Legislative and Executive Newsletter, no. 50, in David Johnson's Russia List, December 28, 1996. ITAR-TASS, November 26, 1996, in David Johnson's Russia List, December 2, 1996.

53. Aleksandr Ashurkov, "Gosudarstvo mnozhit chislo tsennykh bumag" (Government increases the number of bonds), *Finansovye izvestiia*, January 17, 1995, p. III.

54. Vadim Arsen'ev, "Minfin i TsB budut soobshcha uvelichivat' vnutrennii dolg Rossii" (Ministry of Finance and Central Bank will increase internal Russian debt together), *Kommersant Daily*, March 24, 1995, p. 6.

55. The bonds were zero-sum bonds. That is, the face value of the bond was above the amount paid for it, and the "interest rate" was calculated on the difference between the purchase price and the redemption price.

56. John Thornhill, "Markets Give Thumbs-Up to Yeltsin's Ally," *Financial Times*, June 19, 1996, p. 2.

57. A. Vavilov and G. Trofimov, "Stabilizatsiia i upravlenie gosudarstvennym dolgom Rossii" (Stabilization and handling of Russia's national debt), *Voprosy ekonomiki*, no. 12 (1997), p. 67.

58. Thornhill, "Markets Give Thumbs-Up to Yeltsin's Ally," p. 2.

59. "Russia Opens T-Bill Trade," *Wall Street Journal*, January 15, 1996, p. 8.

60. David Hoffman, "Despite Yeltsin's Promises, Workers Remain Unpaid: Speech May Offer Clues on Status of Reform," *Washington Post*, March 6, 1997, p. 24.

61. Carol Matlack, "The High Cost of Easy Money," *Business Week*, December 7, 1998, p. 112.

62. "Lebed: Russian Foreign Debt Close to $210 Billion," Interfax Moscow, September 29, 1998.

63. "Vazhneishie zadachi organov finansovoi sistemy v 1998g" (The most important goals of the financial system bodies in 1998), *Finansy*, no. 3 (1998), p. 10. This was the official journal of the ministry, a magazine foreigners seldom seemed to read.

64. Carol Matlack, "What Happened to the Coal Miners' Dollars?" *Business Week*, September 8, 1997, p. 52.

65. "Russian Pension Fund Ill Again," *Wall Street Journal*, April 3, 1996, p. A10.

66. Alessandra Stanley, "Victor in Russian Election Today Faces Economic Crisis Tomorrow," *New York Times*, July 3, 1996, pp. 1 and 8.

67. Richard W. Stevenson, "I.M.F. Will Delay Money to Russia over Tax Problem," *New York Times*, July 23, 1996, p. 1.

68. "A Polite Warning to Mr. Yeltsin," *New York Times*, July 24, 1996, p. 24.

69. "I.M.F. Pays Installment to Russia" (Reuters), *New York Times*, August 22, 1996, p. 8.; "I.M.F. Eases Terms of Loan to Moscow" (AP), *New York Times*, August 31, 1996, p. 4.

70. Vanora Bennett, "Reforms: New Get-Tough Policy," *Los Angeles Times*, December 28, 1996, p. D1.

71. Aleksey Miashikov, "Provaliatsia li Rossiiskie reformy v propast' mezhdu bogatymi i bednymi?" (Will the Russian reforms collapse into the abyss between the rich and the poor?), *Rabochaia tribuna*, December 7, 1996.

72. V. M. Lebedev, "Razvitie investitsionnoi sfery v rossiiskoi ekonomike" (Development of the investment sphere of the Russian economy), *Finansy*, no. 7 (1998), p. 16.

73. John Thornhill, "Russia's New Deal," *Wall Street Journal*, July 15, 1998, p. 21.

74. Daniel Williams, "Oil-Price Decline Jars Russia," *Washington Post*, March 20, 1998, p. 30.

75. Martin Wolf, "Russian Knife-Edge," *Financial Times*, June 23, 1998, p. 24. See Erik Nielsen, "Russia: Restoring Fiscal and Currency Stability," Goldman Sachs, June 12, 1998.

76. P. A. Neymyshev, "Aziatskii krizis i ego vliianie na rossiiskii finansovyi rynok" (The Asian crisis and its influence on the Russian financial market), *Finansy*, no. 8 (1998), p. 56.

77. Aleksandr Korzhakov, *Boris Yel'tsin: Ot rassveta do zakata* (Boris Yeltsin: From dawn to sunset) (Moscow: Interbuk, 1997), p. 451. Korzhakov reports that from April onward this was a key issue between his team and that of Chubais.

78. Alessandra Stanley, "Brash Capitalist Enters Kremlin's Inner Circle," *New York Times*, August 16, 1996, p. A3.

79. Ibid.

80. Lee Hockstader and David Hoffman, "Yeltsin Rises Again from Political Grave," *Washington Post*, March 17, 1997, p. 13.

81. Daniel Williams, "Shake-Up Strengthens Chernomyrdin," *Washington Post*, November 23, 1997, p. 28.

82. Daniel Williams, "Russia Falls Short on Promise to Pay Back Wages," *Washington Post*, January 8, 1998, p. 24; Daniel Williams, "Yeltsin Returns to Work, Rebukes Prime Minister," *Washington Post*, January 20, 1998, p. 12.

83. Steve LeVine, "Yeltsin Tells Parliament to Fix Economy, and Win I.M.F. Aid," *New York Times*, February 18, 1998, p. 4.

84. In fact, the article was a warning to American policymakers about Chernomyrdin's lack of public support at home. Michael R. Gordon, "Hero to U.S., Yawn to Russia," *New York Times*, March 8, 1998, section IV, p. 18.

85. Thomas W. Lippman, "Gore Carves Unique Post with U.S.-Russia Collaboration," *Washington Post*, March 14, 1998, p. 23.

86. Alessandra Stanley, "The Reformers Did It. No, Blame the Bankers," *New York Times*, March 24, 1998, p. 8; Alessandra Stanley, "After Yeltsin Shake-Up, Business as Usual," *New York Times*, March 25, 1998, p. 8.

87. Michael Specter, "Yeltsin Dismisses His Entire Cabinet in a Show of Power," *New York Times*, March 24, 1998, p. A1.

88. Martin Feldstein, "How to Save the Rouble," *Financial Times*, July 8, 1998, p. 14.

89. Vincent Boland, "Russia Launches 30-Year Issue to Raise $2.5 bn," *Financial Times*, June 19, 1998, p. 30.

90. Edward Luce, "S & P Cuts Russia's Sovereign Rating," *Financial Times*, June 10, 1998, p. 40.

91. John Thornhill, "Chubais Says Russia Needs up to $15bn Aid to Calm Markets," *Financial Times*, June 19, 1998, p. 20.

92. American banks were heavily involved in this action, a fact that subsequently gave rise to a good deal of second-guessing. See Joseph Kahn and Timothy L. O'Brien, "For Russia and Its Bankers, Match Wasn't Made in Heaven," *New York Times*, October 18, 1998, p. 1.

93. John Thornhill and Chrystia Freeland, "Russia 'Has $200m Clandestine Loans,'" *Financial Times*, June 11, 1998, p. 1.

94. John Thornhill, "IMF and Russia in New Loan Accord," *Financial Times*, July 8, 1998, p. 2; John Thornhill, "Cash Crisis Hits Russian Treasury Bills," *Financial Times*, July 9, 1998, p. 3.

95. Chrystia Freeland, "Moscow's Bold Young Reformers View IMF Rescue as 'Absolutely Predictable,'" *Financial Times*, July 22, 1998, p. 2.

96. Chrystia Freeland and Jeremy Grant, "Russia Seals T-Bill Exchange Gamble," *Financial Times*, July 21, 1998, p. 2; and Jeremy Grant and Charles Clover, "Debt Blow to Confidence in Russia," *Financial Times*, August 8, 1998, p. 4.

97. Astrid Wendlandt, "Markets Hit by Dispute over Finance," *Financial Times*, August 11, 1998, p. 2.

98. David Wessel and Bob Davis, "How Financial Crisis Grew Despite Efforts of a Crack U.S. Team," *Wall Street Journal*, September 24, 1999, p. 10.

99. Celestine Bohlen, "Russia Intervenes as Its Currency Takes Sharp Drop," *New York Times*, August 26, 1998, p. 1.

100. Beginning in March 1998, the daily close of the RTS could be found in the "World Markets at a Glance" section of *Financial Times*.

101. "Russia and IMF Say Moscow Is Meeting Conditions on Loan," *Financial Times*, September 24, 1999, p. D1.

102. Arkady Ostrovsky and John Thornhill, "Russia 'Bust' Says Rating Agency," *Financial Times*, September 24, 1999, p. 3.

103. Ibid.

Chapter Eight

1. Douglass C. North, "Epilogue: Economic Performance through Time," in Lee J. Alston, Thrainn Eggertsson, and Douglass C. North, eds., *Empirical Studies in Institutional Change* (Cambridge: Cambridge University Press, 1996), p. 344.

2. Douglass C. North, "The Contribution of the New Institutional Economics to an Understanding of the Transition Problem (Helsinki: UNU World Institute for Development Economics Research, 1997), p. 16. North, "Epilogue," pp. 348–49.

3. Michael Dobbs and Paul Blustein, "Lost Illusions about Russia: US Backers of Ill-Fated Reforms Now Portrayed as Naive," *Washington Post*, September 12, 1999, p. A1; Stanley Fischer, "What Went Wrong in Russia?" *Financial Times*, September 27, 1999, p. 26.

4. This argument is made explicitly in Anders Aslund, *How Russia Became a Market Economy* (Brookings, 1995), pp. 10–11.

5. Robert H. Bates and Anne O. Krueger, "Generalizations from the Country Studies," in Robert H. Bates and Anne O. Krueger, *Political and Economic Interactions in Economic Policy Reform: Evidence from Eight Countries* (Oxford: Blackwell, 1993), p. 459.

6. This is the main argument of Anders Aslund, "Russia's Collapse," *Foreign Affairs*, vol. 78, no. 5 (September/October 1999), pp. 64–77.

7. For such a statement in the late summer of 1999, see Samuel R. Berger, "Getting the New Russia on Its Feet: Our Assistance Is Making the American People More Secure," *Washington Post*, September 5, 1999, p. B7.

8. Lewis B. Namier, *England in the Age of the American Revolution* (London: Macmillan, 1930), pp. 61–65.

9. See David Donald, *An Excess of Democracy: The American Civil War and the Social Process* (Oxford: Clarendon Press, 1960). The election of 1840 was the first with universal white male suffrage, 80 percent turnout, and a modern campaign.

10. Despite the claim of reformers that the communist system was thoroughly politicized, it actually was quite bureaucratized and effective by the mid-1960s. In the words of Samuel Huntington, a man usually accused of being a cold warrior at the time,

> The United States, Great Britain, and the Soviet Union have different forms of government, but in all three systems the government governs. . . .

All three countries have strong, adaptable, coherent political institutions: effective bureaucracies, well-organized political parties, a high degree of popular participation in public affairs, working systems of civilian control over the military, extensive activity by the government in the economy, and reasonably effective procedures for regulating succession and controlling political conflict. . . . In all these characteristics the political systems of the United States, Great Britain, and the Soviet Union differ significantly from the governments which exist in many, if not most, of the modernizing countries of Asia, Africa, and Latin America."

Samuel Huntington, *Political Order in Changing Societies* (Yale University Press, 1968), p. 1.

11. For Weber's use of all these polities as illustrations of patrimonial systems, see his "Patriarchalism and Patrimonialism," in Max Weber, *Economy and Society: An Outline of Interpretive Sociology*, ed. Guenther Roth and Claus Wittich (New York: Bedminster, 1968), vol. 3, pp. 1006–69. For his discussion of the role of Calvinism, see his *The Protestant Ethic and the Spirit of Capitalism* (New York: Scribners, 1950).

12. Mancur Olson, "Dictatorship, Democracy, and Development," *American Political Science Review*, vol. 87 (September 1993), pp. 572–73.

13. Obviously, those in charge of the state—that is, the government—change, often quickly, but what is needed is the assurance that a change in officials will not transform old property rights and institutional rules.

14. Jerry F. Hough, *Democratization and Revolution in the USSR, 1985–1991* (Brookings, 1997).

15. For the way this worked out in the 1993 Duma election, see Michael McFaul, "Russia's Choice: The Perils of Revolutionary Democracy," and Jerry F. Hough, "The Failure of Party Formation and the Future of Russian Democracy," in Timothy Colton and Jerry F. Hough, *Growing Pains: Russian Democracy and the Election of 1993* (Brookings, 1998), pp. 115–40, 703–05.

16. For most of the 1990s, hope was focused more on the party Yabloko, and its leader, Grigory Yavlinsky, was continually praised in the West for maintaining a principled position—that is, for not forming coalitions with Russian insider capitalists. Richard E. Ericson, "Economics," in Timothy J. Colton and Robert Legvold, *After the Soviet Union: From Empire to Nations* (W. W. Norton, 1992), p. 64.

17. James G. March and Herbert A. Simon, *Organizations*, 2d ed. (Oxford: Blackwell, 1993), pp. 4, 161–62.

18. In 1995 the dollar was approaching an exchange rate with the yen of 80 to 1. The IMF thought this threatened financial stability and called for the standard policy of increasing U.S. interest rates. Instead, Alan Greenspan cut rates, and the dollar, instead of weakening further, began rising, eventually reaching

the 140 level. Greenspan and the IMF continued to disagree on interest rates, with the IMF, rightly or wrongly, continually calling for higher interest rates than the Federal Reserve was instituting. Michael M. Phillips, "When It Gives Fed Policy Advice, IMF Gets No Respect—U.S. Tosses Out Prescriptions, While Urging Poor Nations to Take Their Medicine," *Wall Street Journal*, September 30, 1999, p. 1.

19. See Joseph R. Blasi, Maya Kroumova, and Douglas Kruse, *Kremlin Capitalism: The Privatization of the Russian Economy* (Cornell University Press, 1997), pp. 173–76.

20. Maurice Duverger, *Political Parties: Their Organization and Activity in the Modern State* (New York: John Wiley, 1954), p. xxxi.

21. See Susan Rose-Ackerman, "Corruption and Development," in Boris Pleskovic and Joseph E. Stiglitz, eds., *Annual World Bank Conference on Development Economics 1997* (Washington: World Bank, 1998), pp. 35–57.

22. Andrei Shleifer and Robert W. Vishny, *The Grabbing Hand: Government Pathologies and Their Cures* (Harvard University Press, 1998), chap. 5.

23. The general analysis is found in Mancur Olson, *The Logic of Collective Action: Public Goods and the Theory of Groups* (Harvard University Press, 1965); Mancur Olson, "The Logic of Collective Action in Soviet-Type Societies," *Journal of Soviet Nationalities*, vol. 1 (Summer 1990), pp. 13–16.

24. Robert Pear, "State Dept. Moves to Expel Top Kashmir Separatist," *New York Times*, April 22, 1990, p. A17.

25. Frances Fox Piven and Richard A. Cloward, *Why Americans Don't Vote* (New York: Pantheon, 1988), pp. 17–20, 26–63.

Index

Abalkin, Leonid, 60, 114; abolition of industrial ministries, 32, 61–62; bank reform, 37, 38, 62; privatization issue, 69–70

Academy of Sciences, 227

Africa: absence of political parties, 178; economic development, 254

Agrarian lobby, 20

Agrarian party, 170, 171, 227

Agricultural reform: in China, 110, 247; in eastern Europe, 110; lack of, 8, 98, 110, 247; need for, 245, 246; purposes, 110–11; recommended stages, 246–47

Agriculture: banks involved in, 211; collective farms, 79, 172, 246; decline in investment, 14, 54; employment reduction, 22; fertilizer used, 14, 120; government control of trade, 111; industries related to, 111, 112–13; need for investment, 109–10, 112; prices, 246; private plots, 85, 236; privatization, 82; production declines, 14, 54, 110, 111–12, 228, 247; regional differences,

111, 112; in Soviet Union, 110, 124; subsidies, 111, 192. *See also* Food

Alcohol: imports, 47; vodka monopoly, 219

Aleksashenko, Sergei, 205–06

Aleksei II, Patriarch, 158

Alfa Bank, 209

All-Russia Institute of Public Opinion (VTsIOM), 171–72

Amoco, 213

Anarchy, 13

Anpilov, Viktor, 158

Arrow, Kenneth, 12

Asia: corruption, 249; economic development, 16–17, 132, 143, 254; financial crisis (1998), 204

Aslund, Anders, 1–2, 19–20, 58, 77, 184, 196, 225

Atlantic Richfield, 208

Automobile industry: bankruptcies, 55; banks, 37, 65; debt, 216; foreign investment, 213; lack of investment, 100; ministerial "holding companies," 33, 34; stock values, 216; tariffs, 213

295